BUILDING THE JUDICIARY

Princeton Studies in American Politics:
Historical, International, and Comparative Perspectives

Ira Katznelson, Martin Shefter, and Theda Skocpol, Series Editors

Note: the list of series titles is continued at the back of this book

JUSTIN CROWE

Building the Judiciary

LAW, COURTS, AND THE POLITICS

OF INSTITUTIONAL DEVELOPMENT

PRINCETON UNIVERSITY PRESS

Princeton and Oxford

347.73
CRO

Copyright © 2012 by Princeton University Press
Published by Princeton University Press, 41 William Street, Princeton, New Jersey 08540
In the United Kingdom: Princeton University Press, 6 Oxford Street, Woodstock,
Oxfordshire OX20 1TW

press.princeton.edu

Library of Congress Cataloging-in-Publication Data

Crowe, Justin, 1981–

   Building the judiciary : law, courts, and the politics of institutional development / Justin Crowe.
        p. cm. — (Princeton studies in American politics : historical, international, and comparative
perspectives)
   Includes index.
   ISBN 978-0-691-15292-9 (hardcover : alk. paper) — ISBN 978-0-691-15293-6 (pbk. : alk. paper)
   1. Courts—United States—History.   I. Title.
   KF8719.C76 2012
   347.73'109—dc23

                                                                          30.17

                                                                                    2011030845

British Library Cataloging-in-Publication Data is available

This book has been composed in Minion

Printed on acid-free paper. ∞

Printed in the United States of America

10 9 8 7 6 5 4 3 2 1

CONTENTS

ACKNOWLEDGMENTS

For all the important things about which my wife and I agree, we disagree about acknowledgments—namely, I read them, she does not. For her, acknowledgments are nothing more than a waste of time; for me, they are the essential starting point of any book. After all, while books are about ideas, they are written by people— people whose voices become professional and academic while writing, but people whose lives occur in a rich and complex world from which the reader is wholly excluded. Acknowledgments are the one instance in which readers see authors as people—as mothers and fathers, husbands and wives, friends and colleagues; they are the one instance in which authors offer a glimpse of something more than their scholarly pronouncements. These glimpses, I know from recounting my own favorite acknowledgments, come in many shapes and sizes—from amusing anecdotes that illuminate or epitomize the book's origins (James Morone's *Hellfire Nation*) to touching meditations about those who have made the long nights of writing durable (Julian Zelizer's *On Capitol Hill*) to paeans to those whose ideas have encountered, collided with, and shaped the author's own in meaningful ways (Mark Graber's *Dred Scott and the Problem of Constitutional Evil*). I am not sure where my acknowledgments fit along that spectrum or how they measure up to Morone's, Zelizer's, or Graber's, but I have enjoyed writing them nonetheless. If the eight chapters that follow are systematic analysis, then these next several pages are joyous remembrance.

Gary Jacobsohn—more than deserving of first position in any accounting of my intellectual influences—set me on the path to studying the American Constitution and Supreme Court at Williams College more than a decade ago, and, though nothing in here emerged directly out of any conversation I had with him, neither would anything in here exist were it not for him. The more proximate (but by no means more important) source of the spark that became this book came from a group of my Princeton University precept students—specifically Tyler Allard, Anne Louise Bigliani, Jesse Creed, David Korn, Eryck Kratville, and Josh Waldman, all of whom made a habit of asking questions for which I was largely without answers. As I worked my way toward those answers, Paul Frymer nurtured a nascent idea and thankfully confirmed that it could sustain a "project" (rather than just a seminar paper) all its own; Ken Kersch offered enthusiasm, encouragement, and edifying conversation, usually while treating me to lunch in or around Princeton in the process; and a collection of smart and congenial scholars including (but certainly not limited to) Chris Achen, Peri Arnold, Beau Breslin, Steve Burbank, Dan Carpenter, Doug Edlin, Chris Eisgruber, Mark Graber, Fred Greenstein, Ed Hartnett, Scott James, Dave Lewis, George Lovell, Richard Morgan, Carol Nackenoff, Robert Post, Ted Ruger, Kim Scheppele, Gordon Silverstein, Rogers Smith, Jim Stoner, Rick Valelly, and Julian Zelizer probed, poked, and prodded me along in various but uniformly helpful ways. Doug Arnold demanded theoretical precision and analytic rigor, honestly telling me at one point that I had neither a theory nor anything close to a theory before helping me to rebuild it in the same way I argue the federal judiciary was built—piece by piece, from the ground up. Once the theory was complete, Doug lent his keen editorial eye to almost every page, rearranging sentences to say things more elegantly and more economically than I thought possible. Keith Whittington flabbergasted me with his depth of analysis, immediate comments, patience for dumb questions, and thorough guidance on matters large and small. I have no idea where he found the time or energy to read seemingly every book, article, or unpublished masters' thesis that might have been relevant to my work, but I am glad he did and incredibly grateful he gave me access to his encyclopedic store of knowledge while in graduate school and that he has continued to serve as a resource since then. At Princeton University Press, Chuck Myers bred confidence with his excitement and calm with his efficiency, Debbie Tegarden kept things moving smoothly, and Brian Bendlin provided thorough and careful copyediting. Portions of chapters 3 and 6 draw upon material published in *Studies in American Political Development* 24, no. 1 (2010): 90–120, and the *Journal of Politics* 69, no. 1 (2007): 73–87, respectively; both are reprinted here with the permission of Cambridge University Press.

Among friends from various stages of life, Michael Cutrone, Megan Francis, and Dave Glick were always willing to share a cup of coffee and let me distract them with my work in Princeton; Will Barndt, Peter Kung, and Mike Steinberger supplied competition (of the athletic variety), comedy, and camaraderie, respectively, in Claremont; and Karima Barrow and Neil Roberts, Lisa Koriouchkina and Q. Ashraf, and Tara and Will Olney have made dinner about far more than food in Williamstown. Through it all, Emily Zackin displayed a penchant for breaking down an argument and putting it back together—even from half a world away, even on incredibly short notice—with a smile, and Freeden Oeur never stopped believing in me. Time and again, both Emily and Freeden also proved—in unique and evolving ways too multiple to list here—why they are the type of friends one feels blessed to have in life.

From southern California to northwestern Massachusetts, the San Gabriels to the Berkshires, the City of Trees and PhDs to the Village Beautiful, my colleagues in both the Politics Department at Pomona College and the Political Science Department at Williams College have also fulfilled a variety of valuable roles. In Claremont, I was fortunate to find, among other wonderful colleagues, a supremely gracious predecessor (Leo Flynn), a walking book of wisdom and witticisms (Lorn Foster), an inspirational firebrand who continually makes me want to be more like him (John Seery), and a lifelong intellectual soulmate who continually makes me into a better version of myself (Sue McWilliams). In Williamstown, I have been lucky to encounter—again, among other happy things—an unflaggingly supportive chair (Jim Mahon), a sports-obsessed elder statesman (Michael MacDonald), a sophisticated theoretical mind (Mark Reinhardt), an incisive historical interlocutor (Nicole Mellow), a pair of receptive sounding boards and lively lunch companions (Paul MacDonald and Ngoni Munemo), and a trusted and supportive sparring partner (James McAllister). Leaving the first group—especially John and Sue, who made every day of my life at Pomona truly idyllic for two years—was unquestionably the most difficult moment of my (admittedly thus far short) professional life, but the opportunity to come "home" to Williams was too tempting to pass up; luckily for me, the second group—with James in the office next door and the nostalgia of having my mentor's job floating in the air above—has also made it too good to be true.

Colleagues, of course, are—or, at least, have been for me—only half the benefit of being associated with two of the very best educational institutions in the world. It is commonly assumed—especially, I would imagine, by parents who write the tuition checks—that professors educate students. In my case, even as I would like to think I have done that, I know that mine have also educated—and continue, on a daily basis, to educate—me. I wish I could do more than simply name them, but listing the precise ways in which each and every one of them has shaped me as a scholar and a teacher might well double the length of this book; I trust that they, and many others not named here, all know how my fondness for them extends well beyond the words on this page. Especially influential in my perpetual education—to say nothing of my daily enjoyment of my job—at Pomona were Laura Beebe, Sean Beienburg, Dawn Bickett, Greg Carter, Grace Chuchla, Jemel Derbali, Becka DeSmidt, Kevin Frick, Amal Karim, Scott Levy, Dahni Ma, Tom Sprankling, Marlies Talay, Ingrid Vidal, and Jon Zelig; at Williams, my kids are, Darryl Brown, Vera Cecelski, Jen Chan, Rose Courteau, Aimee Dennett, Danielle Diuguid, Kara Duggan, Billy Glidden, Lindsey Graham, Emily Hertz, Tyler Holden, Natalie Johnson, Greg Kim, Chloe Kuh, Alexa Lutchen, Sam Murray, Michelle Noyer-Granacki, Cameron Nutting, Jordan Roberts, Andy Quinn, Chandler Sherman, Nicole Smith, Juliana Stone, Nathaniel Sutton, Stefan Ward-Wheten, and Sam Weinstein. Sean, Natalie, Juliana, and Scott all deserve special mention for sundry forms of research assistance. Sean dutifully performed early copyediting and fastidious fact-checking. Natalie perspicaciously tracked down obscure nineteenth-century information about state populations and congressional committee composition. Juliana—besides often making me laugh and always making me smile—gracefully offered thoughtful feedback and pitch-perfect advice on all manner of aesthetic issues, including the layout of the jacket, the lyricism of the acknowledgments, and the liveliness of the first chapter. Scott single-handedly turned me around on Homer Cummings, but that was only the start: already aware that he is probably more familiar with the strengths and weaknesses of this book than anyone other than me, he should also know—as I firmly do—that those strengths would have been decidedly fewer and those weaknesses unquestionably more glaring in his absence.

Regardless of whether I happened to be dwelling on strengths or weaknesses, triumphs or tribulations, I have purposefully (and perhaps unnecessarily) shielded my family from hearing about my research. That does not mean, of course, I did not garner strength from them along the way. My parents—Bari and Chris Carley, Robert and Rachel Crowe—have always demonstrated, in both word and deed, their confidence in my ability to do whatever I set my mind to and their pride in whatever it was I ultimately did while my siblings—Billy and Madison Crowe and Taylor Carley—have always demonstrated, in both word and deed, that they loved their brother no matter how infrequently he came to visit or how far away from home he moved. I owe all seven of them a debt of gratitude not only for never questioning me but also for never letting me question their support for me.

Of course, my greatest debt is to my wife, best friend, and confidant, Christen Romanick. Her blasphemous views about acknowledgments notwithstanding, I love, respect, admire, and trust her deeply. Over the past few years, Christen let me work when I needed to and happily distracted me when I did not want to. Early in the process, before we started our family, she spent far too many days alone, passed far too many evenings virtually alone, and went to bed far too many nights alone. More recently, even with a toddler in the house, she let me disappear for the occasional long stretch of time when I yearned to focus on research even as she had things—including much-desired rest and much-needed sanity!—to focus on herself. In the meantime, she consoled me when things were going poorly, celebrated with me when they were going well, listened to me brainstorm when I developed new ideas, discovered my errors with her well-honed copyediting skills, picked up the slack on things I forgot (or claimed I lacked time) to do around the house, and invented words with me on a daily basis. I am not yet, and may well never be, certain how to repay her for the myriad ways in which she made this book—in which she makes *everything*—possible, so simply finishing it and at last being more present, in every way possible, for her and our two little men, Everett and Fisher, will need to suffice for the moment. Everett, of course, did much in his first three years of life to make completing this book more difficult (starting with the fact that he ripped the "enter" key off my laptop!) but even more—from wanting to read books to asking to help cook to begging to throw rocks in the river—to make the prospect of completing it more enticing. His little brother, Fisher, may only have arrived after the bulk of work on this book was completed, but that hardly means he—or, more accurately, the prospect of him—did not simultaneously distract and motivate me as I sought to finish. (Inheriting his big brother's love of dilatory techniques, he also steadfastly refused to continue napping in my arms or on my chest while I sought to copyedit during his first few weeks of life.) Simply put, anything done with Christen and the boys is better than anything done without them; they are the ones who give my days meaning and the ones to whom my heart is dedicated.

Finally, there is he to whom this work is dedicated. Long before I knew how this book would end, I knew how it would begin: with a nod to my late friend and teacher Tim Cook. And long before it became clear where I would finish *this* book, I realized—in retrospect—where it became clear that I would someday write *a* book: at a cramped table in a small coffee shop on a snowy street tucked away in the mountains. For it was there on a cold and dusky December afternoon that Tim, an accomplished scholar of political communication and the mass media (among other subjects) whom I first encountered as my unassuming yet generous fresh-man advisor in college, asked about my interest in serving as his research assistant. To this day, I am not sure what prompted Tim's offer, but it intrigued me enough to spend the summer in Williamstown, where I found myself increasingly committed to graduate school in political science and where two doors down from my dorm room I met the woman who would ultimately become my wife. All freshman advi-sors remove registration holds, many guide curricular planning, and some write letters of recommendations; mine gave me both a career I love and a partner I love.

I knew Tim just under seven years—he passed away in August 2006, a few months before I accepted a job at his alma mater (Pomona)—but, even in that relatively short period of time, he taught me innumerable lessons that stick with me to this very day. I can't go to the Thai restaurant without remembering Tim's advice that green curry should be eaten with duck rather than chicken. I can't discuss my syllabus on the first day of class or hold a review session at the end of the semester without repeating—perhaps ad nauseam to my students' ears—Tim's aphorism that "even a final exam can be a learning experience." I can't write about the Supreme Court without embodying Tim's insistence that, despite the impres-sion lent by most scholars of public law, "Congress makes a little bit of law, too." (I'd like to think that point is painfully apparent in this book.) And I can't think about any of those lessons without also thinking about the ones Tim never had the chance to teach me. (One idiosyncratic example: upon reading my senior the-sis acknowledgment that "from the mountains of Massachusetts to the bayous of Baton Rouge, Tim Cook has spent much of the past four years teaching me both what political science was and how to be a political scientist," Tim, who had by that point left Williams for Louisiana State University, simply asked, "Do you even know what a bayou is?")

In the days before brain cancer took Tim from us entirely too soon, I futilely tried to put my feelings about him, my reflections of him, and my gratitude toward him into writing. I have no idea whether my rambling and disorganized electronic "missive" (a word I never use but one of which Tim was inordinately fond) actu-ally reached Tim before he passed, but I wanted him to know, in case he did not already, how much he had meant to me. I wanted him to know that on issues from food to teaching to research, from literature to politics to humanity, he shaped my thinking and influenced my worldview in more ways than I can explain. Most of all, I wanted him to know how he had *literally* changed the course of my life and how I planned to dedicate my first book to him as some small measure of apprecia-tion. Tim never had the chance to read any of the material in this book, a fact that saddens me because he is, among those who cannot read it, the person I most wish could do so. I do not know whether or not he would have agreed with what I have to say, but I know beyond a glimmer of a doubt that I would have enjoyed talking about it with him. So, for one last time, from a roomier table at a shinier version of the very coffee shop on the very (and usually still very snowy) street in the very (and definitely still very tucked away) mountains where it all began, from an Eph who briefly taught Sagehens (and now teaches Ephs) to a Sagehen who long taught Ephs—for one last time: all good things, Tim C—*all good things.*

Justin Crowe
Williamstown, MA
July 2011

BUILDING THE JUDICIARY

CHAPTER ONE

The Puzzle of Judicial Institution Building

When the United States Supreme Court convened for the first time in history at the Royal Exchange Building in New York City on February 2, 1790,[1] it was a sorry scene, and even the justices knew it. With only four of George Washington's initial six nominees bothering to show up and the Court lacking even a single case to hear,[2] Chief Justice John Jay and his three colleagues in attendance—associate justices James Wilson, William Cushing, and John Blair—spent the session devising procedures for the conduct of actual business. The justices could not have known then that they would have no such business for another eighteen months,[3] but, in retrospect, the dearth of activity demonstrated how the Court's institutional beginnings were inauspicious and suggested that its likelihood of exerting any measurable direction on the course of American life was slim.

When, more than two hundred years later, the Court convened for one of the most dramatic moments in its history at its own building in Washington, D.C., on December 11, 2000, it was a stunning spectacle, and all of America knew it. With Chief Justice William Rehnquist at the helm, all nine justices sat at attention for the day's lone case, an election dispute summoned from the Florida Supreme Court, a thorny little matter known as *Bush v. Gore*.[4] The justices steadfastly focused their questions on the arcane interstices of finely wrought election procedures, but, with two of the nation's leading lawyers—future solicitor general Ted Olson and former government litigator David Boies—arguing and many citizens subsequently listening in via an immediately released (and nationally broadcast)

---

[1] The Court's first meeting was actually scheduled for February 1, only to be postponed a day when some of the justices experienced transportation difficulties en route to New York.

[2] Robert Harrison declined the commission, preferring his job as chancellor of Maryland; John Rutledge, though confirmed as a justice, neglected to show up for a single session of the Court before resigning to become Chief Justice of the South Carolina Court of Common Pleas. Washington would subsequently nominate James Iredell to take Harrison's place; Rutledge, replaced in 1791 by Thomas Johnson, would later return to the Court through a recess appointment to the chief justiceship, only to have his nomination rejected by the Senate.

[3] The Court's first decision came in *West v. Barnes*, 2 U.S. 401 (1791) (holding that a writ of error to remove a case from a lower court to the Supreme Court could issue from the clerk of the Supreme Court alone).

[4] 531 U.S. 98 (2000) (declaring the Florida Supreme Court's scheme for recounting presidential election ballots a violation of the Equal Protection Clause of the Fourteenth Amendment).

audio recording,[5] the remarkable and incontrovertible fact that a presidential election hung in the balance raised the possibility that the Court sat at the apex of not just the American judiciary but the entire American political system.

The dissimilarity between these two snapshots in the Court's history could not be more profound. With several distinguished men having refused appointment and the docket languishing without any substantial business,[6] the Court of the late eighteenth century was a feeble institution. It lacked prestige, respect, and power; it had no building, a small budget, and was largely controlled and handicapped by the other branches of government. By contrast, with persistent struggles over judicial nominations and recurrent attempts to restrict jurisdiction over controversial issues (abortion, flag burning, and gay marriage, for instance), the Court of the early twenty-first century is clearly considered significant enough to warrant a fight. It is not only prestigious and revered but also powerful, politically important, and highly contentious; it hears and decides cases in its own "marble temple," has a significant budget, and is sufficiently independent from the other branches to govern its own affairs. How did such a dramatic evolution occur? How did the federal judiciary in general, and the Supreme Court in particular, transcend its early limitations and become a powerful institution of American governance? How, in other words, did we move from a Court of political irrelevance to one of political centrality? Those are the principal questions driving this book.

From Judicial Exceptionalism to Architectonic Politics

The conventional wisdom about—the "textbook" answer to—these sorts of questions emphasizes federal judges, specifically Supreme Court justices, wielding the power of constitutional interpretation. *Marbury v. Madison* is decided, (invalidating Section 13 of the Judiciary Act of 1789 as in conflict with Article III).[7] and judicial review exists. *Cooper v. Aaron* is decided,[8] and judicial supremacy exists. In this understanding, judicial power expands when judges issue opinions that di-

---

[5] The previous week, the Court had agreed, for the first time in its history, to release audiotapes immediately following oral arguments in *Bush v. Palm Beach County Canvassing Board*, 531 U.S. 70 (2000) (requesting clarification from the Florida Supreme Court regarding its decision forbidding Florida Secretary of State Katherine Harris from certifying election results until manual recounts had been completed). Prior to that decision, standard protocol was to release audiotapes of oral arguments only at the conclusion of each term; since *Bush v. Gore*, the Court has considered—and, in many cases, authorized—same-day release of oral argument audiotapes from high-profile cases when specifically asked to do so by a news organization. At the same time, all requests for the Court to provide a live audio feed of oral arguments, including ones made during the 2000 election controversy, have been denied.

[6] Moreover, after only six years as the nation's first chief justice, Jay, while negotiating a treaty overseas, resigned from the Court upon his election as governor of New York.

[7] 5 U.S. 137 (1803).

[8] 358 U.S. 1 (1958) (declaring that the Supremacy Clause of Article VI requires state officers to enforce the decisions of the Supreme Court).

rectly expand it. Courts—and, most often, the Supreme Court—unilaterally determine the contours and extent of judicial power with little or no interference from other political actors. The story of the federal judiciary's transformation unfolds internally, with the Court occupying the central position, constitutional interpretation the central tool, and all other actors and forces relegated decidedly to the background.

In part, this emphasis on judicial prerogative stems from a prevailing but problematic ethos of "judicial exceptionalism." Endemic to far too much scholarly work in public law, judicial politics, and American political development, this ethos manifests itself in the twin suppositions that the judiciary is institutionally separate from and institutionally thin when compared to other political institutions. First, given their lifetime tenure, their officially "nonpartisan" identity, and, most important, their unique role in interpreting the Constitution, we tend to treat judges as though they were endowed with some sort of special status that elevates them above—or at least distinguishes them from—"ordinary" politics and politicians. Conflating the Constitution and the Court,[9] we largely assume—despite sustained political debate over this perspective from the earliest days of the republic to today[10]—that the hallowed status of the former automatically and necessarily redounds to the latter, thereby isolating, insulating, and revering the Court simply because of its contested place as the "Platonic guardian" of the constitutional order. Second, with a few exceptions,[11] we ostensibly think of courts as lacking the com-

[9] There is, of course, Charles Evans Hughes's famous and oft-repeated aphorism, "We are under a Constitution, but the Constitution is what the judges say it is." Though Hughes would subsequently serve two nonconsecutive stints on the Court—as an associate justice (1910–16) and, after a failed presidential bid in 1916 and four years as secretary of state (1921–25) under Warren Harding and Calvin Coolidge, as chief justice (1930–41)—he actually uttered this sentiment while governor of New York. According to Hughes himself, the remark, delivered "extemporaneously" in a speech given before a chamber of commerce in Elmira, New York, on May 3, 1907, was not intended to frame constitutional interpretation as "a matter of judicial caprice" but to emphasize "the importance of maintaining the courts in the highest public esteem as our final judicial arbiters." For the full text of the speech, see Charles Evans Hughes, *Addresses and Papers of Charles Evans Hughes, Governor of New York, 1906–1908* (New York: Putnam's, 1908), 133–46; for Hughes's clarifying statements (accompanied by the relevant portion of the speech), see *The Autobiographical Notes of Charles Evans Hughes*, ed. David J. Danelski and Joseph S. Tulchin (Cambridge, MA: Harvard University Press, 1973), 143–44.

[10] Michael Kammen, *A Machine That Would Go of Itself: The Constitution in American Culture* (New York: St. Martin's Press, 1994); Keith E. Whittington, *Political Foundations of Judicial Supremacy: The Presidency, the Supreme Court, and Constitutional Leadership in U.S. History* (Princeton, NJ: Princeton University Press, 2007).

[11] See, among others, Deborah J. Barrow, Gerard S. Gryski, and Gary Zuk, *The Federal Judiciary and Institutional Change* (Ann Arbor: University of Michigan Press, 1996); Charles M. Cameron, "Endogenous Preferences about Courts: A Theory of Judicial State Building in the Nineteenth Century," in *Preferences and Situations: Points of Intersection Between Historical and Rational Choice Institutionalism*, ed. Ira Katznelson and Barry R. Weingast (New York: Russell Sage Foundation, 2005), 185–215; Peter Graham Fish, *The Politics of Federal Judicial Administration* (Princeton, NJ: Princeton University Press, 1973); Paul Frymer, "Acting When Elected Officials Won't: Federal Courts and Civil Rights Enforcement in U.S. Labor Unions, 1935–85," *American Political Science Review* 97 (2003): 483–99; Howard Gillman, "How Political Parties Can Use the Courts to Advance Their Agendas: Federal Courts in the

plex institutional features—namely, collections of structures and rules that serve to influence behavior and regulate the exercise of power—that make political institutions worth studying. While the legislative branch has a hierarchical system of committees and subcommittees and the executive branch has a vast bureaucracy comprising layers of political appointees and civil servants, the judicial branch has only some courts, some judges, and some clerks—or so the lack of attention to the institutional context of the judiciary would have us believe.[12] The combined effect of these two perspectives—simultaneously overestimating the judiciary's position and underestimating its depth relative to other political institutions—is to obscure the variety of ways in which courts and judges both gain and exercise power.

As we shall see, judicial power grows from more than merely constitutional decisions or the exercise of judicial review; indeed, it more commonly and more foundationally derives from interaction with political elites, from empowering legislation, and from public, media, and interest group support. Judicial power is likewise expressed not simply through jurisprudential constructions such as the "clear and present danger" test or the "state action" doctrine but more frequently (albeit less dramatically and less controversially) through procedural mechanisms such as removal and rule making.[13] Thus, even if the traditional focus on "rule by judges" may be warranted in some respects,[14] it takes for granted the ways in which

---

United States, 1875–1891," *American Political Science Review* 96 (2002): 511–24; Lori A. Johnson, "Institutionalization of the Judicial Branch," paper presented at the 2004 Western Political Science Association Meeting, Portland, Oregon, 2004; Lori A. Johnson, "Who Governs the Guardians? The Politics of Policymaking for the Federal Courts," PhD diss., University of California–Berkeley, 2004; Kevin T. McGuire, "The Institutionalization of the U.S. Supreme Court," *Political Analysis* 12 (2004): 128–42; and Karen Orren, "Standing to Sue: Interest Group Conflict in the Federal Courts," *American Political Science Review* 70 (1976): 723–41.

[12] Although largely ignored by political scientists, the institutional context of the judiciary has received attention from legal academics. Much of this literature, however, has focused on fairly specific legal rules and narrow tracts of judicial administration rather than the causes and consequences of structural and institutional innovation within the judicial branch. Notable exceptions include Stephen B. Burbank, "The Architecture of Judicial Independence," 72 *Southern California Law Review* 315 (1999); Stephen B. Burbank, "Procedure, Politics and Power: The Role of Congress," 79 *Notre Dame Law Review* 1677 (2004); Charles Gardner Geyh, *When Courts and Congress Collide: The Struggle for Control of America's Judicial System* (Ann Arbor: University of Michigan Press, 2006); Judith Resnik, "Managerial Judges," 96 *Harvard Law Review* 374 (1982); and Judith Resnik, "The Programmatic Judiciary: Lobbying, Judges, and Invalidating the Violence against Women Act," 74 *Southern California Law Review* 269 (2000).

[13] For the "clear and present danger" test, see *Schenck v. United States*, 249 U.S. 47 (1919) (upholding the Espionage Act of 1917 against claims that it violated freedom of speech as protected by the First Amendment); for the "state action" doctrine, see *The Civil Rights Cases*, 109 U.S. 3 (1883) (striking down the Civil Rights Act of 1875 as beyond the power granted to Congress by Section 5 of the Fourteenth Amendment).

[14] For recent comparative analyses of "juristocracy," "judicialization," and "constitutionalization," see, among others, Tom Ginsburg, *Judicial Review in New Democracies: Constitutional Courts in Asian Cases* (Cambridge: Cambridge University Press, 2003); Ran Hirschl, *Towards Juristocracy: The Origins and Consequences of the New Constitutionalism* (Cambridge, MA: Harvard University Press, 2004); Martin Shapiro and Alec Stone Sweet, *On Law, Politics, and Judicialization* (Oxford: Oxford University

courts and judges become institutionally equipped to rule.[15] In seeking to understand *how* judges rule, we have largely neglected the conditions that have made it possible *for* judges to rule;[16] in emphasizing how the judiciary acts *upon* politics, we have minimized the ways in which it is equally acted upon *by* politics.[17] Thus, even as we know a great deal about the political consequences of judicial power, its effect on structures of power or individual rights, and its expression through constitutional review, we lack a holistic narrative about the historical processes contributing to the rise of the federal judiciary (or even just the Supreme Court)

Press, 2002); and C. Neal Tate and Torbjorn Vallinder, eds., *The Global Expansion of Judicial Power* (New York: New York University Press, 1995).

[15] Recent attempts to think about these issues have led some scholars to talk about the "institutionalization" of the federal judiciary. See Johnson, "Institutionalization of the Judicial Branch"; Johnson, "Who Governs the Guardians?"; and McGuire, "The Institutionalization of the U.S. Supreme Court." For theories of institutionalization applied to other political institutions, see Nelson Polsby, "The Institutionalization of the U.S. House of Representatives," *American Political Science Review* 62 (1968): 144–68; and Lyn Ragsdale and John J. Thies, "The Institutionalization of the American Presidency, 1924–92," *American Journal of Political Science* 41 (1997): 1280–1318. Largely because the term carries the conceptual baggage of these prior iterations—attempts that are concerned more with identifying the point(s) at which individual institutions satisfy discrete criteria and become "institutionalized" than with tracing the myriad and often non-linear steps in institutional development—I purposefully eschew the language of institutionalization.

[16] There is, of course, a growing—and most impressive—historical-institutionalist literature on the circumstances and conditions surrounding the consolidation, augmentation, and contraction of judicial authority in America, but this work, which seeks to generate strategic explanations of how and why institutions do or do not share, surrender, and grant power to rival institutions, tends to focus almost exclusively on the political foundations necessary for the development and exercise of judicial review. For leading works in this genre, see Gillman, "How Political Parties Can Use the Courts to Advance Their Agendas"; Howard Gillman, "Party Politics and Constitutional Change: The Political Origins of Liberal Judicial Activism," in *The Supreme Court and American Political Development*, ed. Ronald Kahn and Ken I. Kersch (Lawrence: University Press of Kansas, 2006), 138–68; Mark A. Graber, "The Nonmajoritarian Difficulty: Legislative Deference to the Judiciary," *Studies in American Political Development* 7 (1993): 35–73; Mark A. Graber, "Federalist or Friends of Adams: The Marshall Court and Party Politics," *Studies in American Political Development* 12 (1998): 229–66; Keith E. Whittington, "Presidential Challenges to Judicial Supremacy and the Politics of Constitutional Meaning," *Polity* 33 (2001): 365–95; Keith E. Whittington, "'Interpose Your Friendly Hand': Political Supports for the Exercise of Judicial Review by the United States Supreme Court," *American Political Science Review* 96 (2005): 583–96; and Whittington, *Political Foundations of Judicial Supremacy*.

[17] For work that takes account of the political environment surrounding judicial power but is still, at heart, interested in explaining why judges make certain decisions and not others rather than how judges become powerful in the first place, see Cornell W. Clayton and J. Mitchell Pickerill, "The Politics of Criminal Justice: How the New Right Regime Shaped the Rehnquist Court's Criminal Justice Jurisprudence," 94 *Georgetown Law Journal* 1385 (2006); Thomas M. Keck, *The Most Activist Supreme Court in History: The Road to Modern Judicial Conservatism* (Chicago: University of Chicago Press, 2004); Michael J. Klarman, "Rethinking the Civil Rights and Civil Liberties Revolutions," 82 *Virginia Law Review* 1 (1996); Michael J. Klarman, *From Jim Crow to Civil Rights: The Supreme Court and the Struggle for Racial Equality* (Oxford: Oxford University Press, 2004); Kevin J. McMahon, *Reconsidering Roosevelt on Race: How the Presidency Paved the Road to Brown* (Chicago: University of Chicago Press, 2004); J. Mitchell Pickerill and Cornell W. Clayton, "The Rehnquist Court and the Political Dynamics of Federalism," *Perspectives on Politics* 2 (2004): 233–48; and Lucas A. Powe Jr., *The Warren Court and American Politics* (Cambridge, MA: Belknap Press, 2002).

as an independent and autonomous institution of governance in the American political system.[18]

As a result, my central concern in this book is with what might be called "architectonic" politics: the politics of actors seeking to shape the structures of government in order to further their own interests. After all, as political scientists (and sociologists) have recognized since Peter Bachrach and Morton Baratz's seminal 1962 article on the "second face of power,"[19] the processes that define and the structures that surround institutions determine, in no small part, both what those institutions will look like and what they will do. This insight is already central to existing developmental accounts of Congress,[20] the presidency,[21] and the federal bureaucracy.[22] For each of these institutions we know how and why it acquired the role, structure, and powers it did. We know why certain actors delegated specific powers to particular institutions at precise times and how those actors overcame constraints and seized upon opportunities for transformative action. The result is more than isolated conceptions of why the House of Representatives reformed itself, when presidential power is at its greatest, and how the Post Office became autonomous; rather, it is a more holistic and macrolevel understanding of how the growth and evolution of governmental power—how the expansion and refinement of "the state"—shaped and was shaped by politics and policy making at various points in American history. Given the role of the American judiciary in, among

[18] Two attempts that, if read in conjunction, are marginally useful in this regard are Robert G. McCloskey, *The American Supreme Court*, 5th ed., rev. by Sanford Levinson (Chicago: University of Chicago Press, 2010) and Richard A. Posner, *The Federal Courts: Challenge and Reform* (Cambridge, MA: Harvard University Press, 1996); for an older and somewhat more dated account through 1925, see Felix Frankfurter and James M. Landis, *The Business of the Supreme Court: A Study in the Federal Judicial System* (New York: Macmillan, 1928). Of course, there are also historical analyses of these processes (or something akin to them) in specific eras, citations to which are scattered throughout the next six chapters.

[19] Peter Bachrach and Morton S. Baratz, "Two Faces of Power," *American Political Science Review* 56 (1962): 947–52.

[20] Eric Schickler, *Disjointed Pluralism: Institutional Innovation and the Development of the U.S. Congress* (Princeton, NJ: Princeton University Press, 2001); Elaine K. Swift, *The Making of an American Senate: Reconstitutive Change in Congress, 1787–1841* (Ann Arbor, MI: University of Michigan Press, 1996); Julian Zelizer, *On Capitol Hill: The Struggle to Reform Congress and Its Consequences, 1948–2000* (Cambridge: Cambridge University Press, 2004).

[21] Terry Moe, "The Politicized Presidency," in *The New Direction in American Politics*, ed. John E. Chubb and Paul E. Peterson (Washington, DC: Brookings Institution Press, 1985), 235–71; Stephen Skowronek, *The Politics Presidents Make: Leadership from John Adams to Bill Clinton* (Cambridge, MA: Harvard University Press, 1997).

[22] Daniel P. Carpenter, *The Forging of Bureaucratic Autonomy: Reputations, Networks, and Policy Innovation in Executive Agencies, 1862–1928* (Princeton, NJ: Princeton University Press, 2001); Stephen Skowronek, *Building a New American State: The Expansion of National Administrative Capacities, 1877–1920* (Cambridge: Cambridge University Press, 1982). For a theoretically rich but less historically oriented account, see Terry M. Moe, "The Politics of Bureaucratic Structure," in *Can the Government Govern?* ed. John E. Chubb and Paul E. Peterson (Washington, DC: Brookings Institution Press, 1989), 267–329.

other things, spurring the growth of an industrial economy,[23] constituting national citizenship,[24] and advancing certain forms of individual rights and liberties at the expense of others,[25] understanding the historical development of the institution—understanding the process by which its power was constructed—has obvious substantive import.[26] Yet when scholars of American political development speak of the judiciary at all,[27] rarely do they speak of it as an institution that was, in any meaningful sense, a product of architectonic politics.[28]

As this book will demonstrate, however, any view of the judiciary as simply a constitutional abstraction that does not itself develop over time is misguided. As an institution, the federal judiciary is composed of far more varied and complicated

[23] Richard Franklin Bensel, *The Political Economy of American Industrialization, 1877–1900* (Cambridge: Cambridge University Press, 2003), 289–354 (on the judicial construction of an unregulated national market).

[24] Rogers M. Smith, *Civic Ideals: Conflicting Visions of Citizenship in U.S. History* (New Haven, CT: Yale University Press, 1997).

[25] Ken I. Kersch, *Constructing Civil Liberties: Discontinuities in the Development of American Constitutional Law* (Cambridge: Cambridge University Press, 2004).

[26] Cf. Gordon S. Wood, "The Origins of Judicial Review," 22 *Suffolk University Law Review* 1293, 1304 (1988), lamenting that we have "no history of the emergence of the independent judiciary at the end of the eighteenth and beginning of the nineteenth centuries—perhaps because we take a strong independent judiciary so much for granted"; and Mark A. Graber, "Establishing Judicial Review: *Marbury* and the Judicial Act of 1789," 38 *Tulsa Law Review* 609, 646 (2003), noting that we would learn much about the development of judicial power "by examining the legislative debates over the structure of the federal judiciary that have taken place throughout American history." Part of my project, of course, is to begin to write precisely the history to which Wood refers utilizing precisely the sources suggested by Graber.

[27] Although there is an abundance of scholarship approaching the judiciary from the standpoint of American political development, much of it focuses on constitutional law and doctrine to the exclusion of changes in the judiciary as an institution. See, for example, Bruce Ackerman, *We the People: Foundations* (Cambridge, MA: Belknap Press, 1991); Bruce Ackerman, *We the People: Transformations* (Cambridge, MA: Belknap Press, 1998); Pamela Brandwein, *Rethinking the Judicial Settlement of Reconstruction* (Cambridge: Cambridge University Press, 2011); Victoria C. Hattam, *Labor Visions and State Power: The Origins of Business Unionism in the United States* (Princeton, NJ: Princeton University Press, 1993); Keck, *The Most Activist Supreme Court in History*; Kersch, *Constructing Civil Liberties*; George I. Lovell, *Legislative Deferrals: Statutory Ambiguity, Judicial Power, and American Democracy* (Cambridge: Cambridge University Press, 2003); McMahon, *Reconsidering Roosevelt on Race*; William J. Novak, *The People's Welfare: Law and Regulation in Nineteenth Century America* (Chapel Hill: University of North Carolina Press, 1996); Julie Novkov, *Constituting Workers, Protecting Women: Gender, Law, and Labor in the Progressive Era and New Deal Years* (Ann Arbor: The University of Michigan Press, 2001); Karen Orren, *Belated Feudalism: Labor, Law, and Liberal Development in the United States* (Cambridge: Cambridge University Press, 1991); Martin J. Sklar, *The Corporate Reconstruction of American Capitalism, 1890–1916: The Market, the Law, and Politics* (Cambridge: Cambridge University Press, 1988); and Smith, *Civic Ideals*.

[28] For relatively specific treatments of this idea outside the American political development tradition, see Barrow, Gryski, and Zuk, *The Federal Judiciary and Institutional Change*; John M. De Figueiredo and Emerson H. Tiller, "Congressional Control of the Courts: A Theoretical and Empirical Analysis of Expansion of the Federal Judiciary," *Journal of Law and Economics* 39 (1996): 435–462; and Charles R. Shipan, *Designing Judicial Review: Interest Groups, Congress, and Communications Policy* (Ann Arbor: University of Michigan Press, 1997).

components than simply the written opinions of judges; its structural architecture is at least as complex—and its historical development at least as dynamic—as that of Congress, the presidency, or the federal bureaucracy. Indeed, looking back at the indeterminacy of Article III,[29] which declares that a judicial power exists but offers scant guidance about the precise nature, contour, or extent of that power, we see that the development of an active and interventionist third branch of government was far from a foregone conclusion. The American judiciary, that is to say, was not born independent, autonomous, and powerful; rather, it had to become so, largely through a continuous process that was both politically determined and politically consequential.[30] The story of the judiciary's transformation, in other words, is not a single moment of revelation but a series of battles over law, courts, and the politics of institutional development. It is the story of how the judiciary, long outlined in pencil rather than pen, was built—piece by piece, from the ground up, as part and parcel of American political development.

The Puzzle of Judicial Institution Building

At the heart of this book is the puzzle of "judicial institution building"—the puzzle of understanding how the process of "building" the judiciary unfolded over the course of American political development. By "judicial institution building," I mean *the creation, consolidation, expansion, or reduction of the structural and institutional capacities needed to respond to and intervene in the political environment.*[31] In particular, I focus on the construction, destruction, and renovation of three building blocks that are both common and essential to all political institutions[32]: a

---

[29] At a mere 369 words, Article III (the judicial article) is the shortest and vaguest of the articles establishing the three branches of the federal government. For purposes of comparison, Article I (the legislative article) is 2,247 words and Article II (the executive article) is 1,011 words. The entire 1787 Constitution is more than 4,300 words, so Article III accounts for less than one-tenth of the document as a whole. In terms of actual content, the article indicates that there is a "judicial Power of the United States," that such power is "vested in one supreme Court, and in such inferior Courts as the Congress may from time to time ordain and establish," and that it "shall extend" to (among other categories of disputes) "all Cases, in Law and Equity, arising under this Constitution, the Laws of the United States, and Treaties made, or which shall be made, under their authority." At the same time, it gives no indication of how many individuals will compose the Supreme Court and qualifies its grants of jurisdiction "with such Exceptions, and under such Regulations as the Congress shall make."

[30] I borrow this sentence formulation from Gordon S. Wood, *The Radicalism of the American Revolution* (New York: Vintage, 1991), ix: "Americans were not born free and democratic in any modern sense; they became so—and largely as a consequence of the American revolution."

[31] I am influenced here by Stephen Skowronek's definition of state building as the process by which "government officials seeking to maintain power and legitimacy try to mold institutional capacities in response to an ever-changing environment." See Skowronek, *Building a New American State*, 10. For a similar definition of "judicial power," see Cameron, "Endogenous Preferences about Courts," 189.

[32] Although institution building is often conceived strictly as a process of positive growth (empowerment), I include negative growth (limitation) in my conception as well. If our goal is to understand the politics surrounding the development of judicial power, then surely the reduction or abolition of

set of discrete and specific *functions*,[33] which are performed by a group (or variety of groups) of *individuals*,[34] who are themselves aided by a collection of concrete operating *resources*.[35] This tripartite foundation encompasses several features of the institutional judiciary, including—but not limited to—jurisdiction, procedural rules, and judicial discretion (functions); expansion or contraction of courts, organizational structure, and formal institutional entities such as the Judicial Conference or the Administrative Office of the Courts (individuals); and budgets, buildings, and legal reports or books (resources). Together these features allow courts to hear cases, craft and modify legal rules, and render authoritative judgments; in turn, they make it possible for judges to settle political, legal, constitutional, and policy disputes that have concrete effects on citizens, corporations, government, and the nation as a whole.[36]

My goal is to uncover both the causes and consequences of institutional innovation and modification—of changes in functions, individuals, and resources—within the judiciary.[37] As such, I ask three broad questions about judicial reform

particular facets of that power is relevant and important. After all, just as building a structure involves erecting or remodeling certain features, so too might it involve razing others. See Karen Orren and Stephen Skowronek, *The Search for American Political Development* (Cambridge: Cambridge University Press, 2004), 123, eschewing the Whiggish "assumption of progress between past and present" and defining political development as a "durable shift in governing authority." That said, the trajectory of judicial power in America has been consistently and undeniably upward.

[33] *Functions* refers to the number and types of cases that courts can or must hear as well as the manner in which those courts are empowered, encouraged, and permitted to dispose of them.

[34] *Individuals* refers to the number and location of judges and other judicial personnel (clerks, marshals, administrators), as well as the way in which said personnel are hired, fired, organized, and supervised.

[35] *Resources* refers to the amount, source, and type of appropriations granted to the judiciary (including any specific conditions, limits, or incentives placed on or around the use of those appropriations) as well as legal materials and the availability of office space, courtrooms, and courthouses.

[36] On the importance of these seemingly mundane structural features, see Frankfurter and Landis, *The Business of the Supreme Court*, 2: "The mechanism of law—what courts are to deal with which causes and subject to what conditions—cannot be dissociated from the ends that law subserves. . . . After all, procedure is instrumental; it is the means of effectuating policy." For similar assertions applied to legislative development, see Schickler, *Disjointed Pluralism*, 3, noting that "as any legislature evolves through time, little is more fundamental to its politics than recurrent, often intense, efforts to *change*" the body's "complex of rules, procedures, and specialized internal institutions"; and Zelizer, *On Capitol Hill*, 3, arguing that process is "more than a technical backdrop to the *real* political action."

[37] Throughout the book I focus my consideration on Article III courts, largely (though not wholly) leaving aside so-called Article I courts, which include the Tax Court and various administrative law entities that adjudicate disputes over congressionally created rights; Article II courts, which operate as military commissions; and Article IV courts, which exist in American territories such as Guam and the Virgin Islands. While it is no doubt true that these other quasi-judicial bodies are important in the broader landscape of American politics, the fact that they are not established under Article III and therefore neither subject to the constraints (adversarial proceedings for live disputes only) nor in possession of the benefits (life tenure during good behavior) of Article III tribunals raises a somewhat distinct set of analytic issues. For the Supreme Court's official delineation of acceptable uses of non–Article III courts and explication of the key distinctions between Article III and non–Article III courts, see *Northern Pipeline Construction Company v. Marathon Pipe Line Company*, 458 U.S. 50 (1982)

from the commencement of the new government in 1789 through the close of the twentieth century. First, *why* was judicial institution building pursued? Who were the important actors, and what goals were they seeking to attain? Second, *how* was judicial institution building accomplished? What challenges presented themselves, and what events or actions were needed to surmount them? Third, *what* did judicial institution building achieve? What were the concrete and enduring changes in the exercise of judicial power?[38] My focus here is less on what the judiciary does vis-à-vis other political institutions than on what is done to the judiciary both by external actors and by its own members; my interest is less in how the judiciary wields power and authority in any particular jurisprudential or policy area than in the analytically antecedent matter of how it gradually became structurally and institutionally equipped to exert power and authority across a range of areas.

If that process was not overseen by judges, then by whom? If it was not executed through constitutional interpretation and judicial review, then through what? Because of the manner in which Article III effectively delegates judicial institution building to Congress,[39] the chief actors are representatives and senators, the critical actions congressional statutes that are often called (either at the time or in retrospect) "Judiciary Acts." Yet even as the ultimate form of judicial institution building is predominantly legislative, the character of the process leading up to and politics surrounding it is relatively diverse, with presidents, judges, attorneys general, legal academics, bar association leaders, and other notable political actors all playing substantial roles in generating ideas, drafting proposals, and actively working either for or against reform even if, at the conclusion of the process, their actions are validated by and formalized through congressional action. For their part, constitutional interpretation and judicial review are no doubt important, but they are not only less important than action taken by the policy branches but also important less as avenues of institution building than as either context for it, with judicial decisions influencing the strategic environment within which institution building takes place, or extensions of it, with judges frequently acting in the existing stream of politically determined institution building (even if adding their own power-consolidating flourishes to it) and very rarely venturing outside it.

At base, the puzzle of judicial institution building is fundamentally about a series of contested questions of institutional design and delegation. In making choices

---

(invalidating the jurisdiction granted to bankruptcy courts under the Bankruptcy Act of 1978 as an unconstitutional exercise of congressional authority to establish inferior tribunals under Article III).

[38] Although I ask three sets of questions about the politics of institutional development, I offer a theoretical account for only the first two. The third set of questions—focused on consequences rather than causes—is no doubt crucially important (and it receives notable treatment in each subsequent chapter). But, given the context-dependent nature of the consequences of institution building, it is exceedingly difficult—and, indeed, likely undesirable—to craft a generalizable theory to explain them.

[39] Article III, Section 1 vests judicial power in the Supreme Court "and in such inferior Courts as *the Congress* may from time to time ordain and establish" (emphasis added). This follows the enumeration of the power "To constitute Tribunals inferior to the supreme Court" granted to Congress in Article I, Section 8.

about whether, when, and in what way to build the judiciary, political actors are driven by one or more of three goals: satisfying substantive regime commitments (policy), consolidating partisan strength and preserving electoral support (politics), and maintaining a functionally efficient judicial branch (performance).[40] While housekeeping measures are largely uncontroversial, occurring often and easily, more significant policy, political, and performance institution-building efforts face constraints—both practical obstacles and political contestation—that inhibit reform of the institutional judiciary. These constraints are overcome and reform made possible through two catalysts for change: significant political events and strategic political action. While events resulting in increases in judicial workload or a large-scale crisis in American society may help to prompt widely supported change, only pivotal elections that reorder political settings or reorient political incentives are capable of breaking down the constraints that inhibit transformative action. In the absence of such an election, entrepreneurs can overcome the constraints upon reform provided their identity, ideas, and tactics are each carefully tailored to the task at hand.

Over the course of American history, the precise substance of each of these three institution-building aims—policy, politics, and performance—has varied widely, but the overriding purpose has remained constant: to use the judiciary to further some end that would otherwise be difficult or even impossible to realize. Whether hoping to promote the growth of a commercial economy, the protection of minority rights, or the defeat of organized labor, political actors have pursued institution building to reallocate power either horizontally (between branches of the federal government) or vertically (between federal and state governments) in the hope that the federal judiciary would be more amenable than other institutions to their particular policy preferences. Among other plans, institution builders have entrenched their policy preferences past the duration of the current political regime by stacking newly created judgeships with like-minded individuals and expanded federal jurisdiction or broadened the causes for removal from state courts in order to shift particular classes of disputes from hostile forums where their interests are unlikely to be represented to friendlier forums more receptive

---

[40] I should note that, while either policy or political goals might be considered part of a "regime politics" approach to institution building, the two aims do not always act in concert with each other. To say simply that regimes are building the judiciary may be true, but it ignores the process by which different regime interests come to the fore and the ways in which they may conflict, coincide, and combine in unique and often unpredictable ways. For the touchstone of the "regime politics" genre, much of which is concerned with tracking external political influences on judicial decision making at various points of American history, see Robert A. Dahl, "Decision-Making in a Democracy: The Supreme Court as a National Policy Maker," *Journal of Public Law* 6 (1957): 279–95. For more recent iterations, see Clayton and Pickerill, "The Politics of Criminal Justice"; Gillman, "Party Politics and Constitutional Change"; and Pickerill and Clayton, "The Rehnquist Court and the Political Dynamics of Federalism." For a critique of that literature as it applies to the exercise of judicial review, see Thomas M. Keck, "Party, Policy, or Duty: Why Does the Supreme Court Invalidate Federal Statutes?" *American Political Science Review* 101 (2007): 321–38.

to their desired ends.[41] Independent of—or, perhaps in advance of—whatever substantive outcomes they might seek to foster, political actors have also used institution building to consolidate their own power. In this vein, political institution building has alternately been seen as an opportunity to build the party apparatus by distributing patronage positions (judges, marshals, and clerks, for example) to campaign supporters so as to solidify a base of electoral support heading into the next election cycle,[42] and as a mechanism to foist divisive issues onto the judiciary (whether by drafting vague statutes in need of judicial interpretation, including specific provisions authorizing judicial review, or expanding the reach of federal jurisdiction), thereby enhancing electoral prospects by sidestepping contentious and coalition-disrupting political decisions.[43] Finally, political actors have consistently employed institution building to maintain a well-functioning and efficient judicial branch. Such action has often emerged out of the recognition of performance benefits unique to judicial governance (the application of uniform and consistent rules across agencies or states, the information advantage in assessing the concrete effects of policy afforded by being an ex post mover[44]) as well as attempts to solve performance defects of both endemic (rising caseloads) and isolated (sick judges, inconvenient times and locations of court sessions) proportions.[45]

Since—aside from functionalist and nonsubstantive housekeeping measures, which regularly proceed without impediment—institution building holds the potential to be both partial between contending ideological visions (disproportionately benefiting or harming one political party, interest group, or segment of the population) and transformative in scope (fundamentally altering or radically reconfiguring the institution), the process can be quite controversial and encounter substantial resistance from party leaders, organized interests, and ordinary citizens alike. Against both this sort of political opposition and practical obsta-

[41] Gillman, "How Political Parties Can Use the Courts to Advance Their Agendas."

[42] Barrow, Zuk, and Gryski, *The Federal Judiciary and Institutional Change*; Sheldon Goldman, *Picking Federal Judges: Lower Court Selection From Roosevelt Through Reagan* (New Haven, CT: Yale University Press, 1997), citing "personal" as one of three presidential agendas in lower court staffing.

[43] This type of action not only allows elected officials to cast the judiciary as a scapegoat for problematic outcomes but also facilitates their ability to say one thing (to extremists) and simultaneously do another thing (for moderates). See Graber, "The Nonmajoritarian Difficulty"; and Lovell, *Legislative Deferrals*. Of course, Congress regularly delegates power to bureaucratic agencies for similar reasons. See, for example, David Epstein and Sharyn O'Halloran, *Delegating Powers: A Transactions-Cost Approach to Policy Making under Separate Powers* (New York: Cambridge University Press, 1999); John D. Huber and Charles R. Shipan, *Deliberate Discretion? The Institutional Foundations of Bureaucratic Autonomy* (New York: Cambridge University Press, 2002); and Mathew D. McCubbins, Roger G. Noll, and Barry R. Weingast, "Administrative Procedures as Instruments of Political Control," *Journal of Law, Economics, and Organization* 3 (1987): 243–77.

[44] James T. Rogers, "Information and Judicial Review: A Signaling Game of Legislative-Judicial Interaction," *American Journal of Political Science* 45 (2001): 84–99.

[45] To the extent that rectifying these sorts of functional inadequacies is regularly seen as either or both a matter of good governance or a form of constituent service to assuage the frustration of citizens and interest groups, performance-oriented institution building occasionally manifests policy or political concerns indirectly.

cles including the limited time of legislative sessions, the presence of seemingly more pressing matters (both foreign and domestic) on the national agenda, and the technicality of the issues involved, two distinct catalysts—significant political events and strategic political action—have managed to push institution building forward.

Significant events have prompted successful institution building in two distinct ways. Some events, including those contributing to an increase in judicial workload (as in the case of territorial expansion or the passing of significant regulatory legislation) or prompting a crisis in American society (as in the case of economic distress or national political scandal), have helped to facilitate institution building. By prompting calls for, raising awareness about, and generally transcending the inertia and disinterest that might otherwise surround institution building, such events often place on the political agenda largely uncontested initiatives that are likely, though by no means certain, to be viewed favorably by relevant political actors. Beyond merely bringing high-support but low-salience reforms to fruition, other events—specifically, elections that either fundamentally reshape the political environment or substantially alter the calculations of actors within it—have proved independently capable of triggering institution building by surmounting the political barriers surrounding it. Whether by encouraging lame-duck leaders to entrench their substantive policy interests in the judiciary, inviting new leaders to consolidate their electoral support and fortify their party apparatus, substantially weakening an obstructionist minority, elevating politicians with slightly different preferences as their intracoalition predecessors, or convincing moderate actors that the political tides were headed in one direction as opposed to another, pivotal elections have provided ripe opportunities for outgoing, incoming, and existing actors to place their stamp on the shape of the federal judiciary.

When facilitating events have not brought uncontested reform to the fore and triggering events (namely, pivotal elections) have not eliminated potential constraints upon judicial institution building, the entrepreneurship of cautious and strategic political actors has occasionally been successful. Somewhat more difficult—and thus less common—than reforms that emerge in the aftermath of significant events, entrepreneurial reforms have nonetheless proved both transformative and extremely long-lasting.[46] Seeking to resolve rather than simply avoid the collision of rival goals and interests that is endemic to institution building, political entrepreneurs have influenced decisions through and neutralized opposition with some combination of their individual identities, ideas, and tactics. When armed with favorable reputations, embedded in crosscutting networks of support, and possessing a natural constituent base among members of a particular party, region of the country, or substantive interest area, entrepreneurs gain credibility for reform efforts, insulate themselves against certain types of attacks and oppo-

---

[46]Indeed, as we shall see, three of the most important institution-building statutes in American history—the Judiciary Act of 1789 (in chapter 2), the Circuit Courts of Appeals Act of 1891 (in chapter 5), and the Judiciary Act of 1925 (in chapter 6)—were each prompted by political entrepreneurship.

sition, and generally acquire the political capital necessary to enable institution building. Through the articulation of ideas that other actors either support, are neutral toward, or are mildly skeptical of rather than staunchly opposed to, entrepreneurs avoid squandering capital over radical reform proposals. By framing the terms of debate, reconciling contradictory preferences, accommodating and incorporating multiple perspectives, engineering compromises through measured action, building coalitions, constructing political legitimacy, and influencing the media and public perception, entrepreneurs overcome ambivalence and contestation by manipulating actors and the diverse set of interests that surround them.[47] Engaged "in a constant search for political advantage,"[48] entrepreneurs are perpetually looking for "speculative opportunities"—overlays, cleavages, and fissures— that are pregnant with possibilities for change but require an act of leadership in order for any to materialize. And once they find or create such opportunities, entrepreneurs employ targeted strategies sensitive to the surrounding environment at that precise moment in time in order to forge successful political action through politically stable coalitions rather than politically infirm factions.[49]

Conceptualizing the federal judiciary as both a central actor in and an outcome of politics, as simultaneously a participant and object in the struggle for political power, we see that the institution has been designed and constructed in ways that both embody political choice and engendered political change. It has been built because elected politicians consistently and continuously saw it in their interest to build it, and it has been built in ways that converted a woefully inchoate institution into a firmly established one.[50] Far from a clean or consensual process, this transformation of the institutional judiciary did not occur without controversy, without contestation, or without compromise; rather, it emerged from the cauldron of ordinary politics.

Toward a Developmental Account of Judicial Power

Occurring during unified and divided government; under Republicans, Democrats, Federalists, and Whigs; when the Supreme Court was striking down many federal and state laws and when it was striking down few, judicial institution building—far from limited to specific years or spans of years—has been consistent throughout American history and across traditional categories of political analy-

[47] Carpenter, *The Forging of Bureaucratic Autonomy*, 14–17, 27–35; Adam D. Sheingate, "Political Entrepreneurship, Institutional Change, and American Political Development," *Studies in American Political Development* 17 (2003): 188.

[48] Sheingate, "Political Entrepreneurship, Institutional Change, and American Political Development," 186.

[49] Sheingate refers to this as a process of "creative recombination." Ibid., 198.

[50] Throughout much of early American history, in fact, the judiciary lacked the ability to undertake even basic tasks of institutional maintenance, with Congress routinely passing legislation on matters such as the times and locations of court sessions and contingency plans in the event sitting judges grew ill.

sis. The bulk of such institution building, however, has yielded alterations that more closely resembled institutional tinkering than institutional transformation. These reforms have come often, but they have also come piecemeal. Provisional in aim and limited in scope, they modify the problems they address only for a short time and, even then, only at the margins. Frequently, these measures are explicitly framed as temporary expedients—with the promise of more significant reform at a later date—but eventually become fairly permanent (and outdated) fixtures in the landscape of the institutional judiciary. And although it is true that changes that may initially appear insignificant often accumulate and can, with the passage of time, become important in their own right, the development of the institutional judiciary has largely been defined by a small set of transformative—and, for the most part, highly contested—reforms rather than by a larger set of inferior and consensual ones. Inferior episodes are important, but their function is largely to fill in details after landmark episodes outline the role, structure, and powers of the federal judiciary. Given the increased level of political contestation, those land-mark episodes are obviously more atypical, often occurring unpredictably, occa-sionally in fits and spasms after long periods of inactivity and mundane change. Though fewer in number, these episodes are also greater in stature, inducing the "durable shift[s] in governing authority" that denote consequential change in the American political system.[51]

My general approach to creating a developmental account of judicial power, then, embeds case studies of a series of transformative moments within a more deeply contextual understanding of the process in the historical period under con-sideration.[52] In surveying the universe of institution-building episodes,[53] I identify as transformative those episodes that, whether purposefully or inadvertently, in-fluenced either the concrete and tangible state of the institutional judiciary itself or the character of the architectonic politics that surround the building of it in a fash-ion that is both broad-based and enduring.[54] For each such institution-building

[51] Orren and Skowronek, *The Search for American Political Development*, 123.

[52] This means, of course, that I do not treat every conceivable instance of institution building that has occurred since the nation's founding. I do, however, supplement my detailed process tracing of transformative moments by recapping numerous other episodes at the end of each section and by not-ing yet more in assorted footnotes throughout the ensuing chapters.

[53] Using two systematic "sweeps" of American history, I compiled a database of such episodes from 1789 to 2000. Sweep 1 relied on keyword searches—*judge, court, justice,* and *judicia!* (which includes *judicial* and *judiciary*)—of Lexis-Nexis Congressional Universe to locate legislation directly related to courts and judges. Sweep 2 supplemented this already substantial collection with an extensive review of secondary literature, including histories of both the federal courts generally and the Supreme Court specifically, political and constitutional histories of particular time periods, analyses of judicial policy making in discrete areas, legal casebooks and treatises, studies of judicial organization and administra-tion, and empirically grounded arguments for and against judicial power. I borrow this two-pronged strategy from David R. Mayhew, *Divided We Govern: Party Control, Lawmaking, and Investigations, 1946–1990* (New Haven, CT: Yale University Press, 1991).

[54] By *broad-based*, I mean relevant not simply for individual actors, regions, or policy domains but for the nation (and the place of judicial power within it) as a whole. Under this criterion, the authoriza-tion of a single judge—or even several judges—in an individual state or circuit would not be labeled as

episode or set of episodes treated in the successive chapters, I utilize a range of primary source materials (including legislative records, judicial decisions, private correspondence between relevant actors, personal memoirs, and media coverage) to reconstruct the architectonic politics of institutional development—the opportunities seized and wasted, the obstacles overcome and stumbled upon—as they occurred at the time. Drawing upon the work of historians who have pieced together the detailed record behind some of these events, on the one hand, and the work of legal academics who have traced the possible interpretations and concrete ramifications of those events, on the other, I not only integrate the diverse and often uneven treatment of judicial institution building but also bring a historical-institutionalist perspective to bear on the politics of altering the institutional environment of courts and judges in America.

Since institutions operate within a broader political climate that both engenders and constrains action, I endeavor this task with an eye toward other narratives of American political, economic, social, legal, constitutional, and ideological development. Of course, acute events such as the Civil War and the Great Depression are important as potential engines of change, but so too are macrosocial processes such as the rise and fall of political parties; the transformation from an agricultural to an industrial economy; the shifting balance of power between federal and state authorities; the changing nature of citizenship and democratization of political power; the increased solicitude for civil rights and liberties; and the evolution and interaction of intellectual currents such as populism, progressivism, liberalism, and conservatism. For my purposes, these developments are relevant not simply as background history but as forces that bring judicial institution-building initiatives to the agenda, structure debates over them, and serve as possible sites of consonance or friction between advocates and opponents of particular episodes of them. In so doing, they serve to delineate the basic contours of architectonic politics in each era, with distinct periods in the history of institution building defined and demarcated by what I take to be the dominant mode of institution-building activity at the time.[55] To the extent that these modes are inextricably intertwined with—and, indeed, often direct responses to—the overarching tensions and debates of their time, the politics of institution building simply cannot be understood in a historical vacuum.

Ultimately, whatever the animating issues and whatever the resulting mode, transformative and inferior episodes of institution building have combined to pro-

---

transformative while the creation of a slate of new judges or the establishment of an entirely new tier of judges to be distributed across the nation would. By *enduring*, I mean responsible for changes that either persisted for an extended period of time themselves or left a substantial long-term legacy in their wake. Under this criterion, a statute in operation for several decades would be considered transformative while one repealed after only a few years would not—unless it was sufficiently influential in that short time to instigate subsequent changes in political structures, behavior, or outcomes.

[55] As a result of this approach, not every chapter explores each of the three key building blocks—functions, individuals, resources—of the institutional judiciary. Each of those building blocks was a salient feature of reform activity at *some point* but none were especially salient at *all points*.

duce a developmental path for judicial capacity that has been overwhelmingly, though not irreversibly, upward. Largely a function of the fact that—regardless of their specific goals—politicians have often viewed the judiciary as a potential partner in, rather than an obstacle to, their governing coalitions, empowering institution building is usually favored by leaders of the prevailing coalition and resisted by leaders of the opposite coalition. Even when the political majority is at odds with the judiciary, that antagonism generates fewer attempts at limiting judicial power than at reshaping judicial power,[56] often prompting reform proposals from judicial allies hoping to improve judicial performance in such a way that neutralizes opposition.[57] With this recognition that courts and judges can be useful regime partners animating the institution-building impulses of political actors, judicial independence, autonomy, and power have increased steadily and drastically since the founding of the nation. This result, though seemingly obvious today, was, in retrospect, anything but predictable. Indeed, one need look no farther than the heap of discarded, failed, and repealed attempts at judicial reform throughout American history to realize that the shape of the contemporary judiciary was hardly preordained.[58] In other words, a different judiciary—in terms of functions, individuals, or resources—was readily possible. Judicial institution building was not the result of fate or destiny but the architectonic work of influential political actors seeking to advance their own objectives. Indeed, the building of the American judiciary was not at all historically inevitable but, instead, a contingent and continuous political process. It is that process—of policy, politics, and performance; of constraints and catalysts; of elections and entrepreneurship—I attempt to recover here.

• • •

This book proceeds as follows. In chapters 2 through 7, I excavate both the causes and consequences of judicial institution building from the the time of the founding to the close of the twentieth century. In each chapter, I explicate why judicial institution building was pursued, how it was accomplished, and what it achieved in a particular historical time period, characterizing each period according to the central mode of institution building (as expressed in chapter subtitles) during the

---

[56] For further elaboration of this point and a more general treatment of the recurrent strands of hostility to judicial power, see Stephen M. Engel, *American Politicians Confront the Court: Opposition Politics and the Changing Responses to Judicial Power* (Cambridge: Cambridge University Press, 2011).

[57] Although there have been many attempts to limit judicial power, very few have been successful in any meaningful sense. See Stuart S. Nagel, "Court-Curbing Periods in American History," 18 *Vanderbilt Law Review* 925 (1965); and Gerald N. Rosenberg, "Judicial Independence and the Reality of Political Power," *Review of Politics* 54 (1992): 369–98. Of those "court-curbing" measures that have been successful, many were oriented more around controlling litigation than around reducing judicial power. See Dawn M. Chutkow, "Jurisdiction Stripping: Litigation, Ideology, and Congressional Control of the Courts," *Journal of Politics* 70 (2008): 1053–64. For a critique of the prevalence and utility of concepts like "court curbing" in the judicial politics literature, see chapter 8.

[58] Cf. Frankfurter and Landis, *The Business of the Supreme Court*, 4: "Familiarity with political institutions breeds indifference to their origin."

years that constitute it. Taken together, these six chapters offer a historically rich narrative that not only describes the institutional development of the judiciary but also offers analytically grounded explanations of how it happened, why it happened when it did, why it happened in the form it did, and why, from the perspective of American constitutional democracy, it mattered at all. In chapter 8, I synthesize and contextualize within contemporary debates my empirical story about the architectonic politics of judicial institution building as well as reflect upon the lessons of the more than 200 year historical lineage of the institutional judiciary for our understanding of judicial power in America.

In chapter 2, I examine the *establishment* of the judiciary from the beginning of George Washington's first term as president in 1789 to the end of Thomas Jefferson's first term in 1805. Seeking to add flesh to the bare bones of Article III, politicians in the early republic wrestled with the most basic questions of institutional design—what the judiciary should look like, how it should operate, and what it should do. As a result, against the backdrop of the uncertainty surrounding postrevolutionary America and the developing conflict between the rival ideological visions of Hamiltonianism and Jeffersonianism, debates about judicial reform were, at base, debates about the foundations—the core functions, the crucial individuals, and the vital resources—necessary to launch an entire branch of the federal government. Judicial institution building during this era occurred in three stages: a landmark policy compromise guided by a political entrepreneur capable of overcoming political opposition and building a viable coalition in the First Congress (1789); a failed attempt at wholesale performance reform followed by a handful of piecemeal adjustments (1790–99); and, sparked by the emergence of a new governing coalition, a flurry of policy and political institution building that, after much sound and fury, merely reestablished the status quo (1800–1805). In light of these episodes, I argue that judicial institution building in the early republic was motivated by the policy desire of proto-Federalist legislators to encourage a commercial economy, Supreme Court justices' performance-oriented concerns about the propriety and utility of serving on circuit courts, and the Jeffersonian attempt to reconstruct American politics without the interference of a Federalist-dominated judiciary. It was then enabled by the political entrepreneurship of Oliver Ellsworth and by the transfer of power from Federalists to Jeffersonians after the election of 1800; it resulted in the skeleton of what would eventually (and perhaps surprisingly) become an independent, autonomous, and powerful judiciary.

In chapter 3, I examine the *reorganization* of the judiciary from the beginning of Thomas Jefferson's second term as president in 1805 until just prior to the Compromise of 1850. Declining to modify the basic contours of the institutional judiciary established in the early republic, Jeffersonian- and Jacksonian-era politicians attempted instead to manipulate those contours to their own advantage. Intertwined in no small part with territorial expansion and the politics of statehood admission, judicial reform attempts focused primarily on arranging states in circuits and ensuring regional geographic representation on the Supreme Court. Here, judicial institution building occurred in four stages: the initial Jeffersonian expansion of the circuit system to seven circuits and the Supreme Court to seven justices (1805–8), the failed National Republican attempt to add three more circuits and three more justices (1809–28), the failed Whig attempt to consolidate the Third and Fourth Circuits (1829–35), and a quick resolution to multiple decades of stalemate with the Jacksonian establishment of eighth and ninth circuits and eighth and ninth seats on the Court (1836–50). In light of these episodes, I argue that judicial institution building in the ages of Jeffersonian and Jacksonian democracy was motivated by Western complaints about performance problems deriving from the lack of judicial presence in newly admitted states, the proto-Whig National Republican desire to empower the judiciary as a policy-making ally, and the Jacksonian dream of solidifying a Democratic Court. It was then enabled (when it was not impeded by the clash of rival policy and political goals) by a combination of congressional unawareness and Democratic victories in the 1834 midterm and 1836 presidential elections; it resulted in the reorganization of the judicial system so as to privilege Jacksonian, Democratic, and Southern slaveholding interests.

In chapter 4, I examine the *empowerment* of the judiciary from the Compromise of 1850 (admitting California into the Union as a free state and unofficially signifying the beginning of the political crisis leading to the Civil War) to the Compromise of 1877 (settling the disputed 1876 presidential election between Samuel J. Tilden and Rutherford B. Hayes and representing the formal end of Reconstruction). Having seen how Jacksonians reshaped the judiciary according to their interests, Civil War and Reconstruction Republicans set about molding the judiciary according to theirs. Given the increasing sectionalism of the era, satisfying those interests necessitated a judiciary that was more national in outlook and more forceful in the exercise of power. With the conflict over slavery and the remarkable events of the most violent and radical period of American history very much in the foreground, judicial institution building occurred in four stages: the partisan and sectional fight over the structure of the institutional judiciary and the character of judicial power vis-à-vis slavery (1850–64), the Republican reliance on removal provisions and the writ of habeas corpus to protect federal officials and freed slaves from biased Southern courts immediately following the Civil War (1865–67), the consolidation of a Republican-friendly Supreme Court through ameliorative reforms aimed at specific problems of judicial performance (1866–69), and the dramatic nationalization of judicial power and Republican adoption of the federal judiciary as a partner in economic policy making (1870–77). In light of these episodes, I argue that judicial institution building during the Civil War and Reconstruction was motivated mostly by Republicans seeking to transform and then empower the judiciary as a partner in, and enforcer of, national policy making; enabled by Northern and Republican dominance of national politics following the election of Abraham Lincoln and the secession of the Southern states; and resulted in a vast expansion of federal judicial power.

In chapter 5, I examine the *restructuring* of the judiciary during the period of Republican dominance from the inauguration of Rutherford B. Hayes in 1877 to the inauguration of Woodrow Wilson in 1913. Forced to react to the vast wartime and postwar expansion of judicial power in order to maintain a minimal level of judicial effectiveness, Gilded Age and Progressive Era politicians reconsidered and then reconfigured the original 1789 framework. The focus of reform, then, was less the extent of judicial power than the structural logic and internal consistency of the institutional judiciary more broadly. Amid the parallel drives to cement an industrial economy and create an administrative state, judicial institution building occurred in two stages: the Gilded Age attempt to unburden the Supreme Court by appointing a new slate of judges to staff circuit courts (1877–91) and the Progressive Era unification and synchronization of all laws concerning the judiciary in one statute (1892–1914). In light of these episodes, I argue that judicial institution building in the Gilded Age and Progressive Era was advocated by Republicans seeking to satisfy the performance goal of an efficient and expeditious judicial system by alleviating the Supreme Court's workload, Democrats seeking to reduce the judicial workload and limit corporate access to the federal courts, and progressives who favored simplifying, streamlining, and standardizing various features of the institutional judiciary. It was then made possible by the political entrepreneurship of New York senator William Evarts and the widespread (but mistaken) impression that a performance reform was automatically insignificant housekeeping; it resulted in the creation of an entirely new level of the federal judicial hierarchy, the abolition of circuit courts, and the end of circuit riding by Supreme Court justices.

In chapter 6, I examine the *bureaucratization* of the judiciary during the quarter century between the dawn of World War I in 1914 and the dawn of World War II in 1939. With the judiciary having grown substantially in both size and power, and with the Gilded Age and Progressive Era restructuring having failed to alleviate problems completely, interwar and New Deal reformers turned to administrative management. In so doing, they both insulated the federal judiciary from potentially dangerous (and increasingly unnecessary) relationships with the other branches of government and signaled the arrival of a more autonomous and self-governing branch. In conjunction with the vast expansion of regulatory government, judicial institution building occurred in three stages: the forging of judicial autonomy over the Supreme Court's docket and creation of a policy-making body within the judicial branch (1913–29), the realization of a twenty-year American Bar Association goal to vest the authority to promulgate uniform rules of civil procedure in the hands of the justices (1930–35), and the complete separation of the judiciary's budget and administration from the executive branch control of the Department of Justice (1936–39). In light of these episodes I argue that judicial institution building in the interwar and New Deal years was prompted by a variety of performance concerns about the workload and administration of the judicial branch, enabled by separate instances of political entrepreneurship by William Howard Taft and Homer Cummings as well as limited opposition to moderate reform following Franklin Delano Roosevelt's landslide victory in the 1936 presidential election and subsequent ill-fated Court-packing plan, and resulted in the metamorphosis of the federal judiciary into a self-governing policy-making institution with not only its own interests but also the capability to pursue and satisfy those interests.

In chapter 7, I examine the *specialization* of the judiciary from the start of World War II in 1939 to the election of Bill Clinton's presidential successor in 2000. Coming out of the New Deal, when the federal government assumed theretofore unknown powers in American politics and the federal judiciary acquired theretofore unseen control over its own operations, the politicians of modern America broadened the institutional portfolios of courts and judges with a series of specialized functions and individuals. Far from eroding the gains judges had made in terms of centralized administration during the 1920s and '30s, this deepening of the bureaucratic tendency toward division of labor merely cemented the critical role of judicial power in performing the intricate and versatile duties of modern governance. Alongside the growth of (and rising challenges to) both the administrative regulatory state and American political and economic supremacy in the world at large during this time, judicial institution building occurred in three stages: the enhancement and expansion of judicial adjuncts both to execute administrative duties for and to relieve the growing caseload burden on federal district court judges (1939–79), the reorganization of existing courts and judges in order to develop and utilize expertise to handle the particularly complicated matter of patent law (1969–98), and the creation of a new tribunal to provide some measure of judicial scrutiny over the increasingly important domains of domestic surveillance and intelligence gathering (1972–2000). In light of these episodes, I argue that judicial institution building in modern America was pursued by legislators, judges, and academics seeking to modify the judiciary so as to enable it to serve (and, in one case, check) a bigger and (by any measure) more interventionist government more expertly. It was then made possible by the lack of any substantial opposition to seemingly consensus structural innovation, by the recognition of a workload crisis sufficiently threatening to judicial capacity so as to make moderate reform (offered following the failure of more aggressive reform) uncontroversial, and by a facilitating event creating a bipartisan, cross-institutional reform coalition; it resulted in the simultaneous refinement of judicial capacity and adaptation of the federal judiciary to a growing set of institutional responsibilities.

As these modes suggest, the history of judicial institution building has essentially alternated between fundamental transformation (the creation of the judicial system in the early republic, the widespread extension of jurisdiction and broad nationalization of judicial power during the Civil War and Reconstruction, the institutional thickening of judicial administration during the interwar and New Deal years) and more modest adaptations in the aftermath of such transformation (the geographic reshuffling of the circuit system during the eras of Jeffersonian and Jacksonian democracy, the renovation of founding-era judicial hierarchy in the Gilded Age and the Progressive Era, the assignment of various judicial prerogatives according to an elaborate division of labor in modern America). Instead of transforming the institutional judiciary every generation, political actors appear first to adjust it in response to the previous transformation before turning to landmark change once again. If such adjustments fail—or if, as often happens, the political environment changes in such a way that renders them moot[59]—then reformers pursue more widespread and systemic institution-building initiatives. Considered longitudinally, the fact that periods of empowerment were followed by modification rather than retrenchment—the fact that successive periods have, for the most part, built upon rather than torn down or canceled out one another—has resulted in a long-term trend line for judicial capacity marked less by alternating peaks and valleys than by a progressive and consistent increase. Tracing out the evolution of the institutional judiciary as a holistic and ongoing process that has unfolded over the course of American political development, then, we see that judicial independence, autonomy, and power have increased steadily and drastically since the time of the founding.

With this historical trajectory as a foundation, I conclude, in chapter 8, in two ways: first, by looking backward to assess, in empirical terms, the place of the judiciary in America's past; and, second, by looking forward to reflect, in normative terms, on the place of the judiciary in America's future. I illustrate how both political rhetoric and academic exegesis about the Supreme Court embody a fundamentally incorrect presumption about the judiciary being, in any sense, external to politics. In place of that presumption, which leads to a series of faulty and misleading arguments about the relationship between judicial power and democratic politics, I offer a conception that not only locates the judicial branch squarely within the political arena but also places substantially greater emphasis on its cooperation rather than conflict with other actors and institutions in that arena. Such a reality, I contend, should equally be seen as normatively desirable by those seeking to protect judicial independence from democratic politics, those seeking to promote judicial accountability to democratic politics, and those seeking to solidify and revitalize the participation of "the people" in democratic politics.

---

[59] As Frankfurter and Landis, 107, observe, "great judiciary acts, unlike great poems, are not written for all time."

CHAPTER TWO

The Early Republic

ESTABLISHMENT

The early republic was a volatile time.[1] Though a decade had passed from the firing of the first shots of independence at Lexington and Concord, to the opening gavel of the first session of the new government in New York City, the United States was still a work in progress. Since the Treaty of Paris in 1783, Americans had already discarded one governmental framework (that instituted by the Articles of Confederation) and, by 1789, were trying a new, and undoubtedly riskier, one. Swirling around the experiment of constitutional democracy were obstacles both foreign and domestic: avoiding another war with England, establishing credibility on the world stage, jump-starting a national economy, and raising revenue for a military defense. In nearly every realm, the future was uncertain and the possibilities for failure great. America, one might say, was on decidedly tenuous ground. Amid such chaos—amid the lingering hostility of states toward the national government, the developing conflict between agrarian and commercial visions of American political economy, and the rise of political parties—the process of building the federal judiciary into an independent and autonomous branch of governance began in earnest. Indeed, despite the multitude of potential preoccupations, a general reluctance to vest broad powers in unelected officials, and substantial fear about what the judiciary might do in practice, the judiciary, sketched only in the most general terms by the Constitution, began to gain functions, individuals, and resources all its own.

My goal in this chapter is to consider judicial institution building from the beginning of George Washington's first term as president in 1789 to the end of Thomas Jefferson's first term in 1805. In seeking to understand the vitally important first step in the historical process by which the "least dangerous branch" gradually became structurally and institutionally equipped to exert authority in American politics, I ask three questions about the tumultuous politics of institutional design that followed the ratification of the Constitution. First, why was judicial institution building pursued? Second, how was it accomplished? Third, what did it achieve? Judicial institution building in the early republic was, I argue, motivated by the policy de-

---

[1] The definitive history, which offers scarcely a mention of the federal judiciary, is Stanley Elkins and Eric McKitrick, *The Age of Federalism* (New York: Oxford University Press, 1993).

sire of proto-Federalist legislators to encourage a commercial economy, Supreme Court justices' performance-oriented concerns about the propriety and utility of serving on circuit courts, and the Jeffersonian attempt to reconstruct American politics without the interference of a Federalist-dominated judiciary; enabled by the political entrepreneurship of Connecticut senator Oliver Ellsworth and by the transfer of power from Federalists to Jeffersonians after the election of 1800; and resulted in the skeleton of what would eventually (and perhaps surprisingly) become an independent, autonomous, and powerful judiciary. The construction of this skeleton—the establishment of the institutional judiciary—occurred in three stages: a landmark policy compromise guided by a political entrepreneur capable of overcoming political opposition and building a viable coalition in the First Congress (1789); a failed attempt at wholesale performance reform followed by a handful of piecemeal adjustments (1790–99); and, sparked by the emergence of a new governing coalition, a flurry of policy and political institution building that, after much sound and fury, merely reestablished the status quo (1800–1805). After a brief prologue tracing the contours of judicial institutions from the colonial period through the ratification of the Constitution, I examine each of these three stages in turn before concluding with some thoughts on the broader lessons learned about judicial institution building from a study of the early republic.

Prologue: From Colonies to Confederation to Constitution

The judiciary of colonial America was both elaborate and important. Comprising several tiers of general jurisdiction courts as well as a series of specialty courts (for admiralty, chancery, orphans, and probate issues, for example), the judiciary had a substantial effect on the lives of ordinary colonial Americans. Colonial judges not only punished criminals and settled civil disputes over debts and land but also assessed local taxes, allocated tax revenue on public works, approved plans for roads and bridges, adjudicated disputes between slaves and their owners, and issued licenses to innkeepers and merchants. As important as the judiciary was to colonists, it was equally important to the Crown, effectively serving as the administrative arm of the British government in North America. With many colonial judges holding office during the "pleasure" of colonial governors rather than during "good behavior," the judiciary was essentially dependent on the monarch. This offended colonists less because they had a strong norm of "judicial independence"— indeed, most did not—than because they believed that if the judiciary were to be dependent at all (and not everyone agreed that it should be), it should be so on the people and their representatives.[2] The result was that the judiciary occupied an un-

---

[2] See Joseph H. Smith, "An Independent Judiciary: The Colonial Background," 124 *University of Pennsylvania Law Review* 1104 (1976); Jack N. Rakove, "The Origins of Judicial Review: A Plea for New Contexts," 49 *Stanford Law Review* 1031 (1997); Roscoe Pound, *Organization of Courts* (Boston: Little, Brown, 1940), 58–90; Charles Gardner Geyh and Emily Field Van Tassel, "The Independence of

certain place in the political culture of revolutionary America;[3] although colonists recognized the fundamental importance of the institution, they also distrusted its close connection to British authorities.

In the years immediately following the American Revolution, this uncertainty developed into a sharp tension between those who believed judicial power was a dangerous threat to democracy and those who believed it was a necessary check on democracy. Seeking to avoid potentially divisive issues while the nation was still in its infancy, political leaders at both the state and national levels devoted only limited attention to the role of the judiciary. State constitutions treated the judiciary only as it related to tenure and selection issues, and even those provisions varied greatly from one document to the next. With little constitutional guidance, state lawmakers largely adopted the former colonial courts as state courts. Similarly unsure about the role of the judiciary in their new polity, the authors of the Articles of Confederation declined to establish a national court system, choosing instead to leave most judicial business to state proceedings. The only discussion of the judiciary in the Articles occurs in Article IX, which grants Congress the authority to designate federal courts to handle four specific types of disputes—"piracies and felonies committed on the high seas"; "cases of capture"; disagreements "between two or more States concerning boundary, jurisdiction or any other causes whatever"; and "controversies concerning the private right of soil claimed under different grants of two or more States."[4] These courts, however, did not constitute a judicial system but merely a set of ad hoc tribunals.

Acting before the Articles were actually ratified, Congress did establish one standing court—the Court of Appeals in Prize Cases, regarded by some as the "first" federal court in America and designed to replace the five-member congressional committee that had been charged with hearing appeals from state admiralty courts.[5] Established in 1780 at the suggestion of George Washington, the Prize Court was created largely to shift the conduct of international relations from state governments, which had established their own prize and admiralty courts during the Revolution, to the national government. Consisting of three judges commissioned by Congress, any two of whom could conduct business, the court was wholly dependent on state officers to follow and enforce its decisions. Despite congressional encouragement to execute the rulings of the Prize Court, many states

the Judicial Branch in the New Republic," 74 *Chicago-Kent Law Review* 31 (1998); and Richard E. Ellis, *The Jeffersonian Crisis: Courts and Politics in the Young Republic* (New York: Oxford University Press, 1971), 3–9.

[3] On the political culture of revolutionary and postrevolutionary America generally, see Bernard Bailyn, *The Origins of American Politics* (New York: Knopf, 1968); Bernard Bailyn, *The Ideological Origins of the American Revolution* (Cambridge, MA: Belknap Press, 1992); Gordon S. Wood, *The Creation of the American Republic, 1776–1787* (Chapel Hill, NC: University of North Carolina Press, 1969); and Gordon S. Wood, *The Radicalism of the American Revolution* (New York: Vintage , 1993).

[4] Article IX of the Articles of Confederation and Perpetual Union.

[5] See, generally, Henry J. Bourguignon, *The First Federal Court: The Federal Appellate Prize Court of the American Revolution, 1775–1787* (Philadelphia: American Philosophical Society, 1977).

simply refused to obey, and the first federal court limped through a brief and troubled six-year existence.[6]

The vulnerability of federal judicial power revealed by the Articles was not lost on those who gathered in Philadelphia in the summer of 1787, but the founders were still uncertain about the proper role and power of federal courts.[7] It was clear enough that they feared both executive and legislative power more than judicial power and that they believed a judicial system necessary to the proper administration of laws and the settlement of disputes—especially those crossing state lines or involving admiralty, maritime, or international issues. Beyond a general consensus that the new republic would have a federal court system, however, there was not sustained deliberation about the structure of that system. As a result, the minimal debates about various features of the institutional judiciary that did occur, would, of course, reemerge after the Constitutional Convention when the First Congress (1789–91) was faced with the task of implementing the constitutional government.

The constitutional specification of the judicial branch involved a mix of wide agreement, bitter disagreement, and political compromise.[8] On issues implicating the separation of powers, the Convention's delegates were in relative unison. Virtually all delegates acknowledged, for instance, that there should be a Supreme Court and that judges should "hold their offices during good behaviour" and receive a salary that "shall not be diminished during their continuance in office."[9] Determining the method of appointing judges evoked some difference of opinion between those who believed Congress should wield the power and those who thought the president better equipped to make such decisions, but, in the end, a largely uncontroversial compromise[10]—the president would nominate judges, but the Senate would confirm them—satisfied most parties.

On issues concerning federalism, however, the Convention's debates were more contentious. The establishment of inferior federal courts was a point of agreement between the Virginia and New Jersey Plans—each included both trial and appellate courts—but a source of disagreement among the delegates more generally. Those in favor of lower federal courts, including Virginia's James Madison, desired a neutral arbiter to sidestep the local prejudices that state courts might display in

---

[6] Erwin C. Surrency, *History of the Federal Courts* (Dobbs Ferry, NY: Oceana, 2002), 13–14.

[7] On the general debates and themes surrounding drafting and ratifying the Constitution, see Jack N. Rakove, *Original Meanings: Politics and Ideas in the Making of the Constitution* (New York: Knopf, 1996); and Akhil Reed Amar, *America's Constitution: A Biography* (New York: Random House, 2005).

[8] Geyh and Van Tassel, "The Independence of the Judicial Branch in the New Republic," 40–48; David Brian Robertson, *The Constitution and America's Destiny* (New York: Cambridge University Press, 2005), 227–230; Thornton Anderson, *Creating the Constitution: the Convention of 1787 and the First Congress* (University Park: Pennsylvania State University Press, 1993), 148–55.

[9] Article III, Section 1 of the Constitution of the United States of America.

[10] A compromise designed, in Akhil Reed Amar's words, to "produce judges who embodied republican excellence"; Amar, *America's Constitution*, 218.

adjudicating conflicts between citizens of different states.[11] Those opposed, particularly South Carolina's John Rutledge and Connecticut's Roger Sherman, believed such courts were unnecessary, would prove costly, and might encroach upon state judicial prerogatives. After temporary approval for directly establishing inferior courts in the Constitution, Rutledge, later a disgruntled Supreme Court justice and a recess appointment to the chief justiceship, convinced five states to vote for removing the provision (against four states voting to keep it), thereby leaving the issue to the judgment of the First Congress.

The challenge of delineating a jurisdictional grant to the federal court system similarly ended with a compromise between two rival options. The Virginia Plan, introduced by Virginia governor and future attorney general Edmund Randolph, called for jurisdiction over cases involving national revenue, foreigners, citizens from different states ("diversity jurisdiction"), impeachment, admiralty issues, and "national peace and harmony." The New Jersey Plan, introduced by future Judiciary Act of 1789 coauthor and later Supreme Court justice William Paterson, did not grant jurisdiction over impeachments but added jurisdiction over cases involving the construction and interpretation of treaties. The eventual language of Article III, Section 2 excluded cases of revenue, impeachment, and "peace and harmony" but otherwise left the approach of the Virginia Plan intact. At the same time, it broadened the New Jersey Plan's proposal to include all cases "arising under this Constitution, the laws of the United States, and treaties made."[12]

The ultimate result of the Philadelphia Convention's debates about the judicial branch—Article III of the Constitution—was a series of compromises between those who wanted a powerful national judiciary and those who either preferred to leave most judicial business in the hands of state courts or preferred to keep the third branch of the national government dependent on the first two. Effectively functioning as "a compromise by postponement,"[13] the defining feature of Article III is the way in which the framers of the Constitution essentially placed the institutional structure of the judiciary in the hands of Congress, thereby making it inevitable that debate about the structure of the federal judiciary would reemerge in the course of ordinary politics in the future. After all, the language of Article III does more than simply leave questions about judicial structure unanswered; by the very words of Section 1, it entrusts the responsibility both to ask and to answer those questions to Congress. While the Vestiture Clause of Article III ("The judicial power of the United States, shall be vested . . .") initially resembles those of Articles I and II, it takes a sharp turn by vesting a degree of judicial power in the

[11] Madison's support here is reminiscent of his proposal for a "national negative" on state laws. In both instances, the Virginian is deeply concerned with protecting national prerogatives against state laws and officers.

[12] Article III, Section 2, Clause 1 of the Constitution of the United States of America.

[13] Charlene Bangs Bickford and Kenneth R. Bowling, *Birth of the Nation: The First Federal Congress, 1789–1791* (Madison, WI: Madison House, 1989), 45.

Supreme Court "and in such inferior courts as *the Congress* may from time to time ordain and establish."[14] For all the framers did to ensure the "decisional" independence of individual federal judges,[15] the compromise resulting in this clause served to undermine the "branch" independence and institutional autonomy of the judiciary from the outset.[16] In part an attempt to appease Anti-Federalists worried about the federal aggrandizement of state power, in part a reflection of the founding generation's preference for a court system that was dependent (either directly or indirectly) on the people to one that was either dependent on the executive or completely independent,[17] the status of the judiciary as a coequal institution was thus shattered by constitutional text long before it was ever threatened by political practice. Even if it is true, then, that the Constitution exhibits a "strong and remarkable" dedication to the idea of judicial independence,[18] it is also true that it establishes a system that can make the operation of that idea exceedingly difficult in practice. Though it may be correct that the decade following the Revolution began the transformation of political opinion about the desirability and utility of the judiciary, a long and uncertain road still remained until the institution would truly be "an equal and independent entity in a modern tripartite government."[19]

[14] Article III, Section 1 of the Constitution of the United States of America; emphasis added. This language is consistent with Article I, Section 8, Clause 9, which lists "To constitute Tribunals inferior to the supreme Court" as one of the enumerated powers of Congress.

[15] Indeed, with life tenure and a guaranteed salary that could increase but never decrease, the Constitution effectively did what the 1701 English Act of Settlement had purported to do—namely, protect judges from political manipulation. In the process, it also placed federal judges on far more secure ground than state constitutions placed state judges. Gerhard Casper, "The Judiciary Act of 1789 and Judicial Independence," in *Origins of the Federal Judiciary: Essays on the Judiciary Act of 1789*, ed. Maeva Marcus (New York: Oxford University Press, 1992), 285; Amar, *America's Constitution*, 220–21. Of course, the fact that Congress could not legislate a pay decrease does not mean that it could not withhold or dangle a pay increase; Amar, *America's Constitution*, 220–21.

[16] Geyh and Van Tassel, "The Independence of the Judicial Branch in the New Republic," 31–32. The Convention did exhibit some concern for "branch" independence when it struck down the idea of a Council of Revision at least in part because it would have meant federal judges reviewing laws they had helped enact (Geyh and Van Tassel, 46). See also John Ferejohn, "Independent Judges, Dependent Judiciary: Explaining Judicial Independence," 72 *Southern California Law Review* 353 (1999).

[17] Geyh and Van Tassel, "The Independence of the Judicial Branch in the New Republic," 36, 53; Smith, "An Independent Judiciary," 1156; Casper, "The Judiciary Act of 1789 and Judicial Independence," 284. See also Amar, *America's Constitution*, 220–21, which concludes that the colonists had wanted judges independent of unelected executives but not elected legislatures and that the American Revolution, like the Glorious Revolution in England, succeeded in shifting power over the judiciary from the executive to the legislature.

[18] Casper, "The Judiciary Act of 1789 and Judicial Independence," 286.

[19] Gordon S. Wood, "The Origins of Judicial Review," 22 *Suffolk University Law Review* 1293, 1304 (1988) notes that "the part of government that benefited most from the rethinking and remodeling of the 1780s was the judiciary. There in the decade following the Revolution was begun the remarkable transformation of the judges from much-feared appendages of the crown power into one of 'the three capital powers of Government'—from minor magistrates tied to colonial executives into an equal and independent entity in a modern tripartite government." See also Wood, *The Radicalism of the American Revolution*, 323: "The most dramatic institutional transformation in the early Republic was the rise of what was called an 'independent judiciary.'"

Oliver Ellsworth, the First Congress, and the Judiciary Act of 1789

Given the language of Article III, the future of the judiciary was not just in doubt, but highly intertwined with, and perhaps even dependent on, the actions of another branch. If the judiciary was an uncertain institution, it needed the First Congress to make it less so. By the time that Congress convened in March 1789, it was clear that there was great concern about the judicial branch. Of the eighty distinct constitutional amendments proposed by state ratifying conventions, sixteen of them concerned the judiciary.[20] Some of these proposals were motivated by fear that the new judicial system would marginalize—and ultimately displace—the jury system, but the majority of them manifested concern about the balance of power between federal and state governments.[21] Under the new constitutional system, state and local interests were represented in the legislature (through geographic representation and the selection of senators by state legislatures) and the executive (through the Electoral College) but not in the judiciary. With the Supreme Court structured to nationalize disputes by design and having no explicit rules of apportionment or mandated geographic balance, Anti-Federalists were convinced that the institution existed to enforce state compliance to the federal government rather than to represent the states.[22] More specifically, they worried that the judiciary, which, on the eve of the First Congress, consisted of only the Supreme Court, would "vindicate national values against obstreperous states" even as it deferred to Congress.[23] As a result, Anti-Federalists desired a series of major changes[24]: the use of state courts in place of inferior federal courts, extensive limitations on the jurisdiction of the federal judiciary, the establishment of presidential commissioners authorized to override Supreme Court decisions, restricting the Court's appellate power to issues of law rather than fact, guarantees of jury trials for civil cases, and the reduction (or outright elimination) of diversity jurisdiction.[25] With this litany of concerns in the background, many Anti-Federalists considered Article III "the Sore part of the Constitution."[26] As a result, Massachusetts senator Caleb Strong

---

[20] Wilifred J. Ritz, *Rewriting the History of the Judiciary Act of 1789: Exposing Myths, Challenging Premises, and Using New Evidence*, ed. Wythe Holt and L. H. LaRue (Norman: University of Oklahoma Press, 1990), 20.

[21] Even some of the jury concerns were intertwined with issues of federalism. For instance, one of the Anti-Federalist objections to the federal judiciary was that it would deny citizens a trial by a jury of their peers by dragging them away from their homes to be tried according to unknown laws in distant places. Ellis, *The Jeffersonian Crisis*, 11–12.

[22] Amar, *America's Constitution*, 213–14.

[23] Ibid., 213.

[24] Bickford and Bowling, *Birth of the Nation*, 51; Ellis, *The Jeffersonian Crisis*, 11–12.

[25] Diversity jurisdiction, granted to the Supreme Court by Article III, Section 2 of the Constitution, refers to cases involving litigants from different states.

[26] Edmund Pendleton to James Madison, July 3, 1789, reprinted in *The Documentary History of the Supreme Court of the United States, 1789–1800, vol. 4:Organizing the Federal Judiciary: Legislation and Commentaries* [hereafter, *DHSC*], ed. Maeva Marcus (New York: Columbia University Press, 1992), 444.

predicted at the beginning of the First Congress that "one of the first Objects of our Attention will be the Judicial System."[27]

Proving Strong correct, Congress wasted little time filling in the gaps left by Article III. Indeed, in its opening legislative session, it enacted three statutes relating to the federal judiciary—the Judiciary Act of 1789,[28] the Compensation Act of 1789,[29] and the Process Act of 1789.[30] The Judiciary Act of 1789, the monumental legislation that sketched the organization of the federal court system, was not the first of the three—that designation goes to the Compensation Act, signed into law one day earlier—but it was undoubtedly the most important. In essence, the First Congress did in the Judiciary Act precisely what the Convention had declined to do in the Constitution—namely, invent a federal judicial system. As a result, the list of the act's important features is long[31]: constituting the membership of the Supreme Court (five associate justices and one chief justice); designating the terms of the Court (two sessions, beginning in February and August, respectively); dividing the nation into thirteen districts and drawing district lines (made to correspond exactly with state boundaries so that each state was a district); creating thirteen district courts and judges; dividing the nation into three circuits (eastern, middle, southern) and assigning each state to one of the circuits; composing each circuit court of two Supreme Court justices and one district judge from that circuit; regulating the date and location of each district and circuit court session; authorizing the appointment of clerks, marshals, United States attorneys, and an attorney general; outlining both the original and appellate jurisdiction of each court in the tri-tiered (district, circuit, Supreme) judicial hierarchy; delineating the causes for removal from state to federal court; granting the Supreme Court the authority to issue a variety of writs; and empowering the Court to review the final judgments of state supreme courts.

Though the Judiciary Act of 1789 was accomplished quickly, it was not accomplished easily. Indeed, creating and organizing the federal judiciary proved, as a former Virginia judge predicted in a letter to James Madison, "a labour of great difficulty."[32] Part of that difficulty stemmed from the highly technical content of the subject matter,[33] but the central challenge facing the Judiciary Act was the sharp

---

[27] Caleb Strong to John Lowell, March 11, 1789, reprinted in *DHSC*, 366.

[28] 1 Stat. 73 (September 24, 1789).

[29] 1 Stat. 72 (September 23, 1789).

[30] 1 Stat. 93 (September 29, 1789).

[31] The text itself is also quite long. Indeed, at more than 8,400 words, the act is nearly twice the length of the entire 1787 Constitution (approximately 4,300 words) and more than twenty times the length of Article III (a mere 369 words).

[32] Joseph Jones to James Madison, May 10, 1789, reprinted in *DHSC*, 389. See also Richard Bassett to Benjamin Chew, before June 8, 1789, reprinted in *DHSC*, 401, calling the drafting process "Intrigate [*sic*] & Laborious Work"; 1 *Annals of Cong.* 840 (1789) (Michael Jenifer Stone) (admitting that the act was "a work of extreme difficulty").

[33] Gunning Bedford Jr. to George Read, June 24, 1789, reprinted in *DHSC*, 418, regretting that the bill was "too extensive and complicated"; John Dickinson to George Read, June 24, 1789, reprinted in *DHSC*, 419, calling the act the "most difficult to be understood of any Legislative Act I ever read";

THE EARLY REPUBLIC 31

division in the First Congress between those legislators who envisioned a strong centralized judicial system and those who believed the administration of justice should be handled primarily at the state level. Given such extensive disagreement over the need for and substantive effects of the proposed judicial system, submitting the bill for George Washington's signature may have seemed distant at the start of the First Congress.[34] The act's success ultimately depended on the emergence of a catalyst to overcome the constraints upon institution building. With no significant environmental change to break down constraints, that catalyst came in the form of Connecticut senator Oliver Ellsworth. Seizing an opportunity for transformative political action, Ellsworth, the main architect of the proposed judicial system, fashioned a compromise that deliberately diluted the nationalist (and, thus, commercialist) potential of the act in order to assuage his opponents' fears. While Ellsworth's actions did not insulate the Judiciary Act from criticism or guarantee its passage, they did vastly improve its chances in the First Congress. More specifically, Ellsworth's political entrepreneurship—his identity as a moderate nationalist, his ideas about balancing jurisdiction and attending to concerns about judicial geography, and his tactical willingness to compromise and pursue change through measured action—successfully overcame the constraints upon reform. The result was a landmark, precedent-setting episode of judicial institution building that extended judicial power and expanded the judicial apparatus beyond simply the Supreme Court.

Political Contestation in the First Congress

Although often framed in terms of procedural concerns about the balance of power between federal and state governments, the debate between supporters and opponents of the Judiciary Act of 1789 was intricately tied to substantive policy—particularly economic and financial policy—goals that mattered a great deal to both legislators and citizens of the early republic. On one side, those who wished to empower the federal judiciary—in this case, by passing a strong version of the Judiciary Act of 1789—were commercial nationalists. Above all else, they sought to strengthen the federal government and advance the development of a commercial economy by using the judiciary as an arm of centralization, consolidation, and uniformity. They imagined broad grants of federal jurisdiction (including over

---

Thomas FitzSimons to Benjamin Rush, June 2, 1789, reprinted in *DHSC*, 400, lamenting that "we are in our house totally incompetent to such a business and . . . defective it will possibly go down because we are incapable of producing better."

[34] For a thorough, though perhaps flawed, account of the process from conception to presidential signature, including seemingly every amendment (proposed or passed) and minor technical or linguistic modification along the way, see Charles Warren, "New Light on the History of the Federal Judiciary Act of 1789," 37 *Harvard Law Review* 49 (1923). For recent challenges to Warren's history as well as his conclusions, see Ritz, *Rewriting the History of the Judiciary Act of 1789*; and Wythe Holt, "'To Establish Justice': Politics, the Judiciary Act of 1789, and the Invention of the Federal Courts," 1989 *Duke Law Journal* 1421 (1989).

disputes between states, between citizens of different states, and between a state and citizens of another state) wielded by an extensive system of inferior courts that would answer to a centralized Supreme Court authorized to review all decisions occurring below it. On the other side, those who wished to restrict the federal judiciary—in this case, either by not passing the Judiciary Act of 1789 or by passing a diluted version of it—were agricultural localists. At base, they desired to buffer state and local economic prerogatives against national encroachment and resisted the judiciary out of fear that it might become an "effective political engine" for the nationalist vision of a mercantile America.[35] In contrast to nationalists, they preferred utilizing state courts for most judicial business, limiting federal jurisdiction to a small subset of cases, eliminating (or, at least, greatly reducing the number of) inferior courts and circumscribing the power of the Supreme Court.

The policy goals of the act's proponents were the twin commitments of promoting national unity and sparking national economic development. Given the friction that had developed after the Revolution and under the Articles of Confederation between individual states, on the one hand, and between states and the citizens of other states, on the other, nationalists suspected that reliance on state judiciaries would threaten the stability of the Union and function as an impediment to commercial development. In turn, they maintained that "there must be federal Courts to try all matters that are of a federal nature."[36] A national judiciary, nationalists claimed, was "peculiarly necessary" to overcome "local views and partial prejudices"[37] as well as "to secure a Uniformity of Decision thro [sic] the whole."[38] For nationalists, such uniformity was a necessary precondition for reasonable consistency and predictability in social interaction and economic transactions, specifically creditor-debtor relations. "The necessity of uniformity in the decisions of the federal courts," William Smith of South Carolina observed, "is obvious; to assimilate the principles of national decisions, and collect them, as it were, into one focus, appeals from all the State courts to the Supreme Court would

[35] George Lee Haskins and Herbert A. Johnson, *Foundations of Power: John Marshall, 1801–15* (New York: Macmillan, 1981), 145.

[36] Robert Treat Paine to Caleb Strong, May 18, 1789, reprinted in *DHSC*, 392. Cf. Martin Shapiro, *Courts: A Comparative and Political Analysis* (Chicago: University of Chicago Press, 1981), 65–80, on the importance of centralization (of both law and courts) to judicial independence in England.

[37] "A Sketch of the Political State of America by 'Americanus,'" *Gazette of the United States*, June 10, 1789, reprinted in *DHSC*, 402. Cf. Felix Frankfurter and James M. Landis, *The Business of the Supreme Court: A Study in the Federal Judicial System* (New York: Macmillan, 1928), 10, arguing that the federal judicial power was "written into the Constitution whereby the Federal Government could fashion its own judicial machinery for enforcing its claims and safeguarding its agents against the obstructions and prejudices of local authorities."

[38] Richard Law to Oliver Ellsworth, May 4, 1789, reprinted in *DHSC*, 386; Maeva Marcus and Natalie Wexler, "The Judiciary Act of 1789: Political Compromise or Constitutional Interpretation," in *Origins of the Federal Judiciary: Essays on the Judiciary Act of 1789*, ed. Maeva Marcus (New York: Oxford University Press, 1992), 26.

be indispensable."[39] Given that the rulings, doctrines, and procedures of courts in Connecticut had no weight or force on the rulings, doctrines, and procedures of courts in Virginia, a judiciary with a more holistic outlook was needed to impose uniformity on the justice system. Without dependable laws and national courts to enforce them, supporters of the Judiciary Act worried, interstate disputes over trade and maritime commerce would not only rend the nation into parts but also paralyze economic development.[40]

Whereas nationalists sought to further their economic policy aims by empowering the national government against the states, localists conversely sought to protect the states, their economies, and perhaps their distinctive ways of life against the commercial policies of the national government. Chief among the policy issues of importance to localists were the outstanding debts owed British creditors by Southerners. Worried that federal courts would both overrule state court decisions that had allowed debtors to forestall repayment and be more likely to adopt a procreditor approach generally, Southern localists opposed the Judiciary Act out of fear that the judges it created would function much as some colonial judges had—as an administrative apparatus designed to extract money for governmental purposes from ordinary citizens.[41] Moreover, believing that the Judiciary Act "would . . . too strongly mark an inferiority on the State to the federal Courts" and that state judges would "unavoidably feel affected perhaps embarrassed & lessened or burthened [sic] by the Inf. fed. Court,"[42] localists feared that "[t]his new fangled system would eventually swallow up the State courts."[43] "If we establish federal courts, on the principle that the State courts are not able or willing to do their duty," Maryland representative Michael Jenifer Stone argued, "we establish rivals,"[44] a feature that "cannot, in its nature, be agreeable to the State Governments, or to the people."[45] In a letter to James Madison, Edmund Pendleton agreed, dismissing the idea that national judges were needed to overcome state biases and pointing out that "Judges of the State Courts are equally independent, take the same Oaths in Spirit, & have the same law to direct their decisions, as the Foedral

---

[39] 1 *Annals of Cong.* 829 (1789) (William L. Smith). It appears that Smith is specifically referring here to what would become Section 25 of the act, which gave the Supreme Court the authority to review the judgments of state supreme courts in particular instances. This (in)famous provision sparked little debate in 1789 but, as we will see in chapter 3, became the focus of much court-curbing activity in the nineteenth century. See Charles Warren, "Legislative and Judicial Attacks on the Supreme Court of the United States—A History of the Twenty-Fifth Section of the Judiciary Act," 47 *American Law Review* 1 (1913); William M. Wiecek, "*Murdock v. Memphis*: Section 25 of the Judiciary Act of 1789 and Judicial Federalism," in *Origins of the Federal Judiciary: Essays on the Judiciary Act of 1789*, ed. Maeva Marcus (New York: Oxford University Press, 1992), 223–47.

[40] Frankfurter and Landis, *The Business of the Supreme Court*, 7.

[41] Bickford and Bowling, *Birth of the Nation*, 48.

[42] Caleb Strong to Nathaniel Peaslea Sargeant, May 7, 1789, reprinted in *DHSC*, 387; Robert Treat Paine to Caleb Strong, May 18, 1789, reprinted in *DHSC*, 393.

[43] 1 *Annals of Cong.* 852 (1789) (Samuel Livermore).

[44] 1 *Annals of Cong.* 842 (1789) (Michael Jenifer Stone).

[45] 1 *Annals of Cong.* 859 (1789) (Michael Jenifer Stone).

[*sic*]." "Have we any Security," he asked Madison rhetorically, "that Judges of foe-dral [*sic*] appointment, will possess Superior ability or Integrity, to those called into that duty by the States?"[46] Whether or not Southern localists like Pendleton really believed state judges to have "Superior ability or Integrity" to prospective federal judges, they certainly believed that state judges would exercise better judgment regarding important economic policies.

Nationalists, fearing return to a confederation and envisioning the opportunities made possible by a burgeoning mercantile economy, wanted a strong federal judiciary; localists, seeking to prevent consolidation and forestall the growth of a commercial nation, preferred a weak federal judiciary (and no inferior federal courts at all). With the Philadelphia Convention having punted the issue to the First Congress and with many of the same individuals,[47] ideas, and interests carrying over from the Convention's discussion of Article III and the ratification debates to that Congress, this "great Contrariety of Opinion"[48]—this clash of commercial and agricultural policy visions—was not unanticipated. It was, however, potentially paralyzing—unless, of course, it could be overcome by significant changes in the political environment or strategic political entrepreneurship.

"In a Spirit of Moderation": Ellsworth's Compromise

As a member of both the ten-member Senate committee instructed to draft "An Act to establish the Judicial Courts of the United States" and the three-member subcommittee charged with fleshing out the details of that act more specifically, Connecticut senator Oliver Ellsworth took charge in ushering the Judiciary Act of 1789 through the political division and uncertainty of the First Congress.[49] Indeed, in his diary, Pennsylvania senator William Maclay, who ultimately voted against the proposed judicial system, explicitly described Ellsworth as the father of the Judiciary Act: "This vile bill is a child of his, and he defends it with the care of a parent, even with wrath and anger."[50] Though selected to draft the bill because of the

[46]Edmund Pendleton to James Madison, July 3, 1789, reprinted in *DHSC*, 444.

[47]More than three-quarters of the members of the First Congress had participated in either the drafting or ratification of the Constitution. Eleven of twenty-six senators and nine of sixty-five representatives had been delegates to the Philadelphia Convention; sixteen senators (including seven who had been delegates to the Philadelphia Convention) and twenty-nine representatives (including four who had been delegates to the Philadelphia Convention) had attended state ratifying conventions.

[48]Richard Bassett to Benjamin Chew, before June 8, 1789, reprinted in *DHSC*, 401.

[49]In a purposeful and mutually agreed upon division of legislative labor with the House, the Senate took up the project of establishing a national judiciary as its first order of business. A ten-member committee was established both because senators felt that the entire Senate—twenty-two members—was too big to operate as the "Committee of the Whole" and because there were other matters in need of attention.

[50]*Maclay's Journal*, ed. Edgar Maclay (1890), accessed August 1, 2006, at http://memory.loc.gov/ammem/amlaw/lwmj.html, 91. See also *Maclay's Journal*, 101: "Ellsworth has led in this business"; Tristram Lowther to James Iredell, July 1, 1789, reprinted in *DHSC*, 435: "principally drawn up by a Mr Elsworth [*sic*] from Connecticut"; Paine Wingate to Timothy Pickering, April 29, 1789, reprinted in

expertise in technical legal issues he gained while a litigator and state court judge,[51] Ellsworth proved a deft orator and political tactician in the process.[52]

Having been one of Connecticut's delegates to the Philadelphia Convention (where he helped broker several important compromises), Ellsworth understood well the challenges facing the Judiciary Act.[53] Though comforted by the fact that his fellow subcommittee members—William Paterson of New Jersey and Caleb Strong of Massachusetts[54]—were, like him, Northeasterners who strongly supported judicial power, Ellsworth recognized that three potential obstacles remained. The first was the full drafting committee, which included a member from each state (thus ensuring geographic diversity),[55] an equal number of "proadministration" and "antiadministration"[56] members (thus ensuring political diversity),[57]

DHSC, 382: "Mr. Ellsworth seems to be the leading projector"; Abraham Baldwin to Joel Barlow, June 14, 1789, reprinted in *DHSC*, 23n8: "my chum Ellsworth has been at work at [the judiciary bill] night and day all these months." Ellsworth's biographer calls him the bill's "manager and principal defender" and, after a brief review of relevant statements by members of Congress, concludes that it is difficult to dispute the senator's "chief part in creating" the Judiciary Act. See William Garrot Brown, *The Life of Oliver Ellsworth* (New York: Macmillan, 1905),197.

[51]Julius Goebel Jr., *Antecedents and Beginnings to 1801* (New York: Macmillan, 1905), 458–59; William R. Casto, *The Supreme Court in the Early Republic: The Chief Justiceships of John Jay and Oliver Ellsworth* (Columbia: University of South Carolina Press, 1995), 27. See also Brown, *The Life of Oliver Ellsworth*, 186, reasoning that Ellsworth's "great interest in the subject, and his experience on the old committee of appeals, in the great convention, and on the bench, gave him exceptional equipment for the work."

[52]*Maclay's Journal*, 92–93, remarking that, during a debate, Ellsworth heard an adversary "with apparent composure" and then "seemed to batter down all his antagonist had said," displaying "ingenuity in his defense" the entire time.

[53]See Casto, *The Supreme Court in the Early Republic*, describing Ellsworth and Paterson as "immensely practical men" (31–32) who were "fully aware of the concern that the federal courts might swallow up the state judiciaries" (48).

[54]On Paterson, see Daniel A. Degnan, S.J., "William Paterson: Small States' Nationalist," in *Seriatim: The Supreme Court before John Marshall*, ed. Scott Douglas Gerber (New York: New York University Press, 1998), 231–59; Goebel, *Antecedents and Beginnings to 1801*, 457.

[55]New York's designated committee member, Rufus King, did not arrive until late July, one week after the committee's work on the bill was completed.

[56]Given the lack of political parties in the First Congress, it is difficult to label and categorize individual members. Instead of the terms *Federalist* and *Anti-Federalist*, which designate one's view on constitutional ratification but do not necessarily map clearly onto the politics of the First Congress, I use Kenneth Martis's designations of *proadministration* and *antiadministration*. See Kenneth C. Martis, *The Historical Atlas of Political Parties in the United States Congress 1789-1989* (New York: Macmillan, 1989). Martis's labels, which roughly correspond to my own use of *nationalist* and *localist*, attempt to separate those who more often supported and voted in favor of the policy positions of George Washington's presidential administration from those who more often opposed and voted against those positions. In the 1790s, the former largely became Federalists and the latter Democrat-Republicans.

[57]On the proadministration side of the committee sat Ellsworth, Paterson, Strong, Charles Carroll of Maryland, and Ralph Izard of South Carolina; on the antiadministration side sat Maclay, Richard Bassett of Delaware, William Few of Georgia, Richard Henry Lee of Virginia, and Paine Wingate of New Hampshire. With South Carolina's Izard on the proadministration side and both New Hampshire's Wingate and Pennsylvania's Maclay on the antiadministration side, the committee was not strictly divided by North-South sectionalism.

and where the antiadministration forces were ably led by Richard Henry Lee, an ally of Patrick Henry who had previously written (under the pseudonym "Federal Farmer") Anti-Federalist essays against the Constitution. The second was the Senate at large, where, despite a strong 15–7 edge for the proadministration bloc,[58] there was still great uncertainty about precisely how individual members would vote on the establishment of a controversial judicial system. The third was the House of Representatives, where proadministration members constituted a smaller majority (34–25) than in the Senate and where the ten-member Virginia delegation—eight of them regarded as antiadministration—wielded great authority. At each stage, Ellsworth knew, localists would resist any measure—even one as vital as the Judiciary Act—that might threaten state sovereignty or advance commercial interests, going so far as to predict that there would be "[a]ttacks on the General Government that will go to the Very Vitals of it."[59]

Moreover, Ellsworth recognized that his task was not simply to attend to individual complaints but to devise a system more favorable than the alternate plans for the judiciary that were, or would soon be, under consideration by the Senate. Three such alternatives stood in opposition to Ellsworth's bill: Treasury Secretary Alexander Hamilton's plan for an army of powerful judges to bring federal law into every community, Richard Henry Lee's plan to limit federal inferior courts to admiralty and maritime cases and otherwise use state courts in their place, and a plan by Senator William Johnson of Connecticut for one central court to dispatch judges to decide issues of fact locally before returning to the capital to deliberate on issues of law. Although the Lee and Johnson plans would not be formally offered until Ellsworth's own scheme reached the floor (and the Hamilton plan would never be formally offered at all), Ellsworth and his fellow subcommittee members "knew the way the political wind was blowing" and were likely aware of their general contours during the drafting process.[60] Given the numerous obstacles in his path and the existence of alternatives that would undoubtedly hold appeal for some legislators, Ellsworth knew the possible outcomes for the Judiciary Act ranged from passage to evisceration to outright rejection. Realizing he was unlikely to end up with the outcome he desired (a strong federal court system that would further economic progress and empower the central government against the states), he set out to avoid settling for the outcomes he dreaded (either the complete lack of any federal courts other than the Supreme Court or, perhaps even more troublesome, a federal court system that would be subject to state obstruction and resistance at every turn).[61]

That the Judiciary Act of 1789 was ultimately closer to what Ellsworth desired than what he dreaded is a testament to his entrepreneurial identity, ideas, and

---

[58] At this point, the Senate consisted of only twenty-two members because two states—North Carolina and Rhode Island—had not yet ratified the Constitution.

[59] Pierce Butler's notes on Judiciary Bill debate, June 22, 1789, reprinted in *DHSC*, 408.

[60] Holt, "'To Establish Justice,'" 1494.

[61] Cf. Frankfurter and Landis, *The Business of the Supreme Court*, 11: "To press for too much might have endangered what was for them an essential minimum."

tactics, each of which were perfectly tailored to overcome the political contestation of the First Congress. Ellsworth's identity as a spokesman for nationalists who nonetheless appealed to many localists was carefully constructed. As the de facto leader of the proto-Federalists in the Senate,[62] his true base of support was never in question. But, as a senator who occasionally sought the advice and approval of his state's governor, lieutenant governor, and (on legal matters such as the Judiciary Act) chief justice, Ellsworth also had a reputation as a moderate nationalist who was "sensitive and attentive to state interests."[63] Ellsworth's ideas—drawing federal judicial districts to correspond to state lines, using Supreme Court justices to staff circuit courts, carefully delineating jurisdiction to each tier of the federal judicial hierarchy—were similarly balanced; in fact, having been partly adopted from rival proposals rather than created out of whole cloth, they already enjoyed some support. Like his identity and his ideas, Ellsworth's tactics were extremely cognizant of the surrounding political environment. Given the force of the Anti-Federalist critique of Article III, popular fears that a strong judiciary would render the jury system obsolete, and the inevitable objections of congressional localists, compromise—balancing the seemingly widespread desire for a weaker judiciary with his and his allies' preference for potent national judicial power[64]—seemed a prudent course for Ellsworth to follow in the spring and summer of 1789.[65] Indeed, demonstrating his willingness to proceed "in a spirit of moderation,"[66] Ellsworth solicited reactions from lawyers and judges and, hoping to preempt disillusionment with the final act, was not only "wholly sensitive to a variety of criticisms" of the proposed judicial system but also "prepared to meet them."[67]

[62] William R. Casto, "Oliver Ellsworth: 'I have sought the felicity and glory of your Administration,'" in *Seriatim: The Supreme Court Before John Marshall*, ed. Scott Douglas Gerber (New York: New York University Press, 1998), 298.

[63] Casto, *The Supreme Court in the Early Republic*, 50. Cf. Daniel P. Carpenter, *The Forging of Bureaucratic Autonomy: Reputations, Networks, and Policy Innovation in Executive Agencies, 1862–1928* (Princeton, NJ: Princeton University Press, 2001), 4–5, 14–18, detailing the importance of reputations to the construction of "political legitimacy." Although Carpenter's narrative is about bureaucratic (rather than judicial) development and discusses the importance of reputations primarily as they relate to organizations (rather than individuals), his insights are nonetheless useful in thinking about the dynamics of Ellsworth's entrepreneurship.

[64] Ritz, *Rewriting the History of the Judiciary Act of 1789*, 19–20.

[65] See William Smith to Otho Holland Williams, April 23, 1789, reprinted in *DHSC*, 376, suspecting that the framers of the Judiciary Act were "disposed to proceed with great moderation"; and Richard Henry Lee to Samuel Adams, May 10, 1789, reprinted in *DHSC*, 390, expressing hope that the ultimate statute would "quiet the apprehensions of many."

[66] Richard Henry Lee to Samuel Adams, May 10, 1789, reprinted in *DHSC*, 390.

[67] Goebel, *Antecedents and Beginnings to 1801*, 457. See also Casto, *The Supreme Court in the Early Republic*, 28, noting how well Ellsworth treated the bill's opponents on the drafting committee, a conclusion supported by Wingate's claim that Ellsworth was "a very sensible man." Paine Wingate to Timothy Pickering, April 29, 1789, reprinted in *DHSC*, 382. Ellsworth even managed to gain "credit" with Maclay, who thought the Judiciary Act a "vile law system," by taking the Pennsylvanian's objections about chancery under consideration. *Maclay's Journal*, 103–5, 117.

In devising his own plan, Ellsworth tried to eschew the extreme elements in the rival plans and steer a moderate course that might incorporate reasonable features from all of them. In particular, he focused on finding solutions to the three elements of his plan that sparked the most intense criticism: the establishment of inferior federal courts, the geographic arrangement of the judicial system at large, and the reach of federal jurisdiction. Rather than push forward with the judiciary system he thought most suitable to the needs of the new nation and face likely defeat, he decided to compromise on geography and jurisdiction in order to ensure the creation of lower courts, which many (including Ellsworth himself) regarded as "the essence of the whole system."[68]

In order to accommodate concerns about geography, a thorny matter in 1789 that would only grow more difficult as the nation expanded and incorporated more states throughout the nineteenth century,[69] Ellsworth designed his system both to maintain the integrity of individual states and to demonstrate the ability of the federal judiciary to serve state and local communities. First, in order to avoid one source of inevitable geographic controversy, Ellsworth's subcommittee wisely drew district lines to correspond with state lines, establishing a federal district court in each state and alleviating the concern that the new system would drag citizens away to courts far from their homes and families. Second, seeking to overcome fears that a Supreme Court located in Washington, D.C., would be unable to remain in contact with the great number of district courts and judges spread across the nation (occasionally in relatively distant outposts),[70] Ellsworth's plan required Supreme Court justices to "ride circuit"—that is, it required them to travel throughout the nation and join district court judges in hearing circuit court cases.[71] Conceived partly to solve the geography problem and partly to trim costs by eliminating the need for a whole slate of circuit judges, the idea of circuit riding essentially came from Johnson's plan, which itself borrowed heavily from the systems of judicial organization then in operation in England, New York, and

---

[68] "Letter from an Anonymous Correspondent," *Massachusetts Centinel*, August 30, 1789, reprinted in *DHSC*, 505.

[69] See Akhil Reed Amar, "*Marbury*, Section 13, and the Original Jurisdiction of the Supreme Court," 56 *University of Chicago Law Review* 443, 469 (1989): "Geography preoccupied the founding generation." The ramifications of territorial expansion and statehood admission for judicial institution building during the first half of the nineteenth century are discussed in chapter 3. In American political development scholarship more broadly, Richard Bensel's research agenda has been particularly concerned with the theme of political geography and the dynamics of regional difference, though largely in the postbellum era. See, for example, Richard Franklin Bensel, *Sectionalism and American Political Development, 1880–1980* (Madison: University of Wisconsin Press, 1984); Richard Franklin Bensel, *Yankee Leviathan: The Origins of Central State Authority in America, 1859–1877* (Cambridge: Cambridge University Press, 1990); and Richard Franklin Bensel, *The Political Economy of American Industrialization, 1877–1900* (Cambridge: Cambridge University Press, 2000).

[70] Geyh and Van Tassel, "The Independence of the Judicial Branch in the New Republic," 57–59.

[71] Given the combination of original and appellate jurisdiction granted to the circuit courts, these cases could be either trials or appeals of district court rulings.

Massachusetts.[72] Though immediately recognized as an imperfect solution, circuit riding was designed to "unify the court system" and "guarantee systematic interaction" both between Supreme Court justices and district judges as well as between judicial officers and citizens.[73] Given its role in assuaging the fiscal and geographic fears of localists, it is ironic that the practice ultimately provided a means to inculcate nationalism and to educate citizens about the Constitution, the national government, and the role of the judiciary more specifically.[74]

In thinking about jurisdictional grants to the federal courts, Ellsworth ideally wanted the broadest possible base of judicial authority: the entire scope of federal jurisdiction contemplated by the Constitution. Practically, however, he knew this was impossible. As a result, he adopted a more moderate stance in the Judiciary Act of 1789, carefully balancing the jurisdiction the act granted against that which it withheld.[75] To the district courts the act gave original jurisdiction over admiralty and citizenship issues, penalties and forfeitures, and limited criminal cases; to the circuit courts it granted original jurisdiction over diversity claims and appellate jurisdiction over the district courts in only a few instances; and to the Supreme Court it bestowed the original jurisdiction mentioned in the Constitution as well as appellate jurisdiction over all classes of cases—both from lower federal courts and state courts—that could be reviewed.[76] The logic behind Ellsworth's jurisdictional grants here was both practical and strategic. Admiralty cases, for instance, were given to district courts because maritime law was full of technical matters that, although uniform across all jurisdictions, often required consulting legal books and treatises, access to which would be greater for district court judges.[77] Diversity cases, by contrast, were given to circuit courts less because of pragmatic concerns than because of Ellsworth's assumption that Supreme Court justices (sitting as circuit court judges but not tied to any particular state or community) would be more likely than district judges to overcome precisely the type of local bias that might unfairly dictate the outcome of cases between citizens of different states.[78] In addition to some strategic assignment of particular classes of

---

[72] Marcus and Wexler, "The Judiciary Act of 1789," 21; Ritz, *Rewriting the History of the Judiciary Act of 1789*, 15.

[73] Geyh and Van Tassel, "The Independence of the Judicial Branch in the New Republic," 58–59.

[74] Ralph Lerner, "The Supreme Court as Republican Schoolmaster," 1967 *Supreme Court Review* 127 (1967); Warren, "New Light on the History of the Federal Judiciary Act of 1789," 59–61. This would later prove to be one of the Democratic-Republican objections against Federalist judges during the impeachment trials of 1804–5.

[75] See Casto, "Oliver Ellsworth," 297, praising Ellsworth's approach as "masterful" and concluding that, in order to overcome the opposition, Ellsworth needed to "bring to bear the full extent of his remarkable ability to broker compromises."

[76] Frankfurter and Landis, *The Business of the Supreme Court*, 12–13.

[77] On the issue of admiralty jurisdiction generally, see William R. Casto, "The Origins of Admiralty Jurisdiction in an Age of Privateers, Smugglers, and Pirates," *American Journal of Legal History* 37 (1993): 117–57; and William R. Casto, "Additional Light on the Origins of Federal Admiralty Jurisdiction," *Journal of Maritime Law and Commerce* 31 (2000): 143–64.

[78] Ritz, *Rewriting the History of the Judiciary Act of 1789*, 66.

jurisdiction to particular courts, the act was purposefully designed to limit federal jurisdiction to specific categories of cases that were thought to be essential for the maintenance of a national government.[79] As a result, it denied several classes of jurisdiction, including the Supreme Court's ability to review determinations of fact (except in rare instances) or to hear appeals from federal criminal trials. Even more important from the perspective of the bill's skeptics, Ellsworth did not grant the judiciary the general "federal question" jurisdiction—that is, the full scope of jurisdiction stipulated by the first line of Article III, Section 2—that might have truly made the federal court system a powerful agent of nationalization.[80] As a general rule, Ellsworth pursued change through measured action: he was generous to the federal judiciary in areas where strong opposition was unlikely (admiralty cases, for instance) but consciously "chose not to gamble" in instances where he might offend[81]—and likely lose the votes of—legislators fearful of federal, judicial, or federal judicial power.

Together, Ellsworth's compromises on judicial geography and federal jurisdiction succeeded in moderating the more radical tendencies in alternate proposals.[82] While he did not create the army of federal judges Hamilton sought, Ellsworth did establish a federal judge—albeit one with more limited jurisdiction than Hamilton would have hoped—in each district. Yet in keeping with Lee's concerns about the reach of federal jurisdiction and the number of inferior federal courts, Ellsworth outlined discrete categories of cases that would fall under the jurisdiction of these judges and staffed three levels of judicial hierarchy with only two sets of judges. In order to make this hierarchy work properly, Ellsworth borrowed the idea of circuit riding from Johnson and forced Supreme Court justices to perform the "double duty" of hearing cases both inside and outside the capital. By incorporating what he regarded as the reasonable elements of his opponents' plans for a federal judiciary, Ellsworth sketched a judicial system that he hoped would be favorable (or at least neutral) to many and unfavorable to few.

Though it was hardly the mandate for which Ellsworth was hoping,[83] the judiciary bill passed the Senate 14–6 just four months after the start of the First

---

[79] Casto, *The Supreme Court in the Early Republic*, 36–42.

[80] Such jurisdiction, which was not fully granted until the Jurisdiction and Removal Act of 1875 (see chapter 4), is controversial precisely because the clause in question ("The judicial power shall extend to all cases, in law and equity arising under this Constitution, the laws of the United States, and treaties made, or which shall be made, under their authority") is indefinite about the categories of cases to which the judicial power "shall extend."

[81] Casto, *The Supreme Court in the Early Republic*, 43.

[82] Hamilton's proposal was never formally offered in the Senate, but the respective proposals by Lee and Johnson were each rejected by the Senate after approximately one day of debate; Holt, "'To Establish Justice,'" 1490–93.

[83] See Casto, *The Supreme Court in the Early Republic*, 51, noting that Ellsworth was convinced that a substantial vote margin was necessary to establish the national government, and especially the federal judiciary, on firm ground.

Congress,[84] with three members of the drafting committee—Virginia's Lee, Pennsylvania's Maclay, and New Hampshire's Wingate—joining Pierce Butler of South Carolina, William Grayson of Virginia, and John Langdon of New Hampshire in opposition.[85] Upon Senate passage, the bill was sent to the House, where it sat for over a month while the chamber debated proposed amendments to the Constitution.[86] When the bill was finally debated, the sharpest attacks came from three antiadministration representatives: Samuel Livermore of New Hampshire, Thomas Tudor Tucker of South Carolina, and James Jackson of Georgia.[87] Objecting most forcefully to the creation of inferior federal courts, Livermore, Tucker, and Jackson led an unsuccessful charge to strike their establishment from the bill.[88] Once that measure was rejected 31–17, the House left the Senate plan intact and passed it by a voice vote—albeit with more than fifty minor amendments—in mid-September. Returned to the Senate for revision, a peculiar ad hoc committee of Ellsworth (the bill's primary author), Paterson (one of his two deputies), and Butler (an opponent of the bill) met to consider the House amendments. Of the fifty-two amendments proposed by the House, the new subcommittee disagreed with four, further amended one, and accepted thirty-seven; subsequently, the full Senate consented to the bill and the House withdrew the four contested amendments. President Washington signed the final version of the bill into law on September 24, 1789 and, with that, Oliver Ellsworth's child—the federal judiciary—was born.

Sizing Up the Judiciary Act of 1789

With an identity, ideas, and tactics tailored to the political environment of the First Congress, Ellsworth's entrepreneurship overcame the most substantial constraints against the passage of the Judiciary Act of 1789. Consistent with his reputation as a statesman sensitive to state interests, Ellsworth pursued change through measured action and demonstrated a willingness to incorporate opposing viewpoints

[84] Unfortunately, with the exception of the preserved (but often inconsistent and perhaps self-aggrandizing) journal of one senator, there is virtually no documentation of the Senate debate. For the one surviving account of the Senate's consideration of the bill, see *Maclay's Journal*, 85–133. See also Goebel, *Antecedents and Beginnings to 1801*, 494–503 (on the Senate debate) and 503–8 (on the House debate).

[85] The two proadministration members who voted against the bill (Butler and Langdon) were offset by the three antiadministration members (committee members Richard Bassett and William Few along with James Gunn of Georgia) who voted in favor of it. Neither New York senator—Rufus King or Philip John Schuyler—voted.

[86] For detailed chronologies of the act's legislative progress, see Ritz, *Rewriting the History of the Judiciary Act of 1789*, 16–21; Bickford and Bowling, *Birth of the Nation*, 46–48; Holt, " 'To Establish Justice' "; Warren, "New Light on the History of the Federal Judiciary Act of 1789"; and Casto, *The Supreme Court in the Early Republic*, 27–53.

[87] On Jackson, see Marie Sauer Lambremont, "Rep. James Jackson of Georgia and the Establishment of the Southern States' Rights Tradition in Congress," in *Inventing Congress: Origins and Establishment of the First Federal Congress*, ed. Kenneth R. Bowling and Donald R. Kennon (Athens: Ohio University Press, 1999).

[88] Warren, "New Light on the History of the Federal Judiciary Act of 1789," 125.

into the substance of his plan. The result was an act that is usually regarded as a "compromise measure"—an "instrument of reconciliation deliberately framed to quiet smoldering resentments."[89] As is often the case with compromises, the Judiciary Act of 1789 was truly satisfying to almost nobody: the judiciary created was simultaneously not as powerful as the nationalists had hoped and more powerful than the localists had feared. That is to say, although the act's supporters and opponents agreed that Congress could do more, or less, than it did in the Judiciary Act—that Congress could either empower or restrict the federal courts further[90]—they disagreed about who won the battle over the creation of the federal judicial system. Although neither side was satisfied, both left with some spoils of victory. The localists won both because much of the federal jurisdiction granted was, except in admiralty and maritime cases, concurrent with state jurisdiction and because the eventual act complemented the Bill of Rights, particularly the Fifth and Seventh Amendments, to protect the jury system. Indeed, from guaranteeing that juries would decide issues of fact in inferior federal courts to ensuring jury trials in cases against citizens brought before the Supreme Court, from greatly limiting the Court's fact-finding power to mandating that jurors in criminal cases would come from the same county (rather than simply the same state) as the defendant, the act addressed enough of the Anti-Federalists' judiciary-related concerns to make many of their proposed amendments to Article III repetitive.[91] The nationalists won not only because the First Congress created lower federal court judges but also because it allocated significant jurisdiction to the federal judicial branch generally.[92] Thus, although it is certainly true that "some of the measures taken by the Judiciary Act . . . had the effect, even if not fully intended, of tempering judicial power,"[93] it seems an exaggeration to say that the Judiciary Act of 1789 was "a states'-rights document, emblematic of no more than a potential for national judicial action."[94]

In fact, given the surrounding political context—the force of Anti-Federalist opposition during state ratifying conventions, the multitude of potentially crippling amendments to Article III that were proposed in advance of the First Congress,

[89] Goebel, *Antecedents and Beginnings to 1801*, 458. Similarly, Warren, "New Light on the History of the Federal Judiciary Act of 1789," 53, notes the act was "framed as to secure the votes of those who, while willing to see the experiment of a Federal Constitution tried, were insistent that the Federal Courts should be given the minimum powers and jurisdiction."

[90] Marcus and Wexler, "The Judiciary Act of 1789," 16; *DHSC*, 24; William R. Casto, "The First Congress's Understanding of Its Authority over the Federal Courts' Jurisdiction," 26 *Boston College Law Review* 1101 (1985).

[91] Ritz, *Rewriting the History of the Judiciary Act of 1789*, 21; Amar, *America's Constitution*, 234–36.

[92] Cf. Casper, "The Judiciary Act of 1789 and Judicial Independence," 293, noting that the First Congress "withheld much less than it conferred" and pointing out that nearly "every single jurisdictional item listed in Article III, Section 2, was given to some federal court."

[93] Ibid., 292–93.

[94] Kathryn Preyer, "*United States v. Callender*: Judge and Jury in a Republican Society," in *Origins of the Federal Judiciary: Essays on the Judiciary Act of 1789*, ed. Maeva Marcus (New York: Oxford University Press, 1992), 189.

the simultaneous pursuit of a Bill of Rights to limit governmental power,[95] and the two alternative proposals for substantially weaker federal judicial systems—the Judiciary Act of 1789 is more appropriately viewed as a remarkable victory for those with projudicial and pronational sympathies. As the outcome of the Process Act of 1789, a significant defeat for nationalists (and for Ellsworth, the bill's drafter) at the hands of those who preferred reliance on state forms of procedure,[96] suggests, the Judiciary Act could easily have been a setback. The judiciary certainly could have been stronger, but it also could have been weaker—a radically circumscribed Supreme Court, drastic limitations on federal jurisdiction, the absence of inferior federal courts. In this way, to focus only on what was done, rather than what was not done, to the judiciary—to focus on the avenues foreclosed rather than those left open—risks an overly pessimistic interpretation of this crucial episode in judicial institution building. Viewed with an eye toward what might have been without Ellsworth's entrepreneurship, the Judiciary Act both established the foundational pieces of a potentially powerful judiciary and set a historical precedent that was largely friendly to judicial power. Given that the large overlap in membership with the Philadelphia Convention often endowed the work of the First Congress with "quasi-constitutional" status,[97] this was, as we shall see, a particularly forceful and resilient precedent and a "foundation upon which successors could build."[98]

The Quiet Before the Storm, 1790–1799

The immediate response to the Judiciary Act of 1789 was a deafening chorus of critique from localists and nationalists alike. Those who had opposed the act when it was debated in Congress continued to disparage the judicial system it established as "unnecessary, vexatious, and expensive, and calculated to destroy the harmony and confidence of the people."[99] They expressed skepticism about the expansion of national governmental prerogatives at the expense of both state governments and individual rights,[100] and they voiced concerns about the ability of a "people oppressed so severely by the burthens [sic] of the late war" and a nation that had suffered through financial crises and tax revolts (such as Shays' Rebellion) to afford

---

[95] A proposal consisting of twelve constitutional amendments, ten of which would be ratified as the Bill of Rights, was passed by both houses of Congress and submitted to the states for ratification on September 25, 1789—one day after Washington signed the Judiciary Act.

[96] See Goebel, *Antecedents and Beginnings to 1801*, 509–40; "Process Act of 1789" (introduction), in *DHSC*, 108–14.

[97] Mark A. Graber, "Establishing Judicial Review: *Marbury* and the Judicial Act of 1789," 38 *Tulsa Law Review* 609, 637–38 (2003).

[98] Ritz, *Rewriting the History of the Judiciary Act of 1789*, 22.

[99] 1 *Annals of Cong.* 832 (1789) (James Jackson).

[100] 1 *Annals of Cong.* 813 (1789) (Thomas Tudor Tucker): "State courts were fully competent to the purposes for which these courts were to be created"; 1 *Annals of Cong.* 844 (1789) (Aedanus Burke): "the people would . . . express their dislike to a Judicial system which rendered them insecure in their liberties and properties; a system that must be regarded with jealousy and distrust."

an extensive judicial apparatus.[101] Those who had supported the act were worried that it was "defective in both its general structure and many of its particular regulations"[102]—a function, at least to some degree, of the compromises Ellsworth was forced to make in order to preempt localist opposition. Even John Jay, less than a month after being confirmed as the nation's first chief justice, conceded "[o]ur judicial system is not free from difficulties."[103] Given that the Judiciary Act of 1789 had largely been regarded as experimental, such difficulties were not unexpected. Yet, for many, the fact that difficulties were anticipated did not mean that they should be excused.[104] Thus, almost as soon as the bill became law, there was relatively widespread agreement about "the necessity of reforming our judicial system."[105]

As the 1790s would demonstrate, however, agreement about the need for judicial reform could not overcome disagreement about what shape that reform would take. In 1790, a performance-driven attempt at radical overhaul of the entire system by Attorney General Edmund Randolph was unable to overcome the constraints imposed by congressional indifference and opposition. Two years later, the first of several pleas by Supreme Court justices for relief from circuit riding was ignored. With both the Attorney General and the justices themselves unable to spark institution building, little change of any substance occurred in the ten years following Ellsworth's compromise. The story of the 1790s, then, is one of unfulfilled reform; despite repeated attempts at reshaping the institutional judiciary, a series of factors—including unfortunate timing, the legacy of Ellsworth's compromise, opinions issued by the new federal judiciary, and the birth of partisan politics—combined to produce failure, frustration, and a handful of piecemeal performance modification.

The Failure of the Randolph Report

The most comprehensive attempt at reforming the judiciary during the 1790s came from Attorney General Edmund Randolph, a man who considered himself

---

[101] 1 *Annals of Cong.* 827 (1789) (Samuel Livermore). See also "Rusticus," *Independent Chronicle*, August 26, 1790, reprinted in *DHSC*, 536: "Indeed the whole judicial system is a giddy profusion, and quite unnecessary. The business might have been done in the State Courts. . . . And all this unwieldly [*sic*] and useless machinery of Circuit, District, and Supreme Courts might have been omitted; this would have saved about thirty thousand dollars a year."

[102] James Madison to Edmund Pendleton, September 14, 1789, reprinted in *DHSC*, 511.

[103] John Jay to Edward Rutledge, November 16, 1789, reprinted in *DHSC*, 35.

[104] See James Madison to Edmund Pendleton, September 14, 1789, reprinted in *DHSC*, 511: "The most I hope is . . . that the system may speedily undergo a reconsideration"; William Richardson Davie to James Iredell, August 2, 1791, reprinted in *DHSC*, 561: "I sincerely hope something will be done at the next session of Congress with the Judicial law, it is so defective in point of arrangement and so obscurely drawn or expressed, that in my opinion, it would disgrace the composition of the meanest legislature of the States."

[105] Edmund Randolph to George Washington, August 5, 1792, reprinted in *DHSC*, 586.

the government official most in charge of the administration of justice.[106] Authorized by the House to submit a report about the defects of the judicial system,[107]
Randolph offered both critique and suggestion. Feigning embarrassment at being
called "to revise a plan approved by legislative wisdom," claiming at the outset
that he had "examined it with a deference most respectful and sincere," Randolph
nonetheless proceeded to "question the fitness of some of its leading features," offering both "an enumeration of . . . the principal defects" of the present system as
well as a proposed revision—in reality, a whole new bill—of the Judiciary Act of
1789.[108] Although his proposal certainly would have had important substantive effects, Randolph's goal was targeted judicial improvement rather than general judicial empowerment; his motivation was performance rather than policy or politics.

Randolph's reform campaign owed much, at least on the surface, to Ellsworth's
entrepreneurship of 1789—a fact that is not surprising given their respective political identities. Like Ellsworth, Randolph had participated in the American Revolution (as an aide-de-camp to George Washington), served with distinction in the
Philadelphia Convention, played a central role in the Convention's Committee on
Detail, been chosen for a distinguished position within the new government, and
was regarded as a sharp legal mind. Moreover, Randolph's role in coauthoring and
presenting the Virginia Plan at the Philadelphia Convention suggested that he,
like Ellsworth, was both willing and able to serve as a grand architect of institutional design. With a political resume similar to Ellsworth's, Randolph followed
Ellsworth's approach to institution building and relied heavily on compromise and
the balancing of conflicting interests.[109]

Yet despite ostensible similarities in identity and tactics, Randolph's ideas about
judicial reform were fundamentally different from Ellsworth's. Where Ellsworth
sought to protect the one feature—the establishment of inferior federal courts—
that he valued above all else, Randolph set out to rectify two features—the "mixed"
character of jurisdiction and the use of Supreme Court justices as members of
circuit courts—that he viewed as especially problematic. First, Randolph proposed
reconfiguring Ellsworth's allotment of federal and state jurisdiction. Embodying
his belief that the two classes of jurisdiction should be entirely separate and sub-

[106] Even though the Department of Justice was not established until 1870, the position of attorney
general was created by the Judiciary Act of 1789.

[107] It is possible that the House commissioned the Randolph Report in part to regain some of the
control it had relinquished to the Senate by allowing the upper chamber to draft, and essentially dictate
the terms of, the Judiciary Act of 1789. See Bickford and Bowling, *The Birth of the Nation*, 49.

[108] *American State Papers: Miscellaneous* 1:21.

[109] Wythe Holt, "'Federal Courts as the Asylum to Federal Interests': Randolph's Report, The Benson Amendment, and the 'Original Understanding' of the Federal Judiciary," 36 *Buffalo Law Review*
341, 347 (1987), noting that Randolph "consciously sought compromise between Federalist and Anti-
Federalist perceptions of the federal judiciary." But cf. Goebel, *Antecedents and Beginnings to 1801*, 542,
concluding that Randolph's ideal Judiciary Act "was drawn in utter disregard for the criticisms leveled
at a federal judicial system during the ratification struggle, a fact which may account for the cavalier
manner in which the House merely referred the report to the Committee of the Whole, where it rested
in peace."

ject to no overlap whatsoever, Randolph's proposal granted exclusive jurisdiction to the federal courts over six classes of cases that, although either expressly mentioned or implicitly suggested by Article III, were not given to the federal judiciary alone under the Judiciary Act of 1789.[110] In other words, it granted to federal courts the broad federal question jurisdiction that had previously been withheld. Second, Randolph proposed abolishing circuit riding. Rejecting the idea that riding circuit helped the justices by immersing them in state law and ignoring the popular argument that it provided an intimacy between a geographically distant Supreme Court and the increasingly dispersed national bar that made the administration of justice more efficient,[111] Randolph viewed the practice as an impediment to Supreme Court justices becoming "pre-eminent in most endowments of the mind."[112] After all, to "be a master" of various branches of the law required time, energy, and access to libraries, all of which were limited by circuit riding. Even more seriously, by raising the uncomfortable possibility of a justice hearing an appeal of one of his own circuit court opinions, circuit riding threatened the authority of the judicial system. If judgments made riding circuit were reviewed by the Supreme Court, Randolph wondered, would the issuing justices "meet their four brethren unbiassed [sic]?" Between the deleterious effect on the abilities of the justices and the questionable legitimacy of justices reviewing their own decisions, circuit riding was the central defect Randolph perceived in the 1789 system. As a result, his report concluded, "judges of the Supreme Court shall cease to be judges of the circuit courts." Instead, under his revised bill, each circuit court would be composed of panels of the district court judges serving in that circuit.

Although Randolph's proposed jurisdictional revisions and elimination of circuit riding were more favorable to nationalists than to localists, the rest of his report was not. Randolph himself had refused to sign the Constitution in Philadelphia,[113] in large part because he believed that "the power it gave the judiciary was too unlimited and ill-defined."[114] In order to more effectively limit and define judicial power, Randolph proposed eliminating two sections—Sections 14 and 25—of the Judiciary Act of 1789. By eliminating Section 14, which gave federal judges the authority to issue writs not explicitly provided for by statute, Randolph protected his jurisdictional separation by ensuring that judges could not exploit the open texture of the Judiciary Act's language in order to funnel cases into courts to which they did not belong. If judges had unbounded authority to accept any

---

[110] The six categories were "admiralty and maritime jurisdiction," cases in which "the United States are a party defendant," cases in which "a particular State is a party defendant," disputes arising from "lands . . . claimed under grants of different States," treason and "other crimes and offences" created by federal law, and cases involving "rights created by a law of the United States, and having a special remedy given to them in federal courts." *American State Papers: Miscellaneous* 1:22.

[111] Frankfurter and Landis, *The Business of the Supreme Court*, 15–16.

[112] *American State Papers: Miscellaneous* 1:23–24.

[113] Ironically, Ellsworth did not sign the Constitution either, but only because he left the Convention early.

[114] Holt, " 'Federal Courts as the Asylum to Federal Interests,' " 346.

cases they so desired, Randolph reasoned, then there was simply no point in granting specific classes of jurisdiction at all.[115] Even more important, by eliminating Section 25, the controversial provision that gave the Supreme Court jurisdiction over appeals from state supreme courts in certain instances, Randolph would have removed a device that, although probably not widely realized as such in 1790,[116] held enormous potential for federal aggrandizement of state judicial power. Indeed, the nationalizing influence of Section 25 would soon be surrounded by a maelstrom of antijudicial sentiment. By the end of Reconstruction, courts of seven states and legislatures of eight states had declared the provision unconstitutional, and Congress had entertained ten separate attempts—including three in the 1820s alone—to repeal it.[117] Three decades before the real controversy over Section 25 began, Randolph already viewed it as a defect in the judicial system.

    Like Ellsworth, Randolph made concessions to each side—the expansion of jurisdiction and the abolition of circuit riding to nationalists, the elimination of pliable provisions that allowed the expansion of federal judicial power at the expense of state judiciaries to localists—in the hope of gaining widespread support for landmark reform. But where Ellsworth had reconciled tensions between nationalist and localist interests over matters such as geography and jurisdiction, Randolph seemed to aggravate them. Though both sides had expressed displeasure with Ellsworth's compromise, neither seemed willing to budge in order to alter it. With nationalists objecting to the proposed elimination of Sections 14 and 25 as restrictions on judicial power and localists decrying the expansion of federal jurisdiction as a threat to state prerogatives,[118] Randolph's detailed and thoughtful proposal for judicial reform was "immediately consigned to oblivion."[119]

[115] Ibid., 350–52.

[116] But see Charles Warren, *The Supreme Court in United States History*, vol. 1: *1789–1835* (Boston: Little, Brown, 1926), 10–11, noting the House's concern with Section 25.

[117] These developments are discussed in chapter 3. See also Warren, "Legislative and Judicial Attacks on the Supreme Court of the United States," 3–4; Wiecek, "*Murdock v. Memphis*," 223, pointing to Section 25 as the "primary focus for competing theories of the federal union throughout the antebellum and Reconstruction periods" and classifying its nineteenth century history as "one of the most important chapters in the evolution of American federalism."

[118] That nationalists opposed Randolph's report was made clear by a radical counterproposal by New York representative Egbert Benson. A set of constitutional amendments designed to undermine state courts, Benson's proposal would have essentially eliminated the jurisdictional split between federal and state courts by substantially expanding federal jurisdiction and transforming state courts into lower federal courts. Completely national in outlook, Benson's reform proposal came only two days before the end of the legislative session, perhaps suggesting that it was meant as much as symbolic "position taking" than as a substantive policy initiative; *DHSC*, 168. See also John D. Gordan III, "Egbert Benson: A Nationalist in Congress, 1789–1793," in *Neither Separate nor Equal: Congress in the 1790s*, ed. Kenneth R. Bowling and Donald R. Kennon (Athens: Ohio University Press, 2000), 75, describing Benson's proposal as "a reductio ad absurdum of Randolph's restructuring of the federal court system." On the Benson proposal generally, see Holt, " 'Federal Courts as the Asylum to Federal Interests.' " On position taking in Congress, see David R. Mayhew, *Congress: The Electoral Connection* (New Haven, CT: Yale University Press, 1974).

[119] *National Gazette*, December 11, 1792, reprinted in *DHSC*, 587.

What explains Randolph's failure to duplicate Ellsworth's success in judicial institution building? Not a change in congressional membership: the Congress that commissioned Randolph's report was the same Congress that consented to Ellsworth's plan. Not a change in tactics, either—having seemingly learned from Ellsworth's entrepreneurial strategies, Randolph tried to duplicate them. Rather, three factors account for the contrast between Ellsworth's triumph over the political contestation in 1789 and Randolph's inability to overcome the opposition to reform the following year: the timing of the report's appearance, the legacy of the 1789 compromise, and the rise of ideology as a powerful influence in American politics. The first of these three factors was largely out of Randolph's control, but the second and third represent critical flaws in his entrepreneurship—notably, his failure to recognize that the political environment had changed substantially since (and as a result of) Ellsworth's entrepreneurship. Without a keen awareness of the political climate in which he was operating, Randolph's entrepreneurial identity, ideas, and tactics aggravated rather than assuaged the constraints inhibiting reform.

First, the timing of Randolph's report—in terms of both the sequence of the legislative session and the sequence of early American history—made reform difficult. Whereas Ellsworth had the luxury of the Senate taking up the judiciary bill as its first order of business, Randolph's report arrived in the House with fewer than two months remaining in the third session of the First Congress and only two weeks after "another of their secretaries [Alexander Hamilton] made a report on a project infinitely more interesting [the national bank]."[120] "My belief," Fisher Ames wrote in anticipation of Randolph's report, "is that little or nothing will be done (during the session) for the alteration of the law in this regard" for "time will not admit of it."[121] Whether or not time would have permitted action in favor of a less technical and more salient issue is unclear, but there was certainly speculation to that effect. "If the prompt and effectual administration of justice was of as much consequence *as the rise of stocks*," a letter in the *General Advertiser* would later lament, "the court system would probably be treated with more attention."[122]

Moreover, a decrease in the sense of urgency that had accompanied the first year of the new government further complicated Randolph's reform possibilities. Though less than a year had passed, that urgency—at least as it related to the judiciary—had largely receded. In its first session, Congress had tackled the Judiciary Act of 1789 with urgency partly because the situation required urgent action. If Congress failed to pass the Judiciary Act, then the federal judiciary would never have come into being. Even the Supreme Court, the establishment of which was specified in the Constitution itself, would have been unable to operate without its justices—the number of whom was not constitutionally elaborated—or resources

---

[120] Ibid.

[121] Fisher Ames to John Lowell, December 17, 1790, reprinted in *DHSC*, 539.

[122] "Letter from an Anonymous Correspondent to His Friend in Philadelphia," *General Advertiser*, January 25, 1793, reprinted in *DHSC*, 591.

to make the judicial endeavor possible. Sobering even to localists, many of whom supported the creation of a federal judiciary in order to deal with maritime and admiralty issues, the prospect of a completely hamstrung judiciary undoubtedly exerted pressure on legislators, created space for Ellsworth's entrepreneurship, and contributed to the willingness of each side to accept a judicial system that did not entirely satisfy either of their interests. In its second and third sessions, Congress was indifferent to the challenge of building the judiciary largely because it could be. The Judiciary Act of 1789 provided a fallback, or reversionary, plan: even if Congress failed to reform it, the judiciary would still exist, and the nation would survive. Unfortunately for the judiciary, the urgency Ellsworth exploited in 1789 would prove the exception, and the indifference Randolph encountered in 1790—leaving judicial reform until the end of the session, failing to prioritize it over other matters, recognizing the need for relief but then failing to provide any— would soon become the new historical rule.

Second, the hard-fought battle over the Judiciary Act of 1789 had resulted in an uneasy compromise, and, though few were content with that compromise, many were reluctant to disturb it—either because they feared what would replace it or because they preferred a wait-and-see approach to landmark reform of an institution still in its infancy.[123] With nationalists refusing to accept any provisions that might decrease federal judicial power, and localists rejecting any provisions that might increase such power, revising the Judiciary Act of 1789 required energy and political capital that few were willing to expend, especially since the outcome was unlikely to be more auspicious. Obviously, if victory could have been assured, either side would have jumped at the opportunity to remake the judiciary, but without such a guarantee, each camp was content to prevent the other from acquiring the transformative opportunity. Given the inherent unpredictability about the end result of a wholesale reappraisal of the judicial system, nationalists and localists alike preferred the one already in operation to one of imagination. In other words, where Ellsworth was working with a clean slate, Randolph was confronted by the precedent and institutional residue that Ellsworth and the Judiciary Act of 1789 had left behind.[124] Randolph, however, did not pay much attention to this residue

---

[123] Fisher Ames to John Lowell, December 17, 1790, reprinted in *DHSC*, 538, cautioning against "impatient changes" and advising that "prudence requires our waiting till time has more fully disclosed the defects of the System"; Peter Van Schaack to Theodore Sedgwick, December 25, 1791, reprinted in *DHSC*, 568: "I incline to think that it must be left to Time and Circumstances to give it a proper Establishment. Premature Attempts to amend, may check the good and increase the Evils of the present System. We have Seen So little in Practice under the present System, in this State, that We derive no Light from Experience."

[124] On the ideas of institutional residue and layering as they relate to congressional reform, see Eric Schickler, *Disjointed Pluralism: Institutional Innovation and the Development of the U.S. Congress* (Princeton, NJ: Princeton University Press, 2001), esp. 15–16, 252–54; for a broader theory of institutional development incorporating the notion of layering, see Kathleen Thelen, "How Institutions Evolve: Insights from Comparative Historical Analysis," in *Comparative Historical Analysis in the Social Sciences*, ed. James Mahoney and Dietrich Rueschemeyer (New York: Cambridge University Press, 2002), 208–40.

in either his ideas or his tactics. Rather than avoid controversial issues like circuit riding, he confronted them directly; rather than attempt more incremental
reform, his proposal struck at the core of Ellsworth's design. Despite the fact that
his proposal was motivated by concerns about judicial performance rather than
policy or politics, the scope and aggressiveness with which it targeted the 1789
system distinguished its path from the relatively consensual politics surrounding
purely housekeeping initiatives.

Third, even if Randolph could have overcome the poor timing and the precarious balance of Ellsworth's compromise, he was faced with another problem
that made his identity ill-suited for entrepreneurial success in 1790: the growing
intensity of political ideology. Though there were still no formal political parties,
the sharp divergence between Hamiltonian and Jeffersonian visions of America's
political future had nonetheless dichotomized the political sphere.[125] In contrast to
Ellsworth, who was certainly far from neutral between nationalism and localism
(or between Federalism and Anti-Federalism), Randolph was "a genuine middle-
of-the-roader" who felt uncomfortable choosing between the two rival factions.[126]
Though a member of George Washington's proto-Federalist cabinet, Randolph
was uneasy about Hamilton's nationalism; though a Virginian who had initially
opposed the Constitution, he similarly rejected Jefferson's pervading skepticism of
government power. Eschewing both Hamiltonianism and Jeffersonianism for the
above-the-fray and disinterested neutrality of Washington, Randolph's "apparent
ambivalence" about the increasingly contentious ideological divide "rendered his
advice untrustworthy in both camps."[127] That is to say, at a time when ideology
was becoming increasingly influential, Randolph's reputation as a man without an
ideology—even as a man "above" ideology—proved more detrimental than beneficial. Because he lacked a natural constituency or base of support among either
of the predominant factions, Randolph's attempt to triangulate between them was
unable to conquer the great risk that stood in the way of a potentially great reward.

As Randolph's failed reform campaign showed, not just any incident of
entrepreneurship—not just any identity, ideas, or tactics—is a sufficient catalyst to
overcome the constraints against institution building. Rather, in order to be successful, entrepreneurship must be adequately tailored to the environment in which
it operates. After all, entrepreneurs act within an existing political order that may
offer abundant or scarce opportunities for transformative political action. They are

[125] Richard Hofstadter, *The Idea of a Party System: The Rise of Legitimate Opposition in the United States, 1780–1840* (Berkeley and Los Angeles: University of California Press, 1969); William Nisbet Chambers, *Political Parties in a New Nation: The American Experience, 1776–1809* (New York: Oxford University Press, 1963); Elkins and McKitrick, *Age of Federalism*; Cal Jillson, "Fighting for Control of the American Dream: Alexander Hamilton, Thomas Jefferson, and the Election of 1800," in *Establishing Congress: The Removal to Washington, D.C., and the Election of 1800*, ed. Kenneth R. Bowling and Donald R. Kennon (Athens: Ohio University Press, 2005), 6–17; and Bernard A. Weisberger, *America Afire: Jefferson, Adams, and the Revolutionary Election of 1800* (New York: HarperCollins, 2000), 43–116.
[126] Holt, "'Federal Courts as the Asylum to Federal Interests,'" 346.
[127] Ibid.

by no means held captive by their structural surroundings—indeed, entrepreneurship may involve manipulating a hostile or ambivalent political order into a favorable one—but neither are they able simply to stampede over them. In Randolph's case, the unfortunate timing of his report combined with both his tactical failure to recognize the institutional residue of the Judiciary Act of 1789 and his problematic identity relative to the growing ideological contest between Hamiltonians and Jeffersonians to make institutional transformation highly unlikely.

Judicial and Extrajudicial Activities

The death of Randolph's proposal did not end the agitation for judicial reform. By contrast, as the struggle to eliminate the "intolerable labour" of circuit riding demonstrated,[128] it was only the opening salvo in what would prove a continuous battle. A hobbyhorse of Randolph's, circuit riding was the result of having three tiers of a federal judiciary operated by only two sets of judges. Given that the system "pivoted" on having Supreme Court justices double as circuit court judges,[129] it was problematic that the practice raised real questions about the structure of the judicial system in a territorially expanding society. Could the justices handle the physical and emotional burdens of traveling long distances for extended periods of time to hear more cases? Was there something inappropriate or illegitimate about having justices hear appeals of their own decisions? How would territorial expansion—and, with it, expansion in federal judicial business—affect the system of circuit riding? Randolph had provided answers in his report, but they were more prognostication than empirical observation. By the fall of 1792, however, his forecast had come true: the justices were tired of riding circuit and sought relief from Congress.

Walking a fine line between self-preservation and the appearance of selfish indolence, the justices,[130] writing to George Washington in November 1792,[131] were direct in their feelings about the practice: "We really, sir, find the burdens laid upon us so excessive that we cannot forbear representing them in strong and explicit terms."[132] The mismatch between the expanding geography of the new nation and

---

[128] Robert Goodloe Harper to his constituents, February 26, 1801, reprinted in *DHSC*, 715–16. See, generally, Wythe Holt, "'The Federal Courts Have Enemies in All Who Fear Their Influence on State Objects': The Failure to Abolish Supreme Court Circuit-Riding in the Judiciary Acts of 1792 and 1793," 36 *Buffalo Law Review* 301 (1987).

[129] Frankfurter and Landis, *The Business of the Supreme Court*, 14.

[130] The Court at the time comprised John Jay, William Cushing, James Wilson, John Blair, James Iredell, and Thomas Johnson.

[131] This was the second letter written, but only the first sent, from the justices to the president on the topic of circuit riding. After the justices met in August 1790, Chief Justice John Jay penned a letter of objection, but there is no record that it was ever mailed. For a copy of the letter, see John Jay, Draft of Letter from Justices of the Supreme Court to George Washington, September 15, 1790, reprinted in *The Founders' Constitution, vol. 4: Article 2, Section 2 through Article 7*, ed. Philip B. Kurland and Ralph Lerner (Chicago: University of Chicago Press, 1987), 161–62.

[132] *American State Papers: Miscellaneous* 1:51–52.

the relatively small size of the Supreme Court made "holding twenty-seven circuit courts a year, in the different States, from New Hampshire to Georgia, besides two sessions of the Supreme Court at Philadelphia, in the two most severe seasons of the year" decidedly unpleasant. In particular, they complained about a number of personal burdens, including the arduous travel, the extensive time away from their families, and the dangers of compounding those two factors with old age and ill health. Furthermore, they were concerned that compelling "the same men finally to correct in one capacity the errors which they themselves may have committed in another" was "unfriendly to impartial justice, and to that confidence in the Supreme Court which it is so essential to the public interest should be reposed in it."[133] In sum, the negative effects of circuit riding made it a practice that should be utilized only "in cases of necessity."[134] While acknowledging that Congress was "occupied by other affairs of great and pressing importance" and declining "to suggest what alterations of system ought . . . to be formed and adopted," the justices' message was clear: the judicial system was in dire need of modification in order to relieve them "from their present painful and improper situation."

The justices' willingness to complain about, but not assist in, modifying the system perturbed members of Congress, many of whom had assumed that the judicial system would be improved "under the auspices of the Judges who alone will be able to perhaps set it to rights."[135] While Congress expected reform suggestions from judges who witnessed the system's defects firsthand, the justices expected Congress simply to heed their objections and redress their grievances. Unfortunately for the justices, despite Randolph's advice and Washington's urging,[136] Congress simply refused to act—at least in any significant way. Responding to Justice James Iredell's complaints about his brethren's refusal to rotate circuit assignments, Congress passed a small statute mandating precisely the rotation Iredell desired.[137] The following year, in an attempt to alleviate the justices' burdens, Congress passed another statute that, among other things, required only one justice (rather than two) to sit on each circuit court.[138] While ostensibly better than nothing, such

---

[133] In his unsent letter of 1790, Jay warned Washington that the justices could not "be Judges of inferior and *subordinate* Courts, and be at the same time both the *controllers* and the *controlled*." See John Jay, Draft of Letter from Justices of the Supreme Court to George Washington, September 15, 1790, reprinted in *The Founders' Constitution*, 4:162.

[134] *American State Papers: Miscellaneous* 1:51–52.

[135] James Madison to Edmund Pendleton, September 14, 1789, reprinted in *DHSC*, 511.

[136] Prompted by Randolph, Washington included a paragraph in his 1792 address to Congress encouraging judicial reform. See Edmund Randolph to George Washington, December 26, 1791, reprinted in *DHSC*, 569–70: "Perhaps too, in a review which the President takes of the affairs of the Union, at the opening of each Session of Congress, the judicial department will be comprehended."

[137] 1 Stat. 252 (April 17, 1792). In a nutshell, Iredell had initially been assigned the Southern circuit, widely considered the most arduous of the three circuits, and incorrectly assumed the justices would frequently rotate. After his fellow justices repeatedly refused to accommodate him, he made recourse to Congress. For a fuller recounting of the story, see Holt, "'The Federal Courts Have Enemies in All Who Fear Their Influence on State Objects,'" 311–19, 328–30.

[138] 1 Stat. 333 (March 2, 1793).

piecemeal reform did little to improve the situation, and, as suggested by the justices' request for relief in 1794,[139] circuit riding remained an unpleasant ordeal. Moreover, with Iredell turning to Congress instead of settling his objections with his fellow justices, the justices' internal norm of avoiding "political self-help" was betrayed.[140] The combination of the means (a haggard justice begging an unresponsive Congress for relief) and the ends (the Court accepting a congressional dictate about seemingly internal procedures)suggested a radical "cession of power over administration of the branch."[141]

The justices' reluctance to help reform the judicial system can be viewed in two ways. On one level, it was driven by a similar impulse—the desire to avoid political entanglement—as two other controversies of the 1790s: first, the justices' refusal to issue advisory opinions in response to requests by Alexander Hamilton, Thomas Jefferson, and even George Washington;[142] and, second, their multiple declarations, culminating in *Hayburn's Case*,[143] that the Invalid Pensions Act of 1792,[144] which required them to serve as "pension commissioners" while sitting as circuit judges, was unconstitutional.[145] But where these earlier decisions occasioned less political (either congressional or presidential) control over the judiciary, the justices' reluctance to deal with the administrative governance of the judicial branch occasioned more. In this way, then, the reliance on Congress to fix nonstatutory elements of circuit riding was at odds with the justices' long-range attempt to preserve judicial independence through a strict separation of powers.

Raised at the Philadelphia Convention in response to proposals to include federal judges in lawmaking through service on a "Council of Revision," the strategy of protecting judicial independence through rigorous adherence to the separation of powers became central to the justices' avoidance of most extrajudicial activities

[139] *American State Papers: Miscellaneous* 1:77–78.

[140] Goebel, *Antecedents and Beginnings to 1801*, 557.

[141] Geyh and Van Tassel, "The Independence of the Judicial Branch in the New Republic," 69: "What Congress had left to the Court to determine was thus removed by Congress, not only without protest from the judiciary, but at the behest of one of its Justices because several members of the Supreme Court were not prepared voluntarily to share the excessive burdens of riding the southern circuit."

[142] See, generally, William R. Casto, "The Early Supreme Court Justices' Most Significant Opinion," 29 *Ohio Northern University Law Review* 173 (2002); and Stewart Jay, *Most Humble Servants: The Advisory Role of Early Judges* (New Haven, CT: Yale University Press, 1997).

[143] 2 U.S. 409 (1792).

[144] 1 Stat. 243 (March 23, 1792).

[145] On extrajudicial activities, see Jay, *Most Humble Servants*; Wythe Holt, "Separation of Powers? Relations between the Judiciary and the Other Branches of the Federal Government before 1802," in *Neither Separate nor Equal: Congress in the 1790s*, ed. Kenneth R. Bowling and Donald R. Kennon (Athens, OH: Ohio University Press, 2000), 183–210; Casto, *The Supreme Court in the Early Republic*, 173–83; and Mark Tushnet, "Dual Office Holding and the Constitution: A View from *Hayburn's Case*," in *Origins of the Federal Judiciary: Essays on the Judiciary Act of 1789*, ed. Maeva Marcus (New York: Oxford University Press, 1992), 196–222. For a list of other administrative duties imposed upon federal judges by Congress, see *DHSC*, appendix A, 723–29.

throughout the Washington and Adams administrations.[146] In the case of advisory opinions, Chief Justice John Jay, speaking for his fellow justices, referred to the existence of executive and judicial "checks upon each other" as an argument "against the propriety of our extra-judicially deciding the questions alluded to."[147] In the case of the Invalid Pensions Act, two sets of justices, each sitting as circuit judges, emphasized similar themes in separate letters to Congress and the president. In one letter, Jay and Justice William Cushing (along with district judge James Duane) declared that "neither the *legislative* nor the *executive* branch can constitutionally assign to the *judicial* any duties but such as are properly judicial, and to be performed in a judicial manner."[148] In another letter, Justices James Wilson and John Blair (joined by district court judge Richard Peters) concluded that the ability of the secretary of war to overturn the judges' rulings as pension commissioners was "radically inconsistent with the independence of that judicial power which is vested in the courts."[149] Although such rigorous insistence on the separation of powers aided judicial independence in these two episodes, it undoubtedly detracted from it in the case of circuit riding modifications.

Of course, the institutional development of the judiciary during this period was affected not simply by what judges did outside the courtroom but by what they did inside it as well. Although the Supreme Court had relatively little business during much of the 1790s, it did have some, and such business often involved highly controversial subjects such as the governmental power to tax, the repayment of debts, the protection of private property, and the place of the United States in diplomatic affairs.[150] Equally important, from the perspective of judicial institution building, many of these cases implicated contested issues such as state sovereignty and the role of the federal judiciary in assessing the constitutionality of both state and federal laws.

The Court's constitutional rulings throughout the 1790s were controversial precisely because they verified Anti-Federalist and localist fears about both the Court's perceived nationalist bias and the impact of that bias on important issues of economic policy. Indeed, one of the Court's first significant decisions, *Chisholm v. Georgia*,[151] represented a frontal attack on state sovereignty. Involving a federal suit by a South Carolina citizen against the state of Georgia, *Chisholm* evoked a

[146] Of course, the justices did not abstain from all extrajudicial activities. In fact, both John Jay and Oliver Ellsworth were sent on diplomatic missions abroad during their respective tenures as chief justice, a fact that would later feature in Jeffersonian complaints that the judiciary was simply a Federalist appendage.

[147] John Jay to George Washington, August 8, 1793, reprinted in *The Founders' Constitution*, 4:258.

[148] *American State Papers: Miscellaneous* 1:50.

[149] *Ibid.,* 1:51.

[150] Warren, *The Supreme Court in United States History*, 1:91–168. For analyses of the work of the lower courts during this time, see Dwight F. Henderson, *Courts For a New Nation* (Washington, DC: Public Affairs Press, 1971), 55–89; Mary K. Bonsteel Tachau, *Federal Courts in the Early Republic: Kentucky 1789–1816* (Princeton, NJ: Princeton University Press, 1978); and Holt, "'The Federal Courts Have Enemies in All Who Fear Their Influence on State Objects,'" 322–24.

[151] 2 U.S. 419 (1793).

firestorm of criticism by holding that states were not sovereign and that their conduct was not immune from review by a federal court.[152] In fact, the Court's 1793 ruling provoked a reaction so severe that the Eleventh Amendment was passed specifically to overturn it.[153] Three years later, in *Ware v. Hylton* and *Hylton v. United States*,[154] the Court continued what opponents interpreted as its hostility to the states by utilizing something akin to the power of judicial review.[155] In *Ware*, the Court, rejecting the argument of future chief justice John Marshall (who argued the case on behalf of the state of Virginia), concluded that a state law obstructing the payment of debts owed to a British citizen was in conflict with the Treaty of Paris, and struck down a state law for the first time in its (albeit short) history.[156] In *Hylton*, decided the very next day, the Court, also for the first time, considered the constitutionality of a federal law but ultimately upheld the tax imposed on carriages—a tax Jeffersonians believed unwise and unconstitutional—as within congressional taxation power. In addition to their concrete effects,[157] *Ware* and *Hylton* suggested that the Anti-Federalists' fear, articulated since the Philadelphia Convention, that the Court would wield its power unevenly by simultaneously deferring to federal law and attacking state law was not without merit. In contrast to the early views of some members of the emerging (but still minority) Democratic-Republican Party, who had seen the Court and its power of judicial review as a potential bulwark against the excesses of the Federalist majority,[158] the cases of the 1790s—the backlash against *Chisholm* notwithstanding—indicated that judicial power might indeed exist to enforce national prerogatives against state and local interests.

The fact that most judicial decisions during this period were closer to nationalist principles than to localist ones is far from surprising when one considers the ideological makeup of the judiciary. Indeed, despite the fact that openly partisan

---

[152] Support for this holding is found in Article III, Section 2, Clause 1, which extends the judicial power to controversies "between a State and citizens of another State," though there was obvious disagreement about whether or not this meant states could be sued without their consent.

[153] "The judicial power of the United States shall not be construed to extend to any suit in law or equity, commenced or prosecuted against one of the United States by citizens of another State, or by citizens or subjects of any foreign state."

[154] 3 U.S. 199 (1796); 3 U.S. 171 (1796).

[155] Note that *Ware* and *Hylton* occured a full seven years before the conventionally assumed "establishment" of judicial review in *Marbury v. Madison*, 5 U.S. 137 (1803). The work of Mark Graber has been especially illuminating about the relative unimportance of *Marbury* to the establishment of judicial review. See, among others, Graber, "Establishing Judicial Review."

[156] Since the statute was struck down because it conflicted with a federal treaty rather than a constitutional provision, it is not conventionally considered an exercise of judicial review. Two years later, however, in *Calder v. Bull*, 3 U.S. 386 (1798), the Court considered whether a retroactive Connecticut probate law was a violation of the Constitution's prohibition of ex post facto laws in Article I, Section 10 but ultimately upheld the law.

[157] See Warren, *The Supreme Court in United States History*, 1:144, noting that American debts to British creditors totaled more than two million dollars in Virginia alone.

[158] Ellis, *The Jeffersonian Crisis*, 12–13; Warren, *The Supreme Court in United States History*, 1:82.

staffing of the judiciary is usually considered to have begun under John Adams,[159] George Washington's appointments to the Supreme Court were far more geographically than ideologically diverse. Washington's own ideology is difficult to categorize because he transcended ordinary divisions, sought counsel from both Hamiltonians and Jeffersonians, and governed only during the earliest stages of partisan politics, but it is clear from his appointments, which followed careful and thorough consideration, that he sought certain types of individuals—namely, distinguished men who possessed sharp legal minds and were strong, public supporters of the Constitution—for service on the federal bench.[160] Of the ten men Washington named to the Supreme Court,[161] only Samuel Chase (Washington's ninth appointment), a man who would unequivocally prove his Federalist mettle in the first few years of the nineteenth century, had been an opponent of the Constitution.[162] The result was that the initial Court—the Court of the Washington and Adams administrations, the Court before the appointment of the legendary John Marshall—was stacked with two somewhat overlapping categories of Federalists: those who had supported the Constitution (1787 Federalists) and those who supported Adams and Hamilton over Jefferson (1790s Federalists). And, as the Jeffersonians were beginning to notice, since both stripes of Federalists conceived of them as a faction,[163] neither was willing to treat them as "legitimate opposition."[164]

A Decade of Piecemeal Reform

Between the failure of the Randolph Report and the attempts to reform or abolish circuit riding, the decade following the Judiciary Act of 1789—doubtless an eventful and crucially important decade in the history of the American republic—was largely a decade of piecemeal, performance-oriented, and uncontroversial judicial reform. Though Congress passed more than thirty statutes implicating judicial functions, individuals, or resources, most of them were fairly minor: establishing new district courts when North Carolina and Rhode Island ratified the Constitution,[165] regulating the conditions under which a circuit court may be adjourned,[166] providing for the authentication of judicial records,[167] extending and

[159] Amar, *America's Constitution*, 220.

[160] For a summary of Washington's appointments to lower courts as well as his selection of federal marshals and attorneys, see Henderson, *Courts For a New Nation*, 27–34.

[161] This count includes John Rutledge only once, though Washington nominated him twice—first as an associate justice in 1789 and, after Rutledge left the Court for four years, again as chief justice in 1795. The latter appointment occurred during a congressional recess, after which the Senate refused to confirm Rutledge.

[162] Amar, *America's Constitution*, 219.

[163] Bruce Ackerman, *The Failure of the Founding Fathers: Jefferson, Marshall, and the Rise of Presidential Democracy* (Cambridge, MA: Harvard University Press, 2005), 130.

[164] Hofstadter, *The Idea of a Party System*.

[165] 1 Stat. 126 (June 4, 1790); 1 Stat. 128 (June 23, 1790).

[166] 1 Stat. 369 (May 19, 1794).

[167] 1 Stat. 122 (May 26, 1790).

revising the Process Act of 1789,[168] clarifying compensation issues,[169] specifying the locations of particular lower court sessions.[170] Thus, the 1790s were largely characterized by "housekeeping"—low salience and relatively small modifications to the judicial system. As the battle over circuit riding suggested, Congress was generally reluctant to make significant changes to a system that had been in operation only a few short years, so it largely responded with institutional tinkering. In other words, it solved discrete problems but went no further.[171] As a result, congressional action on behalf of judicial reform was simultaneously welcomed and disappointing. On the one hand, as problems arose, Congress usually sought, though not always promptly or successfully, to rectify them through statute. On the other hand, in waiting for problems to arise, Congress expressly declined the opportunity to think through—and, in turn, reform—the role, structure, and powers of the federal judiciary in a holistic or comprehensive fashion.

Why did Congress fail to build the judiciary in any significant way during the 1790s? Without a doubt, the combination of short legislative sessions, the presence of other concerns both foreign and domestic, and the technicality of the issues involved—three factors Ellsworth's entrepreneurship nonetheless overcame in 1789—militated against wide-ranging appraisal of the judicial system and increased the likelihood that, to the extent Congress responded, it would do so with stopgap solutions. Moreover, some of the same factors that had contributed to the failure of Randolph's report in 1790—specifically, the legacy of Ellsworth's compromise and a decreased sense of political urgency—continued to inhibit landmark institution building in the years that followed. But above all of these factors, the interaction of two broad developments in the American political system determined the fate of the 1790s as a decade of institutional tinkering rather than one of institutional transformation: the centrality of political parties to American politics

---

[168] 1 Stat. 123 (May 26, 1790); 1 Stat. 191 (February 18, 1791); 1 Stat. 275 (May 8, 1792). Originally conceived as a "stand-in" until more extensive procedural guidelines could be developed, the Process Act of 1789, much like the Judiciary Act of 1789, was considered defective almost immediately. With Ellsworth and his allies having failed to convince their colleagues that standardized judicial process was vital, the Process Act simply left most issues of federal judicial procedure to be determined by the practices of individual states. After failed attempts at significant reform to the system, it was clear by 1792 that "what had in some quarters been viewed as a temporary expedient was in the way of becoming a fixture"; Goebel, *Antecedents and Beginnings to 1801*, 542.

[169] Most of these issues centered on fee tables and salaries for judicial officers—especially clerks, marshals, and other support staff. Relevant acts include 1 Stat. 216 (March 3, 1791); 1 Stat. 275 (May 8, 1792); 1 Stat. 402 (June 9, 1794); 1 Stat. 419 (February 25, 1795); 1 Stat. 423 (February 27, 1795); 1 Stat. 451 (March 31, 1796); 1 Stat. 492 (June 1, 1796); 1 Stat. 624 (February 28, 1799).

[170] 1 Stat. 335 (March 2, 1793); 1 Stat. 475 (May 27, 1796); 1 Stat. 517 (March 3, 1797).

[171] For instance, Congress resolved the difficulty of petitioning for a stay of circuit court decisions within the allotted time by allowing circuit court clerks, rather than just the clerk of the Supreme Court, to issue writs; addressed concerns about the limited number of locations where federal courts were actually held by requiring district court sessions in additional cities; and expanded federal jurisdiction as necessary to deal with the ramifications of violating new federal criminal or bankruptcy laws. See 1 Stat. 112 (April 30, 1790); 2 Stat. 19 (April 4, 1800); *DHSC*, appendix B, 741.

and greater clarity—indeed, empirical evidence—about how the judiciary would actually function in the new nation.

When Randolph presented his report to the House in 1790, parties were still in their gestational period, but by the latter half of the decade they had matured significantly.[172] Between the continued divergence of Hamiltonian and Jeffersonian worldviews, the emergence of clearer voting patterns in Congress,[173] the retirement of the one man—George Washington—that had been somewhat able to keep the peace between factions, the first contested presidential election in 1796, and the establishment of contending "party presses" as outlets for vitriolic newspaper attacks against ideas and character alike,[174] the Federalist and Democratic-Republican Parties had become central to American political life. And, as they had on a great many issues—including economic development, the Bank of the United States, the location of the capital, the conduct of foreign affairs, the nature of republican government, the size of the federal government, the meaning of sovereignty, and the relationship between federal and state authority—these two parties gradually staked out fundamentally different positions on federal judicial power. At the beginning of the decade, when judicial power was still conceptualized only as an abstraction, Democrat-Republicans had been optimistic that the potentially countermajoritarian power of the judiciary might be used to protect state and individual rights against Federalist incursions.[175] Once the judiciary issued concrete rulings, however, Democratic-Republican support for the institution disappeared rapidly.

The early judicial assaults against Jeffersonian ideology and Democratic-Republican policy positions were significant. Besides the Court's attack on state sovereignty in *Chisholm*, forced repayment of British debts in *Ware*, and approval of a controversial carriage tax in *Hylton*, Democrat-Republicans were enraged by the judiciary's prosecutions under the Sedition Act, partisan jury instructions, denial of American ports to French privateers, invalidation of a 1778 treaty with France, and attempts to incorporate English common law into American federal law.[176] In all of these instances, the Court conveyed the message that it was not ambivalent toward the rival constitutional visions of Federalists and Democrat-Republicans. As a result, Democrat-Republicans were loath to heed the arguments of Federalist justices who felt overburdened by circuit riding or select Federalist legislators who wished to empower the judiciary generally.

[172] Hofstadter, *The Idea of a Party System*; Chambers, *Political Parties in a New Nation*; Elkins and McKitrick, *Age of Federalism*; John Ferling, *Adams vs. Jefferson: The Tumultuous Election of 1800* (Oxford: Oxford University Press, 2004), 56–82.

[173] John H. Aldrich, *Why Parties? The Origin and Transformation of Political Parties in America* (Chicago: University of Chicago Press, 1995), 77–82.

[174] Federalists had John Fenno's *Gazette of the United States* and William Cobbett's *Porcupine's Gazette*; Democrat-Republicans used Philip Freneau's *National Gazette* and Benjamin Bache's *Aurora*.

[175] Warren, *The Supreme Court in United States History*, 1:82.

[176] Ibid., 1:91–168; Ellis, *The Jeffersonian Crisis*, 13–14; Haskins and Johnson, *Foundations of Power*, 126.

While Democrat-Republicans correctly perceived the judiciary as a threat to the Jeffersonian vision, it is not clear that Federalists adequately appreciated the potential of judicial power as a means to advance their own causes—at least not yet. Thus, despite the fact that the judiciary had seemingly supported the Federalist position in the majority of important cases, the party did not aggressively seek to empower the judiciary for reasons of either policy or politics. The best explanation for Federalist inaction in this regard is that the party held a House majority that was both fleeting—Federalists (or their proadministration predecessors) were actually the minority party in the Third (1793–95) and Fourth (1795–97) Congresses[177]—and relatively vulnerable, with no more than a nine-seat edge in any of the first five Congresses.[178] Since not even moderate Democrat-Republicans could be counted on for support, Federalists needed strict party discipline in order to achieve judicial reform. Yet Federalists were far from united over the subject: some eagerly pushed comprehensive change, others believed the Judiciary Act of 1789 needed no revision, some worried about the costs of expanding judicial power, others feared the effects of discontinuing circuit riding on both order and civic pride in areas where a federal presence was generally lacking.[179] Perhaps the largest contingent was dubious that the judiciary could (or would) advance their substantive interests—most notably, commercial economic growth and a neutral (or, perhaps, pro-British) foreign policy—more effectively than legislative policy making. In turn, they were reluctant to spend precious time building an institution that might or might not help them satisfy their long-term policy and political goals. Of course, by the Sixth Congress (1799–1801)—which boasted both the largest Federalist majority (60–46 in the House, 22–10 in the Senate) since the First Congress and the last Federalist majority in American history—most Federalists had come to see the strategic potential of judicial reform, but for much of the 1790s many simply preferred to devote their attention elsewhere.

Thus, the combination of mounting partisan interests and a federal judiciary that was proving itself far from neutral between rival constitutional visions created a 1790s political climate in which the constraints upon institution building trumped the forces promoting it. Minimal institutional housekeeping occurred largely because it was uncontroversial—it neither stimulated attention and opposition from Democrat-Republicans nor required the expenditure of Federalist

[177] In the Third Congress, antiadministration representatives outnumbered proadministration representatives 54–51 in the House; in the Fourth Congress, Democrat-Republicans held a 59–47 edge over Federalists. In both Congresses, however, proadministration legislators/Federalists remained the majority party in the Senate.

[178] The proadministration bloc/Federalists enjoyed the following House majorities from 1789 to 1799: 37–28 in the First Congress, 39–30 in the Second Congress, and 57–49 in the Fifth Congress. Over the same time, majorities in the Senate were relatively comfortable in the First (18–8), Fourth (21–11), and Fifth (22–10) Congresses but slim in the Second (16–13) and Third (16–14).

[179] Holt, "'The Federal Courts Have Enemies in All Who Fear Their Influence on State Objects,'" 313–14, 339–40. On Federalist divisions more generally, see Ellis, *The Jeffersonian Crisis*, 53–57, distinguishing between Hamiltonian "High Federalists" and moderate "Adams Federalists" both before and after the election of 1800.

time and energy—but there was little hope for landmark or highly salient judicial institution building, not even performance initiatives. Just when it seemed that the judiciary was destined to remain largely as it had been created in 1789, however, a momentous event—the impending transfer of power from one governing coalition to another—shocked American politics to the core. With a flurry of activity in only a few short years, the judiciary, which had gone virtually unchanged in the decade following its establishment in the Judiciary Act of 1789, would be undeniably transformed, less by the substance of judicial institution building than by the wave of partisan politics about to engulf it.

The Federal Judiciary and the Birth of Partisan Politics, 1800–1805

Political parties have never been more important—and their vitriol toward each other never more freely exchanged—than in the years surrounding the election of 1800. As the failed attempts to build the judiciary in the 1790s suggested, partisanship was not irrelevant prior to the first pivotal election in American history, but it certainly became more determinative of political behavior during and following that election. Before the waning days of the eighteenth century, party politics had played a somewhat indirect role in judicial institution building. But, with the "Revolution of 1800" imminent, American politics—and, with it, the politics of institutional development—was about to change.[180]

The election of 1800 was not primarily about judges or judicial reform—rather, it was about the clash of broader visions for America's future—but the judiciary was one of many relevant issues.[181] To the extent that the election was, as Thomas Jefferson believed, a referendum on Federalism itself, then it was also a referendum on Federalist judges. In particular, Jefferson and his followers railed against the role of Federalist judges in enforcing the Sedition Act, signed into law by John Adams in 1798. They took umbrage at both judicial decisions—allowing questionable prosecutions and refusing to consider the constitutionality of the statute, for instance—and judicial behavior, especially the demeanor of outright hostility that Federalists assumed during sedition trials. Drawing on the Virginia and Kentucky Resolutions—authored by Madison and Jefferson in 1798 and 1799, respectively—Democrat-Republicans vigorously and consistently denounced sedition in the

[180] On the "Revolution of 1800," see Hofstadter, *The Idea of a Party System*; John H. Aldrich, "The Election of 1800: The Consequences of the First Change in Party Control," in *Establishing Congress: The Removal to Washington, D.C., and the Election of 1800*, ed. Kenneth R. Bowling and Donald R. Kennon (Athens: Ohio University Press, 2005), 23–38; Joanne B. Freeman, "The Election of 1800: A Study in the Logic of Political Change," 108 *Yale Law Journal* 1959, 1969–82 (1999); Dan Sisson, *The American Revolution of 1800* (New York: Knopf, 1974), 343–437; Susan Dunn, *Jefferson's Second Revolution: The Election Crisis of 1800 and the Triumph of Republicanism* (Boston: Houghton Mifflin, 2004), 227–82; Ferling, *Adams vs. Jefferson*, 207–17; and Weisberger, *America Afire*, 278–310.
[181] Warren, *The Supreme Court in United States History*, 1:168.

1800 campaign.[182] With federal courts already unpopular for their nationalism, their perceived invasions of states' rights, their general anti-French stance, and their attempts to incorporate more English common law—"judgemade" law—into American federal law,[183] the attack on judicial conduct was politically prudent, electorally salient, and virtually inevitable. For their part, Federalists were extremely concerned about the ramifications of a possible Democratic-Republican victory. They knew that sedition trials would end and that the Jeffersonian press would be even more unbridled in maligning and disparaging the advocates and adherents of Federalism. More substantively, they assumed that Democrat-Republicans would break with foreign policy neutrality in order to side with France over England, reverse Federalist economic policies designed to stimulate commerce, seize privately-owned property, legislate debt relief, and generally dismantle the strong national government—including the judiciary—that Federalists had sought to build throughout the 1790s and then defend throughout the 1800 campaign.[184]

With these respective interests in the foreground, the election of 1800 actually catalyzed two clusters of judicial institution building: first, a last-ditch effort at long-desired but suddenly urgent performance reform by the outgoing Federalists, and second, an immediate reaction by the incoming Democrat-Republicans to repeal the prior reform and prevent Federalists from subverting the Jeffersonian mandate of 1800. In the first instance, Federalist apprehension about a Jeffersonian future—about Jeffersonian retribution against the judiciary for its complicity in sedition trials and general renunciation of Hamiltonian financial policies—was sufficiently acute that the Democratic-Republican landslide in the 1800 elections and the impending switch in party control of government served to motivate the Federalists' lame-duck agenda.[185] The centerpiece of that agenda was the Judiciary Act of 1801, hurriedly passed legislation that that seized upon an opportunity to entrench Federalist policy interests within the incoming Jeffersonian regime by abolishing circuit riding, expanding federal jurisdiction, broadening the causes of removal from state to federal courts, creating a new tier of sixteen circuit judges, and reducing the size of the Supreme Court from six justices to five. In the second instance, Democrat-Republicans were infuriated by the Federalists' attempt to mute the sweeping changes the new coalition sought. Accordingly, they retaliated by repealing the Judiciary Act of 1801 and returning the judicial system to its 1789 structure with the Judiciary Act of 1802.

---

[182] Donald Grier Stephenson Jr., *Campaigns and the Court: The U.S. Supreme Court in Presidential Elections* (New York: Columbia University Press, 1999), 35–39; Dunn, *Jefferson's Second Revolution*, 95–120; Weisberger, *America Afire*, 200–224. See also Richard N. Rosenfeld, ed., *American Aurora: A Democratic-Republican Returns: The Suppressed History of Our Nation's Beginnings and the Heroic Newspaper That Tried to Report It* (New York: St. Martin's Press, 1997), passim.

[183] Haskins and Johnson, *Foundations of Power*, 126.

[184] Dunn, *Jefferson's Second Revolution*, 153–89; Weisberger, *America Afire*, 227–57; Ferling, *Adams vs. Jefferson*, 135–61; Warren, *The Supreme Court in United States History*, 1:168.

[185] John Rutledge Jr. to Alexander Hamilton, January 10, 1801, reprinted in *DHSC*, 676: "We shall profit of our short lived majority & do as much good as we can before the end of this session."

In both the Federalist offensive and the Jeffersonian counteroffensive, then, members of Congress and federal judges explicitly wrestled with policy, political, and performance goals. Concerns about economic policy and the balance of power between the federal and state governments were still, as they had been since 1789, omnipresent (especially for Federalists), but by 1800 they had become encapsulated in a broader partisan divide that began to recognize how the judiciary could serve both to achieve policy initiatives and to consolidate political power. While policy goals in judicial institution building were familiar, political goals were somewhat novel. The emergence of such goals—and the subsequent realization that the judiciary need not be, if it ever was, "exempt from the partisan imperative"[186]—explains not only how the federal judiciary was transformed twice in only two years but also why, at the end of those two years, it ended up right back where it had been at the close of the First Congress.

The Lame-Duck Federalists and the Judiciary Act of 1801

In early 1801, just a few months after the Democratic-Republican triumph at the polls, former chief justice John Jay, declining outgoing president John Adams's offer to return to his old chair, complained that "[e]fforts repeatedly made to place the judicial Departmt [sic] on a proper Footing, have proved fruitless."[187] Troubled by the reality that there existed "few national institutions of any substance at all" in America,[188] Jay, those who sat with and followed him on the Court, and a few Federalist legislators had unsuccessfully campaigned for judicial reform since the early 1790s. Unfortunately for them, attempts at abolishing circuit riding, simplifying jurisdiction, expanding the federal judiciary, and unifying procedural rules had all become mired in political indifference and opposition (sometimes more than once), with no significant events or strategic political entrepreneurship to catalyze change. Before 1800, the closest Congress had come to landmark judicial reform came in 1798, when the Senate passed two substantial reform bills only to see them linger without attention in the House.[189] Thus, when Congress failed in its attempt to respond to Adams's encouragement of judicial reform in his 1799 message to Congress,[190] there was little surprise. After all, the 1790s were not fertile

---

[186] Graber, "Establishing Judicial Review," 649. See also Stephen Skowronek, *The Politics Presidents Make: Leadership from John Adams to Bill Clinton* (Cambridge, MA: Belknap Press, 1997), 69–81.

[187] John Jay to John Adams, January 2, 1801, reprinted in *DHSC*, 664.

[188] Preyer, "*United States v. Callender*," 189.

[189] Unfortunately, there is little evidence (and no record of the congressional debate) regarding these two failed proposals. The first proposal would have eliminated circuit riding and reorganized the lower courts; the second, stemming from Kentucky and Tennessee joining the Union as the fifteenth and sixteenth states in 1792 and 1796, respectively, would have established the two new states as a circuit and provided for two additional Supreme Court justices to facilitate the expansion of the circuit system. For some speculation about the failure of these proposals, see "Circuit Riding Reform Bills of 1798" (introduction), in *DHSC*, 223–26.

[190] A bill was drafted, proposed, and debated on the floor but ultimately shelved; "Circuit Riding Reform Bills of 1798," in *DHSC*, 284–88.

years for building the judiciary. But, as Federalists were about to demonstrate, the 1800s were an entirely new decade.

By the time Adams opened the second session of the Sixth Congress (1799–1801) in November of 1800, voting in the presidential election of 1800 was complete, but Adams's defeat at the polls was not definitively known. As a result, his plea for Congress to improve the judiciary—a plea made at the behest of and ghostwritten by the secretary of state and soon-to-be chief justice John Marshall—can hardly be regarded as the last-ditch desperate attempt of a lame-duck president to improve his party's lot going forward. Instead, the Federalists' attempt at institution building represented an opportunity not only to remedy defects in the administration but also to do so in a way that would satisfy their policy goals. In other words, despite the conventional emphasis on the timing of the infamous "midnight judges," the Judiciary Act of 1801 was prompted more by a desire to further an economic policy vision than strengthen a partisan or electoral coalition and intended more as a check upon state officers and judges than upon Jefferson and the incoming Democratic-Republican Congress.[191]

More specifically, the chief motivation of the Judiciary Act of 1801 was a familiar Federalist policy goal: furthering commercial economic development by extending "the force and influence of the Judiciary."[192] As they had since 1789, Federalists believed the states had "prejudices against the laws . . . and in favour of all the enemies of the government of the United States,"[193] prejudices that now led the judges of those states to obstruct Federalist financial policies. Two features of the Judiciary Act of 1801, in particular, were designed to overcome such obstruction: the expansion of the causes for removal from state courts and the granting of federal question jurisdiction to lower federal courts. The first increased the number of cases that would begin in federal court; the second increased the number of cases

[191] Cf. Frankfurter and Landis, *The Business of the Supreme Court*, 21:

The history of the federal bench in these early days is thus part and parcel of a fierce party strife. And yet the second major Judiciary Act—the law of the "Midnight Judges"—is apt to be treated too exclusively by historians as merely a piece of stupendous jobbery. Jobbery it was, but by no means the design only of hungry politicians, or the effort of a party to entrench itself on the bench after the country had sent it into the wilderness. Behind the act lay the pressure of solid professional conceptions regarding a judicature appropriate for the new country, reinforced by defects unmistakably revealed in the workings of the initial system.

[192] "Leonidas," *Columbian Centinel*, January 14, 1801, reprinted in *DHSC*, 682. See also John Rutledge Jr. to Alexander Hamilton, January 10, 1801, reprinted in *DHSC*, 676, claiming that the Judiciary Act would "greatly extend the judiciary power, & of course greatly widen the basis of government"; and "A Citizen," *Washington Federalist*, January 28, 1801, reprinted in *DHSC*, 700, predicting that the act would "bring the authority of the Federal Judiciary closer to the feelings, understanding, and affections of all the citizens." Cf. Kathryn Turner, "Federalist Policy and the Judiciary Act of 1801," *William and Mary Quarterly*, 3d ser., 22 (1965): 31, claiming that it was the "underlying purpose of the Federalists to popularize the federal courts throughout the nation." There is an interesting contrast here between the Federalists seeking to bring *judicial* power to the people and, a few decades later, the Jacksonians seeking to bring *political* power to the people.

[193] "A Citizen," *Washington Federalist*, January 26, 1801, reprinted in *DHSC*, 696.

that, although begun in state court, could finish in federal court. Together, these changes facilitated greater citizen access to the federal judicial system and eliminated reliance on state judiciaries to administer and dispense justice; together, that is to say, they "supplied the alternative of a national forum" and "neutralized the power of state courts over a great mass of suits . . . touching the legal interests of a great many citizens."[194] Even the most infamous feature of the Judiciary Act of 1801—the appointment of sixteen new judges—suggests political motivations only if we emphasize who was appointed over why more judgeships were created in the first place. While it is certainly true that Federalists were excited the act would provide "a host of Officers to appoint, before the rising of Congress"[195]— sixteen new judgeships for Adams (rather than Jefferson) to "provide for friends and adherents" he regarded as "safe men"[196]—it nonetheless remains the case that the establishment of an entirely new tier of judges was an immediate substitute for circuit riding (which the act abolished) and thus part of a more general scheme for transforming the federal judiciary into a powerful agent of nationalism.[197]

Of course, expanded citizen access to federal courts was desired by the Federalists not simply out of some abstract concern for a close connection between federal judges and ordinary citizens but because the change dovetailed with Federalist economic policy goals. With expanded citizen access to federal courts would come increased federal judicial business, and with increased federal judicial business, would, Federalists hoped, come greater uniformity in the administration of justice. Uniformity was important chiefly because it enabled stable and predictable economic transactions, thereby encouraging investment, entrepreneurship, and risk—three factors crucial to the development of a robust commercial economy. With their varied procedures, disparate rulings, and general responsiveness to local (rather than national) interests on issues ranging from land policy to debtor-creditor relations, state judiciaries posed a threat to the Federalist economic vision. They inhibited the forging of a national commercial code, treated nonresident landholders harshly, and stunted the development of uniform land policy across states.[198] Effectively serving as an engine of nationalization, the Judiciary Act of 1801 promised to help Federalists overcome these hurdles by relocating litigation to courts where laws were apt to be administered in a more reasonable way and where their own substantive policy interests were more likely to be served.

[194] Turner, "Federalist Policy and the Judiciary Act of 1801," 27, 31.

[195] Thomas B. Adams to John Adams, January 20, 1801, reprinted in *DHSC*, 687.

[196] Gouverneur Morris to Robert R. Livingston, February 20, 1801, reprinted in *DHSC*, 714; Haskins and Johnson, *Foundations of Power*, 129.

[197] See Gouverneur Morris to Robert R. Livingston, February 20, 1891, reprinted in *DHSC*, 714, remarking that the act served "the double Purpose of bringing Justice near to Men's Doors and of giving additional fibres [sic] to the Root of Government." Morris's rhetorical flourish had been a Federalist slogan since 1789. Cf. William Paterson, "Notes for Remarks on Judiciary Bill," June 23, 1789, reprinted in *DHSC*, 416, claiming that circuit courts would "carry Law to their [citizens'] Holmes, Courts to their Doors . . . meet every Citizen in his own State."

[198] Turner, "Federalist Policy and the Judiciary Act of 1801," 22–32; Ellis, *The Jeffersonian Crisis*, 14–16.

Even though the Judiciary Act of 1801, in addition to advancing Federalist pol-icy interests, exhibited some "thoughtful concern for the federal judiciary,"[199] it did so at a moment when Democrat-Republicans could hardly see it as anything other than a partisan power grab.[200] Although they criticized the system created by the act as unnecessary, inconvenient, and exorbitantly expensive on the one hand,[201] and as likely to contribute to the consolidation of the states into a central government on the other hand,[202] the heart of their opposition was that the act was an abuse of power by a lame-duck coalition designed to stymie the incoming regime for an extended period of time. Thinking exclusively about the additional judgeships—the "midnight judges"—created by the act, Jeffersonians feared the potential obstructionism of a Federalist dominated judiciary. For them, the act's central evil was that it "perverted [the judiciary] to the purposes of faction" by intending "to make provision for a set of men who may always have an influence on the politics of the country."[203] In other words, recognizing that "if it now passes Mr Adams will have the Nomination of the Judges to be appointed,"[204] Democrat-Republicans accused their opponents of converting the judiciary into a mere tool of partisan entrenchment. On the eve of Jefferson's inauguration as president, for example, James Monroe, then governor of Virginia, complained, "This party has retired into the judiciary in a strong body where it lives on the treasury, & there-fore cannot be starved out. While in possession of that ground it can check the popular current which runs against them, & seize the favorable occasion to pro-mote reaction, wch [sic] it does not despair of."[205] The problem, as Monroe articu-lated it, was that the life-tenured judges appointed under the act would serve as lasting obstacles to popular government and perpetual thorns in the side of the incoming Jeffersonian regime.

In particular, Jeffersonians feared that more judges would thwart their policy initiatives by expanding the reach of Federalism into areas where Democrat-Republicans were strong—notably, Virginia, Kentucky, Tennessee, North Caro-

---

[199] Frankfurter and Landis, *The Business of the Supreme Court*, 25; see also Turner, "Federalist Policy and the Judiciary Act of 1801," 32, claiming that an "empiric response to their needs had stimulated the Federalist drive for a more comprehensive national judiciary."

[200] See Frankfurter and Landis, *The Business of the Supreme Court*, 25, describing the Democratic-Republican "charges of spoils, politics, extravagance, and judicial entrenchment of discredited political doctrines."

[201] See John Sitgreaves to John Haywood, April 29, 1800, reprinted in *DHSC*, 648, objecting to the "unnecessary Expence [sic] to the public"; and 10 *Annals of Cong.* 900 (1801) (William C.C. Claiborne) (deeming the new judicial system a "shameful profusion of public money").

[202] Robert Williams to his constituents, February 26, 1801, reprinted in *DHSC*, 718, worrying that the act would "infuse the powers of the general government, at the expence [sic] of the state judicial authorities"; Abraham Baldwin to Joel Barlow, March 26, 1800, reprinted in *DHSC*, 640–41, calling the act "a very bold stroke to draw all the powers to the general government and to do away as far as pos-sible not only state powers, but even boundaries."

[203] *Philadelphia Gazette*, February 3, 1801, reprinted in *DHSC*, 710; *Aurora*, February 3, 1801, re-printed in *DHSC*, 709.

[204] Dwight Foster to Timothy Pickering, February 4, 1801, reprinted in *DHSC*, 710.

[205] James Monroe to Thomas Jefferson, March 3, 1801, reprinted in *DHSC*, 720.

lina, and western Pennsylvania. With Democrat-Republicans firmly in control of state and local-level offices in each of these areas, the only way Federalists could frustrate the legislative and popular will—that is to say, the Jeffersonian will—was with unelected and unaccountable judges. Moreover, since those judges would be appointed by a Federalist president, they would surely side against Democrat-Republicans and their interests, which, in western outposts, were largely tied to bitter disputes between absentee or foreign landholders and the actual settlers who lived on the land.[206] Looking back at the Supreme Court's ruling in *Ware* (striking down state legislation about debt repayment to British creditors), Democrat-Republicans could not have been optimistic that Federalist judges would uphold state laws and state judicial rulings permitting the settlers to remain. In general, they were quite pessimistic about how the new judicial system would frustrate their goals, with Jefferson himself admitting to Madison in late December 1800, "I dread this above all the measures meditated."[207]

In short term, Jefferson's dread was well-founded and his party's opposition futile. Once Adams's defeat became clear and Federalists realized that both their days in control of the White House and their congressional majority (22–10 in the Senate, 60–46 in the House) were rapidly coming to an end, the House moved quickly, drafting a bill and debating it only briefly—perhaps because attention was focused on the Electoral College tie between Jefferson and Aaron Burr[208]—before passing it in late January 1801.[209] Moving with comparable celerity and exhibiting similarly little tolerance for extended debate or proposed amendments, the Senate passed the bill within three weeks of receiving it from the House.[210] With less than a month remaining in the Sixth Congress and while the House was balloting on Adams's successor, the president signed the most significant reform of the federal judicial system into law on February 13, 1801.

The Judiciary Act of 1801 did not contain substantially new material;[211] indeed, much of its content drew on Randolph's proposed bill in 1790 as well as the failed reform attempts of 1798 and early 1800.[212] But whether filled with new or recycled ideas, the act was transformative: it abolished circuit riding by creating a tier of circuit court judges (sixteen in all),[213] reorganized judicial districts into six cir-

---

[206] Ellis, *The Jeffersonian Crisis*, 16.

[207] Thomas Jefferson to James Madison, December 26, 1800, reprinted in *DHSC*, 663.

[208] Turner, "Federalist Policy and the Judiciary Act of 1801," 15.

[209] The final vote was 51–43 with one Democrat-Republican (Samuel Goode of Virginia) joining Federalists in voting for the bill, but three Federalists (Benjamin Taliaferro of Georgia, along with George Dent and Samuel Smith of Maryland) voting against the bill.

[210] The Senate vote was also largely along party lines, with only two Federalists (Benjamin Hillhouse of Connecticut and Theodore Foster of Rhode Island) defecting to vote against the bill, which passed 16–11.

[211] 2 Stat. 89 (February 13, 1801).

[212] It did not, obviously, include the localist concessions of Randolph's bill—most notably, the elimination of Section 25.

[213] For an analysis of Adams's selection process for the sixteen new circuit judgeships, see Ackerman, *The Failure of the Founding Fathers*, 130–40.

cuits, reduced the size of the Supreme Court (from six to five justices, including one chief justice),[214] granted federal question jurisdiction to lower courts, and expanded the power of federal court judges to remove cases from state courts. In all, it established (even if only briefly) an expanded and significantly empowered judicial system—precisely the system, in fact, Oliver Ellsworth would have liked to design in 1789 and proto-Federalists like Egbert Benson and Supreme Court justices like John Jay sought in the 1790s. The significance of this achievement was lost on neither the act's supporters, who immediately called it the "most important act of Congress which has passed during the present session,"[215] nor its opponents, who ruefully admitted that it was "one of those bold strokes which has unfortunately struck home."[216]

Yet from the Democratic-Republican lament also came the motivation for action, with rumors of repeal spreading almost immediately after the act's passage—indeed, before Adams had even finished making nominations to the new judgeships—and at least one Democrat-Republican predicting an eventual victory for the Jeffersonian cause. Presaging the upcoming assault on the federal judiciary, Kentucky representative John Fowler posited that the act "will not I trust be durable, and that as it was founded in fraud, the return of a wise system, will release the country from the shame and the imposition."[217] Fowler was, of course, correct that the system imposed by the Judiciary Act of 1801 would not last—it would be repealed in March of 1802 and replaced by a new Judiciary Act the following month—but it was a watershed moment in judicial institution building nonetheless. Despite its potential for nationalization, more efficient administration of justice, and uniformity in economic transactions, though, the Judiciary Act of 1801 was important less for *what* was achieved (which, given its short lifespan, was little) than for *how* it was accomplished—in a lame-duck session following a nasty election. As a result, the Judiciary Act of 1801, even if unintentionally, transformed the judiciary into an object of partisan attention and manipulation, positioning it squarely between Federalists and Democrat-Republicans in what had suddenly become an all-out struggle for political power in the early republic.

The Jeffersonian Repeal and the Judiciary Act of 1802

By the time Thomas Jefferson actually moved into the White House in March 1801, Democratic-Republican frustration with the Judiciary Act of 1801 was palpable. After all, the act effectively meant that the Revolution of 1800 would be incomplete: entrenched with newly appointed Federalist partisans, the judiciary would surely stall—or prevent entirely—a Jeffersonian reconstruction of American poli-

---

[214] Democrat-Republicans claimed that this alteration, which mandated that the next vacancy not be filled, was intended simply to deny Jefferson an appointment to the Court.

[215] Robert Goodloe Harper to his constituents, February 26, 1801, reprinted in *DHSC*, 715.

[216] John Fowler to his constituents, March 6, 1801, reprinted in *DHSC*, 721.

[217] John Fowler to his constituents, March 6, 1801, reprinted in *DHSC*, 722.

tics.[218] Recalling unfavorable decisions throughout the late 1790s, Jeffersonians feared that an empowered judiciary, serving as an arm of Federalism, would stand in the way of state laws that favored resident against nonresident landholders and debtors against creditors. Likewise, they worried that the new judges would continue to draw on English common law precedents, as they did to deny the right of expatriation, and to augment the power of judges to make law more generally.[219] Moreover, the complaints about the new Federalist judiciary went beyond the substance of jurisprudence that was likely to result. Jeffersonians complained, for instance, that the new system would be expensive (and probably require new or higher taxes to offset the cost), that it created needless positions, and that judicial officers (marshals and attorneys, for instance) were likely to bias the administration of justice against Democrat-Republicans.[220] In sum, Jeffersonians viewed the Judiciary Act of 1801 as not only an unnecessary (and perhaps detrimental) attempt at improving judicial functioning but also an illegitimate attempt to preserve a Federalist Supreme Court in a Democratic-Republican government.

Despite widespread consensus about the repugnance of the act, Jefferson's immediate reaction seems to have been measured.[221] Over the course of his first year in office, however, a conglomeration of events gradually converted his stance from conciliatory to bellicose.[222] Those events included the continued attacks on Jefferson by the Federalist press, the general arrogance of Federalist judges while conducting their duties, a common law libel suit initiated by Federalist judges against a Jeffersonian newspaper, the beginning of a litigation campaign by judges whose commissions had been denied by the Jefferson administration,[223] and the growing displeasure of radical Jeffersonians who desired a more aggressive presidential posture toward the judiciary.[224]

With Federalists demonstrating a determination to maintain or regain power and Jefferson having difficulty gaining support for a moderate course from his own party as well as from the very Federalists at whom conciliation was aimed,[225] the president had resolved by the start of the Seventh Congress in December 1801

[218] See William Branch Giles to Thomas Jefferson, June 1, 1801, quoted in Ellis, *The Jeffersonian Crisis*, 20–21: "What concerns us most, is the situation of the Judiciary as now organized. It is constantly asserted that the Revolution is incomplete, as long as that strong fortress is in possession of the enemy." On Jefferson's "reconstruction" generally, see Skowronek, *The Politics Presidents Make*, 62–85.

[219] Warren, *The Supreme Court in United States History*, 1:190–91.

[220] Haskins and Johnson, *Foundations of Power*, 139–40.

[221] Recall that Jefferson famously began his presidency proclaiming that "every difference of opinion is not a difference of principle. We have called by different names brethren of the same principle. We are all republicans—we are all federalists." See Thomas Jefferson, "First Inaugural Address."

[222] See, Ellis, *The Jeffersonian Crisis*, 25–41; Warren, *The Supreme Court in United States History*, 1:195–200; Haskins and Johnson, *Foundations of Power*, 156–61; Ackerman, *The Failure of the Founding Fathers*, 150.

[223] It was this litigation campaign that ultimately resulted in *Marbury v. Madison*.

[224] On the divisions in the Democratic-Republican Party at this time, see, generally, Ellis, *The Jeffersonian Crisis*.

[225] Ellis, *The Jeffersonian Crisis*, 36–41.

THE EARLY REPUBLIC   69

to take direct aim at those Federalists who had "retreated into the Judiciary as a stronghold" by repealing the Judiciary Act of 1801.[226]

As an extensive set of debates in Congress demonstrated,[227] the motivations behind the Democratic-Republican repeal varied from saving money (performance) to reversing the Federalists' partisan trickery (politics) to protecting Congress against executive power (policy). For instance, introducing the repeal bill on the floor of the Senate in January 1802, Kentucky senator John Breckenridge (sponsor of the Kentucky Resolution in 1798 and grandfather of future vice president John C. Breckenridge) questioned the necessity of reconfiguring the judiciary, especially when much of the time and attention of the federal courts had been occupied with prosecutions under the excise law and the unpopular Sedition Act, two sources of litigation that would soon be "forever dried up."[228] Referencing a report by Secretary of State James Madison on workload trends of the federal courts since 1790,[229] Breckenridge was dubious: "Could it be necessary then to *increase* courts when suits were *decreasing*? Could it be necessary to multiply judges, when their duties were diminishing?"[230] Meanwhile, Maryland senator Robert Wright, troubled by the fact that the 1801 act "had arisen from a disposition to provide for the warm friends of the existing administration,"[231] implied that, since the Federalists acted in order to preserve some measure of power in the incoming Jeffersonian regime, the Democrat-Republicans must respond in kind to consolidate their own power base. Finally, Senator Joseph Anderson of Tennessee urged Congress to act in order to avoid enshrining "a precedent dangerous to the independence of this body, and subversive to the true principles of the Constitution." Failing to repeal the act, Anderson maintained, would "countenance the practice which has been adopted, and virtually sanction the right of the President to select members from this body and place them in offices which have been created by their own votes." In turn, it

[226] Thomas Jefferson to Joel Barlow, March 14, 1801, quoted in Warren, *The Supreme Court in United States History*, 1:193.

[227] More so than most issues of judicial reform, the repeal discussion also serves as a rich and fertile illustration of constitutional debate in Congress; see 11 *Annals of Cong.* 23–43, 46–185, 476–81, 510–985 (1802). For recent treatments of this issue, see J. Mitchell Pickerill, *Constitutional Deliberation in Congress: The Impact of Judicial Review in a Separated System* (Durham, NC: Duke University Press, 2004); *Congress and the Constitution*, ed. Neal Devins and Keith E. Whittington (Durham, NC: Duke University Press, 2005). For a set of more reference-like sources on constitutional discourse in Congress during the early republic, see David P. Currie, *The Constitution in Congress: The Federalist Period, 1789–1801* (Chicago: University of Chicago Press, 1997); and David P. Currie, *The Constitution in Congress: The Jeffersonians, 1801–1829* (Chicago: University of Chicago Press, 2001).

[228] 11 *Annals of Cong.* 25 (1802) (John Breckenridge).

[229] For the report itself, see *American State Papers: Miscellaneous* 1: 319–25.

[230] 11 *Annals of Cong.* 26 (1802) (John Breckenridge). See also 11 *Annals of Cong.* 161 (1802) (Stephen Row Bradley): "I shall vote for the repeal, because it seems to me that we have got no use for these courts. The business was decreasing when they were appointed, and the old system seems to me to be much better than the new one." Cf. 11 *Annals of Cong.* 36 (1802) (Gouverneur Morris) (referring to Breckenridge's claims as the "first time I ever heard the utility of courts of justices estimated by the number of suits carried before them").

[231] 11 *Annals of Cong.* 36 (1802) (Robert Wright).

would encourage similar—and similarly injurious—situations in the future. "May we not," asked Anderson, "then expect that some future President, desirous of carrying some favorite point, will have recourse to the same expedient to provide for his warm friends or favorites, and thus, from time to time, by enlisting a sufficient number of members in his interest, may he not acquire a very dangerous ascendancy, and thus most injuriously extend Executive patronage—than which nothing is more dangerous to the principles of a free Government?"[232] Anderson's motivation for repeal, then, was in undoing legislative action that threatened to create a dangerous precedent for executive abuse. Especially in a debate over the composition of the federal judiciary, his fear that such abuse would come in the form of encroachment upon legislative rather than judicial authority placed him in stark contrast with Federalists who opposed the repeal because of the way it made the judiciary subordinate to Congress.

Opposing repeal, Federalists offered precisely that objection—that the measure constituted an assault on judicial independence from the legislature[233]—as well as an affirmative defense of the Judiciary Act itself. Maintaining that the system of 1789 had been defective and would only have grown more so as the burgeoning nation expanded both territorially and commercially, Federalists ignored the Democrat-Republicans' partisan accusations and instead emphasized the tangible improvements resulting from their reforms. Abolishing circuit riding, for instance, eliminated not only the questionable legal practice of justices hearing appeals of their own decisions but also the inconvenience foisted upon justices forced to travel to distant outposts for extended periods and litigants whose business was delayed because "courts were frequently lost."[234] "That the new system remedies all these inconveniences," New Jersey senator Aaron Ogden offered, "has not been disputed, and now it is about to be thrown away to save the community a paltry cent per man; *no, not so much, not a cent.*"[235] In order to justify abolishing the new system, he demanded proponents of the repeal demonstrate that "the new system has not advantages over the old, which will compensate the difference of expense." In other words, from the Federalist perspective, the need for courts outweighed the expense of courts—just as it had done in every attempted instance of judicial institution building leading up to the Judiciary Act of 1801.

With Democrat-Republicans and Federalists battling over whether the 1801 act had been motivated by concerns over performance or partisan politics—and, subsequently, over whether repealing it was constitutional or not—the Seventh Congress was poised for a showdown. Repeal seemed certain to pass in the House,

---

[232] 11 *Annals of Cong.* 168–69 (1802) (Joseph Anderson).

[233] 11 *Annals of Cong.* 163–66 (1802) (James Ross): "By this horrid doctrine, Congress erects itself into a complete tyranny. All the judges of your civil and criminal courts hold their offices at the will of the Legislature. A majority of the two Houses is in reality the national Judiciary." 11 *Annals of Cong.* 36 (1802) (Gouverneur Morris) (objecting that, with the repeal, the good behavior "check established by the Constitution . . . is destroyed").

[234] 11 *Annals of Cong.* 172 (1802) (Aaron Ogden).

[235] 11 *Annals of Cong.* 171–73 (1802) (Aaron Ogden).

where Democrat-Republicans outnumbered Federalists 68–38, but only if it could first get through the Senate, where Democrat-Republicans enjoyed a slim 17–14 majority.[236] The upper chamber debated the bill extensively in early- to mid-January 1801, with each side seeking the support of moderate Democrat-Republicans.[237] From there, the repeal bill had a somewhat circuitous route—including a tiebreaking vote by Vice President Aaron Burr to recommit the bill to committee at one point—to an up-or-down vote in the Senate. When that vote was finally taken in February, the repeal of the Judiciary Act of 1801 passed the Senate by a single vote. In the end, moderates supported the measure almost unanimously, with only one Democrat-Republican, South Carolina's John Ewing Colhoun, breaking ranks to join all fourteen Federalists in opposing repeal. Interestingly, one of the yea votes was cast by Maryland's Robert Wright, a Democrat-Republican who had replaced Federalist William Hindman just three months earlier. Hindman, himself elected to serve the remainder of a resigning Federalist senator's term, had decided not to seek reelection when the original term expired in 1801 but nonetheless agreed to serve until the state legislature could select his successor. If Hindman had sought a term of his own in the 1800 election, if the legislature had waited a few more months to choose his successor, or if he had been replaced with another Federalist, then the repeal of the Judiciary Act very likely would have failed. Having survived Colhoun's defection in the Senate in part because of the peculiar circumstances surrounding the Wright-Hindman seat, the repeal moved on to the House, where it passed by a more comfortable 59–32 vote. As in the Senate, all thirty Federalist representatives that were present voted as a bloc, joined by two New England Democrat-Republicans—William Eustis of Massachusetts and Thomas Tillinghast of Rhode Island. In both houses, then, party line votes dictated the outcome of the repeal: out of the 122 legislators who voted on the repeal, only 3 Democrat-Republicans—and no Federalists—diverged from their party's position.

The repeal of the Judiciary Act of 1801 occurred on March 8, 1802, just thirteen months after John Adams signed the potentially transformative act into law and only twelve months after Democrat-Republicans took control of the federal government.[238] Withdrawing federal question jurisdiction from the lower federal courts, abolishing the new circuit court judgeships, undoing the reorganization of the district and circuit courts, and reinstating circuit riding by Supreme Court justices,[239] the repeal essentially reverted the judicial system to its 1789 structure. The fact that the Federalists' new judicial system had been eliminated not long after it had gotten underway mattered little to Democrat-Republicans, who ignored

[236] New York Democrat-Republican John Armstrong, the thirty-second senator, had resigned by this point in the session and his replacement—ultimately, DeWitt Clinton—had not yet been chosen.

[237] Ellis, *The Jeffersonian Crisis*, 46.

[238] 2 Stat. 132 (March 8, 1802).

[239] By reinstating circuit riding the repeal may have inadvertently exacerbated the long-standing Democratic-Republican grievance against Federalist judges using their positions for partisan propagandizing. Although lower court judges were also targets of Democratic-Republican criticism, partisan speeches by Supreme Court justices riding circuit were viewed as particularly egregious offenses.

denunciations from the partisan Federalist press,[240] angry posturing by Supreme
Court Justice Samuel Chase,[241] analytic essays about the constitutionality of the
repeal by Alexander Hamilton,[242] and "memorials" from the judges whose offices
were abolished.[243] Whether or not the 1801 system might, as claimed by Federalists,
have solved problems that had plagued the federal judiciary for a over a decade,
Democrat-Republicans interpreted the Revolution of 1800 as their turn to govern,
and they had little interest in yielding the power that came with their newfound
status as the majority party.

Yet, as majorities so often discover in politics, numerical advantage does not
always transfer into desirable policy. The ultimate shape of the repeal, in fact, satisfied virtually no one in the Democratic-Republican Party.[244] Radicals wanted a
more aggressive response to the Federalists' pretensions and partisan entrenchment but settled for the repeal as the best they were likely to get. Moderates were
uneasy about the repeal in the first place but did not want to desert the president
in his first major legislative battle. Even Jefferson, who had originally wanted reconciliation and turned to repeal only at the urging of more radical Democrat-
Republicans, was disgruntled by the eventual result.[245] Moreover, the repeal of the
Judiciary Act of 1801 only returned the judiciary to the structure and organization established in 1789; it did not resolve any logistical difficulties caused by that
reversion—for instance, what happened to cases being heard in the courts abolished by the repeal?—or institute any changes in the judicial system. Just over a
month after the repeal of the Judiciary Act of 1801, therefore, the Jeffersonians
acted again, this time passing the Judiciary Act of 1802.[246]

With the new structural outline of the federal judicial system provided by the
Judiciary Act of 1802, the nation was divided into six circuits, each containing
a circuit court—one Supreme Court justice riding circuit and one district judge
residing in that circuit—that would meet for two annual sessions in each of the

[240] Haskins and Johnson, *Foundations of Power*, 164–65.
[241] Chase, a staunch Federalist who would soon find himself the target of impeachment, urged his
brethren to refuse to ride circuit, argued for limits on the Article III power of Congress, and tried to arrange a meeting of the entire Court to discuss what he perceived as a Jeffersonian assault on judicial independence. Cf. Ellis, *The Jeffersonian Crisis*, 62, detailing the threefold Federalist attempt to move the
repeal controversy into the judicial system: convincing the justices to refuse circuit riding, demanding
a redress of grievances for the judges whose offices had been abolished, and challenging the jurisdiction
of the new circuit courts over cases arising under the Judiciary Act of 1801.
[242] Hamilton's essays, authored from January through March of 1802, offer extensive analysis of issues ranging from the separation of powers to the meaning of tenure during "good behavior" to the
distinction between courts and judges. See Alexander Hamilton, "The Examination, No. 6," "The Examination, No. 12," "The Examination, No. 13," and "The Examination, No. 16," all reprinted in *The
Founders' Constitution*, 4:166–67, 175–81.
[243] *American State Papers: Miscellaneous* 1:340.
[244] Ellis, *The Jeffersonian Crisis*, 51.
[245] Ibid.
[246] 2 Stat. 156 (April 29, 1802).

seventeen districts nationwide.[247] More controversially, the 1802 act altered the annual sessions of the Supreme Court, which had recently been changed by the 1801
act from February and August (where they had been set by the 1789 act) to June
and December. Since the repeal did not become operative until July, Jeffersonians
worried that the Court would have a full month to strike down the repeal before
it ever went into effect. Seeking to avoid such a result, they replaced the June and
December terms with a single February term, thereby preventing the Court from
sitting—and, by extension, from passing judgment on the constitutionality of the
repeal[248]—until February of 1803. By the time the justices held forth again, the gap
between Court sessions had been fourteen months and the repeal had been on the
books for almost a year and operational for a full seven months.

Democrat-Republicans defended this system simply by saying that two terms
were unnecessary. "In last June term," Representative Joseph Hopper Nicholson
of Maryland summarized, "there were only eight cases before the Supreme Court.
Now, if it is necessary to call the justices of the Supreme Court together twice a
year from all parts of the Union to try eight cases, I confess I am at a loss to assign
the reason for the necessity."[249] Williams of North Carolina agreed, saying that
two terms of the Supreme Court would "derange the whole system," that Congress needed to "regard the interests of the whole people," and sarcastically predicting that the new system would not "increase the present *monstrous* mass of
business!"[250] In a related but distinct line of thinking, New York representative Lucas Conrad Elmendorf argued that the most pragmatic arrangement was to have
one term of the Supreme Court that would coincide with the term of Congress.
That way, Elmendorf claimed, "the assistance of counsel could be obtained at the
cheapest rate."[251] Insisting that they were acting out of regard for the performance
of the judiciary alone, Democrat-Republicans fastidiously avoided mention of any
partisan or electoral benefits gained by rearranging the terms of the Court.

---

[247] The number six was picked because, with the repeal of the 1801 act, there would once again be six
members of the Supreme Court—one to ride each circuit. Despite "no necessary correlation" between
the number of circuits and the size of an effective Supreme Court, this arrangement meant every new
circuit—and westward expansion put several "on the horizon"—required the expansion of the Court.
However, since it was virtually impossible for any of the justices to sit on their respective circuit court
in all districts for both sessions, such courts were allowed to be held by a single judge. This provision, which was invoked with greater frequency as circuit business increased, meant that circuit courts
gradually "devolved more and more" to individual district judges. Frankfurter and Landis, *The Business
of the Supreme Court*, 32.

[248] But see James M. O'Fallon, "The Case of Benjamin More: A Lost Episode in the Struggle over
Repeal of the 1801 Judiciary Act," 11 *Law and History Review* 43, 53 (1993), noting the unlikelihood that
a question involving the repeal could have ended up in the Supreme Court by June and interpreting
the alteration of terms as a Jeffersonian attempt "to force the Justices to decide whether to comply with
the provision of the repeal act requiring them to resume circuit riding duties, without the benefit of a
face-to-face meeting to discuss the issue."

[249] 11 *Annals of Cong.* 1206 (1802) (Joseph Hopper Nicholson).

[250] 11 *Annals of Cong.* 1209–10 (1802) (Robert Williams).

[251] 11 *Annals of Cong.* 1210 (1802) (Lucas Conrad Elmendorf).

The Democratic-Republican case for the Judiciary Act of 1802 raised the ire of Delaware representative James A. Bayard Sr., who almost single-handedly led the Federalist opposition on the floor of the House. Relentlessly probing both the motives in proposing the measure and the actual substance of the measure itself, Bayard reacted particularly vehemently against what he took to be the act's manipulation of the Court's terms. Dismissing the claims of Nicholson and Williams, Bayard questioned "why the Supreme Court should not be allowed to sit but once a year."[252] Since the elimination of the second session was "in a great measure a denial of justice to suitors, and would operate with peculiar injustices on the present suitors,"[253] he reasoned, the impetus could not possibly have been a desire to improve the administration of justice or to serve those citizens who had cases pending. Instead, he maintained that the Democrat-Republicans were motivated by partisan politics rather than out of any well-meaning concern for citizens, for the administration of justice, or for the constitutional separation of powers:

> This act is not designed to amend the Judicial system; that is but pretence. If amendment had been in view, gentlemen would have contrived a better plan than the present bill proposes, which I panegyrize, by calling a miserable piece of patchwork. No, sir; the design of this bill is, to prevent the usual session of the Supreme Court in next June.
>
> It is to prevent that court from expressing their opinion upon the validity of the act lately passed . . . until the act has gone into full execution, and the excitement of the public mind is abated. I know not that the subject would be brought before the judges, or that they would officially take it up; but it is the fear of their solemn opinion, and a knowledge of the just reverence which the people of this country entertain for judicial decision, which has given birth to the present expedient. Could a less motive induce gentlemen to agree to suspend the sessions of the Supreme Court for fourteen months?

His attack on the Judiciary Act of 1802, however, went further. "Its defects," he said, "are as numerous as its provisions; and it introduces not a single improvement into the system it is designed to amend." With a system full of "incongruities and absurdities," he was not surprised that its proponents could not even "point out a single particular in which it corrects a defect in the old system." Contrasting the bill's official title ("a bill to amend the Judicial system of the United States") with its actual purpose, Bayard asserted that "amendment is not the effect, and nothing is more remote from the design of it."

His distaste for the bill notwithstanding, Bayard seemed cautiously optimistic—at least for the long run—as he concluded his remarks: "The majority, sir, must have their will; but I am deceived, if their triumph is of long duration. The

[252] 11 *Annals of Cong.* 1205–7 (1802) (James A. Bayard Sr.).

[253] 11 *Annals of Cong.* 1213 (1802) (James A. Bayard Sr.). See also 11 *Annals of Cong.* 1207 (1802) (John Dennis): "the Supreme Court may in future be more properly called a court of injustice than a court of justice."

people of America can be governed but a short time by empty words and hollow pretences."[254] Though his prediction recalls Kentucky representative Fowler's correct forecast that the Judiciary Act of 1801 would not long endure, Bayard's party—unlike Fowler's—was doomed to toil as the minority and would not soon have the chance to expose their opponents' "empty words and hollow pretences." Bayard was right about one thing, though: the Jeffersonian majority did have its way. Despite hesitation among some Democrat-Republicans, including James Monroe, that changing the terms of the Supreme Court would both give the impression that the president was afraid of a confrontation with Chief Justice John Marshall as well as allow the Court to seem like the aggrieved party, the Judiciary Act of 1802 passed both houses along party lines—with votes of 16–10 in the Senate and 46–30 in the House[255]—and was signed into law by Jefferson in April 1802.

A Federalist Court in a Jeffersonian Era

Even, or perhaps especially, in the aftermath of the repeal of the Judiciary Act of 1801 and the passage of the Judiciary Act of 1802, there were still members of both parties actively wishing for a clash between the Supreme Court and Congress.[256] Despite their party having been relegated to the minority after losing seven seats in the Senate and twenty-two in the House in the 1800 elections, many Federalists continued to believe that Americans would support a Federalist Court against a Jeffersonian Congress. For their part, some Democrat-Republicans, assuming that the people would side with elected representatives over appointed justices, thought the best way to assert Jeffersonian dominance (and, perhaps, judicial subservience) once and for all was to invite confrontation with the Court. With Congress dismissing the protests of judges whose positions had been abolished by the repeal of the 1801 act,[257] and with litigation challenging various elements of the Jeffersonian counterattack already underway, the clash sought by radical Jeffersonians and High Federalists alike was not far off; rather, a collision between John Marshall and Thomas Jefferson seemed imminent.

By early 1803, it seemed that such a collision would most likely occur in one or both of two Supreme Court cases: *Marbury v. Madison* and *Stuart v. Laird*.[258] *Marbury*, of course, involved a suit by one of Adams's "midnight judges" against

[254] 11 *Annals of Cong.* 1232–36 (1802) (James A. Bayard Sr.).

[255] Once again, only one senator—this time, Vermont Democrat-Republican Stephen Bradley, who had voted in favor of the repeal a month earlier—broke with his party. South Carolina's John Ewing Colhoun, the one Democrat-Republican who opposed the repeal, did not cast a vote on the Judiciary Act of 1802. Of the four Democrat-Republican representatives to vote with the Federalists, only Rhode Island's Thomas Tillinghast had voted against the repeal as well. The other three—Thomas Davis of Kentucky and Ebenezer Elmer and James Mott of New Jersey—had all voted in favor of the repeal. Tillinghast's fellow defector in the repeal vote, William Eustis of Massachusetts, did not vote on the Judiciary Act of 1802.

[256] Ackerman, *The Failure of the Founding Fathers*, 161.

[257] Warren, *The Supreme Court in United States History, Volume One*, 224–26.

[258] 5 U.S. 137 (1803); 5 U.S. 299 (1803).

the Jefferson administration for denying him his commission as a District of Columbia justice of the peace; *Stuart*, decided only a week after *Marbury*, challenged the constitutionality of two aspects of the repeal of the Judiciary Act of 1801—the abolition of circuit court judgeships and the return of circuit riding. Given the political drama surrounding both cases—would Marshall order Jefferson to issue Marbury's commission? would Jefferson obey if Marshall did? would the Court nullify the repeal and reinstate the Judiciary Act of 1801? would the Court be intimidated or emboldened by the Jeffersonian manipulation of its terms in the Judiciary Act of 1802?—the Court's rulings in *Marbury* and *Stuart* were anticlimactic. After all, in both cases, the Court effectively flinched. In *Marbury*, Marshall declared that Marbury was owed his commission but that the Court was not the proper institution from which to seek it.[259] In *Stuart*, the Court—acting without Marshall, who mysteriously recused himself because he had tried the case while riding circuit[260]—limited the scope of the question presented but implicitly upheld the repeal as constitutional nonetheless. In neither case, then, did any real "collision" occur. Since Marshall did not lecture or dictate orders to Jefferson, as Federalists had hoped, Jefferson could not defy, punish, or humble Marshall, as Democrat-Republicans had planned.

Accordingly, both *Marbury* and *Stuart* are significant less for what they did (little more than strike down a minor provision of the Judiciary Act of 1789) than for what they did not do[261]—namely, provoke a constitutional crisis that might have resulted in a weakened Supreme Court or diluted the power of the federal judiciary more generally. In a highly charged political environment where there was a real chance of defiance by Jefferson, the Court's decision to roll over averted what seemed like an inevitable, and probably unwinnable, fight with a more powerful branch. In this view, Marshall's deftness in *Marbury* was in avoiding making a potentially destructive mistake rather than, as is commonly assumed, in establishing the power of judicial review. Especially when read in light of the following week's capitulation in *Stuart*, *Marbury* did almost nothing to establish judicial review and said almost nothing that was not already accepted as uncontroversial. As Mark

---

[259] Marbury's suit, requesting that the Court order the Jefferson administration to provide him with his commission by issuing a writ of mandamus, was filed under Section 13 of the Judiciary Act of 1789, which granted the Court original jurisdiction over certain classes of mandamus cases. Unfortunately for Marbury, Marshall asserted that, since the Court's original jurisdiction was constitutionally specified by Article III and could not be expanded by statute, Section 13 was unconstitutional. In turn, Marshall concluded, the Court was simply without power to issue the writ sought by Marbury under its original jurisdiction.

[260] The recusal is mysterious because justices often heard appeals to rulings they had made while riding circuit; indeed, the awkwardness resulting from this arrangement was one of the prime objections against the practice of circuit ruidingin the first place. Moreover, Marshall's recusal in *Stuart* but not in *Marbury* is peculiar given his greater role—as Adams's secretary of state he was responsible for delivering Marbury's commission in the first place but, in the midst of simultaneously serving as secretary of state and chief justice, neglected to do so—in the latter case.

[261] Cf. Alexander M. Bickel, *The Least Dangerous Branch: The Supreme Court at the Bar of Politics*, 2nd ed. (New Haven, CT: Yale University Press, 1986), 111–98, on the "passive virtues."

Graber has noted, the case provided support for only the "most limited" form of judicial review.[262] Together with *Stuart*, it allowed the president to deny appointed judicial officers their commissions and allowed Congress to abolish judicial offices as well as prevent the Court from meeting.[263] If it occasioned any "durable shift of governing authority,"[264] it did so in a way that weakened rather than strengthened the judiciary vis-à-vis the other branches of government.

As purported episodes of institution building in the aftermath of the repeal of the Judiciary Act of 1801 and the passage of the Judiciary Act of 1802, then, the Marshall Court's decisions in *Marbury* and *Stuart* are hardly noteworthy. Rather than asserting new powers, they merely sought to preserve existing ones; rather than demonstrations of judicial might, they stand as admissions of judicial vulnerability. As such, the cases verify rather than disconfirm the idea that Congress, not the Court, was effectively in charge of building the judiciary in the early republic.

The Spirit of 1789

Just over a year after Jeffersonians took control of the federal government, they had spearheaded two significant judicial institution-building initiatives: one to undo the crowning achievement of the outgoing Federalist majority, another to mitigate the damage the Federalists might be able to exact in return. These were the first two acts relating to the federal judiciary passed after Jefferson's inauguration, and they would be the only two until a statute adjusting the time of holding federal court in Kentucky was passed in March 1803.[265] Judicial reform arrived in a burst only when a significant event overcame constraints and catalyzed transformative action; it came at precisely the moment, in fact, when it became clear that power would switch hands from one party to the other. Once that transition was complete—once the Democrat-Republicans had undone what they perceived as Federalist excesses and settled into their own as the majority party—the legislative endeavor of building the judiciary came to a screeching halt. A handful of low-level and performance-oriented institutional modifications—reorganizing circuit assignments,[266] altering the time and place of district court sessions in three states,[267] allowing a marshal to adjourn court in the absence of a judge,[268] revising the process of authenticating records of judicial proceedings,[269] providing for an additional judge in the Mississippi Territory,[270] and expanding the jurisdiction

[262] Graber, "Establishing Judicial Review," 629–30.
[263] Ibid., 638–39.
[264] Karen Orren and Stephen Skowronek, *The Search for American Political Development* (Cambridge: Cambridge University Press, 2004), 123.
[265] 2 Stat. 242 (March 2, 1803).
[266] 2 Stat. 244 (March 3, 1803).
[267] 2 Stat. 273 (March 23, 1804).
[268] 2 Stat. 291 (March 26, 1804).
[269] 2 Stat. 298 (March 27, 1804).
[270] 2 Stat. 301 (March 27, 1804).

of certain territorial courts[271]—occurred during the remainder of Jefferson's first term, but the most significant events of the period were those that occurred in the wake of the 1800 election.

By the beginning of Jefferson's second term in March 1805, the spirit of 1789— the spirit of Oliver Ellsworth's compromise—had been restored. After all, in addition to ensnaring the judiciary in the intense ideological disputes of the early republic, the Judiciary Act of 1801 had upset the tenuous compromise between projudicial nationalists and antijudicial localists struck by Ellsworth in the First Congress. With the repeal of that act, the Jeffersonians had essentially reinstituted Ellsworth's compromise and returned the judiciary to its old moorings; with the passage of the Judiciary Act of 1802, they removed the most immediate threat— nullification by the Supreme Court—to their repeal. Yet while the Jeffersonians succeeded in reversing the Federalist trend toward judicial empowerment and consolidation, the fact that the system reverted to its 1789 form, rather than being restricted even further, as some radical Jeffersonians had wished and expected, meant that the conflict between advocates of nationalism and localism, of a strong judiciary and a weak one, remained—without a clear winner.[272] The tensions inherent in judicial institution building—tensions between conceptions of the judicial role in American politics—were not reconciled but pushed back and defused for the time being. With the gradual accretion of federal judicial power during the antebellum period and growing uneasiness—first of Jeffersonians, then of Jacksonians, and eventually of Southerners more generally—about the role of federal courts in national consolidation, the issue would resurface soon enough.

In the meantime, the controversy surrounding the judiciary that raged from the final days of the Adams administration through Jefferson's first term left several lasting imprints on the course of future judicial institution building in America. First, it suggested the relative weakness and vulnerability of the judiciary as a co-equal branch of the federal government. Though the idea of judicial independence was alive, it was inchoate at best. At this early stage of American democracy, the federal judiciary was still an uncertain institution and though its role, structure, and powers would gradually evolve over the course of American political development, the embryonic stages of its institutional development offered little hope for a powerful third branch. In other words, although the development of an independent and autonomous judiciary is taken for granted in the twenty-first century, it may not have seemed possible, let alone probable or inevitable, during the early years of the nineteenth century. If the judiciary was to be built, it would almost

---

[271] 2 Stat. 338 (March 3, 1805).

[272] On the idea that the true winners were political moderates, see Ellis, *The Jeffersonian Crisis*, 233– 49, 278–84. Agreeing with Ellis's view of the 1801–2 controversy, O'Fallon, "The Case of Benjamin More," describes the outcome as "a victory of the moderates over judiciophobic radical Republicans and demophobic high Federalists" (45) and notes that the "best reading of the state of affairs may be that in between the most vocal partisans of High Federalism and Jeffersonianism were a body of citizens . . . who were politically sympathetic to the president, but attached to the principle of a politically independent judiciary" (57).

certainly take a sustained and committed effort by other political institutions, especially Congress.

Second, the events of 1801–2 demonstrated how partisan politics could be used as a way of conducting governmental business, even governmental business about the judiciary. Partisan goals—unknown to some of the nations founders, despised by others—were suddenly in vogue. Whether or not the Federalists' motivations in pushing the Judiciary Act of 1801 through a lame-duck session of Congress were exclusively (or even predominantly) motivated by partisan and electoral politics, the perception that they were opened up judicial institution building to similar action in the future. Of course, the Democrat-Republicans immediately seized upon the opportunity to erase one political initiative with another, lending further credence to politically-driven institution building in the process. Building the judiciary, that is to say, did not preclude the pursuit of partisan or electoral regime goals any more than substantive policy goals; in fact, the process might even be used to advance them.

Third, and finally, the controversy provided a cautionary tale for would-be judicial reformers in the future. The Judiciary Act of 1801 had attempted wholesale reform, only to be repealed a year later. The moral was that transformative reform is a difficult and challenging project, perhaps one requiring a serendipitous combination of structural conditions, political actors, and collective interests. At the very least, any reform more significant than housekeeping inevitably faces political controversy and can be achieved only when significant environmental change or strategic political action transcends that controversy. Even when such reform initially succeeds, it may nonetheless remain vulnerable. Indeed, achieving reform that would prove durable in the early republic demanded not only overcoming constraints but also some sort of coalition building—whether through the reconciliation of multiple interests or the neutralization of opposing factions. Forged in the wake of the defining political event of the early republic, the Federalist attempt to remake the judicial system in 1801 eschewed compromise and, as a result, overestimated the possibility of pure partisan entrenchment. If they had any hope of significantly restructuring the judiciary, future reformers would need to recognize that purely partisan foundations for institution building required a party that was itself both strong and stable.

Of course, as the process of judicial institution building continued, new developments would alter and remake the political climate for reform activity, but coming out of the controversy of the early nineteenth century, these were the best guidelines available for the process of building the judiciary.

• • •

The history of judicial institution building in the early republic unfolded in three stages: the policy compromise of 1789, the stalemate preventing large-scale reform in the 1790s, and the flurry of policy and political initiatives of the early 1800s. In examining each of these stages, I have explored both the causes and consequences of judicial institution building. That is to say, I have answered three questions: first, why judicial institution building was pursued; second, how it was accomplished; and, third, what it achieved.

Why was judicial institution building in the early republic pursued? It was pursued (though not always successfully) by a variety of actors—presidents, members of Congress, the Attorney General, Supreme Court justices—motivated to build the judiciary by a diverse collection of policy, political, and performance goals. The Judiciary Act of 1789 was motivated primarily by the policy goals of members of the First Congress. The attempts to abolish circuit riding and generally improve the judicial system during the 1790s were prompted by the performance goals of not only representatives and senators but also the attorney general and the justices of the Supreme Court, especially Chief Justice John Jay. The events of the 1801–2 crisis—the Judiciary Act of 1801, its repeal the following year, and the subsequent Judiciary Act of 1802—were each pursued by presidents (the first by John Adams, the second and third by Thomas Jefferson) and legislators with a mix of policy, political, and performance goals. More specifically, the Federalists' aggressive 1801 reform was driven mostly by the desire to improve judicial administration by abolishing circuit riding and to promote commercial economic growth by empowering the federal judiciary to decide more cases whereas the Jeffersonian counterattack sought to eliminate the Federalists' ability both to make public policy and to retain power in a Democratic-Republican government.

How was judicial institution building in the early republic accomplished? In 1789, the political entrepreneurship of Connecticut senator Oliver Ellsworth overcame the constraints imposed by localist opposition to strike a compromise that, although entirely pleasing to neither cost-conscious localists nor commercially minded nationalists, was sufficiently unobjectionable to facilitate passage of the first Judiciary Act. In the 1790s, the campaign for comprehensive reform gave way to more piecemeal reform largely because the entrepreneurship of Attorney General Edmund Randolph was not sufficiently sensitive to the political dynamics of the First Congress. In 1801–2, bitter political disagreement was conquered, and institution building realized, as a result of the election of 1800, which prompted judicial reform by both the outgoing party and, in response, the incoming party.

What did judicial institution building in the early republic achieve? It provided a new institution with functions, individuals (including eighteen lower court judges and six Supreme Court justices) to perform those functions, and resources to assist them in doing so. More succinctly, it constructed the bare-bones skeleton of a *potentially* powerful judiciary. Although, as evidenced by both the perpetual murmurings of discontent and the periodic attempts at reform, neither side was completely satisfied with the outline of the federal judiciary that emerged, that outline was virtually settled by the end of Jefferson's first term in the White House. By avoiding confrontations over contentious issues with no simple solutions and by not definitively settling the issues in favor of any one side, judicial institution building in this era succeeded in establishing and then preserving the foundational elements of the institutional judiciary. The desire to remove the divisive issues from the table for the time being, however, not only precluded a potential resolution over those issues but also left them squarely on the table for the future. In exchange for getting the judiciary off on the right foot, it appears this was an acceptable, if not necessary, risk for advocates of judicial power to assume.

In addition to period-specific answers to these three central questions, the three stages of judicial institution building in the early republic also offer some insight into the broader relationships among legislators, presidents, and judges over the politics of institutional development. Above all, they illustrate how judicial authority is politically constructed—how the empowerment of courts and judges is "an ongoing political choice, not a fait accompli."[273] The construction of judicial power, that is to say, "depends on cooperation from other governing officials" who have identified concrete policy or political reasons to support such power.[274] Although judges do possess some self-empowering capability, more often than not their power flows out of a political process. In the period from 1789 to 1805, Congress made more decisions about the judiciary's role, structure, and powers than the judiciary made for itself. From the Judiciary Act of 1789 to the circuit riding modifications of the 1790s to the back-and-forth between Federalists and Democrat-Republicans after the election of 1800, the judiciary was built by political actors looking to satisfy political goals.

The process by which those actors pursue those goals, the judicial institution building of the early republic further suggests, is highly uncertain. Building the judiciary has historically been a slow and difficult undertaking, with spurts of activity mixed in with extended periods of quiescence or frustration, and the early republic was no exception. The attention given to judicial reform during this period was uneven and the analysis of the issues surrounding such reform was far from comprehensive.[275] In part, this is a function of constitutional design: Article III gives Congress, an institution charged with a fair number of functions, the primary authority to build the federal judiciary but offers little guidance about what tools to use or what type of structure to erect. Building a judiciary of this sort—a complex one with multiple tiers of judges, varying grants of jurisdiction, and both trial and appellate functions—was an unprecedented task, one that few members of Congress understood intuitively. The result, as we see throughout the 1790s, is a punctuated and often uncertain process characterized by false starts, failed

---

[273] Graber, "Establishing Judicial Review," 649.

[274] Ibid., 618.

[275] See Erwin C. Surrency, "A History of Federal Courts," 28 *Missouri Law Review* 214, 244 (1963), noting the "glaring failure of Congress to give any mature deliberation to the needs and proper organization of the courts." Surrency's statement is in reference to the entire history of the federal judiciary but applies particularly well to the early republic.

attempts, and frequent congressional "give-and-take"[276]—both with the judiciary and between internal interests and factions.

Yet perhaps because the process is uncertain, individual moments loom large and carry great precedential value. The Judiciary Act of 1789, for example, was almost immediately regarded as quasi-constitutional in stature and subsequently acquired an aura of respect and deference from lawmakers that made it difficult to reform. In turn, nearly every time reformers attempted to modify a feature of the 1789 system, they were met with accusations of disrespect toward the First Congress and its landmark enactment. In that case, an episode of judicial institution building established a benchmark of agreement sufficiently precarious that most attempts to alter it were destined to fail; in other cases—the cautionary tale about the Judiciary Act of 1801, for instance—an episode of judicial institution building served to guide subsequent behavior both by offering reform opponents a ready club to wield against future proposals and by suggesting to reform advocates tactics that might wisely be avoided. In both instances, however, one episode of institution building had a substantial effect on the course of similar activity in the future. Far from simply isolated occurrences that seek to instigate some immediate alteration and then recede from memory once the ultimate result has been determined, individual reforms (or attempts at reform) can leave institutional residue capable of influencing the course of institution building for years to come. Prior political action structures the opportunities, choices, and incentives for future action; big successes and big failures become arguments for and against later attempts at change.

For the same reasons, the timing of any individual institution-building episode is critically important. As suggested by the contrast between Ellsworth's success in framing the Judiciary Act of 1789 and Randolph's failure to convince Congress to undertake radical reform in 1790, similar tactics attempted at even slightly different times—or by slightly different individuals—may yield vastly divergent results. The lesson is that the political climate for judicial institution building—indeed, for any type of governmental action—can change quickly, drastically, and unexpectedly. Sometimes, as in the case of Randolph, this change in the political environment results from slow-building processes such as the rise of partisanship; other times, as in the case of the Judiciary Act of 1801 and its repeal, it follows on the heels of a more punctuated event such as an election or transfer of power. In the latter example, Federalists transformed the institutional judiciary only to see their work washed away by Jeffersonians. Just as the sequence of events surrounding the lame-duck session of a Federalist-dominated Congress had made the act's genesis possible, so too did it make its demise probable. Thus, whether or not the act was

---

[276] See Casper, "The Judiciary Act of 1789 and Judicial Independence," 294–95, calling the task "perhaps the most puzzling of all the challenges faced by the Framers' generation." Cf. Frankfurter and Landis, *The Business of the Supreme Court*, 1, explaining the successive Judiciary Acts as a "continuous process of empiric legislation by which the federal judiciary has been adapted, more or less, to the changing needs of time and circumstance."

an improvement on the judicial system as it had existed since 1789, the timing of its passage virtually sealed its disappointing fate.

While the fate of the Judiciary Act of 1801 may have been sealed at nearly the moment John Adams signed it into law (if not before), the fate of judicial institution building in America more generally was not entirely clear in the aftermath of the Jeffersonian counterattack on the federal judiciary. With the frenzied urgency of the Federalists' last days and Jefferson's first years now in the past, it seemed probable (though by no means assured) that a stable Democratic-Republican majority would simply let the judiciary remain as it then existed. After all, Jeffersonians had succeeding in rolling back the Federalist expansion and empowerment of the judiciary as well as reinstituting the compromise of the Judiciary Act of 1789. Although the radical wing of the party may have wished to push further, most signs pointed to a settlement in the institutional development of the judicial branch. The task of building the judiciary would undoubtedly continue but, at least for a moment in 1805, it seemed that the outline of the federal judiciary was set and the turbulence that characterized institution building in the early republic was, at long last, over.

CHAPTER THREE

Jeffersonian and Jacksonian Democracy

REORGANIZATION

If the early republic was America's infancy, then the first half of the nineteenth century was its adolescence. The government had survived its early years—the uncertainty of the First Congress, the farewell of George Washington, the rise of political
parties, the emergence of contested elections, and the first transfer of power from
one coalition to another—but a new set of challenges had surfaced.[1] Many of those
challenges were the result of the vast territorial expansion that occurred during the
period. From the Louisiana Purchase in 1803 to the annexation of Texas in 1845 to
the vast tracts of land acquired as a result of the Mexican-American War in 1848,
the area owned by the United States had swelled greatly from the thirteen colonies that declared independence from George III. As these open swaths of land
attracted settlers, their populations grew steadily, and as their populations grew,
territories were admitted into the union as states. After the incorporation of only
four new states in the two decades following the First Congress—Vermont (1791),
Kentucky (1792), Tennessee (1796), Ohio (1803)—thirteen more, including one in
each year from 1816 through 1821, followed before 1850.[2]

Raising concerns about the economic and social direction of the nation, the
politics of territorial expansion and statehood admission served as an accelerant

[1] For political histories focusing on various aspects of the period, see Sean Wilentz, *The Rise of
American Democracy: Jefferson to Lincoln* (New York: Norton, 2005) on the consolidation of democratic norms and practices; Charles Sellers, *The Market Revolution* (New York: Oxford University Press,
1991) on the development of a capitalist economy; William W. Freehling, *Road to Disunion*, vol. 1,
Secessionists at Bay, 1776–1854 (New York: Oxford University Press, 1990) on slavery, the South, and
the seeds of secession; Merrill D. Peterson, *The Great Triumvirate: Webster, Clay, and Calhoun* (New
York: Oxford University Press, 1987) on three influential legislators and regional leaders; and Michael
F. Holt, *The Rise and Fall of the American Whig Party: Jacksonian Politics and the Onset of the Civil War*
(New York: Oxford University Press, 1999) on party politics and the development of an anti-Jacksonian
coalition. For the previous generation of historical scholarship on this period, see George Dangerfield,
The Era of Good Feelings (New York: Harcourt, Brace, 1952); George Dangerfield, *The Awakening of
American Nationalism, 1815–1828* (New York: Harper and Row, 1965); and Arthur M. Schlesinger Jr.,
The Age of Jackson (Boston: Little, Brown, 1945).
[2] The following states were admitted in this period: Louisiana (1812), Indiana (1816), Mississippi
(1817), Illinois (1818), Alabama (1819), Maine (1820), Missouri (1821), Arkansas (1836), Michigan (1837),
Florida (1845), Texas (1845), Iowa (1846), and Wisconsin (1848).

for both sectional and intergovernmental tension. As North and South fought over control of the West, their divergent economic paths and contrasting views on slavery were magnified and exacerbated. Northerners, of course, continued to argue for financial policies designed to promote a bustling commercial economy and against the extension of slavery to the territories and new states. Southerners, meanwhile, still dreamt of an agrarian nation and supported the maintenance of their "peculiar institution." At the same time, with the growth of national government running parallel to the growth of national boundaries, state officials increasingly assumed postures of active resistance toward the exercise of centralized federal (including federal judicial) authority. Such resistance came from the North as well as the South, from Federalists and Whigs as well as Democrat-Republicans; it was prompted by dissatisfaction with foreign as well as domestic policy, by judicial as well as legislative and executive action. As a result, the defiance—much of which invoked the spirit and ideas of the Virginia and Kentucky Resolutions of 1798—varied from debates over secession (at the Hartford Convention in late 1814 and early 1815) to proclamations of nullification (by John C. Calhoun and the state of South Carolina in response to the Tariff Act of 1828) to calls for state interposition and citizen obstruction (against the enforcement of the Fugitive Slave Act of 1850 in Wisconsin and Illinois, among other states).[3] Neither of these debates was unknown in earlier decades; indeed, each had been omnipresent at the Philadelphia Convention and through the early republic. Nor were they as hostile as they would prove to be in subsequent decades, when proslavery advocates grew more aggressive in protecting their property and abolitionists more militant in response, thereby sharpening the conflict between the federal government and the states in the process. Yet, in a manner that was equally novel and noteworthy, territorial expansion infused them both with renewed salience, urgency, and importance.

Relative to the federal judiciary specifically, territorial expansion also posed a pair of concrete performance problems. First, since states were not automatically incorporated into one of the nation's judicial circuits upon joining the Union, new states were effectively excluded from the federal judicial system. Second, with populations growing within and spreading across all states rapidly, judicial workload was simultaneously increasing and becoming more diffuse, thus making it increasingly difficult for judges—especially Supreme Court justices, who were still forced to ride circuit[4]—to dispatch judicial business efficiently. Although the early nine-

[3] In terms of the judiciary specifically, this undercurrent of defiance initially boiled over in the aftermath of the Supreme Court's assertion of jurisdiction over appeals from state supreme courts in *Martin v. Hunter's Lessee*, 14 U.S. 304 (1816), and *Cohens v. Virginia*, 19 U.S. 264 (1821), but ultimately settled as Andrew Jackson's appointees came to dominate the Court in the late 1830s and 1840s.

[4] Circuit riding was the practice of having Supreme Court justices join district court judges in hearing circuit court cases. A function of the fact that the landmark Judiciary Act of 1789 had established three tiers of courts but provided for only two sets of judges, this arrangement—which required arduous and time-consuming travel and placed justices in the uncomfortable position of being forced to hear appeals of their own decisions—was an unremitting source of judicial aggravation from its establishment in the early republic through its effective abolition in the Gilded Age.

teenth century is traditionally regarded as a key period when the Court increased its own power,[5] the Court's canonical decisions about contracts, commerce, and federalism—important as they may have been for the development of constitutional law—did little to fix these problems of the institutional judiciary. Indeed, with judicial review and legal doctrine orthogonal to the structural problems facing the judiciary, the task of building the judiciary yet again fell to Congress.

With the tension between the thickening government associated with territorial expansion, on the one hand, and state-level resistance to central governmental consolidation, on the other, as a background, this chapter focuses on judicial institution building from the beginning of Thomas Jefferson's second term in 1805 until just prior to the Compromise of 1850. In chronicling the politics of institutional development over this period, I focus on the myriad attempts—more failed than successful—at reorganizing the judicial system to accommodate territorial expansion. As with the early republic, I ask three questions about the politics of institutional development up to the brink of the political crisis of the 1850s. Why was judicial institution building pursued? How was it accomplished? What did it achieve? Here, the answers to these questions are that judicial institution building in the ages of Thomas Jefferson and Andrew Jackson was motivated by Western complaints about performance problems deriving from the lack of judicial presence in newly admitted states, the proto-Whig National Republican desire to empower the judiciary as a policy-making ally, and the Jacksonian dream of solidifying a Democratic Court; enabled (when it was not impeded by the clash of rival policy and political goals) by a combination of congressional unawareness and Democratic victories in the 1834 midterm and 1836 presidential elections; and resulted in the reorganization of the judicial system so as to privilege the Southern slaveholding interests of Jacksonian Democrats. More specifically, although judicial institution building in the early to mid-nineteenth century was originally motivated by the exigent needs for judicial administration in newly admitted Western states, it soon became a battle over legislators' desire to create (or prevent their opponents from creating) new seats on—or to appoint (or prevent their opponents from appointing) particular individuals to— the Court. This switch in the character of judicial reform from a fairly uncontroversial subject to a highly politicized one subsequently divided reform coalitions so as to make meaningful change virtually impossible for three decades. Yet, though characterized less by its success in reforming the judicial system than by its perpetual failure to do so, the era was ultimately defined by two significant reforms—one that established a basic (if largely unworkable) formula for expanding the judiciary and one that exploited that formula to the advantage of particular partisan and sectional constituencies. In what follows, I examine the four stages of this struggle—the initial Jeffersonian expansion of the federal circuit system to seven circuits and the Supreme Court to seven justices in 1807, the failed National Republican attempt to add three more circuits and three more

_____

[5] This was, after all, the era when the legendary John Marshall served as chief justice.

justices in the mid-1820s, the failed Whig attempt to consolidate the circuits in 1835, and a quick resolution to multiple decades of stalemate with the Jacksonian establishment of the Eighth and Ninth Circuits and eighth and ninth seats on the Court in 1837—before explicitly connecting this chapter to the dynamics of institution building that preceded it in the early republic and those that would follow it in the Civil War and Reconstruction.

New States, New Circuits, and New Supreme Court Justices, 1805–1808

When Ohio joined the Union on March 1, 1803, it joined on unequal terms. After all, like its fellow Western states Kentucky and Tennessee, Ohio was not included in one of the six circuits in the federal judicial system. The reason for Ohio's exclusion traced back to the Judiciary Act of 1802, which rearranged the circuit system in such a way that excluded the Western states,[6] largely because circuit riding was once again required of the justices and because traveling across the Appalachian Mountains was a time-consuming and arduous task. In practical terms, this meant that the three Western states were reduced to a scheme whereby certain district courts possessed both district and circuit court jurisdiction;[7] in symbolic terms, it meant they were relegated to second-class status.

The remedy for both the practical and symbolic woes of the Western states was the Judiciary Act of 1807.[8] Passed after persistent complaints by the aggrieved states, the act established the Seventh Circuit comprising Kentucky, Tennessee, and Ohio, created a seventh seat on the Supreme Court, and required that the newly created seat be filled by an individual residing in the newly created circuit. At first glance, the legislation looks pedestrian and unimportant, an observation supported by the fact that the entire legislative history of the bill seems to unfold over just seven weeks of the lame-duck session of the Ninth Congress and without any recorded debate in either chamber. While it is certainly true that the act was politically uncontroversial, passed largely to deal with performance concerns (growing caseloads, citizen dissatisfaction) about the administration of justice in

---

[6] Although the Judiciary Acts of both 1801 and 1802 organized the federal judiciary into six circuits, the two acts differed in the precise arrangement of those circuits. Under both acts, two circuits (the First and Second) were allotted to New England states and two (the Third and Fourth) to mid-Atlantic states, but where the 1801 act provided for one Southern circuit (the Fifth) and one Western circuit (the Sixth), the 1802 act provided for two Southern circuits (the Fifth and Sixth). The 1802 act accomplished this by shifting Delaware from the Third Circuit to the Fourth, Virginia from the Fourth to the Fifth, and South Carolina and Georgia from the Fifth to the Sixth. The 1802 act also excluded Maine, which was then still part of Massachusetts but had nonetheless been included in the First Circuit (along with New Hampshire, Massachusetts, and Rhode Island) by the 1801 act, from the system. For further discussion of the Judiciary Acts of 1801 and 1802, see chapter 2.

[7] Courts of this type would prove common through the beginning of the Civil War, largely for territories that had district courts but had yet to be incorporated into the circuit system. Erwin C. Surrency, *History of the Federal Courts* (Dobbs Ferry, NY: Oceana, 2002), 36.

[8] 2 Stat. 420 (February 24, 1807).

the Western states and to blunt criticism that the circuit system did not treat all states equally, it nonetheless served to connect new states, new circuits, and new Supreme Court justices in a way that would effectively paralyze judicial reform for three decades.

A Performance Problem with a Consensus Solution

As the lack of real debate or controversy over it suggests, the Judiciary Act of 1807 was a performance-oriented response to the immediate problems posed by the exclusion of three states from the circuit system. These problems—the distant and inefficient administration of justice in the frontier, restricted appellate options for Western citizens, a growing number of direct appeals to the Supreme Court— were not subject to judicial resolution. Whatever powers John Marshall may have invented, consolidated, or exercised in the early part of his tenure, he could not expand the circuit system to include the Western states, and he could not fix the structurally-based workload problems created by Western expansion. Instead, the task was a legislative one, and legislators had salient performance motivations to reform the system. Particularly in the West, where the complicated nature of land deeds and titles—and the battles between absentee landholders and resident settlers over them—was a constant agitation, citizens needed judges to resolve disputes and maintain a sense of order. District judges, especially when there was only one per state, were regarded as less capable of performing this function on their own than when joined by circuit-riding Supreme Court justices, who were more knowledgeable about the law, more skilled in educating citizens, and more respected as agents of the central government.[9] Furthermore, to the extent that a well-functioning judicial system was an issue about which citizens cared, judicial reform was a type of constituent service that might strengthen legislators' popularity in their respective districts.

Far from the concerns of partisanship, the performance goal of a well-functioning judicial system was consistent across different groups of legislators. Whether noble or self-interested, Democrat-Republicans and Federalists alike had incentives to alleviate the problems that plagued Western justice and irritated Western citizens.[10] Moreover, aside from the fact that the proposed reform—the creation of a seventh circuit for the West and a seventh seat on the Supreme Court for a Westerner—offered Thomas Jefferson an additional Supreme Court appoint-

[9] 16 *Annals of Cong.* 46 (1807).

[10] Federalists had suffered a consistent and precipitous fall in popularity since 1800, but the Ninth Congress (1805–7) represented the largest Democratic-Republican majority to that point—twenty seats in the Senate (27–7) and eighty-six seats in the House (114–28). The incoming Tenth Congress (1807–9) marked a slight increase to twenty-two seats in the Senate (28–6) and ninety seats in the House (116–26). On the Federalist Party after the "Revolution of 1800," see David Hackett Fischer, *The Revolution in American Conservatism: The Federalist Party in the Era of Jeffersonian Democracy* (New York: Harper and Row, 1965); and Shaw Livermore Jr., *The Twilight of Federalism: The Disintegration of the Federalist Party, 1815-1830* (Princeton, NJ: Princeton University Press, 1962).

ment, it neither disproportionately favored one party or population (except the West) over another nor fundamentally transformed the judicial system as it then existed. As a result, it was relatively easy for Democrat-Republicans and Federalists to agree on both the need for reform and the type of reform that would rectify existing problems. With fairly widespread consensus about the benefits of expanding the circuit system to the West, political opposition was minimal; with minimal opposition, there were no obstacles in the path of reform. Accordingly, regarding the reform as a simple, straightforward solution to a concrete problem of judicial performance, neither chamber gave the bill any more than cursory attention before passing it—the Senate without a recorded vote,[11] and the House of Representatives by a margin of seventy-five votes (82–7).[12] Because it was the first time the circuit system needed to be modified to incorporate states that would not naturally fit into existing circuits,[13] simply expanding the system by creating a new circuit and new Supreme Court justice to ride that circuit was a reasonable idea. It was also, however, an idea with potential ramifications of which Congress seemed completely unaware.

A New Model for Judicial Reform

As the first instance in which a new circuit and a new justice were added simultaneously, the Judiciary Act of 1807 not only integrated the Western states into the circuit system and expanded the Supreme Court beyond its original 1789 size but also established a model for future institution building.[14] This model had two crucial features. The first was a connection between the circuit system and the Supreme Court—or, more precisely, between the number of circuits and the number of Supreme Court justices. Such a connection was not unprecedented, but neither was it clearly established by constitutional text or political practice. For example, by simultaneously constituting a Court of six justices and requiring the attendance of two of those justices at circuit courts in each of the nation's three judicial cir-

[11] 16 *Annals of Cong.* 46 (1807).

[12] 16 *Annals of Cong.* 499 (1807). Fifty-three members of the House—more than one-third of the entire chamber—did not vote on the bill. Of the seven nay votes, five (James M. Garnett, David Meriwether, John Randolph, Richard Stanford, and David R. Williams) were Democrat-Republicans from the South, one (Joseph Stanton) was a Democrat-Republican from Rhode Island, and one (Benjamin Tallmadge) was a Federalist from Connecticut.

[13] Between 1789 (when the circuit system was established) and 1807, three states—original colonies North Carolina and Rhode Island (which had delayed ratifying the Constitution) as well as Vermont (which was carved out of existing portions of New York and New Hampshire)—had joined the Union, but perhaps because they were each part of the original American landmass and geographically surrounded by states already included in a circuit, all three were immediately incorporated into the circuit system. 1 Stat. 126 (June 4, 1790) (North Carolina); 1 Stat. 128 (June 23, 1790) (Rhode Island); 1 Stat. 197 (March 3, 1791) (Vermont).

[14] See Felix Frankfurter and James M. Landis, *The Business of the Supreme Court: A Study in the Federal Judicial System* (New York: Macmillan, 1928), 34: "Thus began the periodic increase in the membership of the Supreme Court as the territorial needs of the country for more circuits were met."

cuits, the Judiciary Act of 1789 drew a de facto parallel between the number of circuits and the number of justices—at least until the circuit-riding reform of 1793 required only one justice to sit on each circuit court.[15] Similarly, with the repeal of the Judiciary Act of 1801 having resurrected circuit riding and returned the Court to a six-member body, Democrat-Republicans chose to preserve the Federalist idea of six circuits in the Judiciary Act of 1802, thus guaranteeing one justice for each of the nation's six circuits. Precisely because the Democrat-Republicans sought to return the judiciary to a slightly modified form of the pre-1801 system, however, it was not clear whether the parallel between circuits and justices established by the 1802 act was meant as a prescription for future action or a reactionary move to reclaim the previous status quo. With the Judiciary Act of 1807, then, the Democratic-Republican Congress affirmed and strengthened the 1802 parallel.

The second feature, prompted by the explicit statement in the Judiciary Act of 1807 that the newly created vacancy on the Court be filled by an individual that would "reside in the seventh circuit,"[16] required the president to heed concerns about geographical representation when choosing new justices. Congress had raised the matter of residency twice before—allotting circuit assignments based on the residence of the justices in the Judiciary Act of 1802 and again in an amendment to that act in 1803[17]—but it had never been so bold as to require that an appointed justice hail from a specific state or region.[18] And even though the statutory basis for this requirement applied only to the Seventh Circuit justice, once Thomas Jefferson obeyed it by appointing Kentuckian Thomas Todd to the new seat, the pressure exerted via senators chosen by state legislatures on future presidents made geographic representation for other circuits the expectation for other Supreme Court appointments.[19]

The effect of these two features on the future of the Supreme Court was twofold. First, by tying population growth to Supreme Court growth such that, provided the former continued, the latter was effectively required to keep pace with it, the con-

---

[15] 1 Stat. 333 (March 2, 1793).

[16] Explaining this feature, Frankfurter and Landis, *The Business of the Supreme Court*, 34n94, write that the "necessity of bringing into the Supreme Court a member familiar with the land law of the Western states was keenly felt."

[17] 2 Stat. 244 (March 3, 1803).

[18] It is not even clear that Congress possessed the constitutional authority to do so. After all, since the Constitution does clearly forbid individuals "who shall not, when elected, be an Inhabitant of that State in which he shall be chosen" from serving in either the House (Article I, Section 2) or the Senate (Article I, Section 3), one might reasonably interpret the absence of such qualifications for Supreme Court justices to suggest not only that no such qualifications existed but also that none could be added except through a constitutional amendment.

[19] Indeed, histories of the appointment process suggest that, for *every vacancy* in the first half of the nineteenth century, presidents considered themselves sufficiently bound by this expectation that they only even *considered* appointing individuals from the geographically appropriate region. See Henry J. Abraham, *Justices, Presidents, and Senators: A History of U.S. Supreme Court Appointments from Washington to Bush II*, 5th ed. (Lanham, MD: Rowman and Littlefield, 2008), passim; Charles Warren, *The Supreme Court in United States History*, vol. 1, *1789 1835* (Boston: Little, Brown, 1926); and Charles Warren, *The Supreme Court in United States History*, vol. 2, *1836–1918* (Boston: Little, Brown, 1926).

Table 3.1.
Circuit Organization and Supreme Court Representation
Judiciary Act of 1807

Circuit	States	Supreme Court Justice
First	Massachusetts, New Hampshire, Rhode Island	William Cushing (MA)
Second	Connecticut, New York, Vermont	Henry Brockholst Livingston (NY)
Third	New Jersey, Pennsylvania	——
Fourth	Delaware, Maryland	Samuel Chase (MD)
Fifth	Virginia, North Carolina	John Marshall (VA) Bushrod Washington (VA)
Sixth	Georgia, South Carolina	William Johnson (SC)
Seventh	Kentucky, Ohio, Tennessee	Thomas Todd (KY)

Note: There was no Third Circuit justice until 1830 due to John Adams's appointment of Virginian Bushrod Washington to replace Pennsylvanian James Wilson in 1799—a geographically "inappropriate" appointment before the post-1807 norm of geographic representation was established.

nection between circuits and justices infused political considerations about new judicial appointments into an issue that had previously been dictated by apolitical performance concerns. Without such an arrangement, the circuit system could have evolved routinely, uncontroversially, and without broader ramifications for the Court. Under the system inaugurated by the Judiciary Act of 1807, however, circuit reform occurred rarely and only in exceptional circumstances because such reform held the potential for exploitation by a partisan coalition looking to gain new seats on the Court. In that way, the system did not recalibrate the natural partisan politics surrounding appointments so much as it forced their emergence on issues where such politics would have otherwise been absent, a development that greatly increased the stakes of, made perpetual the debates over, and substantially delayed success in changing the size of the Court.

Second, the fact that new states required new circuits, that new circuits required new justices, and, that those new justices were—as a result of the norm of geographically representative appointments—expected to come from one of the new states in the new circuit meant that the composition of the Court was inextricably tied to the politics of regionalism and statehood admission. Which territories were admitted to the Union when and how they—together with existing states—were organized once included in the circuit system suggested who could be appointed to the Court and, in turn, what type of body the Court was likely to be. While this practice of geographically representative appointments was—with the exception of Jefferson's appointment of Todd pursuant to the Judiciary Act of 1807 itself—an informal norm rather than a statutory rule, it nonetheless operated with both consistency and force, successfully limiting the appointment options for and constraining the appointment preferences of presidents for more than five decades. Moreover, with North, South, and West sufficiently divergent in terms of policy preferences and preferred way of life, disparate regional views on the proper scope of federal judicial power should not have been surprising. And just as justices from New Hampshire, Georgia, and Ohio were likely to differ about the place of judicial power in American democracy, so too were they likely to differ about the ends to which—about the policies for which—such power should be used. Thus, to the extent that individuals from different corners of the rapidly expanding nation were influenced by local or regional concerns and values, sectionalism and territorial expansion shaped not only the makeup but also the jurisprudence of the nineteenth-century Court.

With decisions about judicial structure suddenly decisions about the composition and jurisprudence of the Supreme Court, about the force and reach of judicial power, and about the battle between Northern abolition and Southern slavery, circuit organization was transformed from a mundane procedural matter into a substantive issue about the shape of national government and the future of national politics. The Supreme Court did not require expansion at any point in the first four decades of the nineteenth century—the size of the Court caused no problems of judicial performance. The circuit system, however, did require reform and, once the two features were connected, it meant that Supreme Court expansion was inevitable because circuit system reform was inevitable. The only question that remained was one of timing; the only matters left to be determined were when exactly reform would occur and who exactly would stand to benefit from it. As we shall see, the link between circuits and justices—embedded in the framework established by the Judiciary Act of 1807 and inescapable unless and until that framework was jettisoned—dictated the answer to that question, not only making substantial judicial reform in the 1820s and '30s exceedingly difficult and extremely rare but also delaying it until the potential for exploitation was especially ripe.

Judicial Reform in the Era of Mixed Feelings, 1809–1828

The remedy offered by the Judiciary Act of 1807 solved the immediate problem posed by the exclusion of Kentucky, Tennessee, and Ohio from the circuit system, but it did not solve the recurring problem. That problem, of course, was that, while the nation expanded, the judicial system remained frozen. Indeed, with the admission of five states—Louisiana (1812), Indiana (1816), Mississippi (1817), Illinois (1818), and Alabama (1819)—making the second decade of the nineteenth century the single most active decade for statehood admission in American history, the judicial system was under constant strain. If the addition of three new states had previously necessitated one new circuit, then what type of reforms might five—or seven, if we include the admission of Maine (1820) and Missouri (1821)—new states require? In each new state, a judicial district was established, but, without broader reorganization, each of the new districts (except Maine[20]) remained outside the circuit system and, thus, the judge of each district was granted both district and circuit court jurisdiction.[21] Encompassing more area than it could reasonably cover and facing more cases than it could reasonably decide, the judiciary was once again ill-equipped to serve the needs of the nation, and geographic expansion was once again the root cause.[22]

Although the federal judiciary itself was active during this period, often considered the "golden age" of John Marshall, it was not active in a way that addressed the structural problems caused by territorial expansion and statehood admission. Rather, it was active as a centrifugal force, interpreting the Constitution and federal statutes so as to create and sustain the broadest possible expanse of central governmental authority. Indeed, most significant judicial decisions of the first quarter of the nineteenth century—sustaining Jefferson's embargo in 1807;[23] asserting the power to declare state law unconstitutional in *Fletcher v. Peck*;[24] legitimating statutes passed to prosecute the War of 1812;[25] declaring the federal gov-

---

[20] Within a month of admission to the Union in 1820, Maine was immediately made part of the First Circuit. 3 Stat. 554 (March 30, 1820).

[21] 3 Stat. 390 (March 3, 1817) (Indiana); 3 Stat. 413 (April 3, 1818) (Mississippi); 3 Stat. 502 (March 3, 1819) (Illinois); 3 Stat. 564 (April 21, 1820) (Alabama); 3 Stat. 653 (March 16, 1822) (Missouri).

[22] Cf. Frankfurter and Landis, *The Business of the Supreme Court*, 34: "New territory brings new judicial needs coincident with a rise in the volume of judicial business in the old districts and circuits."

[23] The embargo controversy (at least as it concerned the judiciary) arose when one of Jefferson's own appointments to the Court, William Johnson, declared the president's specific instructions regarding enforcement of the Embargo Act of 1808, 2 Stat. 499 (April 25, 1808), unsupported by the original statute in *Ex parte Gilchrist*, 5 Hughes 1 (1808). Johnson's decision, issued while riding circuit in staunchly Jeffersonian South Carolina, sparked widespread Democratic-Republican outrage, Federalist joy, and hostile recriminations from those legislators who had expected Johnson to serve as a bulwark of Jeffersonianism on an otherwise Federalist-dominated Court. While Johnson and the Jefferson administration publicly debated the validity and force of Johnson's decision, however, Massachusetts district judge (and committed Federalist) John Davis upheld the constitutionality of Jefferson's embargo, viewed by many Federalists (especially those in New England) as the most odious of Democratic-Republican policies, with a capacious construction of congressional powers in *United States v. The Brigantine William*, 28 Fed Cas. 622 (1808). Although the embargo was sustained, its enforcement was severely impeded—and its effectiveness weakened—by a slate of judicial decisions dismissing indictments for obstruction and denying the force of state laws designed to aid enforcement in federal courts. These obstacles helped to prompt Democrat-Republicans to pass the Enforcement Act of 1809, 2 Stat. 506 (January 9, 1809). For a recap of the entire episode, see Warren, *The Supreme Court in United States History*, 1:324–56.

[24] 10 U.S. 87 (1810) (striking down a Georgia law repealing a fraudulent land sale approved by a corrupt previous legislature as a violation of the Contracts Clause). Contrary to popular belief, *Fletcher* was not the first instance in which the Court struck down a state law. That distinction goes to *Ware v. Hylton*, 3 U.S. 199 (1796) (invalidating a Virginia law inhibiting the repayment of debts to British creditors because it conflicted with the Treaty of Paris and, thus, violated the Supremacy Clause). The Court also considered a constitutional challenge to a state law in *Calder v. Bull*, 3 U.S. 386 (1798), but ultimately upheld the statute.

[25] Warren, *The Supreme Court in United States History*, 1:426–31 (referring to more than twenty cases in which the Supreme Court upheld the nonintercourse acts necessary for the conduct of "Mr. Madison's War"); Surrency, *History of the Federal Courts*, 138–39.

ernment supreme in its own sphere in *McCulloch v. Maryland*;[26] striking down state action in *Sturgis v. Crowninshield*,[27] *Dartmouth College v. Woodward*,[28] and *Gibbons v. Ogden*[29]—were characterized by a steadily increasing and intensifying nationalism.[30] In other words, these expressions of judicial nationalism were significant not because they represented unilateral judicial action in the service of institution building—they did not—but because they altered the strategic environment within which such institution building was already occurring.

Even the Court's highly controversial decisions in *Martin v. Hunter's Lessee* and *Cohens v. Virginia*[31]—cases that have been called "the keystone of the whole arch of Federal judicial power"[32]—were important less for the institutional changes that resulted (or failed to result) than for situating the judiciary firmly on the nationalist side of the suddenly resuscitated debate between nationalists and localists. After all, the central question raised in both *Martin* and *Cohens*—whether or not Section 25 of the Judiciary Act of 1789, which explicitly authorized federal courts to review state court judgments, was constitutional—was not novel; rather, it was asked (albeit in general more than specific terms) at the Philadelphia Convention and during the First Congress as nationalists and localists fought over what types of power the federal judiciary should have and what type of institution the Supreme Court should be. Nor were the answers offered (in *Martin* and *Cohens*) unprecedented.[33] The Court's rulings did not announce a new doctrine or invent a new power; they merely applied an existing provision, a provision that had been ap-

---

[26] 17 U.S. 316 (1819) (affirming congressional authority to establish the Bank of the United States and rejecting Maryland's contention that a state could tax an organ of the national government).

[27] 4 Wheat 122 (1819) (nullifying state bankruptcy laws that retroactively applied to existing contracts).

[28] 17 U.S. 518 (1819) (extending the protection of the Contracts Clause to a corporate charter).

[29] 22 U.S. 1 (1824) (invalidating a New York steamboat licensing law as inconsistent with congressional legislation).

[30] Notable exceptions include the federal judiciary denying common law jurisdiction over criminal offenses in *United States v. Hudson and Goodwin*, 11 U.S. 32 (1812) and *United States v. Coolidge*, 14 U.S. 415 (1816), as well as restricting the ability of corporations to sue in federal court in *Bank of United States v. Deveaux*, 9 U.S. 61 (1809).

[31] 14 U.S. 304 (1816); 19 U.S. 264 (1821).

[32] Warren, *The Supreme Court in United States History*, 1:449.

[33] *Martin* originated when the Virginia legislature voided a loyalist land grant and transferred a tract of property back to the state. When the original landholder appealed, the Court, in *Fairfax's Devisee v. Hunter's Lessee*, 11 U.S. 603 (1813), declared that he was entitled to the land, but Virginia Court of Appeals judge Spencer Roane refused to obey the higher court's ruling. In his own defense, Roane—a close ally of Jefferson and longtime rival of Marshall—simply claimed that Section 25 was unconstitutional and that, as a result, the Supreme Court had no legitimate authority over the case at hand. Taking direct aim at the defiance by a lower court and an inferior judge, Justice Joseph Story's opinion in *Martin* flatly rejected Roane's claims. Not only was Section 25 constitutional, Story asserted, but even if it did impugn state sovereignty (as Roane contended), the goal of protecting federal sovereignty and supremacy trumped. *Cohens*, decided five years later, entertained the issue once more, with the Court—this time through Chief Justice John Marshall, who had recused himself in *Martin*—again declaring that Section 25 was legitimate and that the federal courts could indeed exercise jurisdiction over state court decisions. On Marshall's tactics in *Cohens*, see Mark A. Graber, "The Passive-Aggressive

proved by democratic majorities as part of the legislative process. The application of that provision may have been controversial, but the Court's willingness to apply it was not unpredictable and its reasoning for defending it was not unfounded. Since *Martin* and *Cohens* occurred within the prevailing stream of congressional action—perhaps doing little more than providing a judicial voice for a legislative enactment—it seems emphatically false to claim that Marshall broadened judicial power on his own, "*without* the aid of a specific statute."[34] Thus, despite a slate of decisions that increased judicial power as part of increasing federal power against the states, there was no decision—nor could there feasibly be—that integrated the West into the circuit system or alleviated the growing caseload pressures on federal judges. In other words, regardless of how the Marshall Court's judicial nationalism may have shaped constitutional jurisprudence, it did not convert the judiciary into an institution that could effectively administer justice in a growing nation.

With the judiciary ill-equipped to deal with the defects in its own structure and organization, the task inevitably fell to Congress. Although there was occasional attention to institution building during James Madison's presidency and James Monroe's first term,[35] it was not until a caseload crisis threatened to paralyze the Seventh Circuit in 1823 that legislators began to think seriously about the possibility of reform. By that point, there seemed to be wide agreement that something needed to be done about the judiciary,[36] but different factions of the Democratic-Republican Party and different regions of the country disagreed about precisely what needed to be done.[37] As three years of debate over a multitude of proposed bills unfolded, it was precisely this disagreement, filtered through the structure

Virtues: *Cohens v. Virginia* and the Problematic Establishment of Judicial Review," 12 *Constitutional Commentary* 67 (1995).

[34] *The Documentary History of the Supreme Court of the United States, 1789–1800*, vol. 4, *Organizing the Federal Judiciary: Legislation and Commentaries*, ed. Maeva Marcus (New York: Columbia University Press, 1992), 295; emphasis added.

[35] For a summary of these occasional attempts, see Frankfurter and Landis, *The Business of the Supreme Court*, 35n98. Justice Joseph Story and Daniel Webster had attempted to motivate landmark reform in 1816—with the former drafting, and the latter proposing, a bill that would have given circuit courts the "full sweep of judicial power contained in the Constitution" (Frankfurter and Landis, 36)—but it went nowhere. See also Robert V. Remini, *Daniel Webster: The Man and His Time* (New York: Norton, 1997), 213. In addition, it was during this period that Congress began what would become a century-long project of regulating the terms of federal courts, passing multiple statutes specifying the time and place of court proceedings during each legislative session. Congress had passed a handful of such statutes in the 1790s, but, as the judicial system expanded throughout the nineteenth century, they became a consistent feature of judicial institution building. See, for example, 2 Stat. 815 (March 3, 1813) (concerning the district of New York); 3 Stat. 411 (March 19, 1818) (concerning the district of Virginia); 4 Stat. 186 (May 20, 1826) (concerning the district of North Carolina).

[36] See, for example, 2 *Cong. Deb.* 1142 (1826) (Daniel Webster): "The necessity of some reform in the Judicial establishment of the country, has been presented to every Congress, and every session of Congress, since the peace of 1815."

[37] Cf. Frankfurter and Landis, *The Business of the Supreme Court*, 41–42, noting that the "need for judicial organization was recognized by all parties" but referring to substantial disagreement about the "methods by which judicial organization should be kept abreast of national development."

imposed by the Judiciary Act of 1807, that inhibited the campaign to reform the judiciary.

A Factionalized Party and a Multiplicity of Interests

As the dichotomy between Hamiltonianism and Jeffersonianism collapsed and the Democratic-Republican Party fractured in the second decade of the nineteenth century,[38] the distinct motivations for judicial reform multiplied. Indeed, even during an era conventionally known as one of the most ideologically unified and uncontested in American history, three different segments of the Democrat-Republican coalition—proto-Whig "National Republicans," proto-Jacksonian "Old Republicans," and Westerners—were each motivated to pursue a different type of judicial reform for different reasons. The existence of three distinct (and, to a great extent, mutually exclusive) reform agendas meant not only that the so-called Era of Good Feelings might more appropriately be labeled the Era of Mixed Feelings but also that judicial institution building during that era stood as a contested and precarious project,[39] impeded by the clash of interests and constrained by the presence of substantial political opposition.

First, National Republicans—a combination of Federalists who were disenchanted with the radical secessionist talk at the Hartford Convention and Democrat-Republicans who were increasingly dissatisfied with the party's focus on agrarian economic development[40]—sought to resurrect the system established by the Judiciary Act of 1801, which they reasoned was repealed "not from an objection to its structure, but to the mode of its execution."[41] Acting primarily to satisfy performance goals jeopardized by the increasing caseload, National Republicans considered the 1801 system—the establishment of an entirely new tier of circuit courts, the appointment of separate circuit judges to staff such courts, the elimination of circuit riding, and a reduction in the size of the Court from seven members to five—the sweeping change necessary to remedy the continual defects in the

---

[38] See Mark A. Graber, "Federalist or Friends of Adams: The Marshall Court and Party Politics," *Studies in American Political Development* 12 (1998): 232, arguing that the importance of the Hamiltonian-Jeffersonian divide—a divide that had, in one way or another, structured American politics and society since the late 1780s—broke down in the second decade of the 1800s, when the "American political universe disintegrated and was reconstituted." On the factionalized nature of the Democratic-Republican Party generally, see Richard E. Ellis, *The Jeffersonian Crisis: Courts and Politics in the Young Republic* (New York: Oxford University Press, 1971).

[39] Cf. Wilentz, *The Rise of American Democracy*, 181–217, examining the period as an "era of bad feelings."

[40] Ibid., 141–78. On the rise of the "National Republicans," see Dangerfield, *The Awakening of American Nationalism*; Livermore, *The Twilight of Federalism*; William Nisbet Chambers, *Political Parties in a New Nation: The American Experience, 1776–1809* (New York: Oxford University Press, 1963), 191–208; and Richard Hofstadter, *The Idea of a Party System: The Rise of Legitimate Opposition in the United States, 1780–1840* (Berkeley and Los Angeles: University of California Press, 1969), 170–211.

[41] 2 *Cong. Deb.* 1128 (1826) (Charles F. Mercer).

administration of justice.[42] As early as 1816, Madison, in his eighth annual message to Congress, cited "the accruing business which necessarily swells the duties of the Federal courts" and the "great and widening space within which justice is to be dispensed" as reasons to consider "the expediency of a remodification of the judiciary establishment." Specifically, he urged "a relief from itinerary fatigues" (circuit riding) for Supreme Court justices and "a more convenient organization of the subordinate tribunals."[43] Eight years later, Monroe agreed with his predecessor, drawing attention to the effect of territorial expansion on the judicial system and calling again for the abolition of circuit riding:

> The augmentation of our population with the expansion of our Union and increased number of States have produced effects in certain branches of our system which merit the attention of Congress. Some of our arrangements, and particularly the judiciary establishment, were made with a view to the original 13 States only. Since then the United States have acquired a vast extent of territory; eleven new States have been admitted into the Union, and Territories have been laid off for three others, which will likewise be admitted at no distant day.
>
> An organization of the Supreme Court which assigns the judges any portion of the duties which belong to the inferior, requiring their passage over so vast a space under any distribution of the States that may now be made, if not impracticable in the execution, must render it impossible for them to discharge the duties of either branch with advantage to the Union. The duties of the Supreme Court would be of great importance if its decisions were confined to the ordinary limits of other tribunals, but when it is considered that this court decides, and in the last resort, on all the great questions which arise under our Constitution, involving those between the United States individually, between the States and the United States, and between the latter and foreign powers, too high an estimate of their importance can not be formed. The great interests of the nation seem to require that the judges of the Supreme Court should be exempted from every other duty than those which are incident to that high trust. The organization of the inferior courts would of course be adapted to circumstances. It is presumed that such an one might be formed as would secure an able and faithful discharge of their duties, and without any material augmentation of expense.[44]

[42] A similar plan, though without a reduction in the size of the Court, had passed the Senate in 1819, but the House did not act on the bill. Curtis Nettels, "The Mississippi Valley and the Federal Judiciary, 1807–1837," *Mississippi Valley Historical Review* 12 (1925): 210–211.

[43] James Madison, Eighth Annual Message to Congress (December 3, 1816). See also 1 *Cong. Deb.* 535 (1825) (James Barbour) (referring to the "impossibility of men, advanced in years, being able to undertake a journey of two or three thousand miles" while riding circuit); 1 *Cong. Deb.* 534 (1825) (James Barbour) (noting that the abolition of circuit riding would allow the justices "full time to deliberate on the important causes which necessarily came before them").

[44] James Monroe, Eighth Annual Message to Congress (December 7, 1824).

For National Republicans, then, the plan to replace circuit-riding justices with an entirely new tier of circuit court judges solved two performance problems: it allowed the justices to focus on their growing docket in Washington, D.C., and it staffed regional circuit courts with judges whose sole duty would be to dispatch judicial business in those courts. Both of these developments, of course, promised to consolidate judicial power in ways that skeptics of the federal judiciary were likely to find objectionable.

Second, Old Republicans—that is to say, those who had not been converted to the need for a strong executive by the pressure of war and those who opposed both the rechartering of the Bank of the United States and the Tariff of 1816—pursued a variety of restrictive reform measures, including the removal of judges by a vote of both houses of Congress,[45] an age limit for federal judges,[46] restricting admiralty jurisdiction,[47] requiring a supermajority of the Court to nullify a state or federal law,[48] increasing the size of the quorum needed for Supreme Court business,[49] allowing appeals to the Senate in cases where a state was a party,[50] demanding individual seriatim opinions from each judge (rather than an official "opinion of the Court," as became the custom under Marshall),[51] and, most significantly, repealing the Court's appellate jurisdiction over state court decisions as provided by Section 25 of the Judiciary Act of 1789.[52] Seeking to advance their own policy interests and stunt those of National Republicans, Old Republicans viewed these court-curbing measures as powerful tools to bring judges under stricter political control and limit the reach of federal judicial authority generally.

Third, Westerners in both the House and the Senate, some of whom were either National Republicans or Old Republicans, desired to continue along the path established by the Judiciary Act of 1807 by increasing the number of circuits—and, in turn, the number of Supreme Court justices—from seven to ten. Deeming the way the existing circuit system excluded the six newest Western states and combined

---

[45] 20 *Annals of Cong.* 480 (1809).

[46] 20 *Annals of Cong.* 479–80 (1809).

[47] 38 *Annals of Cong.* 44–47 (1821).

[48] 42 *Annals of Cong.* 2635–48 (1824); 1 *Cong. Deb.* 365–71 (1825); 2 *Cong. Deb.* 1119–49 (1826).

[49] 22 *Annals of Cong.* 961–62 (1811); 2 *Cong. Deb.* 1119–49 (1826).

[50] David P. Currie, *The Constitution in Congress: The Jeffersonians, 1801–1829* (Chicago: University of Chicago Press, 2001), 335.

[51] Warren, *The Supreme Court in United States History,* 1: 653.

[52] Charles Warren, "Legislative and Judicial Attacks on the Supreme Court of the United States—A History of the Twenty-Fifth Section of the Judiciary Act," 47 *American Law Review* 1 (1913); Warren, *The Supreme Court in United States History,* 1:554–59, 633–34, 653, 663. Although the provision had sparked little debate in the First Congress, and despite the fact that it had been the basis of the Court's jurisdiction in sixteen separate cases prior to 1816, Section 25 was viewed as particularly noxious in the South, largely because it subjected state court decisions on matters of *state* law to review by justices of the federal Supreme Court. Cf. William M. Wiecek, "*Murdock v. Memphis*: Section 25 of the Judiciary Act of 1789 and Judicial Federalism," in *Origins of the Federal Judiciary: Essays on the Judiciary Act of 1789,* ed. Maeva Marcus (New York: Oxford University Press, 1992), 225, referring to antebellum fear that Section 25 would make the Supreme Court the "principal agency promoting power drain out of the states."

the other three into one unmanageable circuit to be "essentially inadequate,"[53] as well as the cause of "great vexation and distress,"[54] Westerners—particularly Kentuckians Henry Clay, Richard Buckner, and Richard Johnson—saw the possibility of integrating their states and constituents into the circuit system as a means of satisfying both political and performance goals.[55] In terms of politics, Westerners, believing that "the principle of representation was not more important in legislation itself, than in the administration of justice,"[56] longed for "their due representation in the Supreme Court" and the judicial system more broadly.[57] Such representation was important because it both offered access to circuit-riding justices who might gain exposure to (and knowledge of) the laws and customs of Western communities and—provided continued presidential obedience to the norm of geographically representative appointments—presented an opportunity for additional Western justices to shape the jurisprudence of the Court.[58]

In terms of performance, inclusion in the circuit system promised more efficient administration of justice for citizens. Additional Western circuits, for instance, offered the possibility of reducing the burden on the Seventh Circuit, which was sufficiently large in area and sufficiently heavy in workload stemming from complicated litigation involving titles to Western lands that it was perpetually backed

[53] 1 *Cong. Deb.* 369 (1825) (Daniel Webster).

[54] 42 *Annals of Cong.* 575 (1824) (Isham Talbot).

[55] It was also seen as a way to fulfill the explicit words in congressional acts authorizing or declaring statehood, which often ended with a comment indicating that the state in question was admitted to the Union upon the same or equal footing as the original states in all respects whatsoever. See, for example, 2 Stat. 641 (February 20, 1811) (authorizing Louisiana statehood). For similar arguments about the importance of equal status to regional pride, see 2 *Cong. Deb.* 1009 (1826) (Edward Livingston): "We desire it, sir, because we are States! entitled to equality! the most perfect equality with the oldest, the most populous, the most influential, the best represented State among the first thirteen of the Union! Rights, privileges, honors, burthens [sic], duties, every thing, by the structure of our Government, must be participated in by every member of it, on the broadest principle of equality"); and 2 *Cong. Deb.* 1002 (1826) (Richard A. Buckner): "Do not these six States contribute their due proportion to meet the expenditures of the Government? and have not they, and all the Western states, most valiantly and magnanimously defended the rights of our common country?"

[56] 1 *Cong. Deb.* 370 (1825) (Henry Clay). See also 2 *Cong. Deb.* 1002 (1826) (Richard A. Buckner) (regarding the exclusion of Western states from the circuit system as equivalent to telling those states "that they may send delegates to Congress who may present their petitions and explain their grievances, but that they shall be entitled to no vote.")

[57] 1 *Cong. Deb.* 528 (1825) (Richard M. Johnson).

[58] 1 *Cong. Deb.* 529 (1825) (Richard M. Johnson) (supporting circuit riding as a way for the justices both to escape the politically corrupting influence of the capital and to "mingle with those whom they serve, and learn the manners, habits, and feelings of the people"); 1 *Cong. Deb.* 370 (1825) (Henry Clay): "In the present state of things, the Judges of the Supreme Court know as little about the local laws of some of the Western and Southern states, as if they did not belong to the confederacy." Through Monroe's first term, Westerners supported the abolition of circuit riding, but after judicial decisions they believed reflected the justices' ignorance about and indifference to the concerns of the West, those feelings essentially vanished. Nettels, "The Mississippi Valley and the Federal Judiciary," 210–11, 217.

up and delayed in issuing judgments.[59] Similarly, as "memorials" (formal written complaints and pleas for action) from various Western states illustrated, the lack of a circuit court (and the presence of only a district judge exercising circuit court jurisdiction) caused manifold problems in criminal and civil cases alike.[60] Among such problems were the fact that, if the district judge was forced to recuse himself or was otherwise unable to hear a case, the only recourse was to plead for a hearing in a neighboring circuit court (a tactic which seldom worked[61]) and the fact that, if litigants disagreed with the judgment of the district judge, the only option was a costly appeal to the Supreme Court.[62] Regarding their states and constituents as "deprived of those immunities which every other section of our confederacy has the felicity to share,"[63] and with "not a case of more crying injustice to be found in the Union,"[64] Western leaders considered it "time, high time, that something should be done" about their exclusion from the circuit system.[65]

In sum, National Republicans longed to abolish circuit riding and establish a new tier of circuit court judges, Old Republicans hoped to cabin the exercise of judicial power with any number of court-curbing measures, and Westerners sought the extension of the circuit system to the new states. Such divergent positions on judicial reform, especially those of the National Republicans and Old Republicans, were largely a function of divergent opinions about the Supreme Court and judicial nationalism. For National Republicans like Madison and Monroe—presidents who had, after all, appointed like-minded individuals to the Marshall

[59] The Seventh Circuit was reported to be so large that Justice Thomas Todd simply excluded Tennessee from his circuit riding schedule altogether. See 31 *Annals of Cong.* 419 (1817) (Thomas Claiborne): "The time of the judge was so divided that it made it impossible for him to devote the necessary time to the court in Tennessee." There is also some belief that Seventh Circuit duties may have been sufficiently arduous so as to accelerate Todd's death; Warren, *The Supreme Court in United States History*, 1:301. 2 *Cong. Deb.* 1016 (1826) (Ralph I. Ingersoll): "Kentucky, we are told, has six hundred cases annually commenced in the Federal Courts; Ohio has four hundred; Tennessee has three hundred and twenty suits undecided; and the dockets of the Federal Courts in Indiana, Illinois, and Missouri, are so lumbered up as to call loudly for relief. Does any thing like this mass of business exist in the Atlantic States, where the Judicial system acts freely and unembarrassed?" See also Nettels, "The Mississippi Valley and the Federal Judiciary," 203. Indeed, according to a table presented by Ohio representative John C. Wright, approximately 1,700 suits were filed each year in the Seventh Circuit. The next highest number of suits filed in one circuit was 130, in the First Circuit; the first six circuits combined received fewer than 600 suits. In other words, the Seventh Circuit received more than *ten times* the number of suits annually as any other circuit and nearly *three times* the number of all suits as all six other circuits combined. 2 *Cong. Deb.* 1047 (1826) (John C. Wright).

[60] Nettels, "The Mississippi Valley and the Federal Judiciary," 206–8.

[61] 2 *Cong. Deb.* 1042 (1826) (John C. Wright).

[62] 2 *Cong. Deb.* 1011 (1826) (Edward Livingston); 2 *Cong. Deb.* 413 (1826) (Martin Van Buren). Moreover, there was apparently some concern that district judges were "not men of the highest honor, nor had they the capacity to make a correct decision in an intricate case," the consequence of which was a judicial system lacking "the confidence of the people." 1 *Cong. Deb.* 586 (1825) (William Kelly).

[63] 1 *Cong. Deb.* 527 (1825) (Richard M. Johnson).

[64] 1 *Cong. Deb.* 370 (1825) (Henry Clay).

[65] 1 *Cong. Deb.* 528 (1825) (Richard M. Johnson).

Court[66]—cases like *Martin*, *McCulloch*, *Cohens*, and *Gibbons* were consistent with their moderate mercantile and thoroughly nationalist policy preferences; for Old Republicans they were simply proof that judicial power had run amok; for Westerners they were at best orthogonal to the structural problems that plagued the judiciary. Accordingly, National Republicans provided the justices with "the political space necessary" to develop constitutional meaning as they saw fit,[67] demonstrated a willingness to empower them further,[68] and attended to their institutional needs;[69] Old Republicans helped orchestrate a series of congressional and state attacks on various facets of the Court's authority; and Westerners, though irked by the Court's invalidation of state laws protecting settlers in land disputes and nullification of state laws that allowed repayment of debts in paper money rather than exclusively gold and silver,[70] continued to push for reform that might actually ameliorate the ills of the existing system.

[66] Madison's appointment of the young Joseph Story in 1810, for instance, came over vocal objections from those who thought the death of William Cushing offered an opportunity to rein in the Court that would be wasted on a moderate New Englander like Story. Monroe went even further, nearly appointing strong Federalist James Kent in 1823 before settling on Kent's protégé, New York judge Smith Thompson, instead. Even Thomas Jefferson, from whose ideology Madison and Monroe broke but whom both still considered their mentor, nominated as justices three men—William Johnson, Henry Brockholst Livingston, and Thomas Todd—from the moderate wing of the Democratic-Republican Party. Combined with John Marshall and Adams appointee Bushrod Washington, these justices anchored the Court's nationalism. See Graber, "Federalist or Friends of Adams," 242; and Warren, *The Supreme Court in United States History*, 1:415–19.

[67] Graber, "Federalist or Friends of Adams," 248.

[68] For example, when the New England states defied the embargo and obstructed the war effort, Congress included provisions in the Non-Intercourse Act of 1815, 3 Stat. 195 (February 4, 1815), and the Collection of Duties Act of 1815, 3 Stat. 231 (March 3, 1815), allowing for removal of suits against federal officers from state to federal court. Such provisions, which would later serve as a model for the nullification and Civil War removal statutes, protected customs officials and duty collectors from local hostility and biased prosecutions by state courts opposed to the substance of the federal law those officials were charged with enforcing, but they expired naturally on their own and did not effect any lasting change in the character of judicial power.

[69] In the first two decades of the nineteenth century alone, National Republicans extended the power to issue injunctions in circuit court cases to district court judges, 2 Stat. 418 (February 13, 1807); provided for circuit judges to perform the duties of district judges when the latter were unable to do so, 2 Stat. 534 (March 2, 1809); established new judges in understaffed locations, 2 Stat. 563 (March 2, 1810), 2 Stat. 719 (April 29, 1812), 3 Stat. 95 (January 27, 1814); granted circuit courts jurisdiction over patent cases, 3 Stat. 481 (February 15, 1819); and furnished the Supreme Court with a paid court reporter, 3 Stat. 276 (March 3, 1817). This latter development made the justices' opinions more broadly accessible to both lawyers and citizens and subsequently diminished the importance of newspapers (and unreliable, highly impressionistic reports) in shaping public opinion about the Court. See Warren, *The Supreme Court in United States History*, 1:455. For John Marshall's approval of the idea of a paid Court reporter, see *American State Papers: Miscellaneous* 2:419–20.

[70] On land disputes, see, for example, *Green v. Biddle*, 21 U.S. 1 (1823) (striking down Kentucky's occupancy law as a violation of an earlier compact between Kentucky and Virginia that was protected by the Contracts Clause). On the nullification of state laws that allowed repayment of debts in paper money, see Nettels, "The Mississippi Valley and the Federal Judiciary," 217.

Webster, Van Buren, and Bicameral Stalemate

Although the divergent interests of National Republicans, Old Republicans, and Westerners offered a range of reform options (and a range of opinions about the Supreme Court) in the mid-1820s,[71] the debate over judicial institution building largely focused on the Western plan for three new circuits and three new justices, perhaps because Westerners held the greatest personal stake and thus pressed both the issue and their preferred resolution of it continuously. Urging caution against the Western-sponsored reform were assorted non-Westerners[72]—particularly conservative National Republicans from the South—who favored the abolition of circuit riding, questioned the causes of the caseload increase in the West,[73] objected to the notion of "judicial representation,"[74] and opposed the idea of a large Court filled with Western justices who might overrule precedents friendly to National Republicans.[75] In favor of the reform were Westerners and their allies, who saw new circuits (and new justices to attend to those circuits) as the quickest way for the West to gain substantial influence in the federal judiciary and, by extension, in American politics more generally. Chief among these allies was Massachusetts representative Daniel Webster, chairman of the House Judiciary Committee and a

[71] A fourth alternative, raised from time to time but never with much support among legislators, proposed the addition of two circuit courts in the West and two circuit judges who would exercise authority equivalent to Supreme Court justices without creating a new circuit or a new seat on the Court. A slight variant of this plan effectively designated the new circuit judges as "backup" justices in case there was a vacancy on the Court. Since neither plan offered the West the judicial representation it desired, both were wholeheartedly opposed by Westerners.

[72] 42 *Annals of Cong.* 576 (1824) (James Barbour) (reminding his colleagues that it was "much more easy to adopt than to get rid of any new judiciary system which might be adopted"); 2 *Cong. Deb.* 1136 (1826) (Dudley Marvin) (cautioning legislators that "what shall be done to-day cannot be revoked to-morrow" and hoping that any reform be "the result of cool deliberation").

[73] 2 *Cong. Deb.* 1127 (1826) (Charles F. Mercer): "sudden augmentation of business in the Courts of the seventh Circuit, did not arise from the alleged defects of the present Judicial System of the United States, but from transient causes, either multiplying the claims of non-residents, of the Bank of the United States, and of merchants of the East; or from a course of legislation which induced the plaintiff to prefer the Federal to the State Courts."

[74] 2 *Cong. Deb.* 1137 (1826) (Dudley Marvin): "This Court, sir, is the common property of the whole American People. It belongs not exclusively to the West or to the East, the North or the South"; 2 *Cong. Deb.* 976 (1826) (Alfred H. Powell): "Judges should have no political opinions or sectional feelings. Like the emblem they represent, they ought to be blind to the party or sectional policy or views of the Government under which they administer the laws."

[75] Cf. Nettels, "The Mississippi Valley and the Federal Judiciary," 217, noting that calls for judicial representation caused "many Easterners of conservative cast of mind to believe that one purpose of enlarging the Court was to add enough western judges for reversing its recent anti-Western decisions." On the size of the Court more generally, see 2 *Cong. Deb.* 1130 (1826) (Charles F. Mercer): "*Seven* Judges, and more especially *five*, will perform the duties of an Appellate Court, in much shorter time than *ten*"; and 2 *Cong. Deb.* 1139 (1826) (Dudley Marvin): "But what is the system of the bill? To meet the increase of business in the inferior Courts, it increases the number, not of the inferior, but of the Supreme Court judges; it makes the Supreme Court subordinate and secondary, and burthens [*sic*] it with a number of Judges confessedly too large for its own business, that they may attend to the business of Courts below!"

leader of what would ultimately become the Whig Party.[76] Though more nationalist than most Western legislators, Webster nonetheless abandoned his previous
support of a plan to abolish circuit riding in favor of the plan for Western expansion of the circuit system.[77] His conversion represented tactical calculations about
appointment and sectional politics. First, since the Western plan would result in
three new Court vacancies to be filled by John Quincy Adams, it presented an opportunity to cement the Marshall Court's judicial nationalism for years to come.
Second, recognizing that the "close union . . . between the Southern Atlantic and
the Western States" had caused "the East much mischief," Webster agreed with
his friend Jeremiah Mason that a "union of sentiment between the East and the
West . . . ought to be carefully cultivated."[78] With an influential member and former
advocate of abolishing circuit riding now leading the charge, the Western plan for
three new circuits and three new justices earned easy passage in the House (132–
59) in 1826.

Unfortunately for Webster and Westerners, however, bicameralism stunted the
drive for reform. When the Webster-sponsored bill crossed the Capitol to the Senate, it was received by New York's Martin Van Buren, chairman of the Senate Judiciary Committee (and future architect of the Democratic Party), who "reported
two seemingly harmless amendments."[79] The first amendment made a slight alteration to the composition of circuits as proposed by the House, shifting Missouri
from the House-proposed Seventh Circuit to the Eighth Circuit and returning
Ohio from the House's Eighth Circuit back to the Seventh Circuit.[80] The second
amendment established an 1807-style residency requirement, mandating that each
justice reside in the circuit to which he was assigned and thus explicitly continuing
the tradition of geographically representative appointments. The full Senate ac-

---

[76] Webster's first stint in Congress (1813–17) was actually as a representative from New Hampshire;
after six years practicing law, he returned to the House as a member of the Massachusetts delegation in
1823, serving two terms before moving to the Senate in 1827.

[77] 2 *Cong. Deb.* 877 (1826) (Daniel Webster): "but then, whether it be desirable, upon the whole, to
withdraw the Judges of the Supreme Court from the Circuits, and to confine their labors entirely to the
sessions at Washington, is a question which has most deeply occupied my reflections, and in regard to
which I am free to confess, some change has been wrought in my opinion." For Webster's original 1824
proposal to abolish circuit riding, a proposal drafted after conferring with Justice Joseph Story, see 42
Annals of Cong. 2617 (1824). On Webster's consultation and friendship with Story, see Remini, *Daniel
Webster*, 213–14, 257.

[78] Cf. Jeremiah Mason to Daniel Webster, February 4, 1826, quoted in George Ticknor Curtis, *Life of
Daniel Webster*, vol. 1, 4th ed. (New York: D. Appleton, 1872), 264.

[79] Nettels, "The Mississippi Valley and the Federal Judiciary," 222. For Van Buren's amendments, see
2 *Cong. Deb.* 409 (1826).

[80] The House bill grouped Kentucky and Missouri in the Seventh Circuit and Ohio, Indiana, and
Illinois in the Eighth Circuit; the Senate bill combined Ohio and Kentucky in the Seventh Circuit and
Indiana, Illinois, and Missouri in the Eighth Circuit. Both plans added Tennessee, which had been
joined with Kentucky and Ohio as part of the Seventh Circuit since 1807, to Alabama in the Ninth
Circuit and paired Louisiana and Mississippi in the Tenth Circuit.

cepted both amendments (32–4) and, after a week of debate, the entire bill (31–8),[81] but the divergent House and Senate versions of the reform necessitated a compromise that did not emerge. Instead, the House rejected the Senate's amendments, the Senate reiterated its amendments, the House requested a conference, and the Senate refused, prompting Webster to wonder aloud on the House floor whether one chamber had ever before refused to conference with the other.[82] With no clear end in sight and Ohio representatives displeased with the Senate plan because it combined the two largest Western states (Ohio and Kentucky) in one circuit, the House ultimately voted to postpone the reform bill indefinitely.[83]

The story of judicial institution building in the 1820s, then, is a story about how reform did not occur. That story, however, is less about partisanship and more about geography than it might first appear. Indeed, even though the failure to reach a mutually agreeable reform bill was a failure of bicameralism, and even though the two chambers were controlled by different wings of the fraying Democratic-Republican coalition,[84] the stalemate was not solely (or even mostly) caused by differences between Webster's proto-Whigs and Van Buren's proto-Jacksonians. Although it is true that the structure established by the Judiciary Act of 1807 implicated the disparate political goals of the two groups within the otherwise uncontentious performance issue of circuit expansion, it was actually the demands of Westerners and the constraints of geographic representation that prevented reform.

Obviously, on some level, Webster and Van Buren were jockeying over whether proto-Whigs or proto-Jacksonians would benefit from the appointments associated with expansion of the circuit system, but both leaders seemed more than willing to cooperate on what partisan politics would suggest was the most important and most controversial issue—the number of new Supreme Court seats—and both were limited in what they wished to do by geographic forces and considerations. While Webster certainly hoped to secure the vacancies for Adams, both he and Adams actually preferred two new seats on the Court instead of three—actually preferred *fewer* seats to *more*—in order to avoid the potential of tie votes on a

[81] Nettels, "The Mississippi Valley and the Federal Judiciary," 223, claims that Van Buren succeeded in sustaining the amendments by building a coalition of three groups—"the anti-administration senators of the South, the eastern conservatives who were opposed to tampering with the Supreme Court and perceived in the amendments the hope of defeating the bill, and the senators from the interested western states"—but only four senators, including both of Ohio's and one of Kentucky's, voted against the amendments, so it is difficult to draw any certain conclusions about voting patterns.

[82] 2 *Cong. Deb.* 2602 (1826) (Daniel Webster).

[83] Nettels, "The Mississippi Valley and the Federal Judiciary," 223. If necessary to pass the reform bill, Webster was willing to accede in the Senate amendments, but the loss of the Ohio representatives apparently foreclosed that possibility. See Daniel Webster to Jeremiah Mason, May 2, 1826, quoted in Warren, *The Supreme Court in United States History*, 1:683n1: "If the Senate do not yield their amendment probably we shall agree to it."

[84] In the Nineteenth Congress (1825–27), supporters of Adams held a slim 109–104 edge over supporters of Jackson in the House while supporters of Jackson owned a 26–22 majority in the Senate.

Court with an even number of justices.[85] Acknowledging that his opponents "did not wish to give so many important appointments to the President,"[86] Webster expressed willingness to pass a bill authorizing only two new seats, but the majority of his committee, especially Western representatives John C. Wright of Ohio and James Clark of Kentucky, insisted on three so that two (instead of one) could be allotted to wholly Western circuits.[87] For his part, Van Buren, while predictably loathe to place one-third of the seats on the Court in the hands of an opposition president who had won the White House under questionable terms,[88] seemed prepared either to give Adams two appointments or to agree to the circuit composition proposed by Webster's committee but reluctant to yield on both the number of justices and the organization of circuits.

The latter issue proved a particularly thorny question of geographic politics, with the Ohio representatives demanding that Ohio (the most populous Western state) and Kentucky (the most politically powerful Western state, on account of leaders like Henry Clay) be placed in different circuits.[89] Far from disagreeing with the Ohio delegation, Webster actively desired to facilitate the appointment of an Ohioan—Adams's Postmaster General, John McLean—to one of the proposed new seats on the Court.[90] Unfortunately for both the Ohio representatives and Webster, though, Ohio, as part of the Seventh Circuit, was already represented on the Court by Kentuckian Robert Trimble. For Webster, McLean's prospective appointment promised twin benefits. On the level of partisan strength, it delicately removed an individual who was increasingly suspected to possess strong Jacksonian tendencies from one of the central organs for distributing patronage,[91] and it did so

---

[85] Remini, *Daniel Webster*, 258.

[86] See Daniel Webster to Joseph Story, May 8, 1826, quoted in Remini, *Daniel Webster*, 259n29.

[87] Remini, *Daniel Webster*, 258 n24.

[88] In the 1824 presidential election, the infamous "corrupt bargain" between then secretary of state John Quincy Adams and Speaker of the House Henry Clay threw the Electoral College vote—and, thus, the presidency—to Adams over Jackson even though the latter had won the national popular vote.

[89] Nettels, "The Mississippi Valley and the Federal Judiciary," 223.

[90] For the details of this remarkable incident, I draw on Nettels, "The Mississippi Valley and the Federal Judiciary," 222–23; Warren, *The Supreme Court in United States History, Volume One*, 683; Remini, *Daniel Webster*, 258–60; Robert V. Remini, *Martin Van Buren and the Making of the Democratic Party* (New York: Columbia University Press, 1959), 114, 229n1; and Frankfurter and Landis, *The Business of the Supreme Court*, 42.

[91] Indeed, when McLean—who had remained on good terms with supporters of both Adams and Jackson during the 1828 election but soon came to be affiliated with the John C. Calhoun wing of the proto-Democrats—did make it to the Court in 1829, it was as a Jackson appointee. Jackson, however, was uneasy about placing someone as ideologically iconoclastic as McLean on the Court, ultimately doing so largely to remove a potential presidential rival from the electoral sphere. With McLean waging active campaigns for the presidency four times on four different party lines (including, finally, as a Republican) during his thirty-two years on the Court, Jackson's ploy did not work; Abraham, *Justices, Presidents, and Senators*, 78–79. On the work of John McLean as postmaster general and the role of the early Post Office in American society, see Richard R. John, *Spreading the News: The American Postal System from Franklin to Morse* (Cambridge, MA: Harvard University Press, 1995). On patronage and the "clerical" bureaucracy, including the Post Office, during the first half of the nineteenth century more generally, see Daniel P. Carpenter, *The Forging of Bureaucratic Autonomy: Reputations,*

without alienating potential supporters in the West generally or McLean's important home state of Ohio specifically.[92] On the level of personal advancement, it allowed Adams to name more moderate Jacksonian representative Samuel Ingham of Pennsylvania—the chair of the Committee on the Post Office and Post Roads and a potential Speaker of the House[93]—as McLean's replacement in the Postmaster General's Office, thus helping to clear the field for Webster himself to become Speaker.[94] In order both to satisfy the Ohio delegation's wishes and to overcome the geographic restrictions forbidding McLean's appointment to the Court (thus serving his party as well as his own career advancement), Webster attempted to divorce Ohio from Kentucky, a tactic that prompted Van Buren to amend the bill not only to keep the two states together but also explicitly to require circuit residency (so as to prevent Webster and Adams from disregarding the post-1807 norm of geographically representative appointments and appointing McLean anyway).[95]

Networks, and Policy Innovation in Executive Agencies, 1862–1928 (Princeton, NJ: Princeton University Press, 2001), 37–64.

[92] See Martin Van Buren to Benjamin F. Butler, May 15, 1826, quoted in Warren, *The Supreme Court in United States History*, 1:683n1: "The great object is to get McLean out of the Post Office which can only be effected by his promotion, as they dare not displace him." The general consensus of the era seemed to be that, even though McLean was untrustworthy, unpredictable, and self-serving, he was sufficiently popular in the West that politicians were careful not to offend him. Ohio representative Thomas Corwin, for example, warned that any slight to McLean would "have the effect to rouse all his minions and the howl of prosecution would resound throughout the Union"; Corwin, quoted in Francis P. Weisenburger, *The Life of John McLean: A Politician on the United States Supreme Court* (Columbus: Ohio State University Press, 1937), 61. Jackson apparently weighed similar factors in eventually appointing McLean to the Court. See Abraham, *Justices, Presidents, and Senators*, 78–79.

[93] Ingham would later become Jackson's first secretary of the treasury, only to resign after two years as part of the Petticoat Affair.

[94] See Martin Van Buren to Benjamin F. Butler, May 15, 1826, quoted in Warren, *The Supreme Court in United States History*, 1:683n1: "It is also said that Ingham is to be made P. M. G. and Webster, Speaker. There may be some mistake about this latter part although I am not certain that there is." Nettels, "The Mississippi Valley and the Federal Judiciary," 222, states that McLean's move to the Court would enable, in succession, the Speaker of the House "to be advanced to the Cabinet" and Webster to "step into the speaker's chair," but Ingham, though a prominent member viewed as a potential Speaker, never actually served in that role. (Rather, the Speaker during the Nineteenth Congress (1825–27) was Democrat-Republican John W. Taylor of New York, an ally of Adams.)

[95] But see 2 *Cong. Deb.* 410 (1826) (Martin Van Buren) (claiming that he "was absent, on account of indisposition" when the amendment altering circuit composition "was discussed and decided in the committee" and that he had previously introduced a bill with the exact same circuit composition as proposed by the House). Van Buren's public statements, however, are contradicted by sentiments expressed in private correspondence. See Martin Van Buren to Benjamin F. Butler, May 15, 1826, quoted in Warren, *The Supreme Court in United States History*, 1:683n1:

> There has been a great deal of shuffling on the part of Webster & Co. to let the Bill die in conference. This plan we have defeated by a pretty strong course. With characteristic Yankee craft, he has, though defeated in his main object, seized upon some clumsy expressions of Holmes (who reported the bill or rather amendment during my sickness) to hide the true ground of collision, the union of Kentucky and Ohio, by raising another question upon the form of the amendment. But, the matter is perfectly understood here. Unless they can have a Judge in Kentucky (who is already appointed) and one in Ohio also, they wish to defeat the bill, in hopes of getting a better one next year.

The intensity and complexity of this "subterranean maneuvering" suggests that the failure to build the judiciary in the 1820s was not because there was a lack of "powerful, concentrated economic, political, or social interest[s]" but, rather, because there were too many.[96] Chief among them, it seems, was the emergence of the West and the desire of both parties to court the region's support. Geography was not sole, supreme, and absolute in this episode; there were, of course, partisan imperatives at work. Yet even as Webster and Van Buren may have sought to do what was best for their respective coalitions, the extent to which they were able to accomplish purely partisan motivations was complicated, compromised, and constricted by the influence of the rapidly growing (in population and, thus, in potential political importance as well) West on national politics. Indeed, the actions of both Webster and Van Buren reflect a delicate balance between defeating the partisan opposition and not alienating Western constituencies. By emphasizing the Western desire for circuit expansion (as opposed to the old Federalist-National Republican desire to abolish circuit riding) and carefully considering how best to manage the popular (but politically dangerous) Westerner McLean, all while remaining open to a compromise with Van Buren's proto-Jacksonians that Westerners might oppose, Webster was perpetually looking for ways to benefit (or, at least, avoid actively antagonizing) both proto-Whigs and Westerners. By first expressing conditional willingness to add new (Western) circuits and new (Western) justices to the Court but later introducing amendments that ultimately killed the reform bill, Van Buren was simultaneously able to triumph over Webster and maintain to Western allies that he had tried to extend the circuit system to their states. The link between circuits and justices and the norm of geographically representative appointments—both products of the Judiciary Act of 1807—had made judicial reform potentially transformative and undoubtedly controversial, but the addition of a veto point independent of partisanship threatened to paralyze the task entirely. Absent a significant event to alter the political environment or a strategic political entrepreneur to navigate the land mines within it, the constraints imposed by the changing sectional politics of antebellum America, by the clash of proto-Whig and proto-Jacksonian political goals, and by the structure of the 1807 system poisoned any real chance of compromise.

The Failure of the 1820s

With much argument but little action, the debate over judicial reform in the early to mid-1820s thus "spent itself in talk."[97] By the time John Quincy Adams declared in his third annual message to Congress in 1827 that "the extension of the judicial administration of the Federal Government" to the newly admitted states

---

[96] Nettels, "The Mississippi Valley and the Federal Judiciary," 224; Frankfurter and Landis, *The Business of the Supreme Court*, 42.

[97] Frankfurter and Landis, *The Business of the Supreme Court*, 44.

was a subject "of deep interest to the whole Union,"[98] even the "talk" had virtually disappeared. Indeed, before Andrew Jackson's election to the presidency in
1828, Congress took three remedial and largely uncontroversial measures to deal
with specific problems of judicial administration[99]—lengthening the session of the
Supreme Court by one month,[100] establishing procedures for taking evidence and
issuing subpoenas,[101] and applying the forms of judicial procedure established in
the Judiciary Act of 1789 to all states admitted since[102]—but the opportunity for an
overhaul, extension, or reorganization of the entire system had evidently passed.
Although the pressure placed on the existing system by territorial expansion, on
the one hand, and the convergence between the National Republican administrations of James Madison, James Monroe, and John Quincy Adams and the nationalist impulses of John Marshall, Joseph Story, and their Court brethren, on the
other hand, had made substantial reform seem promising for almost a decade,
landmark institution building found itself doomed by the structural rigidity of the
1808 system.

The failure of reformers to overcome that structural rigidity during the 1820s
meant that the judicial system continued to disintegrate under the weight of a
growing caseload and the area of a growing nation. The defects of 1810–1829 did
not disappear on their own; in fact, they grew worse, and Westerners—having
begged for full inclusion in the circuit system for two decades—grew more dissatisfied. Within a decade, the West would finally gain the circuits it long demanded,
but the failure to reform the federal judiciary before the Jacksonian ascent meant
that the resulting reform would occur at the expense rather than benefit of the
nationalist, Northern, and abolitionist interests that appeared so close to victory
in 1826.

Democrats, Whigs, and the Possibility of Supreme Court Vacancies, 1829–1835

Like Jefferson's defeat of Adams in 1800, Andrew Jackson's defeat of John Quincy
Adams in 1828 fundamentally reshaped the landscape of American politics.[103] Jack-

[98] John Quincy Adams, Third Annual Message to Congress (December 4, 1827).

[99] In the midst of debates over judicial reorganization, Congress also passed the Crimes Act of 1824, which extended federal admiralty jurisdiction to crimes aboard American vessels in foreign waters. 4 Stat. 115 (March 3, 1825).

[100] 4 Stat. 160 (May 4, 1826). As Frankfurter and Landis, *The Business of the Supreme Court*, 44, note, lengthening the Supreme Court's term both served as a "corrective for the arrears of cases" and decreased justices' circuit court attendance.

[101] 4 Stat. 197 (January 24, 1827).

[102] 4 Stat. 278 (May 19, 1828).

[103] On Jackson's "reconstruction" of American politics, see Stephen Skowronek, *The Politics Presidents Make: Leadership from John Adams to Bill Clinton* (Cambridge, MA: Belknap Press, 1997), 130–54. On the election of 1828 itself, see Florence Weston, *The Presidential Election of 1828* (Washington, DC: Ruddick Press, 1938).

son, of course, had become a powerful figure on the national political stage four years prior, when he won a plurality of both the popular and electoral votes only to see the House vault Adams to the White House instead.[104] After effectively running against Adams for the latter's entire presidential term, Jackson got his revenge in 1828, trouncing his nemesis by greater than a 2–1 margin in the Electoral College (an institution Jackson had campaigned to abolish since his 1824 defeat). The result was a regime that was unabashedly hostile to most National Republican commitments. Jacksonian Democrats, for instance, favored Indian removal and opposed the Bank of the United States. They generally preferred a strict constitutional reading to a broad one and a narrow sphere of federal government authority to an expansive one. They envisioned a society where the common man had power and respect and an America where Northern financiers held no more influence than Southern or Western farmers and laborers. Unlike John Marshall and the justices of the Supreme Court, they were not especially concerned with protecting private property or the sanctity of contracts; unlike the National Republicans that preceded them and the Whigs that had emerged to oppose them, they were against sweeping internal improvements and Henry Clay's "American System." In many ways, Jacksonian Democrats renewed and updated the Jeffersonian tradition, shifting it away from the nationalism that had consumed it since the War of 1812 and back toward the small government, agricultural roots of the late 1790s and early 1800s.[105]

As much as the political environment and the likely public policies changed from the Era of Good (or Mixed) Feelings to the Age of Jackson, the plight of the judiciary remained much the same. Although territorial expansion had come to a temporary halt—Missouri's admission in 1821 would be the last until Arkansas joined the Union in 1836—the problems of the first quarter of the century had not gone away. Six Western states remained outside the circuit system; the Seventh Circuit—still the sole Western circuit—remained immense in both land mass and caseload; and Westerners remained indignant at their continued exclusion from the judicial system afforded the rest of the nation. Though the Supreme Court was issuing important decisions and developing constitutional law in areas such as commerce, contracts, business, and bankruptcy, none of these decisions were related to the structural problems faced by the judicial system, so the task of judicial institution building fell once again to Congress. As had been the case during the Monroe and Adams administrations, congressional attempts at judicial reform during Jackson's terms were characterized by seeming consensus about the general need for reform but sharp disagreement about the specific type of reform

[104] On the election of 1824, see Robert V. Remini, *The Election of Andrew Jackson* (Philadelphia: Lippincott, 1963), 11–29; and Jeffrey A. Jenkins and Brian R. Sala, "The Spatial Theory of Voting and the Presidential Election of 1824," *American Journal of Political Science* 42 (1998): 1157–79.

[105] One important point of convergence between Whigs and Jacksonian Democrats during this era was the desire to keep the issue of slavery out of the national political arena. See, for example, Mark A. Graber, "The Nonmajoritarian Difficulty: Legislative Deference to the Judiciary," *Studies in American Political Development* 7 (1993): 35–73, 46–50. I address this subject in chapter 4.

that was most necessary or would be most beneficial. While the source of this disagreement—the prospect of additional seats on the Supreme Court—was familiar, the relevant partisan coalitions had reversed positions from where they had been in the 1820s: the previous Old Republican minority had become the Democratic majority, and the previous National Republican majority had become the Whig minority. Though both Democrats and Whigs sought to satisfy Western demands for circuit expansion and judicial representation, the link between circuits and justices imposed by the Judiciary Act of 1807 meant that the performance-oriented matter of Western justice was intertwined with the politics of prospective Supreme Court appointments. Thus, despite widespread interest in fixing problems afflicting the judicial system and multiple attempts at reform, the continued attachment of political concerns about judicial appointments to the performance issue of circuit expansion left the early to mid-1830s as simply "another decade of legislative sterility."[106]

The Politics of Prospective Appointments

Having reclaimed the White House in 1828, Democrats were eager to reward supporters and entrench their policy preferences in the judiciary by creating new Supreme Court vacancies for Andrew Jackson to fill with Democratic partisans. Jackson himself was a strong supporter of reform, urging legislators to act on the matter in three of his first four annual messages to Congress. In each address, he emphasized the inequity of excluding the West from the benefits of the circuit system, questioned why reform had yet to occur, and exhorted Congress to act. In 1829, he called the organization of the judiciary a "subject of high importance" and encouraged Congress to "extend the circuit courts equally throughout the different parts of the Union."[107] Two years later, he reminded legislators that the new states "demand circuit courts as a matter not of concession, but of right."[108] "If the existing system be a good one," he asked in 1832, "why should it not be extended? If it be a bad one, why is it suffered to exist?"[109] As a Westerner himself,[110] Jackson desired reform for the West whether or not it meant additional Court appointments,[111] but he preferred a reform plan that would allow him to pack the Court with like-minded Democrats.

After all, additional Democratic appointees on the Court likely meant more pro-Jacksonian and fewer anti-Jacksonian judicial decisions. With ostensibly pro-

[106] Frankfurter and Landis, *The Business of the Supreme Court*, 44.
[107] Andrew Jackson, First Annual Message to Congress (December 8, 1829).
[108] Andrew Jackson, Third Annual Message to Congress (December 6, 1831).
[109] Andrew Jackson, Fourth Annual Message to Congress (December 4, 1832).
[110] Though born and raised in South Carolina, Jackson spent most of his adult life in Tennessee.
[111] See Jackson, First Annual Message to Congress: "If an extension of the circuit court system to those States which do not now enjoy its benefits should be determined upon, it would of course be necessary to revise the present arrangement of the circuits; and even if that system should not be enlarged, such a revision is recommended."

Jacksonian decisions in *Willson v. Blackbird Creek Marsh Company*,[112] *Providence Bank v. Billings*,[113] and *Barron v. Baltimore*,[114] it was clear that Jackson's defeat of Adams—and the concomitant realization by Marshall Court justices that they were no longer supported by the dominant coalition—had brought the golden age of John Marshall and judicial nationalism to an "abrupt halt,"[115] but Democrats desired to solidify a true Jacksonian majority. Indeed, far from the impression given by Jackson's hostile (and almost certainly apocryphal) response to the Supreme Court's decision in *Worcester v. Georgia* ("John Marshall has made his decision, now let him enforce it"),[116] Jacksonians, who lacked a firm view on any public policy issue except Indian removal (hence Jackson's opposition to *Worcester*), did not oppose judicial power per se.[117] They had never mentioned restricting federal jurisdiction in their national party platforms, and, once in office, they did not cooperate in the aggressive and repeated attempts to curb judicial power.[118] In fact, during the Nullification Crisis,[119] Jacksonians empowered the judiciary by passing the Force Act of 1833 to overcome Southern defiance of the Tariff Acts of 1828 (the "Tariff of Abominations") and 1832.[120] Although the proximate goal was to suppress state uprising, the willingness to use the judiciary in the propagation of Jacksonian policy aims demonstrates that Jackson and his allies were hardly opposed to the exercise of judicial power or the enhancement of judicial capacity. Jacksonians did, however, object to instances where such power was used to

[112] 27 U.S. 245 (1829) (upholding state regulation of commerce as a valid exercise of police power).

[113] 29 U.S. 514 (1830) (strictly construing a corporate charter to allow state taxation of banks).

[114] 32 U.S. 243 (1833) (limiting the application of the Bill of Rights to federal government action).

[115] Graber, "Federalist or Friends of Adams," 262. This supports the idea that the Court has "seldom lagged far behind or forged far ahead of America." See Robert G. McCloskey, *The American Supreme Court*, 5th ed., rev. by Sanford Levinson (Chicago: University of Chicago Press, 2010), 261.

[116] 31 U.S. 515 (1832) (striking down a Georgia law allowing prosecution of Cherokee Indians on the grounds that only the federal government could regulate intercourse between American citizens and Indian nations).

[117] I draw here on Mark A. Graber, "The Jacksonian Origins of Chase Court Activism," *Journal of Supreme Court History* 25 (2000): 17–39; and Mark A. Graber, "The Jacksonian Makings of the Taney Court," unpublished article, accessed December 20, 2009, at http://papers.ssrn.com/sol3/papers.cfm?abstract_id=842184.

[118] See Mark. A. Graber, "James Buchanan as Savior? Judicial Power, Political Fragmentation, and the Failed 1831 Repeal of Section 25," unpublished article, accessed December 20, 2009, at http://papers.ssrn.com/sol3/papers.cfm?abstract_id=1356075.

[119] On the constitutional dimensions of the tariff dispute and nullification crisis, see Keith E. Whittington, *Constitutional Construction: Divided Powers and Constitutional Meaning* (Cambridge, MA: Harvard University Press, 1999), 72–112.

[120] 4 Stat. 632 (March 2, 1833). The legislation, which is sometimes referred to as the Bloody Bill Act, granted Jackson the authority to close ports and harbors, expanded the jurisdiction of the federal courts over cases arising under the Tariff Acts, and broadened the causes for which federal officers could remove cases from state to federal courts. Much like the predecessor removal statutes during the embargo and the War of 1812 and the successor removal statutes during the Civil War and Reconstruction, the Force Act assisted the enforcement of unpopular federal action in recalcitrant states by protecting federal marshals and collectors against biased or overzealous prosecution by state officials. For the extensive debate over the bill, see 9 *Cong. Deb.* 243–462 (1833).

expand or consolidate the power of the federal government. More concerned with limiting national power than with empowering states,[121] Jacksonians imagined a small sphere of federal authority trumping a larger sphere of state authority. To the extent that they could shift the balance of power on the Court—either by replacing existing National Republican justices with Democratic appointees or by creating new seats to be filled by a Democratic president—the Jacksonian vision of limited federal government could be implemented more quickly.

It was the idea of a Democratic Supreme Court legitimating precisely this Jacksonian vision that prompted Whigs to pursue a different type of judicial reform. Like Democrats, Whigs wanted to improve the administration of justice and satisfy Western demands for the extension of the circuit system. Yet, as much they wanted to place Western states on equal judicial footing with their Eastern counterparts, Whigs also wished to prevent Andrew Jackson from remaking the Court in his own image. With the 1807 link between circuits and justices still in operation, however, decoupling the performance benefits of Western reform from the political advantage Democrats would gain from a slate of new judicial appointments required expanding the scope of the judicial system and the area covered by it without adding new circuits.

The January 1835 resignation of Justice Gabriel Duvall, a Maryland resident who was responsible for the Fourth Circuit, and Jackson's nomination of Roger Taney, also a Maryland resident, to replace Duvall provided both an opportunity and additional motivation for such a plan. Jackson had, for several years, desired to appoint Taney to the Court as repayment for his Cabinet service, once noting that he owed him "a debt of gratitude and regard which I have not the power to discharge."[122] Jackson's "debt" stemmed from Taney's loyalty first in advising the president (as attorney general) to remove government deposits from the Bank of the United States and then subsequently in carrying out (as acting secretary of the treasury) the president's controversial orders to do so,[123] two actions that gave rise to Whig accusations that Taney was merely a Jacksonian sycophant.[124] Regardless of the depth of Jackson's affection for Taney or Whig enmity toward him, the matter of his appointment to the Court had largely been moot while Duvall—a fellow Marylander—remained on the bench. Regarding himself as bound by the post-1807 norm of geographically representative appointments, and reluctant to be ac-

---

[121] Jacksonians were not ardent states' rights advocates; while they were committed to a limited central government, they firmly believed the federal government was supreme within the limits of its power and were emphatic that state actors could not interfere with national policy making.

[122] Andrew Jackson to Roger Taney, June 25, 1834, quoted in Samuel Tyler, *Memoir of Roger Brooke Taney* (Baltimore: Murphy, 1872), 222–23.

[123] Indeed, Jackson's orders were sufficiently controversial that two previous treasury secretaries—Samuel D. Ingham and Louis McLane—had refused to implement them. Ultimately, Jackson replaced McLane with Taney, who served a recess appointment as acting treasury secretary for nine months before resigning when Congress refused to confirm him to the position on a permanent basis.

[124] On the Whig response to Taney's nomination, see Warren, *The Supreme Court in United States History*, 1:798–800.

cused of pressuring an aged Supreme Court justice to leave the bench, Jackson maneuvered to facilitate Taney's appointment by gently inducing Duvall's retirement.
Seizing upon the evidently widespread knowledge that Duvall, who had been deaf
for quite some time and had grown increasingly infirm during the 1830s but had
delayed his retirement almost a decade out of fear about who might be appointed
to replace him, was quite fond of Taney, Jackson seemingly authorized a "careful"
leak from the Court's clerk to Duvall that the president was ready to nominate
Taney to replace him.[125] Upon hearing the news, Duvall retired immediately.

Whether or not they were aware of the president's back-channel politicking to
enable Taney's nomination, Whigs were determined to forestall the appointment
and utilized circuit reorganization—or, more precisely, circuit consolidation—to
accomplish the task. The Whig consolidation plan, offered by New Jersey senator
Theodore Frelinghuysen, proposed three changes.[126] First, it would combine two
Eastern circuits—the Third (New Jersey, Pennsylvania) and the Fourth (Delaware,
Maryland)—into one circuit. Second, it would establish one new Western circuit
to include Louisiana, Mississippi, Illinois, and Missouri. Third, it would annex
Alabama to the existing Sixth Circuit (South Carolina, Georgia) and Indiana to
the existing Seventh Circuit (Kentucky, Tennessee, Ohio).

Under this plan, all states then admitted to the Union would be incorporated in
the circuit system and the vacancy created by Duvall's resignation would be filled
with a justice from—and a justice who would ride circuit in—the new Western
circuit. With this new circuit effectively replacing the old Fourth Circuit, the number of circuits would remain at seven and, thus, the number of seats on the Court
would remain at seven as well. Delaware and Maryland would no longer receive
their own justice; rather, they would share one with New Jersey and Pennsylvania.[127] Thus, to the extent that Jackson felt bound by the norm of geographically
representative appointments, the proposed fusion of the Third and Fourth Circuits
effectively prohibited the appointment of a resident of New Jersey, Pennsylvania,
Delaware, or Taney's home state of Maryland to the Court.[128]

[125] Atkinson, *Leaving the Bench*, 28. See also Irving Dillard, "Gabriel Duvall," in *The Justices of the
United States Supreme Court 1789–1969: Their Lives and Major Opinions*, vol. 1, ed. Leon Friedman and
Fred L. Israel (New York: Chelsea House, 1969), 427; and Ward, *Deciding to Leave*, 60.

[126] 11 *Cong. Deb.* 287–88 (1835) (Theodore Frelinghuysen).

[127] In turn, Duvall's Fourth Circuit responsibilities would revert to the Third Circuit justice, Henry
Baldwin of Pennsylvania, who was said (perhaps surprisingly, perhaps falsely) to "most cheerfully accept the proposed delegation of more extended duties." 11 *Cong. Deb.* 288 (1835) (Theodore Frelinghuysen). Notably, since Frelinghuysen himself was from New Jersey, his plan effectively diminished
the chances that a resident of his state would be appointed to a vacancy on the Court and reduced the
amount of time spent in New Jersey by the justice assigned to its circuit. His willingness to do this, then,
suggests the depth of enmity Whigs felt toward Taney.

[128] Daniel Webster, having moved from the House to the Senate in 1827, privately confirmed that this
was at least a welcome consequence, if not an explicit goal, of the Whigs' consolidation plan. See Daniel
Webster to Jeremiah Mason, February 1, 1835, quoted in Warren, *The Supreme Court in United States
History*, 1:800n2: "Mr. Taney's case is not yet decided. A movement is contemplated to annex Delaware
and Maryland to Judge Baldwin's Circuit and make a Circuit in the West for the Judge now to be ap-

In sum, Democrats and Whigs each sought judicial reform for both performance and political reasons. On the level of performance, the two parties agreed that the extension of the circuit system to the West and some level of Western representation on the Supreme Court was a necessity. On the level of politics, however, the two parties vigorously disagreed, with Democrats seeking additional Court vacancies for Jackson to fill and Whigs desperately working to thwart the creation of those vacancies. The prospect of additional Court vacancies and the possibility of a Court dominated by Jackson appointees thus dominated debates about judicial reform during the early to mid-1830s. To the extent that Democrats and Whigs expressed any concern about the actual mechanics of the rival reform plans—the number of new circuits or the arrangement of states within those circuits, for instance—they did so largely because such mechanics had potentially transformative effects for the character of the Supreme Court and the future of federal judicial power more generally.

The Whigs' Last Stab

Though Jackson encouraged judicial reform on multiple occasions in the early 1830s, a slim Democratic Senate edge (25–23) in the Twenty-First Congress (1829–31), a deadlocked Senate (24–24) in the Twenty-Second Congress (1831–33), and a Whig Senate majority (28–20) in the Twenty-Third Congress (1833–35) meant that reform authorizing new Jacksonian appointments stood little chance of success.[129] Indeed, though the Senate Judiciary Committee tackled the issue in 1829,[130] and the House debated a plan offered by Judiciary Committee Chairman James Buchanan in 1830,[131] the closest Congress came to reform prior to the Twenty-Fourth Congress (1835–37) was the Whig consolidation plan of February 1835. Offered during the lame-duck session of the Twenty-Third Congress, the plan was debated in the final month of the Whigs' Senate majority and represented their last attempt at forestalling pro-Jacksonian reform. Indeed, two months earlier, in the wake of the 1834 midterm elections, Jackson's sixth annual message suggested that judicial reform was likely to be on the agenda in the Twenty-Fourth Congress:

> It is undoubtedly the duty of Congress to place all the States on the same footing in this respect, either by the creation of an additional number of as-

pointed. If we could get rid of Mr. Taney on this ground, well and good; if not, it [Taney's confirmation] will be a close vote."

[129] In contrast to the closely divided Senate, Jacksonians in the House outnumbered the anti-Jacksonian coalition of National Republicans, Anti-Masonics, and Nullifiers by fifty-nine seats (136–77) in the Twenty-First Congress, thirty-nine seats (126–87) in the Twenty-Second Congress, and forty-six seats (143–97) in the Twenty-Third Congress.

[130] Among the alternatives considered were expanding the 1807 system, reviving the disgraced 1801 system, appointing a handful of circuit judges who would be elevated to the Supreme Court in the event of a vacancy, and staffing circuit courts exclusively with district judges. Frankfurter and Landis, *The Business of the Supreme Court*, 46.

[131] 6 *Cong. Deb.* 540–605 (1830).

sociate judges or by an enlargement of the circuits assigned to those already appointed so as to include the new States. What ever may be the difficulty in a proper organization of the judicial system so as to secure its efficiency and uniformity in all parts of the Union and at the same time to avoid such an increase of judges as would encumber the supreme appellate tribunal, it should not be allowed to weigh against the great injustice which the present operation of the system produces.[132]

To Democrats, Jackson's forceful statement, issued on the first day of the lame-duck session, was a directive to resume the campaign for new vacancies once the Senate returned to Democratic hands;[133] to Whigs it was a warning that their period of obstructing Democratic reform—and their possibilities for pursuing their own reform—was about to end. Knowing that they were about to be out of power and that Democrats were likely to succeed in packing the Court with new Jacksonian appointments, Whigs offered the consolidation plan as their last stab at judicial reform.

Despite clear political motivations—namely, preventing the creation of several new Supreme Court vacancies and foiling Jackson's appointment of Taney—on the part of the Whigs, Frelinghuysen offered performance arguments in favor of the consolidation plan. Emphasizing that it was the Whig fear of an unwieldy Court, more so than the prospect of a thoroughly Jacksonian Court, that served as the "great and serious obstacle . . . in the way of the claims of the West," Frelinghuysen maintained that consolidation circumvented the "difficulties and dangers of enlarging the Court to the number that was desired."[134] Moreover, he claimed, the plan not only remained within the structure of the 1807 system but also had the capacity to serve as a long-term corrective to the problems posed by territorial expansion and statehood admission: "Look a little further, sir, in prospect of the Territories becoming States, and requiring further provision. When the fifth circuit shall become vacant, at a far distant day, I trust, then, sir, may the States of Virginia and North Carolina, that compose it, be attached to South Carolina and Georgia; and the Western States receive the judicial labors of three justices of the Supreme Court, while the fifteen on this side of the mountains will have four—a distribution fair, equal, and just."[135] Avoiding any talk of Taney or the possibility of new Court seats, Frelinghuysen attempted to convince the Senate that he had succeeded where others failed. The consolidation plan, he argued, solved the problems of judicial structure with an eye toward both present and future as well as concessions to both Westerners who demanded judicial representation and non-Westerners who worried about a large and unruly Court. "A door is now opened,"

---

[132] Andrew Jackson, Sixth Annual Message to Congress (December 1, 1834).

[133] The Senate of the Twenty-Fourth Congress was actually evenly divided (26–26), but, with Vice President Martin Van Buren breaking ties, officially Jacksonian.

[134] 11 *Cong. Deb.* 288 (1835) (Theodore Frelinghuysen).

[135] Ibid.

he hopefully remarked, "by which all these dangers are avoided, and a full and healthful operation shall be given to our judicial system."[136]

Westerners, however, saw more problems than solutions. Even setting aside their most visceral objection—that the consolidation plan would provide only one Western circuit (and only one Western justice)[137]—Westerners failed to see Frelinghuysen's plan as either a permanent solution or a quick fix. As one of the West's more prominent politicians, Missouri's Thomas Hart Benton, for instance, objected to the size of the new circuits under Frelinghuysen's plan, commenting, "It gave them a judicial circuit which was to extend—where? Why, almost from the Gulf of Mexico to Lake Michigan—from the torrid to the frigid zone; and a term was to be held once a year. The senator had better at once have proposed that a court should be held once in twenty or thirty years."[138] With such a sprawling circuit area to cover and not much time to cover it, Benton sarcastically wondered if "the judge might, in his journeys south, be transported by one of those flights of wild geese which periodically emigrate from the north, if he could manage to have his car attached to them."[139] In addition, he complained that the senators from Indiana, Illinois, and Alabama—all states affected by Frelinghuysen's plan—were not consulted,[140] that such an important measure was "brought up here during a short session, and at the eleventh hour,"[141] and that the plan deprived Louisiana—with its French-inspired civil law system—of having a circuit justice who could understand its laws.[142] As an alternative, Benton proposed establishing a Southwestern circuit composed of Louisiana, Alabama, and Mississippi; adding an eighth justice to the Court; and waiting until the census of 1840 before attending to the other Western states.[143]

Understanding that the Whig plan was simply a convenient way of disrupting the president's pending nomination of Taney to replace Duvall on the Court and eagerly awaiting their own return to the majority, non-Western Democrats in the Senate joined their Western colleagues in mobilization against consolidation.[144] Whether genuine or simply masking their desire to create new seats that would be filled by Jackson, Southerners, in particular, were vociferous in their opposition: Louisiana's Alexander Porter seconded Benton's worry about the absence of

---

[136] Ibid.

[137] Since Westerners had objected to the idea of *two* circuits (and two justices) in 1826, it should be no surprise that they strongly objected to the idea of *one* circuit (and one justice) in 1835.

[138] 11 *Cong. Deb.* 584 (1835) (Thomas Hart Benton).

[139] 11 *Cong. Deb.* 585 (1835) (Thomas Hart Benton). See also 11 *Cong. Deb.* 589–90 (1835) (George M. Bibb).

[140] 11 *Cong. Deb.* 584 (1835) (Thomas Hart Benton): "It is the first time in the history of the American Senate, of a bill having been framed, making provision for three entire States, without consultation with the six Senators of those States".

[141] 11 *Cong. Deb.* 584–85 (1835) (Thomas Hart Benton).

[142] 11 *Cong. Deb.* 585 (1835) (Thomas Hart Benton).

[143] 11 *Cong. Deb.* 585–86 (1835) (Thomas Hart Benton).

[144] For a summary of the surrounding politics, including Jackson's broken promise to appoint another man to Duvall's seat, see Warren, *The Supreme Court in United States History*, 1:797–820.

a justice who understood Louisiana's civil law system[145]; Alabama's John P. King preferred circuit organization to remain "permanent in character";[146] Mississippi's John Black threatened to abstain voting for the appointment of judges until the West was fully included in the circuit system.[147] Following his complaint with a suggestion, Pennsylvania's James Buchanan argued that the proposed Western circuit was "far too extensive" with too many court sessions "very remote from each other" and instead proposed adding one Western circuit and one Southwestern circuit for a total of nine.[148]

In response to Buchanan's plan, Frelinghuysen, fearing the effects of allowing Jackson to fill two new justiceships (in addition to Duvall's vacant seat) and still hoping to preempt Taney's appointment, promptly offered an amendment to fuse his idea for combining the Third and Fourth Circuits with Buchanan's plan for two new circuits.[149] While still providing a circuit and justice for both the West and the Southwest, this revised plan would have reduced the number of circuits and justices from nine (under Buchanan's plan) to eight, limited Jackson to two (rather than three) new appointments, and prevented Taney's appointment. After passing the Senate with a surprisingly bipartisan 36–10 vote in late February 1835,[150] the modified consolidation plan moved on to the House with precisely one week left in the Twenty-Third Congress. Following a short debate about whether the measure should be committed to the Judiciary Committee or the Committee of the Whole, the House opted for the latter,[151] but the bill was not actually debated until March 3—the final day of the session—and, even then, the House was preoccupied with interchamber negotiations over an appropriations bill.[152] With substantial disagreement about the Senate plan—Kentucky's Benjamin Hardin wanted nine circuits rather than eight,[153] Maryland's Francis Thomas referred to the consolidation of the Third and Fourth Circuits as a "monstrous injustice" against the people of his state,[154] New York's Samuel Beardsley suggested constituting his state as its own circuit[155]—and other matters in need of attention, the House simply tabled the reform bill, foreclosing yet another opportunity at substantial judicial institution building.[156]

As in the 1820s, then, judicial institution building in the early to mid-1830s was characterized by failure; as in the 1820s, the interaction of divided govern-

[145] 11 *Cong. Deb.* 587–88 (1835) (Alexander Porter).

[146] 11 *Cong. Deb.* 589 (1835) (John P. King).

[147] 11 *Cong. Deb.* 590 (1835) (John Black).

[148] 11 *Cong. Deb.* 591–92 (1835) (James Buchanan).

[149] 11 *Cong. Deb.* 593 (1835) (Theodore Frelinghuysen).

[150] 11 *Cong. Deb.* 594 (1835).

[151] 11 *Cong. Deb.* 1647, 1649 (1835).

[152] 11 *Cong. Deb.* 1646 (1835) (Benjamin Hardin).

[153] Ibid.

[154] 11 *Cong. Deb.* 1646 (1835) (Francis Thomas).

[155] 11 *Cong. Deb.* 1654–55 (1835) (Samuel Beardsley).

[156] On the very same day, the Senate voted to postpone indefinitely Taney's nomination as associate justice; it would confirm him as chief justice the following year.

ment and the structure imposed by the Judiciary Act of 1807—a structure that divided reform coalitions between those who were members of the president's party and those who were members of the opposition party—was once again largely responsible for that failure. Seeking to capitalize on their lame-duck majority, Senate Whigs pushed a modified version of judicial reform that would have denied Jackson a handful of new appointments, but House Democrats, realizing that their compatriots would reclaim control of the Senate in just a few weeks, strategically delayed consideration of the Whig plan until the last day of the session before killing it. With Whigs in control of the lame-duck Senate in the Twenty-Third Congress, judicial reform that offered new judicial vacancies for Jackson to fill was improbable; with Democrats in control of the House and set to regain control of the Senate in the Twenty-Fourth Congress, judicial reform that did not offer new judicial vacancies for Jackson to fill was equally improbable. Not least since Westerners remained dissatisfied with their continued exclusion from the circuit system and their lack of adequate representation on the Supreme Court, Whigs and Democrats agreed about the desirability of extending the circuit system to the West, but until they also agreed about the desirability (or lack thereof) of consolidating the Jacksonian majority on the Supreme Court (or until one party controlled the White House and both houses of Congress and thus could overcome partisan disagreement while appealing to Westerners at the same time), performance-oriented judicial reform remained trapped within a debate about the politics of prospective appointments.

The End of an Era and the End of the Stalemate, 1836–1849

By the time Martin Van Buren was set to succeed Andrew Jackson as president in March 1837, the campaign to reform the judiciary had lasted three decades. Precisely thirty years earlier, the Judiciary Act of 1807 had created the first Western judicial circuit and provided for the first Western justice. Four presidents (Madison, Monroe, Adams, and Jackson), a war (the War of 1812), a financial crisis (the Panic of 1819), and a sectional dispute (the Nullification Crisis) later, that system of seven circuits and seven justices remained unchanged, in large part due to the details of the authorizing act. Indeed, by establishing a link between the number of circuits in the judicial system and the number of justices on the Supreme Court as well as a norm of geographic representation on the Court, the 1807 system had obstructed numerous future attempts at modification. Though repeatedly proposed and frequently debated, attempts to extend the circuit system to the West were continuously foiled. With the possibility of new Court appointments dangling in front of political actors and the future character of constitutional jurisprudence in the balance, the issue of judicial reform had seemingly reached a stalemate.

In the midst of this stalemate, in the midst of the series of false starts and close calls that characterized judicial institution building throughout the eras of Jeffersonian and Jacksonian democracy, an unexpected thing happened at the close of the Twenty-Fourth Congress in 1837: the House and Senate actually agreed on a plan for judicial reform, the president signed it, and the judicial system was—at long last!—revised and extended to include the Western states. The Judiciary Act of 1837,[157] the most sweeping reform of the circuit system since 1801, added two new circuits to the federal judicial system and two new (geographically unrestricted) justices to the Supreme Court, bringing the total of circuits and justices to nine each. Doing so required slight geographic reorganization of existing circuits,[158] but the result was that, for the first time since Louisiana joined the Union in 1812, every state—twenty-six in all—was included in the circuit system. Although this reform, or variants of it, had been stalled repeatedly throughout the 1820s and '30s, a combination of four events—the Democratic Senate victories in the 1834 midterm elections, Van Buren's victory over William Henry Harrison in the 1836 presidential election, the admission of Arkansas to the Union in 1836, and the admission of Michigan to the Union in 1837—finally catalyzed transformative action in 1837. As subsequent decades would demonstrate, the product of that action was nothing less than the creation of the Court that would safeguard slavery, anger Abraham Lincoln, and push the nation ever closer to the brink of Civil War.

Consolidating the Jacksonian Judiciary

While the performance-oriented desire to fix the structural problems that had plagued the federal judiciary since the Jefferson administration was undoubtedly a factor in prompting judicial reform, legislators sought reform when they did because of political concerns. That is to say, while extending the circuit system to the excluded Western states was still on the minds of legislators, judicial reform was pursued in 1837 primarily because Democrats hoped to consolidate the Jacksonian takeover of the Supreme Court. The Court, after all, had gradually grown more Jacksonian during the 1830s as Jackson consistently replaced Federalist and National Republican justices with Democratic ones. Indeed, with four deaths (Robert Trimble in 1828, Bushrod Washington in 1829, William Johnson in 1834, and John Marshall in 1835) and one resignation (Gabriel Duval in 1835) over the first seven years of his presidency, Jackson had the opportunity to fill five high court vacancies prior to the Judiciary Act of 1837.

On all five occasions, Jackson followed Jefferson's precedent of geographic representation, though it was not always as simple as replacing the departing justice with an individual residing in the same circuit. Trimble, who had filled the "Kentucky seat" previously held by Thomas Todd, was replaced by former postmaster general John McLean, a resident of Ohio rather than Kentucky, but a resident

---

[157] 5 Stat. 176 (March 3, 1837).

[158] Ohio remained in the Seventh Circuit, joined by Indiana, Illinois, and newly admitted Michigan; Kentucky and Tennessee were moved from the Seventh Circuit to the Eighth Circuit, where they were joined by Missouri; and Louisiana, Mississippi, Alabama, and Arkansas were established as the Ninth Circuit.

of a Seventh Circuit state all the same. Washington, an Adams appointee whose time on the Court exceeded even that of Marshall's, was replaced by Pennsylvania's Henry Baldwin, a supporter of Jackson's 1828 presidential bid and a moderate politician whose appointment corrected a nearly three-decade-old geographic imbalance caused by the appointment of Virginia's Washington to replace Pennsylvania's James Wilson in 1799.[159] Johnson, the justice who had defied Jefferson in the embargo dispute, was replaced by James Wayne, a congressman and former judge from Georgia. Marshall, the chief spokesman of the Court's nationalism, was replaced in the Court's center chair by Maryland's Roger Taney. Finally, Duvall, who had resigned (with some gentle encouragement from Jackson) due to deafness, and who Jackson had originally tried to replace with Taney only to have the Senate postpone consideration of the nomination (and attempt to eliminate the seat entirely), was replaced by Virginian Philip Barbour, a former Speaker of the House. Demonstrating the strength of the post-1807 norm of geographically representative appointments particularly clearly, Taney and Barbour arrived as a coupling, with Jackson, foiled in his first attempt to place Taney on the Court but determined to succeed on the second try, naming a Virginian (Barbour) to replace a Marylander (Duvall) in order to balance his simultaneous decision to name a Marylander (Taney) to replace a Virginian (Marshall).

With this gradual but consistent replacement of the Court's members, the later Marshall Court and then the Taney Court became more likely to limit the sphere of central government authority, carve out greater room for the exercise of state police power, and shift the emphasis of the Court's work from protecting individual property rights to providing for the welfare of the general community.[160] Recognizing that Democratic justices could shape the constitutional landscape in a way that advanced their regime goals, Democrats were willing, eager, and suddenly able to guarantee that their appointees remained the majority, to extend the reach of Democratic ideology further into the future, and to make it virtually impossible for their Whig opponents (should they ever become the majority) to balance the Court by adding more seats. Indeed, by converting a three-member majority (five Democrats out of seven justices) into a five-member majority (seven Democrats out of nine justices), Democrats hoped to ensure that the Court's decisions remained favorable to Jacksonian aims for a prolonged period of time.

Despite the renewed Democratic desire for reform, both pragmatic and political constraints plagued institution building. Pragmatically, reform was inhibited by the fact that judicial organization was often left for the end of the legislative

[159] Although Adams's appointment was geographically "inappropriate" in the sense that it left the Court with two Fifth Circuit justices and no Third Circuit justice for three decades, it occurred before the 1807 norm of geographic representation was established.

[160] For evidence that such changes did indeed occur, see *Mayor of New York v. Miln*, 36 U.S. 102 (1837) (upholding a state law ostensibly regulating interstate commerce as a constitutional exercise of the state's "police power" to protect the health, safety, and welfare of its citizens); *Charles River Bridge v. Warren Bridge*, 36 U.S. 420 (1837) (narrowly construing a public charter so as to deny the existence of implied exclusive rights to a private corporation in favor of the public good).

session or even the end of a particular Congress. Given the inevitable scramble in the closing days of a session to pass needed appropriations measures, arrange conferences with the Senate over differing versions of bills, and send approved legislation to the president for his signature, the time and attention for judicial reform was limited. Politically, though the party system was still partly in flux, the Whigs had emerged as a potent minority party with a counterargument to Jacksonian and Democratic orthodoxy. With the two parties holding different policy positions on issues ranging from Indian removal to the Bank of the United States, they held different preferences about the types of judges that should be appointed to the Court. And, with the 1807 link between circuits and justices inextricably linking judicial reform to additional Court appointments, Whigs were hesitant to provide Jackson an opportunity to pack the Court with Democrats.[161] Embroiled in the familiar politics of patronage appointments and against the backdrop of dwindling legislative time, judicial reform remained stalled until the final months of the Twenty-Fourth (1835-1837) Congress.[162]

The Sudden Whig Surrender

When reform ultimately occurred on the last day of Jackson's presidency in 1837, it did so quietly rather than contentiously, with Democrats quickly pushing a bill through both houses of Congress and onto the president's desk with nary an obstacle or even a word of opposition from their Whig rivals.[163] While the historical record on Whig thinking about and intentions surrounding this episode is remarkably thin, it seems likely, given the Whig political outlook at the time, that some combination of three motivations—resignation, nobility, and strategy[164]— were instrumental in compelling the sudden Whig surrender.[165]

[161] See Nettels, "The Mississippi Valley and the Federal Judiciary," 225, referring to the Whigs' "hostility to allowing President Jackson to appoint the new judges and thereby determine the character of the Court for many years to come," especially so close to the 1836 election, which Whigs hoped would catapult them back into the White House.

[162] It is also possible that Congress may have purposely delayed acting in the early to mid-1830s because the admission of three new states (Arkansas, Michigan, and Florida) seemed imminent. Ibid., 224.

[163] In terms of the actual legislative history of this landmark reform, there is little surviving record. Neither the *Register of Debates* nor the *Congressional Globe* nor the House and Senate journals indicate anything more than that the bill was proposed and passed quickly, with little deliberation in between. To the extent that biographies of the relevant actors (Jackson, Van Buren, Buchanan, Webster) mention judicial reform at all, they peculiarly omit discussion of the Judiciary Act of 1837, the one landmark Jacksonian era reform that actually succeeded.

[164] Given that Whigs (and their Federalist and National Republican predecessors) had been engaged in these sorts of political battles for years, cluelessness—which is often an explanation for how meaningful judicial reform is accomplished—seems unlikely in this instance. On the other hand, with the Whig decision to surrender looking foolish and naive in retrospect, it is not clear the extent to which the party's thinking should be treated as particularly astute.

[165] Unfortunately, the scantiness of both primary and secondary literature on the subject—indeed, even the definitive history of the Whigs, Holt's nearly 1,000-page *The Rise and Fall of the American*

First, having lost control of the Senate in the 1834 midterm elections, there was, in a pragmatic sense, relatively little Whigs could do to obstruct Democratic will. Although Whigs could have engaged in dilatory techniques, the partisan balance was such that even delay would eventually be overcome, regardless of how much, how loudly, or how persuasively they resisted. Besides, by that point, Jackson had already appointed five of the seven justices—only Madison appointee Joseph Story and Monroe appointee Smith Thompson remained from the National Republican epoch—so "there no longer existed the fear that the addition of two new judges would change the complexion of the Court."[166] In other words, with or without new appointments, the direction of the Court seemed clear, and there was no longer anything Jackson's opponents could do to stop it. In this line of thinking, Whigs surrendered because there was no sense in fighting when they were almost certainly destined to lose anyway.

Second, with the prospect of Van Buren's defeat of William Henry Harrison in the presidential election of 1836 guaranteeing four more years of Democratic rule (thus dashing Whig hopes of filling any new justiceships themselves), there was some concern that expansion of the circuit system to the West could not be delayed until a Whig occupied the White House,[167] a point brought into stark relief by the admission to the Union of Arkansas (in June 1836) and Michigan (in January 1837), the seventh and eighth states excluded from the circuit system. In the thirty years that had passed since the creation of the original Seventh Circuit, nine new states had been incorporated into the nation, but only Maine had fully been incorporated into the federal judicial system. In addition to emphasizing the legislative inaction of the 1820s and '30s, the admission of new states underscored the fact that, though a solution had not yet been found, the problem would not soon go away—indeed, without action, it would only get worse. The previous years had witnessed massive growth in trade, finance, and transportation in the Western states; factories had been built, canals dug, crops planted.[168] Yet while the need for the administration of justice inevitably grew, the apparatus for administering justice remained as it had been when the nation barely extended into Appalachia. The admission of new states, therefore, brought with it not only a reminder of past failures and renewed calls for reform but also a concrete increase in judicial

Whig Party, lacks a single reference to either the reform or the debate surrounding it—forecloses the possibility of carefully and systematically adjudicating between these motivations.

[166] Nettels, "The Mississippi Valley and the Federal Judiciary," 225.

[167] Ironically, Whig political fortunes improved considerably not long after the passage of the Judiciary Act of 1837. Owing in part to the Panic of 1837, Whigs made gains in the 1838 midterm elections for both the House and Senate, even coming to control the House Judiciary Committee (as the minority party, no less!) for a period in 1838–39. Two years later, in a rematch of the 1836 presidential contest, Harrison defeated Van Buren, meaning that Whigs would have needed to delay only four more years—a period during which no other states were admitted—to have one of their own serve as president. Of course, since Harrison died exactly one month after he took office and his successor John Tyler repeatedly clashed with Whig leaders, the party controlled the presidency for only a brief moment.

[168] See, for instance, Frederick Jackson Turner, *The Frontier in American History* (New York: Holt, 1920), which includes Turner's famous essay "The Significance of the Frontier in American History."

business that could not be left unaddressed for much longer. In this line of thinking, Whigs surrendered because circuit disparities were sufficiently egregious and Western states sufficiently frustrated that they could not bear to stand in the way of much-needed and long-desired change simply because it would yield two new Supreme Court appointments for a Democratic president.

Third, with Western population steadily rising—increasing almost twelvefold since 1800, a period during which Northern population only tripled and Southern population barely doubled—and the recognition that a "union of sentiment" (as Webster phrased it in 1826) with the West would be desirable in various ways, Whigs no doubt saw strategic value in placating Western politicians. Whether because of the possibility of a Whig rebirth in Western states or because a friendly Western bloc could only serve to advantage the North vis-à-vis the South, Whigs may have seen serving Western interests (even if it also meant satisfying, at least on this particular issue, Democratic and Southern interests) as a short-term sacrifice for the potential of a long-term gain. In this line of thinking, Whigs surrendered because the costs of giving Jackson two new appointments in 1837 were considerably less than the costs of alienating Westerners when their support might be needed in larger battles for years to come.

Whether out of resignation, nobility, or strategy, the Whig surrender in early 1837 enabled landmark reform to overcome the multitude of pragmatic and political constraints upon it. Perhaps under different circumstances, an entrepreneur—a man like then senator James Buchanan, who was perhaps uniquely equipped with the knowledge, experience, reputation, affiliations, and networks to usher institutional transformation through a contested political environment—might have emerged to negotiate those constraints, but the two decades of failed reforms that preceded the Judiciary Act of 1837 meant that there were few new ideas to pursue and few new tactics with which to pursue them. Indeed, Buchanan himself had attempted reform on multiple occasions[169]—actively campaigning for Webster's reform bill as a young House member in 1826, putting forth his own plan as House Judiciary Committee chairman in 1830, and then leading the charge against Frelinghuysen's consolidation plan as a senator in 1836—without much success.[170] Though characterized by consensus about the need for improvements in the administration of justice, debates about judicial reform in the Jacksonian era were sufficiently replete with clashes over rival political goals that only the arrival of unified Democratic government, the slow erosion of Western patience, and the Whig realization that reform was either inevitable, necessary, or desirable were able to shatter the stalemate that had surrounded the subject for three decades.

---

[169] Frankfurter and Landis, *The Business of the Supreme Court*, 44n23, also credit Buchanan with leading the charge against an 1831 attempt to repeal the perpetually controversial Section 25 of the Judiciary Act of 1789. For a deconstruction of that argument, see Graber, "James Buchanan as Savior?"

[170] Though Frelinghuysen's consolidation plan was ultimately defeated, it was killed by the House rather than the Senate, so any "credit" for preventing it properly belongs with House Democrats rather than with Buchanan.

The Making of the Southern Slaveholding Supreme Court

The partisan alignment of both houses of Congress and the president—and the subsequent convergence of legislative and executive preferences about new Supreme Court vacancies—resulted in two new circuits, two new justices, and a wholesale reorganization of the circuit system. Three decades in the making, it was the most significant piece of judicial institution building since the repealed Judiciary Act of 1801. Yet, in terms of lasting effects on the exercise of judicial power in antebellum America, the Judiciary Act of 1837 was important less because it extended the circuit system to the West than because it did so in a way that privileged not only Jacksonian Democratic interests but also Southern slaveholding ones heading into the sectional crises of the 1840s and '50s.

Consider the following: of the twenty-six states in post-1837 America, thirteen were slave states and thirteen free states,[171] but of the nine circuits in the 1837 judicial system and the nine seats on the 1837 Supreme Court, five were allotted to slave states and four to free states (with one each of the slave and free circuits devoted to Western states).[172] In fact, of virtually all the circuit arrangements considered in the 1820s and '30s, the one implemented in 1837 was the single most favorable to slaveholding interests. The only scenario in which slave states would have fully composed more circuits was Daniel Webster's 1826 reform proposal. Under that plan, slave states would have fully composed six circuits, but, with the newly created seats set to be filled by John Quincy Adams, a president decidedly less concerned with Southern sensibilities than Andrew Jackson, the likely appointees may not have proved reliably proslavery. Instead, with the statutory creation of the Court's eight and ninth seats occurring in 1837, Jackson was given the opportunity to fill the sixth and seventh high court vacancies of his presidency and to buttress the Court's existing Jacksonian majority with two Democratic—and, likely, proslavery—appointees. Though he was only able to fill one of these two new seats (appointing John Catron from his own home state of Tennessee),[173] Jackson's six

---

[171] The slave states were Alabama, Arkansas, Delaware, Georgia, Kentucky, Louisiana, Maryland, Mississippi, Missouri, North Carolina, South Carolina, Tennessee, and Virginia; the free states were Connecticut, Illinois, Indiana, Maine, Massachusetts, Michigan, New Hampshire, New Jersey, New York, Ohio, Pennsylvania, Rhode Island, and Vermont. By 1849, the additions of slave states Florida (1845) and Texas (1845) and free states Iowa (1846) and Wisconsin (1848) had raised the numbers of slave and free states to fifteen each.

[172] The slave circuits were the Fourth (Delaware, Maryland), Fifth (North Carolina, Virginia), Sixth (Georgia, South Carolina), Eighth (Kentucky, Missouri, Tennessee), and Ninth (Alabama, Arkansas, Louisiana, Mississippi); the free circuits were the First (Maine, Massachusetts, New Hampshire, Rhode Island), Second (Connecticut, New York, Vermont), Third (New Jersey, Pennsylvania), and Seventh (Illinois, Indiana, Michigan, Ohio).

[173] Catron's confirmation actually occurred during the initial days of Van Buren's presidency, but his name was placed into nomination by Jackson, so he is usually considered a Jackson appointee. Jackson offered the second seat to former South Carolina Senator and Democratic vice presidential candidate William Smith, but Smith declined to serve. As a result, that seat was filled by Jackson's successor, Martin Van Buren, who chose Alabama Senator John McKinley.

Table 3.2.
Circuit Organization and Supreme Court Representation
Judiciary Act of 1837

Circuit	States	Supreme Court Justice
First	Maine, Massachusetts, New Hampshire, Rhode Island	Joseph Story (MA)
Second	Connecticut, New York, Vermont	Smith Thompson (NY)
Third	New Jersey, Pennsylvania	Henry Baldwin (PA)*
Fourth	Delaware, Maryland	Roger Taney (MD)*
Fifth	Virginia, North Carolina	Philip Barbour (VA)*
Sixth	Georgia, South Carolina	James Wayne (GA)*
Seventh	Illinois, Indiana, Michigan, Ohio	John McLean (OH)*
Eighth	Kentucky, Missouri, Tennessee	John Catron (TN)*
Ninth	Alabama, Arkansas, Louisiana, Mississippi	John McKinley (AL)*

Note: *Indicates a Jackson—or, in the case of McKinley, a Van Buren—appointee.

appointments—the third-most of any president in American history[174]—served a combined 138 years on the bench, with four of them lasting into the Civil War. Even with the Court's ninth seat still vacant, Jackson left office having appointed six of the Court's eight members. Viewed in these terms, it becomes clear that the Judiciary Act of 1837 marked more than the culmination of the long-standing campaign to reform the circuit system; indeed, it also marked the culmination of the Jacksonian reconstitution of the federal judiciary.

Rather than merely an instance of partisan entrenchment by Democrats, the Jacksonian reconstitution was enabled, first and foremost, by Westerners. It was Western insistence on three (as opposed to two) new justices for the Court and the placement of Ohio and Kentucky in separate circuits, not proto-Jacksonian resistance to granting new seats to Adams, that killed reform in 1826. It was Western opposition to the consolidation plan because it provided for only one additional Western circuit as much as or more than it was Democratic anger about the transparent Whig attempt to keep Taney off the Court that doomed reform in 1835. In both instances, the Western influence suggests that the appointment politics—or, perhaps more accurately, the *pre*appointment" politics—of antebellum America

[174] Together with William Howard Taft, who appointed six justices in just his one term as president, Jackson trails only George Washington, who appointed eleven justices (including the first six all at once), and Franklin Roosevelt, who—after being denied the opportunity to name a new member to the Court in his first term—spread nine appointments over his second and third terms in the White House. Abraham Lincoln and Dwight Eisenhower each appointed five justices.

were more forcefully driven by geography than partisanship, that the debates over judicial reform were not simply (or even mostly) a matter of one party against the other. By effectively exercising a veto in both 1826 and 1835, Westerners delayed reform until the point when Northern-sympathizing Whigs were no longer in power and no longer able to prevent Southern-sympathizing Democrats from simultaneously providing Westerners with the representation they desired and exploiting the system to their own advantage. Indeed, throughout this period, it is clear that Westerners, a powerful enough constituency to facilitate or forestall legislative action, were simply looking for the plan that promised them the greatest influence and most meaningful representation; as a result, they were willing to support either a Whig plan or a Democratic plan if it satisfied their desires and interests. While which plan (Northern or Southern) Westerners accepted mattered little to the West or its fortunes, the decision did have enormous ramifications for whether the system as a whole would benefit the North, as it later would under Lincoln, or the South, as it imminently would under Jackson.

Judicial reform did not end in 1837. Indeed, as the judicial system transitioned from seven circuits comprising seventeen states to nine circuits comprising twenty-six states, it required further institutional modification,[175] administrative housekeeping,[176] and sundry performance reforms.[177] In response to an increase in both circuit and Supreme Court work and inevitable rumblings about the inadequacy of the existing system,[178] legislators introduced resolutions about studying the judicial system and proposed bills to revise the circuit system further,[179] but, as had been the case since 1801, circuit riding endured. Congress did, how-

[175] In a flurry of institution building during 1842, for example, Congress extended the judicial procedure established by the Judiciary Act of 1789 to all states admitted since 1828 (when Congress had last authorized such an updating), 5 Stat. 499 (August 1, 1842); expanded the power of the Supreme Court to adopt rules governing lower court procedures regarding modes of discovery, admitting evidence, and issuing decrees, 5 Stat. 518 (August 23, 1842); and empowered the Court to grant writs of habeas corpus to foreign citizens in American custody, 5 Stat. 539 (August, 29, 1842). For a summary of the extensive debate over this last bill and related issues, see David P. Currie, *The Constitution in Congress: Descent into the Maelstrom, 1829–1861* (Chicago: University of Chicago Press, 2005), 56–64.

[176] Throughout the late 1830s and '40s there were a series of acts attending to the organization and structure of district courts. Some states were awarded new districts, others had their districts separated into divisions, still more gained new cities where court sessions would be held. Urged to act by local groups and citizens desiring cheaper and easier access to the administration of justice, Congress made these changes frequently but on a state-by-state basis. See Surrency, *History of the Federal Courts*, 65–70.

[177] In 1845, Congress extended—without debate—federal admiralty jurisdiction to include lakes and navigable inland waters rather than just the high seas, 5 Stat. 726 (February 26, 1845). It was the constitutionality of this statute that the Court sustained in its controversial decision in *The Propeller Genesee Chief v. Fitzhugh*, 53 U.S. 443 (1851), which overruled the Court's earlier decision limiting admiralty jurisdiction to the "ebb and flow of the tide" in *The Steamboat Thomas Jefferson*, 23 U.S. 428 (1825).

[178] Frankfurter and Landis, *The Business of the Supreme Court*, 48–52.

[179] For a summary of these resolutions and bills, including proposals in 1848 to temporarily suspend circuit riding for one or two years, see Frankfurter and Landis, *The Business of the Supreme Court*, 48n162, 50n164, 51nn169–70.

ever, make two remedial changes related to the practice. First, largely to appease Justice John McKinley (who had complained that the Ninth Circuit—Alabama, Arkansas, Louisiana, and Mississippi—was too large for one justice to cover[180]) and Martin Van Buren (whose third annual message to Congress suggested a remedy for the "great inequality in the amount of labor assigned to each judge"),[181] it redistributed the delicate circuit organization of states by shifting Fifth Circuit states Virginia and North Carolina into the Fourth and Sixth Circuits, respectively, and establishing Ninth Circuit states Alabama and Louisiana as the new Fifth Circuit.[182] Although this rearrangement merely shifted the organization of states within wholly slave circuits and thus did nothing to alter the balance of power between free states and slave states in the circuit system more generally, it did leave the Court with two justices (Maryland's Roger Taney and Virginia's Peter Daniel) from the slaveholding Fourth Circuit and no justice from the slaveholding Ninth Circuit, thereby disturbing the post-1807 tradition of one justice—and one justice only—from each circuit.[183] Each of the six subsequent appointments to the Court in the 1840s and '50s, however, continued to respect the post-1807 norm by replacing each departing justice with a resident of a state from the same circuit,[184] thus perpetuating the Southern advantage in the Court's membership into the Civil War.[185] Second, Congress required justices to attend only one term annually of each circuit court in their respective circuits and extended the Court's session by one month, thereby allowing the justices to spend more time disposing of the Court's many backlogged cases in the capital.[186] Both of these reforms addressed a concrete and specific problem—a geographically sprawling circuit or an overcrowded docket, for instance—but neither induced enduring changes in the character of federal judicial power. That character, of course, had been firmly

[180] Erwin C. Surrency, "A History of Federal Courts," 28 *Missouri Law Review* 221 (1963).

[181] Martin Van Buren, Third Annual Message to Congress (December 2, 1839): "The number of terms to be held in each of the courts composing the ninth circuit, the distances between the places at which they sit and from thence to the seat of Government, are represented to be such as to render it impossible for the judge of that circuit to perform in a manner corresponding with the public exigencies his term and circuit duties."

[182] 5 Stat. 507 (August 16, 1842).

[183] By separating Mississippi from Alabama and Louisiana in the Fifth Circuit, the 1842 arrangement also marked the first time in history that all the states in one circuit were noncontiguous.

[184] In sequence, John Tyler appointed Samuel Nelson to replace fellow New Yorker Smith Thompson as the Second Circuit justice in 1845; James Polk named Levi Woodbury of New Hampshire to succeed Joseph Story of Massachusetts as the First Circuit justice in 1845 and tapped Robert Grier to replace fellow Pennsylvanian Henry Baldwin in 1846; Millard Fillmore appointed Benjamin Curtis of Massachusetts to replace Woodbury in 1851; Franklin Pierce selected Alabama's John Campbell to fill the Fifth Circuit seat of John McKinley, also of Alabama, in 1853; and James Buchanan replaced Curtis with Maine's Nathan Clifford in 1858.

[185] On the sequence of events leading to the dismantling of the Southern slaveholding Court in the early 1860s, see chapter 4.

[186] 5 Stat. 576 (June 17, 1844).

established by the Judiciary Act of 1837, and it was fundamentally Jacksonian, disproportionately Southern, and undeniably slaveholding.[187]

• • •

The history of judicial institution building in the eras of Jeffersonian and Jacksonian democracy unfolded in four stages: the performance-oriented but extremely influential Judiciary Act of 1807, the stalemate over National Republican attempts to extend the circuit system to the West in the mid-1820s, the failed Whig consolidation plan of 1835, and the triumph of reform in the Judiciary Act of 1837. In examining each of these stages, I have explored both the causes and consequences of judicial institution building (or the lack thereof). As in the previous chapter, I have answered three questions about the historical period at hand: first, why judicial institution building was pursued; second, how it was accomplished; and, third, what it achieved.

Why was judicial institution building in the eras of Jeffersonian and Jacksonian democracy pursued? In 1807, it was pursued by Democrat-Republicans seeking to respond to performance problems caused by westward expansion. From the second decade of the 1800s through the late 1820s, judicial institution building was pursued by various constituencies—by proto-Whig National Republicans who sought to abolish circuit riding and empower a nationally oriented judiciary to carry out its regime commitments, by proto-Jacksonian Old Republicans who not only detested the Supreme Court's attack on state sovereignty and authorization of sweeping federal power but also wished to prevent National Republican presidents from entrenching judicial nationalism any further, and by Westerners who complained that the failure of the judiciary to keep up with the pace of territorial expansion and statehood expansion both deprived them of rightful judicial representations and caused defects in the administration of justice. In the late 1820s and 1830s, institution building was pursued by Democrats who viewed judicial expansion as a means to cement a Democratic majority on the Court, by Whigs who sought to forestall the transformation of the Court into a wholly Jacksonian institution, and by even more Westerners who amplified their earlier complaints about the operation of the judicial system.

How was judicial institution building in the eras of Jeffersonian and Jacksonian democracy accomplished? For much of the period between 1805 and 1849, institution building was not accomplished but impeded by constraints—most notably the 1807 link between circuits and justices and the subsequent legislative resistance to creating Supreme Court vacancies to be filled by a president of the opposing party. Indeed, with each party regarding seats on the Court as simply too permanent and

[187] For an elaboration of this point, see Justin Crowe, "Westward Expansion, Preappointment Politics, and the Making of the Southern Slaveholding Supreme Court," *Studies in American Political Development* 24 (2010): 90–120.

too valuable—both for their potentially lasting effect on law and policy as well as for their ability to strengthen coalitions by rewarding friends and supporters with plum positions—"to leave to its adversary,"[188] judicial reform failed more often than it succeeded. In the first significant instance of successful institution building, the Judiciary Act of 1807, landmark reform was accomplished largely because there was a concrete problem with an ostensibly simple solution and because there was seemingly a complete lack of awareness about the potential ramifications of that solution. In the second significant instance of successful institution building, the Judiciary Act of 1837, landmark reform was accomplished because Democratic victories in the 1834 midterm and 1836 presidential elections combined with the admission of two new states into the Union to force the Whigs to concede that their hope of regaining the White House could not deter reform any longer.

What did judicial institution building in the eras of Jeffersonian and Jacksonian democracy achieve? At specific moments—the embargo, the War of 1812, the Nullification Crisis—institution building resulted in the fortification of federal and executive power and a stronger synergy between party politics and judicial power, but the repeated failure to extend the circuit system mostly achieved Western frustration with a system that had long been severely and undeniably broken. Of course, with the passage of the Judiciary Act of 1837, the federal court system was extended to include the Western states and reshaped in a way that favored Democrats, Southerners, and slaveholders. Perhaps equally important is what judicial institution building during this era did not achieve: limitations on the independence of federal judges or restrictions on the exercise of judicial power. That is to say, with the same dynamics that prevented progressive reform until 1837 also inhibiting restrictive reform, the judiciary was neither built up nor torn down but, instead, preserved as it existed. Given the strong current of dissatisfaction stemming from the Court's application of Section 25 and nullification of state laws, the fact that the Court emerged from the 1840s with its authority intact (by repelling court-curbing attacks) and its capacity enhanced (by accepting ad hoc instances where Congress expanded jurisdiction or broadened the causes for removal) was a significant development. As a result, it is possible that the structural rigidity of the 1807 system may have been just as much a safeguard for judicial power as an obstacle to it.

More broadly, the troubles encountered by judicial reformers during the first half of the nineteenth century reinforce a number of general lessons about the process of judicial institution building. First and foremost, they remind us that judicial reform is difficult, and that, the flurry of activity in the early republic notwithstanding, landmark institution building is unquestionably the exception rather than the rule. Even when there is ostensibly broad support for it, institutional transformation does not happen easily; rather, it is characterized by false starts, close calls,

---

[188] Martin Van Buren to Andrew Jackson, August 7, 1834, quoted in Warren, *The Supreme Court in United States History*, 1:800n3.

unpredictable constraints, and unexpected opportunities. From one chamber of Congress refusing to submit to a conference with the other to landmark enactments passing virtually without debate, judicial reform rarely follows a traditional script or charts a preordained course. To say that judicial institution building is seldom fated, however, is not to say that it is idiosyncratic or beyond the scope of meaningful conclusions. Indeed, the fundamental lesson of the early republic—that the federal judiciary was initially built by legislators and executives looking to satisfy a variety of their own policy, political, and performance goals—continued to govern the process of building the judiciary in the eras of Jeffersonian and Jacksonian democracy. Whether the relevant partisan divide was between Federalists and Democrat-Republicans, National Republicans and Old Republicans, or Democrats and Whigs, progressive institution building was favored by leaders of the prevailing coalition and resisted by leaders of the opposing coalition.

Aside from the realization that judicial reform is difficult and the idea that judicial power is politically constructed, other insights drawn from the early republic are equally applicable to the half-century that followed it. For instance, as was the case from the First Congress through Jefferson's first term, past attempts—both successful and failed—loomed large in the politics of institution building from 1805 through 1849. Whether it was the Judiciary Act of 1801 continuing to serve as an example of how *not* to build the judiciary,[189] the Judiciary Act of 1807 establishing an overarching structure within which future issues would be debated and according to which future decisions would be made, or the Judiciary Act of 1837 providing the foundation for Southern slaveholding dominance of the Supreme Court, the legacies—the institutional residue—of landmark events served to hinder and facilitate different possibilities for action. Similarly, the importance of timing, contingency, and the surrounding political environment persisted throughout the period. For more than two decades, judicial reform was stunted by one party or faction refusing to consent to plans that would allow another party or faction to reap the benefits of additional Supreme Court appointments. Here, the identity of the president, the nature of partisan conflict, and the personalities and ambitions of key actors altered the calculus for reform. Ideas and strategies that held promise at one time under one set of circumstances provoked controversy at some other time under a different set of circumstances.

In addition to highlighting continuity with the early republic in these four realms (the difficulty of institution building, the political construction of judicial power, the precedential value of individual moments, and the critical importance of timing and contingency), the dynamics of judicial reform during the eras of Jeffersonian and Jacksonian democracy also suggest a new lesson about the process of

---

[189] See, for example, 33 *Annals of Cong.* 93 (1819) (James Barbour): "Sir, in a measure so important as this, it behooves Congress to advance with extreme caution and circumspection. This scene has already been acted in the United States. The sixteen, by some called the midnight judges, were created only to be destroyed." Arguments of this kind—cautionary tales, of a sort—were common in nearly every debate about significant judicial reform during this era.

building the judiciary. At base, that lesson is that, at least in structural and organizational terms, the judiciary does not and cannot adapt itself to sociodemographic changes through the exercise of judicial review or the disposition of constitutional cases. With the words of Article III and the legacy of the Judiciary Act of 1789 effectively placing Congress in charge of the institutional judiciary, legislators must act on behalf of courts and judges in this regard. Just as Congress must enlarge its own ranks to include representation for new states, so too must it expand the judiciary to provide for the administration of justice in new states. With the judiciary incapable of performing this self-preservationist and self-updating function itself, congressional inaction—as was the case for much of the 1820s and '30s—is almost certain to leave the judiciary outmoded, outdated, and ill-suited to the changing nation it is designed to serve. In other words, whether the first branch chooses to address the third branch or neglect it—and, perhaps more important, precisely *how* it chooses to address it or neglect it—determines, in large part, the shape and extent of judicial power.

With the 1840s coming to a close and one of the most turbulent decades in American history about to begin, the federal judiciary was not, except in isolated areas, any more powerful than it had been at the end of the early republic. It was, however, both more resilient (from having fought off attacks against its authority) and better adapted to the area and population of the rapidly expanding nation (as a result of the Judiciary Acts of 1807 and 1837). Moreover, though the role, structure, and powers of the judiciary in 1849 largely resembled those of the judiciary in 1805, the pro-Southern bias of judicial organization and the limited government emphasis of the constitutional jurisprudence that followed marked a dramatic shift in the character of the institution. By the time the first shots were fired on Fort Sumter in 1861, the judiciary—reorganized by Jacksonians, supported by antebellum Democrats, and dominated by slaveholding interests—was at the center of a firestorm over slavery and secession, over the rights of citizens and the nature of the Union. Sparking the rise of Abraham Lincoln and the birth of the Republican Party, it was a firestorm that effectively led to a wholesale reconstitution of judicial power during the Civil War and its aftermath.

The Civil War and Reconstruction

EMPOWERMENT

The twenty-eight years from the passage of the infamous Fugitive Slave Act of 1850 to the removal of Northern troops from the South in 1877 witnessed nothing less than the dissolution of one political order and the reconstitution of another.[1] From the mounting sectional tensions swirling around antebellum politics to the internecine bloodshed at Gettysburg and Antietam to the Northern division of the South into five occupied military districts, American society was in legitimate upheaval for nearly three decades. Prompted by the explosion of disagreements over slavery, states' rights, and economic development—founding-era contradictions that had simmered beneath the surface of the republic for more than a half century—the citizenry, the government, and the nation prepared (and then proceeded) to rend itself in half. As a result, the years preceding, encompassing, and following the Civil War marked the most violent, most radical, and most transformative period in American history.

Those years—the 1850s, '60s, and most of the '70s—were also some of the most formative in the development of federal judicial power. Contrary to the view that the election of Abraham Lincoln and the ascendance of Radical Republicans effectively resulted in a circumscribed and cowering Supreme Court,[2] the events of the Civil War and Reconstruction empowered rather than dismantled the federal courts.[3] Indeed, by 1877, the federal judiciary was undoubtedly transformed, but it

---

[1] For general histories of the period, see Sean Wilentz, *The Rise of American Democracy: Jefferson to Lincoln* (New York: Norton, 2005); Michael F. Holt, *The Political Crisis of the 1850s* (New York: Wiley, 1978); David M. Potter, *The Impending Crisis, 1848–1861* (New York: Harper and Row, 1976); James M. McPherson, *Battle Cry of Freedom: The Civil War Era* (Oxford: Oxford University Press, 1988); James M. McPherson, *Ordeal By Fire: The Civil War and Reconstruction* (New York: Knopf, 1982); Eric Foner, *A Short History of Reconstruction, 1863–1877* (New York: Harper and Row, 1990); and C. Vann Woodward, *Reunion and Reaction: The Compromise of 1877 and the End of Reconstruction* (New York: Oxford University Press, 1991).

[2] See, for example, Charles Warren, *The Supreme Court in United States History,* vol. 2, *1836–1918* (Boston: Little, Brown, 1926), 421–97; and Walter F. Murphy, *Congress and the Court: A Case Study in the American Political Process* (Chicago: University of Chicago Press, 1962), 35–43.

[3] This view is roughly consistent with Stanley I. Kutler, *Judicial Power and Reconstruction Politics* (Chicago: University of Chicago Press, 1968); William M. Wiecek, "The Reconstruction of Federal Judicial Power, 1863–1875," *American Journal of Legal History* 13 (1969): 333–59; and William M. Wiecek,

was transformed in a way that made it more powerful than ever before. Moreover, this empowerment was effected by Congress through statute rather than by the Court through statutory or constitutional interpretation. The Court was certainly a partner in Congress's attempt to enhance judicial power, but the justices emphatically did not make a "power grab." Instead, Republican, Northern, and nationalist politicians, recognizing that matters of judicial structure and organization had serious ramifications for slavery, the nature of the Union, and industrialization, actively fortified the judiciary as a partner against the South. With such empowerment occurring in the absence of appreciable antijudicial fervor, the Civil War and Reconstruction periods stand as evidence not of judicial weakness but, instead, of judicial resilience.

In this chapter, I examine judicial institution building from the Compromise of 1850 (admitting California into the Union as a free state and signifying the beginning of the "political crisis"[4]) to the Compromise of 1877 (settling the disputed 1876 presidential election between Samuel J. Tilden and Rutherford B. Hayes and representing the formal end of Reconstruction). Unlike the previous epoch, the Civil War and Reconstruction were frenzied periods of institution building that resulted in lasting changes to the federal judiciary. Simply put, if the judiciary at the close of the Jacksonian era was essentially the Federalist era judiciary captured by Democrats and updated to reflect the growth of the nation, then the judiciary at the close of Reconstruction was, except for the lingering problem of crowded dockets, scarcely the same institution. In seeking to explain the causes and consequences of the changes embodied in this sweeping reform of the institutional judiciary, I once again ask why judicial institution building was pursued, how it was accomplished, and what it achieved within the context of mid-nineteenth century American politics. Civil War and Reconstruction era institution building was, I argue, motivated mostly by Republicans seeking to transform and then empower the judiciary as a partner in, and enforcer of, national policy making; enabled by Northern and Republican dominance of national politics following the election of Abraham Lincoln and the secession of the Southern states; and resulted in a vast expansion of federal judicial power. This substantial empowerment of the judicial branch and the accompanying transformation of that branch from a Jacksonian-Democratic-Southern institution into a Lincolnian-Republican-Northern one occurred in four stages: first, the partisan and sectional fight over the structure of the institutional judiciary and the character of judicial power vis-à-vis slavery (1850–64); second, the Republican reliance on removal provisions and the writ of habeas corpus to protect federal officials and freed slaves from biased Southern courts immediately following the Civil War (1865–67); third, the consolidation of a Republican-friendly Supreme Court through ameliorative reforms aimed at specific problems of judicial performance (1866–69); and, fourth, the dramatic

---

"The Great Writ and Reconstruction: The Habeas Corpus Act of 1867," *Journal of Southern History* 36 (1970): 530–48.

    [4]I borrow this phrase from Holt, *The Political Crisis of the 1850s.*

nationalization of judicial power and Republican adoption of the federal judiciary as a partner in economic policy making (1870–77). After considering each stage in turn, I summarize the lessons of Civil War and Reconstruction era institution building and assess the state of the institutional judiciary as it entered the Gilded Age and approached the dawn of the twentieth century.

Slavery and the Fight for the Soul of Judicial Power, 1850–1864

Southern and Democratic suspicion of the federal judiciary was at its nadir in 1850. After all, slave states still controlled five of the nine seats on the Supreme Court, and, as a result of the pro-Southern structural bias of the Judiciary Act of 1837, knew that, even if the Southern influence on national politics was diminishing (and with population shifts from the South to the North and West, that seemed a likely development), the South would maintain a strong foothold in the Court. With Southern justices guaranteed—regardless of the nominating president and the confirming Senate—to be replaced by other Southerners, the Court, once viewed antagonistically by Jefferson and cautiously by Jackson, had effectively been converted into a Democratic institution.[5] In fact, by the time California was admitted to the Union in September 1850, all nine of the Court's justices had been appointed by Democratic presidents.[6] Since the Court was favorably predisposed toward their interests, Democrats were willing to empower it to settle controversial debates—particularly on the issue of slavery.[7]

As perhaps the only issue capable of single-handedly disturbing the Second Party System, slavery was a subject that Jacksonian era moderates had long sought to remove from national electoral politics.[8] To this end, Democrats and Whigs alike encouraged and actively attempted to facilitate judicial resolution of the slavery question on multiple occasions. In 1848, for example, the Senate passed a bill (the so-called Clayton Compromise) permitting the appeal of all slavery-related cases from territorial courts directly to the Supreme Court, but the legislation was tabled in the House. The Compromise of 1850 and the Kansas-Nebraska Act of 1854 each allowed appeals on slavery questions to be taken to the Court regardless of the monetary value of the suit. Throughout the late 1840s and early 1850s, politi-

---

[5]See chapter 3; and Justin Crowe, "Westward Expansion, Preappointment Politics, and the Making of the Southern Slaveholding Supreme Court," *Studies in American Political Development* 24 (2010): 90–120.

[6]This counts John Tyler, who, after succeeding William Henry Harrison as president in April 1841, appointed one justice (New York's Samuel Nelson). Although Tyler had been elected on the Whig ticket, he had been a lifelong Democrat-Republican and broke with the Whigs soon after becoming president.

[7]On the "constitutional politics of slavery," see Mark A. Graber, *Dred Scott and the Politics of Constitutional Evil* (Cambridge: Cambridge University Press, 2006), 91–171.

[8]Mark A. Graber, "The Nonmajoritarian Difficulty: Legislative Deference to the Judiciary," *Studies in American Political Development* 7 (1993): 35–73.

cians such as Stephen Douglas and Sam Houston framed the slavery question as a constitutional (rather than "political") one and argued that national leaders were powerless to settle it.[9] Assuming that the Democratic-dominated Court of Roger Taney would agree with them, and reasoning that political resolution of the issue would serve only to weaken party unity, Democrats simply made the Court the "national institution responsible for choosing between antislavery, proslavery, and popular sovereignty policies."[10]

As Democrats delegated resolution of the slavery dispute to the federal judiciary, westward expansion and population growth continued to exact their toll on judicial performance. California's statehood meant that the nation officially stretched from the Atlantic seaboard—traversing Appalachia, the Mississippi River, the Great Plains, and the Rocky Mountains—to the Pacific Ocean. Across this yawning area, the federal judiciary was "carrying a load beyond its capacity."[11] Given the number and distribution of judges, there were simply too many cases to hear and too large a landmass to travel in order to hear them. In response, President Franklin Pierce, whose first annual message to Congress declared federal judicial organization "confessedly inadequate,"[12] presented to the Thirty-Third Congress (1853–55) a judicial reform plan meticulously prepared by Attorney General Caleb Cushing.[13] Attempting to provide the judiciary with the means to dispose of its increasing business without upsetting the Western attachment to judicial representation, Cushing's plan formally retained circuit riding but recommended the appointment of a separate set of nine circuit judges to ease the burden of circuit work on Supreme Court justices. With extensive experience in both Massachusetts and the federal government as well as a concerted effort to consult justices and lobby influential legislators,[14] Cushing possessed both the identity and tactics necessary for successful political entrepreneurship, but the absence of suitable ideas— namely, a compromise on sectional disagreements over circuit riding (the North and South wanted to abolish the practice, the West demanded it continue)—and a proposed amendment by then Ohio senator and future chief justice Salmon Chase to reduce the size of the Court (supported by the North, opposed by the South and West) prevented the bill's passage.

---

[9] Ibid., 47.

[10] Ibid., 48. See also Don E. Fehrenbacher, *The Dred Scott Case: Its Significance in American Law and Politics* (New York: Oxford University Press, 1978); and Wallace Mendelson, "Dred Scott's Case— Reconsidered," 38 *Minnesota Law Review* 16 (1953–54).

[11] Felix Frankfurter and James M. Landis, *The Business of the Supreme Court: A Study in the Federal Judicial System* (New York: Macmillan, 1928), 52.

[12] Franklin Pierce, First Annual Message to Congress (December 5, 1853).

[13] For an account of the origins of and debate over the Cushing plan, see Kermit L. Hall, "Federal Judicial Reform and Proslavery Constitutional Theory: A Retrospect on the Butler Bill," *American Journal of Legal History* 17 (1973): 166–84.

[14] While drafting his plan, Cushing sought the advice of Supreme Court Justice Benjamin Curtis; while attempting to steer it through Congress, he carefully courted the support of Senate Judiciary Committee chairman Andrew Pickens Butler of South Carolina and Western Democratic leader Stephen Douglas of Illinois.

After failing to overhaul the system completely, Congress offered two smaller innovations in early 1855: the creation of a separate California circuit,[15] and the establishment of a Court of Claims.[16] Both reforms were stopgap measures directed at specific problems of judicial performance. The California Circuit, for instance, was created because the state's two district courts, each of which wielded district court, circuit court, and specialized jurisdiction,[17] were severely overburdened with cases. Given the size, distance, and caseload of California, it would have been impossible to include it in any other circuit, so Congress created a new one. It structured that circuit in such a way, however, that sharply distinguished it from the nine existing circuits in the federal judicial system. Although it exercised the same jurisdiction as all other circuits, it received neither a numbered designation nor an additional Supreme Court justice to staff it.[18] Instead, the president was authorized to appoint a single 1801-style "circuit judge"—the only one in the entire nation—to dispose of California's appellate business. Far from a significant change to rectify the faults of post-1807 judicial structure then, the creation of the California Circuit was little more than an ad hoc adjustment to the existing system.

Similarly, the Court of Claims was established in large part because all previous arrangements for adjudicating citizens' claims against the government had proved both inefficient and constitutionally dubious.[19] Conceived as an improvement upon previous systems, which had successively relied upon the Treasury Department, upon statutorily created administrative bodies, and upon congressional committees for hearing and deciding claims, the Court of Claims was hardly a court at all. Despite the fact that many of its mechanics—adversarial proceedings, subpoena power, testimony taken on both direct and cross-examination, life-tenured judges appointed by the president and confirmed by the Senate—resembled those of an Article III tribunal, the Court of Claims was required to report its findings and conclusions to Congress and to draft legislation in cases where the plaintiff should prevail.[20] Absent authority to resolve cases one way or the other, it could do little more than advise Congress on how to deal with particular claims.[21] As a result, the Court of Claims more closely resembled a legislative advisory council and the "old problems connected with congressional adjudication of claims remained unsolved."[22]

---

[15] 10 Stat. 631 (March 2, 1855).

[16] 10 Stat. 612 (February 24, 1855).

[17] More specifically, they had jurisdiction over appeals from a commission charged with determining the validity of land grants issued by the Spanish and Mexican governments.

[18] It was simply called the "California Circuit."

[19] For a summary of the three phases of claims determination—executive-administrative (1789–1820), legislative (1820s–1855), and judicial (1855–66)—see William M. Wiecek, "The Origin of the United States Court of Claims," 20 *Administrative Law Review* 387 (1967–68). For a summary of the congressional debate over the Court of Claims, see David P. Currie, *The Constitution in Congress: Democrats and Whigs, 1829–1861* (Chicago: University of Chicago Press, 2005), 195–203.

[20] Currie, *The Constitution in Congress*, 201–2. Unlike those of Article III judges, the salaries of Court of Claims judges were not irreducible.

[21] Ibid., 202.

[22] Wiecek, "The Origin of the United States Court of Claims," 395.

The combined failure of Cushing's plan for comprehensive reform in 1853 and the minimal effect of the 1855 acts meant that the defects of federal judicial organization remained until the Civil War.[23] Of course, with Democrats and Southerners preferring a judicial rather than political resolution to the thorny question of slavery in the territories, any attempts to remedy those defects inevitably implicated partisan and sectional interests. Thus, rather than being "partly engulfed by" or "subordinated to" the political crisis surrounding slavery,[24] judicial reform became entangled with it.[25] Indeed, it was precisely this intersection of the slavery debate and the pressing need for improvements to existing judicial machinery that structured debates over institution building in the late 1850s and early 1860s. It was in those years, after repeated Democratic attempts to delegate the slavery question to the judiciary effectively produced *Dred Scott v. Sanford*,[26] that the nascent Republican Party sought to break the Southern stranglehold on the Supreme Court. Soon after Abraham Lincoln's election as president in 1860 prompted the secession of Southern states and the subsequent creation of artificially large Republican majorities, these attempts succeeded, resulting in two significant judicial reforms: the Judiciary Act of 1862,[27] which reorganized the circuits to incorporate six new states into the system, and the Judiciary Act of 1863,[28] which replaced the California Circuit with a new Tenth Circuit and added a tenth justice to the Court. Together, these two enactments altered the circuit system so as to shatter Southern slaveholding dominance of the federal judiciary once and for all.

Breaking the Southern Stranglehold

Despite the fact that, by 1856, nearly all national political leaders, including then former Illinois congressman and soon-to-be Senate candidate Abraham Lincoln, had agreed that the Supreme Court was the proper body to determine the status

---

[23] Although neither the California Circuit nor the Court of Claims significantly improved judicial performance, both foreshadowed more fundamental institutional changes—the establishing of intermediate appellate judgeships in 1869 and 1891 and the creation (and reauthorization) of a truly judicial Court of Claims in 1863 and 1866, respectively. In the meantime, Congress did fix one perpetual defect in the administration of justice by providing better space for lower court proceedings—often relegated to public buildings, private homes, and even the public rooms of taverns—through appropriations for the purchase, construction, and renovation of courthouses and by reserving spaces in customs houses for courtrooms. See Michael Kammen, "Temples of Justice: The Iconography of Judgment and American Culture," in *Origins of the Federal Judiciary: Essays on the Judiciary Act of 1789*, ed. Maeva Marcus (New York: Oxford University Press, 1992), 248–80.

[24] Cf. Frankfurter and Landis, *The Business of the Supreme Court*, 54.

[25] Cf. Hall, "Federal Judicial Reform and Proslavery Constitutional Theory," 166, noting that judicial reform became "subtly linked to sectional expectations and demands on the slavery-extension question."

[26] 60 U.S. 393 (1857) (declaring that no descendant of a slave could ever be a citizen and striking down the Missouri Compromise as beyond congressional authority to regulate the territories).

[27] 12 Stat. 576 (July 15, 1862).

[28] 12 Stat. 794 (March 3, 1863).

of slavery in the territories,[29] Roger Taney's declarations in *Dred Scott*—that African Americans were not citizens, that Congress could not constitutionally prohibit slavery in the territories, and that the Missouri Compromise (which prohibited slavery north of the Thirty-Sixth Parallel) was unconstitutional[30]—sent shockwaves throughout America. While Southern slaveholders rejoiced, the Northern press as well as both radical and moderate Northern politicians immediately condemned the decision.[31] For Northerners and abolitionists, *Dred Scott*—together with *Prigg v. Pennsylvania* before it and *Ableman v. Booth* after it[32]—symbolized slaveholding control of the federal judiciary.[33] Regardless of the South's fortunes in national electoral politics, the proslaveholding bias of the Judiciary Act of 1837 and the two decades of Democratic dominance that followed had created a Southern (or, at least, Southern-sympathizing) cabal in the Supreme Court. And though radicals like New Hampshire senator John P. Hale turned their attention in the years to follow toward vanquishing the last remaining national vestige of Southern constitutional ideals with aggressive court-curbing measures,[34] most Republicans—including Lincoln—preferred renovation to demolition.[35] In part, Republicans continued to view the judiciary as an "indispensable part of the American constitutional system"[36]; in part, they "recognized the Court as a desirable prize."[37] After all, if Democrats had succeeded in making the judiciary a partner in their coalition, Republicans would surely be able to do the same. The problem, then, was less judicial power per se than the existence of structural arrangements that biased the exercise of that power toward Jacksonians, Democrats, Southerners, and slaveholders.

Solving this problem—that is to say, fashioning a Court that was simultaneously receptive to Republican interests and powerful enough to help satisfy them—required altering the membership of the Court, which, by virtue of the post-1807

---

[29] Graber, "The Nonmajoritarian Difficulty," 48.

[30] On *Dred Scott*, see Graber, *Dred Scott and the Politics of Constitutional Evil*; Austin Allen, *Origins of the Dred Scott Case: Jacksonian Jurisprudence and the Supreme Court, 1837–1857* (Athens: University of Georgia Press, 2006); and Don E. Fehrenbacher, *The Dred Scott Case: Its Significance in American Law and Politics* (New York: Oxford University Press, 1978).

[31] See Barry Friedman, "The History of the Countermajoritarian Difficulty, Part One: The Road to Judicial Supremacy," 73 *New York University Law Review* 333 (1998).

[32] 41 U.S. 539 (1842) (nullifying a state "personal liberty law" as in conflict with the federal Fugitive Slave Act of 1793); 62 U.S. 506 (1859) (denying the right of state courts to obstruct enforcement of federal judicial business, including that pursuant to the Fugitive Slave Act of 1850).

[33] Collectively, the three cases placed slavery beyond the legitimate reach of abolitionist legislatures in the North (*Prigg*), prevented the federal government from reducing slavery to an exclusively Southern relic (*Dred Scott*), and required not only state obedience to the constitutionality of slavery but also active cooperation in enforcing national laws protecting it (*Ableman*).

[34] In 1861, Hale proposed abolishing the existing Supreme Court and establishing a new one in its place.

[35] Cf. Kutler, *Judicial Power and Reconstruction Politics*, 11, noting that Republicans sought "[c]reative reform, not denunciation or destruction."

[36] Ibid.

[37] Ibid., 162.

norm of geographic appointment,[38] required rearranging the circuits as organized by the Judiciary Act of 1837. That organization had favored slave states over free states since Andrew Jackson signed it into law, but the inequity grew wider during the 1850s. In 1849, only four states—two free (Iowa and Wisconsin) and two slave (Florida and Texas)—were excluded from the circuit system; by 1860, the admission into the Union (but not incorporation into the circuit system) of California (1850), Minnesota (1858), and Oregon (1859) meant that five of the seven excluded states were free states. In 1849, the fifteen slave states controlled five circuits whereas the fifteen free states controlled four; by 1860, there were three more free states than slave states (and roughly 2.5 million more free state residents than slave state residents) but still one fewer free circuit than slave circuit and, in turn, one fewer Supreme Court justice hailing from a free circuit than a slave circuit. Eliminating—or, at the very least, reducing—this disproportionate Southern influence on the exercise of federal judicial power was the central factor motivating Republican efforts at judicial reform in the late 1850s.

Behind the Republican desire to remake the judicial system rested a simple policy goal: halting the spread of (and ultimately eliminating) slavery. After all, this was a party that had emerged to fight for free soil, free labor, and free men,[39] so it could scarcely tolerate a Court beholden to slaveholders. Ohio representative Benjamin Stanton had expressed this view one month before *Dred Scott*, proposing a circuit reorganization that, rather than protect the "partial and sectional" slaveholding interests of the South, would "command the confidence and respect and obedience of the people of the free States."[40] Two years later, the *New York Tribune* criticized slaveholders for using the Court as their "final hiding-place from the avenging spirit of Freedom" and encouraged Republican officials to reclaim for the Court "the confidence of the people by adapting it to the ends for which it was created."[41] The following year, Ohio representative James Ashley similarly denounced the "Calhoun conspiracy" to entrench support for "this monstrous wrong of human slavery" in the judiciary through biased structural arrangements (such as the Judiciary Act of 1837) and carefully screened appointments.[42] Only by freeing the Court from the shackles of Southern dominance, Republicans reasoned, could they free African Americans from the shackles of their owners.

---

[38] All three presidents to appoint justices in the 1850s—Millard Fillmore, Franklin Pierce, and James Buchanan—made geographically appropriate choices. Fillmore appointed Benjamin Curtis of Massachusetts to replace Levi Woodbury of New Hampshire as the First Circuit representative in 1851; Pierce tapped Alabama's John Campbell to fill the Fifth Circuit seat of John McKinley, also of Alabama, in 1853; and Buchanan replaced Curtis with Maine's Nathan Clifford in 1858.

[39] Eric Foner, *Free Soil, Free Labor, Free Men: The Ideology of the Republican Party before the Civil War* (New York: Oxford University Press, 1970).

[40] *Cong. Globe*, 34th Cong., 3rd Sess. 300–301 (1857) (Benjamin Stanton).

[41] *New York Tribune*, March 26, 1859, quoted in Kutler, *Judicial Power and Reconstruction Politics*, 16.

[42] *Cong. Globe*, 36th Cong., 1st Sess., appendix, 365–77 (1859) (James M. Ashley) (accusing Calhoun, who served as John Tyler's secretary of state, of making the respective slavery views of Peter Daniel and Levi Woodbury "a test of their promotion" to the Court).

Of course, for all the reasons Republicans desired circuit reorganization, Democrats, particularly those from the South, opposed it. With Republicanism and Northern abolitionism set to sweep the nation, protecting the status quo—a Court that had gradually been shaped to reflect Southern interests—was slaveholders' best chance to continue exerting power over national policy making. And, at least through the Thirty-Fifth (1857–59) and Thirty-Sixth (1859–61) Congresses, slaveholders succeeded in forestalling reform. Even when Democrats lost control of the House and lost three seats in the Senate in the 1858 election, they still controlled one chamber of Congress and had one of their own (James Buchanan) in the White House. Accordingly, with Republicans realizing significant reform stood little chance under a Democratic administration, calls for reform came "primarily from spokesmen outside Congress" while Republican officeholders waited and hoped for a more propitious partisan climate.[43]

The Election of 1860 and the Rise of Republican Government

As Republicans may have suspected, the presidential election of 1860 served as the catalyst needed to create that more propitious partisan climate and enable institution building. By election day, the result was all but a foregone conclusion. With the hopelessly divided Democrats offering two candidates—the popular sovereignty Northern wing nominated Illinois senator Stephen A. Douglas while the committed proslavery Southern wing supported incumbent vice president John C. Breckenridge—and Southern Whigs joining border-state moderates to support Constitutional Union Party candidate John Bell of Tennessee, Abraham Lincoln swept all free states except New Jersey (which pledged four electoral votes to Lincoln and two to Douglas) en route to a greater than two-to-one Electoral College margin over his closest rival.[44] The ramifications of Lincoln's victory were extraordinary—both for the future of the nation generally and for the course of judicial institution building over the next seventeen years more specifically. Before Lincoln could even assume office in March 1861, seven Southern states—South Carolina, Mississippi, Florida, Alabama, Georgia, Louisiana, and Texas—had seceded from the Union and established the Confederate States of America; by early June, Virginia, Arkansas, North Carolina, and Tennessee had all followed.[45] The result was that as the months of 1861 passed by, secession—and the subsequent withdrawal by or expulsion of Southern legislators—provided House and Senate

---

[43] Kermit L. Hall, "The Civil War Era as a Crucible for Nationalizing the Lower Federal Courts," *Prologue* 7 (1975): 180.

[44] Of 303 possible electoral votes, Lincoln claimed 180, Breckenridge 72, Bell 39, and Douglas a mere 12. The popular vote was noticeably closer, with Lincoln winning just under 40 percent to almost 30 percent for Douglas, 18 percent for Breckenridge, and over 12 percent for Bell.

[45] By the end of November, rival groups (sometimes known as "rump governments") in Missouri and Kentucky had also declared secession. The Confederacy accepted both states as members, but secessionists never actually controlled either one.

Republicans in the Thirty-Seventh Congress (1861–63) with larger legislative majorities than they had actually earned in the election of 1860.[46]

Despite striking a defiant tone toward *Dred Scott* in both his Illinois Senate debates with Stephen Douglas and his inaugural address, Lincoln, presumably occupied by the disintegration of the Union and the onset of the Civil War, said little about the judiciary during his first nine months in office. When he finally did address the judiciary in his first annual message to Congress in December 1861, it was not as a would-be "court-curber." Instead, Lincoln surveyed the existing judicial system, argued that the nation had "outgrown" it, and proposed structural and organizational reforms that left judicial authority and independence untouched:

> Three modifications occur to me, either of which, I think, would be an improvement upon our present system. Let the Supreme Court be of convenient number in every event; then, first, let the whole country be divided into circuits of convenient size, the Supreme judges to serve in a number of them corresponding to their own number, and independent circuit judges be provided for all the rest; or, secondly, let the Supreme judges be relieved from circuit duties and circuit judges provided for all the circuits; or, thirdly, dispense with circuit courts altogether, leaving the judicial functions wholly to the district courts and an independent Supreme Court.[47]

Far from irate denunciations of the Taney Court or support for punishing the Court in any sense, Lincoln's suggestions were "mild, indisputably constitutional, and hardly original."[48] The creation of independent circuit judges (albeit as an addition to, rather than replacement for, circuit riding) had been at the heart of Caleb Cushing's reform plan in 1853, and dividing the circuits into "convenient size" had been the stated purpose of Benjamin Stanton's 1857 proposal. In other words, Lincoln's suggestions aligned with the mainstream Republican view that the Court was to be reshaped rather than rebuked.

Prompted by Lincoln's encouragement and reassured by their sizable majorities, congressional Republicans immediately added judicial reform to their legislative agenda. In fact, within three weeks of Lincoln's address, Senate Judiciary Committee Chairman Lyman Trumbull of Illinois promptly dispensed with John P. Hale's radical plan to abolish the Supreme Court and instead reported a bill "to reorganize and equalize the judicial circuits according to population."[49] Despite Hale's

---

[46] At the beginning of the Thirty-Seventh Congress in March 1861, Republicans outnumbered Democrats 108–44 in the House (not including twenty-six Unionists, two Constitutional Unionists, two Union Party members, and one Independent Democrat) and 31–15 in the Senate (not including three Unionists and one vacant seat), thereby marking the first time Democrats had been the minority in both houses since the Twenty-Seventh Congress (1841–43). Since four more states would secede in the first three months of the legislative session, these numbers effectively represent the low watermark of the Republican majority in the Thirty-Seventh Congress.

[47] Abraham Lincoln, First Annual Message to Congress (December 3, 1861).

[48] Kutler, *Judicial Power and Reconstruction Politics*, 13.

[49] *Cong. Globe*, 37th Cong., 2nd Sess. 155 (1861) (Lyman Trumbull).

warning that the plan was "far short" (in terms of punishment for the Court) of what it should have been and that it was likely to "meet with some opposition,"[50] the general approach of the Senate bill—to incorporate new states and reorganize the allotment of existing ones so as to convert one slave circuit into a free circuit[51]—was widely accepted.[52]

The precise reorganization outlined in the bill, however, was significantly more controversial, as the Midwestern delegations jockeyed over which states belonged together in which circuits. Among other preferences, Ohio wished to remain in a circuit with Indiana and Michigan (rather than Kentucky), Illinois wanted to be joined with upper Midwest states Michigan and Wisconsin (rather than Missouri), and Iowa sought a separate and unified circuit for states west of the Mississippi River (Iowa, Kansas, Minnesota, and Missouri).[53] In general, the Midwestern delegations wanted circuits to be a reasonable size (in both population and area) and to "encompass states with mutual legal and business interests."[54] Since these concerns, unlike those of the 1820s and '30s, were not motivated by partisan disjuncture between Congress and the president and did not implicate the politics of prospective Supreme Court appointments, they were not insuperable obstacles. Rather, following several months of haggling and a friendly reminder of Lincoln's stated reluctance to fill two of the three vacancies on the Court before a reorganization bill passed,[55] Congress agreed in July 1862 on a compromise plan that created three Midwestern circuits amenable to all parties involved.[56] Although the Midwestern delegations were

---

[50] *Cong. Globe*, 37th Cong., 2nd Sess. 155 (1861) (John P. Hale).

[51] Under the terms of the plan, only three circuits (the Fifth, Sixth, and Ninth) would have been altered. The slave Ninth Circuit (Arkansas and Mississippi) would have been reconstituted as a free circuit consisting of five formerly excluded states (Illinois, Iowa, Kansas, Minnesota, and Wisconsin). In turn, Arkansas and Mississippi would have joined Alabama, Louisiana, and formerly excluded Texas in the slave Fifth Circuit. Florida would have been added to the slave Sixth Circuit (Georgia, North Carolina, and South Carolina).

[52] Indeed, working on advice from Attorney General Edward Bates, who was particularly concerned that sweeping reform might open the Court to a frontal attack by more radical Republicans, the Senate Judiciary Committee deliberately followed the most moderate of Lincoln's three suggested reforms (circuit reorganization, the elimination of circuit riding, the abolition of circuit courts entirely). Hall, "The Civil War Era as a Crucible for Nationalizing the Lower Federal Courts," 181.

[53] *Cong. Globe*, 37th Cong., 2nd Sess. 187–88, 288, 469, 2914, 3088–3091 (1862).

[54] Hall, "The Civil War Era as a Crucible for Nationalizing the Lower Federal Courts," 181.

[55] Peter Daniel had died in May 1860, John McLean had died in April 1861, and John Campbell had resigned in April 1861, but Lincoln deliberately waited to fill the Daniel and Campbell seats. (To replace Ohioan and *Dred Scott* dissenter McLean, he appointed Noah Swayne, also of Ohio, in January 1862.) *Cong. Globe*, 37th Cong., 1st Sess. 188 (1862) (Lyman Trumbull): "The Supreme Court has but six judges upon the bench. The other three ought to be appointed, but I presume they will not be appointed until some bill passes on the subject." In his first annual message, Lincoln explained that he had "so far forborne making nominations to fill these vacancies" because "[t]wo of the outgoing judges resided with the States now overrun by revolt" and it would be difficult to find men willing to ride circuit under such conditions. Lincoln, First Annual Message to Congress.

[56] Specifically, Indiana and Ohio constituted the Seventh Circuit; Illinois, Michigan, and Wisconsin the Eight Circuit; and Iowa, Kansas, Minnesota, and Missouri the Ninth Circuit. Within seven months, however, this configuration was altered twice, with Michigan and Indiana switching circuits, 12 Stat.

seemingly thinking only of their respective states, the plan devised to satisfy their various interests actually weakened the South even further than the original Senate bill would have. Indeed, under the terms of the Judiciary Act of 1862, five slave circuits were consolidated into three,[57] one new free circuit was created,[58] and one "mixed" circuit was established.[59] With Southern delegations absent from Congress and thus unable to object, this radical transformation of the circuit system—from five slave circuits and four free circuits to five free circuits, three slave circuits, and one (free-leaning) mixed circuit—attracted scarcely any opposition.

The absence of Southerners from Congress resulted in virtually uncontested pro-Northern institution building again the following year, when Republicans sought to add a tenth circuit to the system and a corresponding tenth justice to the Court. Part of their quest to "make national institutions more responsive to the needs of the dominant section" of the nation (namely, the North),[60] the Judiciary Act of 1863 was essentially the coda to the Judiciary Act of 1862. The latter had succeeded in reorganizing the circuits in a way that diminished Southern influence, but it still remained the case that the Court comprised five justices who had voted the proslavery position in *Dred Scott* (Roger Taney, Samuel Nelson, Robert Grier, James Wayne, and John Catron) as well as "doughface" Nathan Clifford,[61] who had replaced *Dred Scott* dissenter Benjamin Curtis in 1858. Moreover, the 1862 arrangement left the California Circuit intact and left Oregon as the lone state not included in any circuit. In order to alleviate both the remaining proslavery majority on the Court and judicial performance in the far West, Republicans proposed and passed—without debate or a recorded vote—a bill abolishing the California Circuit, joining California and Oregon in a newly created Tenth Circuit, and authorizing the appointment of a tenth justice responsible for representing and riding circuit on the Pacific coast.

Lincoln's Proto-Yankee Court

Rather than pack the Court in the immediate term, the Judiciary Acts of 1862 and 1863 served to set up the end of Southern slaveholding dominance of the federal judiciary in the long term. Seeking to reform a Supreme Court they saw as section-

---

637 (January 28, 1863), and Wisconsin shifting into the Ninth Circuit, 12 Stat. 648 (February 9, 1863). By the close of the Thirty-Seventh Congress, the Seventh Circuit comprised Michigan and Ohio; the Eight Circuit comprised Illinois and Indiana; and the Ninth Circuit comprised Iowa, Kansas, Minnesota, Missouri, and Wisconsin.

[57] The three remaining slave circuits were the Fourth (Delaware, Maryland, North Carolina, and Virginia), the Fifth (Alabama, Florida, Georgia, Mississippi, and South Carolina), and the Sixth (Arkansas, Kentucky, Louisiana, Tennessee, and Texas).

[58] The former Seventh Circuit (Illinois, Indiana, Michigan, and Ohio) was split into two circuits—the Seventh (Indiana and Ohio) and the Eighth (Illinois, Michigan, and Wisconsin).

[59] The Ninth Circuit included three free states (Iowa, Kansas, and Minnesota) and one slave state (Missouri).

[60] Kutler, *Judicial Power and Reconstruction Politics*, 16.

[61] The term *doughface* was late-nineteenth-century parlance for a Northerner who supported the South (and slavery) during the Civil War.

ally biased and corrupted by Democratic machinations, Republicans opted for a "substantive change . . . conceived within a traditional framework."[62] That is to say, rather than limit the reach of the Court's power or authority, Republicans tried to make the exercise of that power more receptive to their (antislavery) policy interests;[63] rather than dismantle the post-1807 system of judicial representation that Democrats had manipulated in the Judiciary Act of 1837, Republicans simply reappropriated it to their own advantage. Although circuit reorganization and the creation of the Tenth Circuit undoubtedly improved judicial functioning by more equitably distributing population (and workload) across circuits, the two acts were a deliberate attempt to reconfigure the judicial branch into an institution that would be more favorable to Republican views on slavery.

In focusing on the concrete problem of Southern judicial bias, however, the Judiciary Acts of 1862 and 1863 left numerous other growing problems unsolved.[64] They did not, for instance, provide Supreme Court justices relief from circuit riding, which became increasingly arduous as new states were incorporated into the judicial system and the land mass of individual circuits grew, or alleviate the backlogged dockets of district court judges, who faced an increase in litigation from wartime legislation.[65] Nor did they satisfy the concerns of businessmen and creditors worried about the settlement of prewar debts or attend to the "pro-slavery oligarchy" that dominated Southern state courts and mistreated Unionists and freedmen by confiscating property and instituting Black Codes.[66] In general, the judicial reorganization of the early 1860s was not a comprehensive renovation of the federal judicial system or a panacea to all defects in the administration of justice. Those defects would be addressed in the years to come, but they went unequivocally unaddressed in the Judiciary Acts of 1862 and 1863.

Moreover, by manipulating the idea of judicial representation to serve the sectional interests of the North and Midwest, the Judiciary Acts of 1862 and 1863 facilitated *Northern* rather than *national* dominance of the federal judiciary. In fact, the reforms reduced rather than enhanced "the federal judicial presence in the area where it would prove most necessary" after the Civil War: the South.[67] Though this seeming oversight may make Republicans of the early 1860s appear "surprisingly shortsighted" seekers of immediate gain rather than visionary architects of

[62] Kutler, *Judicial Power and Reconstruction Politics*, 14.

[63] Ibid., 29, arguing that the Republicans' "preoccupation with reorganization amounted to creative reform, reflecting a practical regard for the Court's potentiality as a power phenomenon."

[64] For a summary of these problems, see Hall, "The Civil War Era as a Crucible for Nationalizing the Lower Federal Courts," 182–83.

[65] At Lincoln's urging, Congress did, however, create a genuinely judicial Court of Claims—one whose decision making was separate from Congress and final—in 1863; 12 Stat. 765 (March 3, 1863). After the Supreme Court denied the Article III status of the Court of Claims in *Gordon v. United States*, 69 U.S. 561 (1865), Congress confirmed the judicial character of the Court of Claims yet again in 1866; 14 Stat. 9 (March 16, 1866).

[66] Hall, "The Civil War Era as a Crucible for Nationalizing the Lower Federal Courts," 182.

[67] Ibid.

Table 4.1.
Circuit Organization and Supreme Court Representation
Judiciary Acts of 1862 and 1863

Circuit	States	Supreme Court Justice
First	Maine, Massachusetts, New Hampshire, Rhode Island	Nathan Clifford (ME)
Second	Connecticut, New York, Vermont	Samuel Nelson (NY)
Third	New Jersey, Pennsylvania	Robert Grier (PA)
Fourth	Delaware, Maryland, North Carolina, Virginia	Roger Taney (MD)
Fifth	Alabama, Florida, Georgia, Mississippi, South Carolina	James Wayne (GA)
Sixth	Arkansas, Kentucky, Louisiana, Tennessee, Texas	John Catron (TN)
Seventh	Indiana, Ohio	Noah Swayne (OH)*
Eighth	Illinois, Michigan, Wisconsin	David Davis (IL)*
Ninth	Iowa, Kansas, Minnesota, Missouri	Samuel Miller (IA)*
Tenth	California, Oregon	Stephen Field (CA)*

Note: *Indicates a Lincoln appointee.

grand design,[68] it reflects the degree to which they were still fighting the previous battle (the sectional wars of the 1850s) rather than preparing for the next one (Reconstruction). Simply put, the Republican judicial reforms of the early 1860s were aimed less at the ambitious goal of subjugating and controlling the South (which would become the project of Reconstruction) than at the more targeted goal of removing the judiciary from the Southern grip.

While the Judiciary Acts of 1862 and 1863 did not fully accomplish this goal, they did effectively lay the groundwork for it. To the extent that constitutional decisions on slavery in the 1860s were in large part a function of the men making them,[69] the transformation of Jackson's Dixie Court into Lincoln's Yankee Court depended on securing reliably abolitionist Northern and Western justices in the future, and the reforms of the early 1860s facilitated the appointment of precisely those sorts of justices. Even after Lincoln's appointment of Noah Swayne to replace the deceased John McLean in January 1862, two vacancies—those of Peter Daniel

[68] Ibid.
[69] Cf. Kutler, *Judicial Power and Reconstruction Politics*, 20, noting the Republican "faith that constitutional decisions are brought by men, not storks."

(Virginia) and John Campbell (Alabama)—remained. As a lame-duck president, James Buchanan had tried to replace Daniel with secretary of state (and former attorney general) Jeremiah Black, but Republicans, knowing that Lincoln would have the opportunity to fill the vacancy with one of their own in due course, rejected the nomination.[70] Had Lincoln, who—despite fighting the Civil War— seemed to regard himself as bound by the norm of geographically representative appointments obeyed by every president since Jefferson, filled the Daniel vacancy immediately upon assuming office, he would have been forced to appoint a resident of a slave state.[71] Instead, by waiting until after the Judiciary Act of 1862, Lincoln was able to avoid appointing a Southerner. With the reorganized circuit system containing three slaveholding circuits (the Fourth, Fifth, and Sixth) and the Court already containing three slave state residents (Roger Taney of Maryland, James Wayne of Georgia, and John Catron of Tennessee), Lincoln effectively appointed two Northern Republicans—Samuel Miller of Iowa and David Davis of Illinois—to replace two Southern Democrats.[72] By the time Lincoln tapped Californian Stephen J. Field—a pro-Union, antislavery Democrat—to fill the Tenth Circuit seat created by the Judiciary Act of 1863 and named Ohio's Salmon Chase to replace the deceased Taney as chief justice the following year,[73] the transformation of the Court into a Northern Republican institution was well underway. Even after Chase's appointment, however, the Court's ten justices were evenly split on the issue of slavery, with five in favor (Clifford, Nelson, Grier, Wayne, and Catron) and five opposed (Chase, Swayne, Davis, Miller, and Field).[74] Future appointments (or perhaps reform) were still needed to overcome this deadlock, but, with judicial reform providing more than twice as many seats for free states (seven) as slave states (three), it seemed that Lincoln and the Thirty-Seventh Congress had placed the Court safely on the path to Republicanism.[75]

[70] Warren, *The Supreme Court in United States History*, 2:363–65.

[71] Because of the 1842 circuit reorganization, Lincoln actually had the option of appointing a resident from either Daniel's Fourth Circuit (Delaware, Maryland, and Virginia) or, since Maryland resident Chief Justice Taney also represented the Fourth Circuit, the unrepresented Ninth Circuit (Arkansas and Mississippi).

[72] With Miller representing the trans-Mississippi Ninth Circuit (Iowa, Kansas, Minnesota, and Missouri) and Davis representing the new Eighth Circuit (Illinois, Michigan, and Wisconsin), Lincoln's appointments actually restored full and equal geographic representation to the Court—one justice for each and every circuit—for the first time in twenty years.

[73] Lincoln's decision not to replace Taney with a resident of the Fourth Circuit deprived that circuit of representation, instead giving the Seventh Circuit two justices. Thus, only two years after his appointments of Miller and Davis had restored circuit-justice geographic symmetry, Lincoln's appointment of Chase disturbed it.

[74] Grier and Wayne, however, did side with the Lincoln administration on other issues, notably voting to sustain the president's blockade of Southern ports in *The Prize Cases*, 67 U.S. 635 (1862).

[75] But see Mark A. Graber, "The Jacksonian Origins of Chase Court Activism," *Journal of Supreme Court History* 25 (2000): 17–39, explaining Chase Court (1864–73) activism as the result of justices who held much narrower conceptions of federal power than the Republican Congresses of the era.

Removal, Habeas Corpus, and Postwar Reform, 1865–1867

The process of converting the Supreme Court into a fully Republican institution would (as we shall see in the next section) continue in 1866, but the immediate aftermath of the Civil War also witnessed a distinctly different type of judicial institution building. Unlike the Judiciary Acts of 1862 and 1863, these reforms were not concerned with empowering the North at the expense of the South or Republicans at the expense of Democrats. Instead, they were concerned first and foremost with empowering the federal judiciary at the expense of state courts, particularly Southern state courts. In other words, while the judicial reforms of the early 1860s were directed at the organization of the circuit system and the membership of the Court, a similarly transformative series of reforms in the years that followed were directed squarely at bolstering federal judicial power vis-à-vis the recalcitrant and rebellious states of the vanquished Confederacy.[76]

This gradual shift of power was produced by an assortment of statutes designed to maintain the rule of law in the postwar South. Whether explicitly procedural legislation about judicial process and federal court jurisdiction or substantive legislation (about revenue collection or civil rights, for example) that included enforcement provisions enlarging judicial power,[77] these statutes reflected not only Republican impatience with "state harassment of national policy" but also the willingness to do something to stop it.[78] That something was a determined effort to shift cases involving favored Republican constituencies from hostile state courts to more fair-minded and impartial federal courts through two mechanisms: expanding the causes for removal and extending the reach of the writ of habeas corpus. Whether or not legislators conceived removal and habeas corpus as parts of a broader scheme of either nationalization or judicialization, the "cumulative effect" of postwar legislation was a marked increase in the ability of federal courts to hear cases that had long been the province of state judges.[79] Given this continuous and multifaceted congressional empowerment of the federal judiciary, it seems clear that federal courts after the Civil War were neither "thrust into the background and rendered unable to defend judicial liberty" nor made "impotent and acquiescent in the face of a supposed congressional onslaught."[80] Rather, though judicial-legislative interactions were not without tensions, federal courts became integral and influential partners in the Republicans' postwar regime.

[76] Despite their temporal overlap with the Judiciary Act of 1866 (discussed in the next section), I discuss these reforms in a separate section here because they were aimed at distinct goals and utilized distinct tools to accomplish them.

[77] See Wiecek, "The Reconstruction of Federal Judicial Power," 338, distinguishing between legislation that provided an "auxiliary procedural device for protecting the enforcement of substantive policies" and legislation with the "explicit and primary objective of expanding federal judicial power."

[78] Kutler, *Judicial Power and Reconstruction Politics*, 151. See also Wiecek, "The Reconstruction of Federal Judicial Power," 338, citing the "growing Republican disenchantment with state courts."

[79] Kutler, *Judicial Power and Reconstruction Politics*, 144.

[80] Wiecek, "The Great Writ and Reconstruction," 537.

Protecting Unionists and Freedmen

Republican institution building during the aftermath of the Civil War was aimed at satisfying one of the party's policy goals: protecting Unionists and freedmen from harassment, discrimination, and maltreatment in the South. After all, most legislation passed by the federal government in the 1860s was wildly unpopular throughout the South. Seeking to thwart the enforcement of national policy, Southern judges, politicians, and citizens confiscated property owned by Union sympathizers, approved Black Codes established to oppress freed slaves, subjected Republicans to prejudiced judicial proceedings, and manipulated litigation so as to deny Northern supporters the chance to have their grievances heard in federal courts. To Republicans, these obstructions were unacceptable. Without a "supporting body of enforcement procedures" to protect Unionists (who had supported the Republican cause),[81] federal officials (who were charged with carrying out the work of national policy makers), and African Americans (on whose behalf the war was partly fought), the decision to resist Southern secession looked overly costly in retrospect.

As a solution to these problems and as a way to validate the aims of the war, Republicans turned to the federal judiciary. The key, of course, was getting cases out of biased state judicial systems and into the impartial (at least from the Northern perspective) federal judiciary. Two jurisdictional mechanisms—removal and the writ of habeas corpus—were capable of implementing such a shift, and Republicans made use of both. Removal permitted citizens to transfer cases that were already underway from state court to federal court; the writ of habeas corpus (the "Great Writ") allowed detained or imprisoned citizens to petition for a judicial hearing about whether their rights had been violated. Neither tool had been particularly common prior to the 1860s—apart from the Federalists' ill-fated Judiciary Act of 1801, removal was used only in rare and very specific instances;[82] the writ of habeas corpus was employed almost exclusively as a challenge to detention ordered by an executive officer rather than a court of law—but together they offered Republicans an opportunity to bypass state judicial proceedings, ensure equal treatment for their favored constituencies, and overcome local obstruction of federal policies.

Republicans first attempted to expand the causes for removal and extend the reach of habeas corpus during the war itself. Though best known for retroactively authorizing Lincoln's 1861 suspension of the writ of habeas corpus, the Habeas Corpus Act of 1863 actually protected individuals acting "under color of any authority derived from or exercised by or under the President of the United States, or any act of Congress" from prosecution in state courts.[83] After the surrender at Appomattox, Republicans passed numerous statutes with a similar purpose. The

---

[81] Kutler, *Judicial Power and Reconstruction Politics,* 147.

[82] To quell Northern resistance to the War of 1812 or to aid enforcement of the Tariffs of 1828 and 1832 in South Carolina, for example.

[83] 12 Stat. 755 (March 3, 1863).

Separable Controversies Act of 1866 attempted to prevent Southern citizens from manipulating lawsuits and forestalling removal by allowing litigants to separate, or "split," causes of action.[84] The Internal Revenue Act of 1866 provided for the removal of cases against any "officer on account of any act done under color of his office," allowed an action to begin anew in federal courts if the state court obstructed removal, and gave the federal courts jurisdiction "over the body of the defendant" in addition to his case.[85] The Civil Rights Act of 1866 authorized removal of cases stemming from actions "done or committed by virtue or under color of authority derived" from either itself or the Freedmen's Bureau Act.[86] An 1866 amendment to the Habeas Corpus Suspension Act sought to punish disobedient state actors by not only voiding any and all state court proceedings that occurred after removal had been authorized but also making the obstructing party "liable in damages . . . to the party aggrieved."[87] The Local Prejudice Act of 1867 permitted removal to federal court upon the simple filing of an affidavit that a state court failed to provide an impartial forum for the administration of justice.[88] Finally, in the most transformative (of judicial power) statute of them all,[89] the Habeas Corpus Act of 1867 allowed federal judges to grant the writ "in all cases where any person may be restrained of his or her liberty in violation of the constitution, or of any treaty or law of the United States."[90]

Considered collectively, these statutes portended a vast increase in both the number of cases that could be heard in federal court and the extent to which federal judicial power could reach into the justice systems of individual states, yet virtually all of them passed with relatively little (if any) opposition or controversy.[91] The Separable Controversies Act, for instance, was passed in the Senate within one day of being introduced and engendered only minimal Democratic opposition in the House, even after it was amended to offer removal from the courts of all states rather than simply those of the Confederacy. Debate over the Civil Rights Act focused on the definition of citizenship, virtually ignoring the removal provision completely. Like the Separable Controversies Act, the Local Prejudice Act was uncontroversially amended to expand removal to citizens in all state courts, passing

---

[84] 14 Stat. 306 (July 27, 1866). Exploiting *Strawbridge v. Curtiss*, 7 U.S. 267 (1806), which required all parties on one side of a lawsuit to have different citizenship from all parties on the other in order to remove a case to federal court, Southerners routinely joined a "nominal resident party to the real and nonresident defendant" in order to preempt the possibility of removal." Wiecek, "The Reconstruction of Federal Judicial Power," 340.

[85] 14 Stat. 98 (July 13, 1866).

[86] 14 Stat. 27 (April 9, 1866).

[87] 14 Stat. 46 (May 11, 1866).

[88] 14 Stat. 558 (Marc 2, 1867).

[89] The Civil Rights Act of 1866 was obviously landmark legislation in other ways.

[90] 14 Stat. 385 (February 5, 1867).

[91] See Kutler, *Judicial Power and Reconstruction Politics*, 147–52. The wartime Habeas Corpus Act of 1863 elicited some resistance from Democrats and conservative Republicans concerned about the expansion of federal power, but most of this resistance was sparked by the act's ex post legitimation of Lincoln's wartime suspension of habeas corpus.

both houses without debate and receiving Andrew Johnson's signature on the last day of the term. The debate over the Habeas Corpus Act of 1867 was characterized by "scantiness and opacity,"[92] with seemingly divergent remarks from two influential Republicans—House Judiciary Committee member William Lawrence of Ohio and Senate Judiciary Committee chairman Lyman Trumbull of Illinois—on the bill's objectives and a laughter-inducing query from a House member about "whether anybody in this House, when he gives his vote on these amendments, knows what he is voting on,"[93] but little opposition and no recorded vote.

Given the partisan and sectional composition of the Thirty-Ninth Congress (1865–67), the unchallenged passage of these statutes is far from surprising. After all, those most in favor of the systematic disempowerment of Southern state courts were Republicans, who maintained strong majorities in both houses;[94] those most likely to oppose such measures were Southerners, few of whom had returned to Congress by 1867,[95] and Northern Democrats, who presumably found it difficult to justify state court obstruction of federal authority. Moreover, encompassing the end of the war and the beginning of Reconstruction, the Thirty-Ninth Congress was a particularly eventful one. Between proposing and debating the Fourteenth Amendment and passing the Civil Rights Act of 1866, the first Reconstruction Act,[96] and the Tenure of Office Act,[97] legislators were busy. Though protecting Unionists and freedmen and facilitating enforcement of national policies was undoubtedly an important element of Reconstruction, it nonetheless seems that other exigencies of occupying and rebuilding the postwar South may have taken precedence over judicial reform. To the extent that time was scarce and ostensibly more pressing issues were in need of resolution, the Republican campaign to expand the causes for removal and extend the reach of the writ of habeas corpus received less attention and stimulated less debate than Democrats and absent Southerners might have hoped.

Opting for Federal Justice

The effect of the removal and habeas corpus statutes of the Thirty-Ninth Congress was twofold. First, they substantially augmented federal judicial power. By including removal provisions in substantive legislation as well as passing explicit removal statutes, Republicans not only made federal judges the "primary enforcers of the

[92] Wiecek, "The Great Writ and Reconstruction," 538.

[93] *Cong. Globe*, 39th Cong., 2nd Sess. 899 (1867) (Edwin R.V. Wright).

[94] In the Senate, Republicans held a twenty-eight-seat advantage (39–11) over Democrats (not including three Unconditional Unionists and one Unionist); in the House, Republicans held a ninety-eight-seat advantage (136–38) over Democrats (not including thirteen Unconditional Unionists, five Unionists, and one Independent Republican).

[95] Indeed, the only former Confederate state to rejoin the Union—and, thus, have its representatives and senators resume their seats—by this point was Tennessee, which had been readmitted in July 1866.

[96] 14 Stat. 428 (March 2, 1867).

[97] 14 Stat. 430 (March 2, 1867).

growing confiscation, anti-disloyalty, and conscription" campaigns underway in the South but also expanded federal court jurisdiction over state court proceedings well beyond diversity cases.[98] Before the Civil War, "justice, even when federal constitutional standards were at issue, was overwhelmingly state justice."[99] No federal court order to a state court could shift the case to the federal level, and no federal judge could intervene once a state trial was underway; defendants were, in essence, limited to state courts unless and until they faced an adverse ruling.[100] Beginning in 1866, however, defendants in a wide variety of criminal cases from across the nation were effectively allowed to choose between state and federal justice.

Moreover, because Congress had also liberalized the situations in which federal judges could grant a writ of habeas corpus, citizens could choose federal justice even if they had mistakenly chosen state justice first. That is to say, by making the writ into "a means of reviewing *judicial* confinement" and recasting it as a "post-conviction form of relief,"[101] the Habeas Corpus Act of 1867 offered citizens a second chance at obtaining their freedom. Prior to this point, federal habeas corpus "could not reach the man held under the order of a state court" regardless of "how outrageous the violation of his rights" under the Constitution or federal law; federal judges, in effect, lacked the authority to "question the judgment of a jurisdictionally-competent court."[102] Once the purposes and extent of the writ was transformed in 1867, however, habeas corpus empowered federal courts to oversee the behavior of state court judges.

Second, in significantly increasing federal judicial power, the postwar removal and habeas corpus statutes also prompted a mild confrontation between Congress and the Supreme Court. Republicans had empowered the federal judiciary not because they viewed judicial power as intrinsically beneficial but because they saw federal courts in the late 1860s as a potential ally against obstructionist Southern states. Once federal judges—and Supreme Court justices, in particular—began to use their enlarged power for purposes other than enforcing preexisting national policies and protecting Unionists and freedmen from biased state prosecutions, Republican dissatisfaction emerged. This dissatisfaction famously came to a head when, following the Court's decision to accept *Ex parte McCardle*,[103] a challenge to the first Reconstruction Act brought under the Habeas Corpus Act of 1867, congressional Republicans repealed (over Andrew Johnson's veto) the part of the latter act expanding the Court's jurisdiction and authorizing it to hear McCardle's case.[104] A hostile action by legislators who feared they had created a monster they could no longer control, the

---

[98] Harold M. Hyman and William M. Wiecek, *Equal Justice under Law: Constitutional Development, 1835–1875* (New York: Harper and Row, 1982), 260.

[99] Ibid., 261.

[100] Ibid.

[101] Wiecek, "The Reconstruction of Federal Judicial Power," 342, 346.

[102] Ibid., 342–43.

[103] 74 U.S. 506 (1867).

[104] 15 Stat. 44 (March 27, 1868).

"*McCardle* repealer" was a blatant attempt to bring the Court under political control and prevent it from making a decision the majority party would not like.[105] Yet the repeal was essentially targeted at one specific case and, compared to the vast jurisdiction granted to the federal judiciary during the first few years after the Civil War, the sliver of possible cases taken back by it relatively inconsequential.[106] The new and improved writ of habeas corpus remained fully available to lower federal court judges, and the Court's jurisdiction remained untouched except for one specific section of one specific act. Thus, the supposedly defining action of Republican antipathy toward Reconstruction era judicial power was committed not "with a cleaver but with a surgical knife."[107] With federal courts still more of a partner to Republican legislators than an enemy of them, the *McCardle* repealer signified "merely a temporary intermission" in an otherwise friendly and mutually beneficial legislative-judicial relationship that would continue well into the next decade.[108]

In fact, the judicial reforms of the Thirty-Ninth Congress would presage an even greater expansion of federal jurisdiction in the 1870s. By that point, the substantive interests for which Republicans sought to increase judicial power had changed, but the core insight of postwar institution building—that providing federal justice as an easily obtainable alternative to state justice could efficiently serve national policy aims—remained. This insight was, as we shall see later in this chapter, the central premise behind the sweeping Jurisdiction and Removal Act of 1875.

Judicial Performance and Judicial Politics, 1866–1869

Together with the slow beginnings of industrial economic growth and a transportation revolution spurred by the spread of railroads, the secessionist embers of obstruction in the wartime and postwar South greatly contributed to a significant increase in federal judicial business.[109] Despite the fact that the continuous expan-

---

[105] On the interaction between law and politics in both congressional and judicial decision making surrounding *McCardle*, see Lee Epstein and Thomas G. Walker, "The Role of the Supreme Court in American Society: Playing the Reconstruction Game," in *Contemplating Courts*, ed. Lee Epstein (Washington: CQ Press, 1995), 315–46; and Mark A. Graber, "Legal, Strategic or Legal Strategy: Deciding to Decide during the Civil War and Reconstruction," in *The Supreme Court and American Political Development*, ed. Ronald Kahn and Ken I. Kersch (Lawrence: University of Kansas Press, 2006), 33–66.

[106] In fact, even while affirming Congress's authority under the Exceptions and Regulations Clause of Article III, Section 2 to repeal the Court's appellate jurisdiction, Chase's opinion of the Court in *McCardle* makes clear that the repealer relates exclusively to cases on appeal from circuit courts under the Habeas Corpus Act of 1867 and has no relevance whatsoever to any other jurisdiction the Court may exercise.

[107] Wiecek, "The Reconstruction of Federal Judicial Power," 357–58.

[108] Ibid., 352.

[109] Cf. Howard Gillman, "How Political Parties Can Use the Courts to Advance Their Agendas: Federal Courts in the United States, 1875–1891," *American Political Science Review* 96 (2002): 515, referring to federal judges as the "first line of defense—or offense—for the federal government when confronting challenges to national authority."

sion of federal jurisdiction had resulted in bloated dockets throughout the nation, Congress had yet to provide substantial relief to assist judges in the performance of their duties. Though circuit riding was required less often, the circuits were more populous and more geographically sprawling than ever before. Thus, despite the fact that their time and attention were desperately needed in Washington, D.C., where the accumulation of Supreme Court cases meant a delay of well over a year, justices were still, as they had since they 1789, traveling the nation and dispatching local judicial business. In sum, with both district judges and Supreme Court justices overworked and (in some opinions, at least) underpaid, the Republican plan to empower the federal judiciary had created an unworkable situation.

Fixing that situation was the primary motivation behind two Republican reforms in the late 1860s: the Judiciary Act of 1866,[110] which reduced the membership of the Court to seven justices by mandating that the next three vacancies not be filled, and the Circuit Judges Act of 1869,[111] which increased the size of the Court to nine justices and provided for the appointment of nine circuit judges to handle the vast majority of circuit court business. With the former occurring shortly after Andrew Johnson succeeded Abraham Lincoln as president and the latter occurring shortly before Ulysses S. Grant succeeded Johnson, the two acts are often regarded as companion pieces of a Republican attempt to manipulate Supreme Court appointments for partisan advantage.[112] According to this conventional wisdom, Republicans reduced the size of the Court in order to deny Johnson, a lifelong Democrat who frequently clashed with the Republican Congresses of the 1860s, any appointments and then subsequently increased the size of the Court in order to provide Grant, a loyal Republican who had led the Union army in the Civil War, the opportunity to appoint like-minded jurists. In reality, the political agenda of solidifying Lincoln's Yankee Court was less the cause behind the two acts than the chief consequence of them. Instead, the Judiciary Act of 1866 and the Circuit Judges Act were motivated by practical and mundane performance goals—specifically, returning the Court to a workable (and odd) number of justices, alleviating the circuit court stress on both district judges and Supreme Court justices by creating a new tier of judges, and increasing the federal judicial presence in the South. To the extent that Republicans hoped that the federal judiciary would continue to serve as a partner in (or enforcer of) their postwar regime, it was imperative that judges have the ability and resources to perform their duties effectively.

A Court of Convenient Size

The standard interpretation of the Judiciary Act of 1866—that Republicans reduced the size of the Court in order to prevent the untrustworthy and Southern-sympathizing Andrew Johnson from exercising any control over the makeup of the

[110] 14 Stat. 209 (July 23, 1866).
[111] 16 Stat. 44 (April 10, 1869).
[112] See, most notably, Warren, *The Supreme Court in United States History*, 2:421–23, 501–8.

Supreme Court—ignores three crucial facts, each of which casts substantial doubt on the centrality of crassly political motivations. First, Johnson, who showed little compunction in vetoing landmark Reconstruction legislation,[113] actually signed the bill into law. Second, the justices, who presumably did not want the Court used as a pawn of ordinary politics, were themselves either in favor of or neutral to the proposed reduction,[114] with Chief Justice Chase even presenting his own reduction plan.[115] Third, the (admittedly limited) legislative record of the act includes neither a single expression of Republican vitriol toward Johnson nor a single Democratic accusation of Republican impropriety or partisan manipulation.[116] In other words, there appears to be little evidence that the reduction of the Court in 1866 was prompted by the Republicans' desire to forestall judicial appointments by a president they despised. Moreover, since the legislation was drafted and debated before the Court provoked Republican ire with its decision in *Ex parte Milligan* or its decision to accept jurisdiction in *McCardle*,[117] interpreting the reduction as a gesture of Republican and congressional hostility toward judicial power—interpreting it as an act of "Court-curbing"—is similarly misguided.[118]

Far from a strike against either the executive or the judiciary, the Judiciary Act of 1866 was designed as a much-needed corrective for a Court that was too large and at risk of issuing deadlocked opinions. It had been only three years since Republicans, seeking both to transform the Court into a Northern institution and to provide judicial representation for the Pacific coast states, added a tenth justice, but there was nonetheless some concern that the 1863 expansion had been a mistake. With the argument that too many justices might be "rather detrimental to the business of that court," the impression that "some of the members of that court are confirmed in that opinion that the court is too large,"[119] and the knowledge that the Court's membership was set at an even number for the first time since the Jefferson administration,[120]

[113] Most significantly, Johnson vetoed the Civil Rights Act of 1866, the Freedmen's Bureau Act of 1866, and the Tenure of Office Act of 1867. In all three cases, however, the Republican Congress overrode his veto.

[114] Chief Justice Salmon Chase and Justice Samuel Miller actively encouraged Congress to pass it; Justice David Davis, who did express his opposition to plans calling for the abolition of circuit riding, expressed no disapproval of a reduction in the Court's size; and Justice Stephen Field failed to mention the reduction plan in the chapter of his autobiography focusing on hostility toward the Court. Kutler, *Judicial Power and Reconstruction Politics*, 55–56.

[115] A modified version of the proposal Chase made as a senator in 1855, the chief justice's plan called for a reduction of the Court to seven members in exchange for an increase in judicial salaries. Kutler, *Judicial Power and Reconstruction Politics*, 54–55.

[116] Contrast this with Democrat-Republicans' outrage following the Federalist Judiciary Act of 1801. See chapter 2.

[117] *Ex parte Milligan*, 71 U.S. 2 (1866) (striking down military trials of civilians in areas where civil courts remained in operation).

[118] Kutler, *Judicial Power and Reconstruction Politics*, 52–53.

[119] *Cong. Globe*, 39th Cong., 1st Sess. 1259 (1866) (James F. Wilson).

[120] Though retirements and deaths obviously relegated the Court to an even number of justices from time to time, the permanent size had been an odd number since Congress added a seventh justice in the Judiciary Act of 1807.

House Judiciary Committee Chairman James Wilson of Iowa stated simply that the "purpose of the bill" was to "reduce the number of judges and again constitute the court of an odd number."[121]

With little debate and essentially no floor opposition, both the House and Senate—still without a single legislator from a former Confederate state—accepted Wilson's characterization of the bill as an initiative aimed at performance rather than politics. Even when Senate Judiciary Committee Chairman Lyman Trumbull of Illinois moved to amend the House bill to reduce the Court to seven members rather than nine,[122] the Senate debate focused not on the size of the Court but on the size of, and particular arrangement of states within, the circuits.[123] The parallel debate in the House featured clarifying questions about whether the House Judiciary Committee (rather than just Wilson) had approved the Senate amendment and whether the reduction would preempt "the judge whose appointment the President sent to the Senate the other day,"[124] but not a single objection to the idea of reducing the membership of the Court. Eight days after the Senate had passed the bill without a recorded vote, the House passed it 78–41, with twenty-one Republicans (including both radicals and moderates) opposing the bill;[125] five days later, Johnson, armed with the ability to pocket veto the reduction,[126] signed it

[121] *Cong. Globe*, 39th Cong., 1st Sess. 1259 (1866) (James F. Wilson).

[122] *Cong. Globe*, 39th Cong., 1st Sess. 3697 (1866) (Lyman Trumbull): "But the Committee on the Judiciary have instructed me further to report an amendment not to fill the vacancies until the whole number is reduced to seven." Though Wilson similarly preferred "further reducing the number," the plan he presented on behalf of the House Judiciary Committee called only for the existing Court vacancy—caused by the death of John Catron—not to be filled. *Cong. Globe*, 39th Cong., 1st Sess. 1259 (1866) (James F. Wilson).

[123] *Cong. Globe*, 39th Cong., 1st Sess. 3697–98 (1866). In order to maintain symmetry between the number of justices and the number of circuits, the reduction plan consolidated the ten existing judicial circuits into nine, the same number of justices that would sit on the Court once the bill became law. Because the Court would be reduced to seven members only as existing justices retired or passed away, Trumbull admitted that, in order to maintain the symmetry, the circuits would need "to be modified as from time to time the number of judges decreases." *Cong. Globe*, 39th Cong., 1st Sess. 3697 (1866) (Lyman Trumbull).

[124] *Cong. Globe*, 39th Cong., 1st Sess. 3909 (1866) (John Wentworth). After clarifying that the bill had "passed the House before any nomination was made," Wilson conceded that it did indeed nullify Johnson's nomination of Henry Stanberry. *Cong. Globe*, 39th Cong., 1st Sess. 3909 (1866) (James F. Wilson). Stanberry, however, was confirmed the following week as Attorney General, making it extremely unlikely that Republicans reduced the size of the Court simply to prevent his appointment. See Kutler, *Judicial Power and Reconstruction Politics*, 50n5, noting that, since Stanberry was a Republican and had argued on behalf of the government in *Milligan*, it is "difficult to imagine that Congress had any misgivings" about him personally.

[125] After comparing individual representatives' votes on the reduction bill to their votes in four other significant roll calls, Kutler, *Judicial Power and Reconstruction Politics*, 51, concludes that "there is little correlation between 'supporting' the President on Court reduction and general support for him in opposition to congressional policies. More specifically, such evidence indicates little reason to cast this issue into a simple 'pro' and 'anti' Johnson dichotomy."

[126] The bill passed the Senate on July 10, the House on July 18, and was enrolled by both houses on July 19—nine days before the close of the first session of the Thirty-Ninth Congress.

into law instead. In existence for only three short years, the ten-member Supreme Court would never appear again.

Reinforcements on the Way

Though more systemic in approach and more transformative in outcome, the other significant episode of judicial institution building in the late 1860s—what would become the Circuit Judges Act of 1869—was also motivated by the desire to improve judicial performance on the ground. Three concerns, in particular, prompted Republicans to pursue judicial reform. First, only three years after Congress attempted to make the Court more efficient by reducing the number of Supreme Court justices by one-third, the Court had actually become less efficient. The deaths of John Catron and James Wayne, whose seats were effectively abolished by the Judiciary Act of 1866, combined with the lack of any other departures had reduced the Court to an even eight members, which once again raised the specter of a series of deadlocked decisions. Moreover, with two of the remaining eight justices—septuagenarians Samuel Nelson and Robert Grier—afflicted by the "infirmities of age" and one of them (Grier) "not able . . . to reach the bench without being borne to it by the hands of others,"[127] only six of the Court's eight members were operating at full physical and mental strength.[128] Second, with the Judiciary Acts of 1862, 1863, and 1866 all having reduced the influence of the South by consolidating Southern states in fewer circuits, there existed a "want of proper judicial force in South."[129] Indeed, the expansion of causes for removal and the extension of the writ of habeas corpus had increased Southern citizens' recourse to federal courts, but they did not establish more federal courts in the South. As a result, federal judicial presence in the South was weaker than it had ever been. Third, and most important, dockets at all three levels of the federal judiciary—Supreme, circuit, and district—were severely backlogged. Torn between their own rising caseloads and their circuit court duties, Supreme Court justices and district court judges alike were struggling to keep up with the double responsibility the 1789 judicial system demanded of them.

In order to correct these problems, Republicans combined two remedies—without either completely abolishing circuit riding, which many legislators and citizens still regarded as a virtue,[130] or creating "a large number of additional ju-

---

[127] *Cong. Globe*, 41st Cong., 1st Sess. 337 (1869) (John A. Bingham).

[128] See also Artemus Ward, *Deciding to Leave: The Politics of Retirement from the United States Supreme Court* (Albany: State University of New York Press, 2003), 75–79.

[129] *Cong. Globe*, 40th Cong., 3rd Sess. 1486 (1869) (William M. Stewart).

[130] See, for example, *Cong. Globe*, 40th Cong., 3rd Sess. 1367 (1869) (George F. Edmunds): "The judges of the Supreme Court have been, from the first, the judges of the circuit courts. They have been allotted, by an arrangement among themselves, to this duty, this one going to this circuit and that one to that. They have held courts, they have administered justice, and nobody has complained of the method in which they have administered it." See also *Cong. Globe*, 40th Cong., 3rd Sess. 1483 (1869) (George F. Edmunds):

dicial districts,"¹³¹ which was perceived to be costly.¹³² First, in order to buttress the Court and sidestep the possibility of a voting stalemate,¹³³ they simply added another justice, thereby fixing the number at nine. Second, in order to "give quiet and peace to the southern country,"¹³⁴ to "enable the justices of the Supreme Court to relieve the docket,"¹³⁵ and to provide a sufficient "judicial force to discharge the duties . . . devolved upon" the district courts,¹³⁶ they created a panel of "separate and independent" circuit judges.¹³⁷ The cornerstone of the repealed Judiciary Act of 1801 and a frequently suggested reform in the Jeffersonian and Jacksonian eras, the idea of circuit judges, which had last been seriously entertained during the debate over Caleb Cushing's 1853 proposal,¹³⁸ had long been seen in some quarters as the only way to improve judicial administration at the Supreme Court, in the circuit courts, and in the district courts all at once. By relieving both district court judges and Supreme Court justices of most duties involving the mounting circuit court caseloads,¹³⁹ circuit judges, proponents argued, would simultaneously en-

[O]ne of the chief elements of success in this system, as history demonstrates, has been that the people who are interested in the daily administration of justice have found the highest judges of the realm, of the country, of the Commonwealth, coming to their own localities to sit in judgment upon their trials, and they feel a respect and a confidence in the judicial disposition of their disputes which they cannot otherwise feel. They feel that one of the members of the court of last resort has come into their locality, having no acquaintance with the parties, no prejudices, and has brought something of the dignity and repose and fairness that belong to an entire absence of prejudice or acquaintance with the particular circumstances or parties. And in such a case . . . they feel that at least they have had a perfectly impartial and unprejudiced disposition of their affairs.

¹³¹ *Cong. Globe*, 40th Cong., 3th Sess. 1366 (1869) (Lyman Trumbull).

¹³² *Cong. Globe*, 41st Cong., 1st Sess. 208 (1869) (Lyman Trumbull).

¹³³ See *Cong. Globe*, 40th Cong., 3rd Sess. 1487 (1869) (Charles R. Buckalew): "In the first place that court ought not to be composed of an even number of judges. The number ought to be uneven in order that cases should not fall by an equal disagreement among them."

¹³⁴ *Cong. Globe*, 41st Cong., 1st Sess. 337 (1869) (Lyman Trumbull). See also *Cong. Globe*, 40th Cong., 3rd Sess. 1486 (1869) (John Sherman): "The bill will enable at least circuit courts to be held throughout the United States, and especially in the southern States where the United States courts alone can administer justice as it ought to be administered, without regard to person, race, color, or previous condition of servitude." And see *Cong. Globe*, 40th Cong., 3rd Sess. 1486 (1869) (William M. Stewart): "I believe if we give to the South a judiciary who can perform the duties devolving upon them it will do more to settle that country, do more to establish law, order, and peace, than anything else."

¹³⁵ *Cong. Globe*, 40th Cong., 3rd Sess. 1366 (1869) (Lyman Trumbull).

¹³⁶ *Cong. Globe*, 40th Cong., 3rd Sess. 1486 (1869) (William M. Stewart).

¹³⁷ *Cong. Globe*, 41st Cong., 1st Sess. 337 (1869) (Charles D. Drake). The act also included a provision allowing judges with ten years of judicial service to retire and receive their salary for life upon reaching seventy years of age. See Ward, *Deciding to Leave*, 75–78.

¹³⁸ The act creating the California Circuit also established a circuit judgeship, but that was an ad hoc response to a particular anomaly, and it did not apply anywhere else. Besides, the separate California circuit judgeship was in operation for only eight years before being abolished by the Judiciary Act of 1863.

¹³⁹ Supreme Court justices were still required to attend a circuit court in each district within their assigned circuit once every two years.

able Supreme Court justices to focus on the growing docket in the capital,[140] provide circuit courts with a more consistent judicial presence, and unburden district
court judges to focus on local judicial proceedings in their respective districts. In
turn, all federal courts (including those in the South) would be able to dispatch
judicial business more quickly, more effectively, and more fairly.

Despite widespread agreement that such ends were valuable, there was substantial debate about whether the Republican plan of expanding the Court and
creating circuit judges was the most desirable means of attaining them. Indeed, beginning with a pair of nearly identical proposals offered by Lyman Trumbull and
fellow Republican senator David Harris of New York in 1865 and 1866, respectively,
the reform campaign that finally produced the Circuit Judges Act was impeded
by disagreement at multiple points. Trumbull's 1865 proposal was raised largely
to stimulate legislative discussion of judicial reform,[141] but Harris's subsequent
bill—which called for the consolidation of the district and circuit courts into one
trial-level court, the establishment of nine intermediate courts of appeals as the
final appellate authority in most nonconstitutional cases,[142] and an increase in the
minimum monetary value necessary to appeal a trial court decision—passed the
Senate only, inexplicably, to be ignored by the House.[143] Having noted the opposition to both raising the jurisdictional minimum and creating nine new courts,[144]
Trumbull ditched the jurisdictional modification and substituted circuit judges in
place of circuit courts when he reintroduced his reform plan during the lame-duck
session of the Fortieth Congress (1867–69). Although these changes did not forestall all opposition, they did enable the bill to pass the Senate with relative ease and
the House without debate before Andrew Johnson pocket vetoed it on his final day
in office.[145] With Ulysses S. Grant having reclaimed the White House for Republicans in the 1868 election and another strong Republican majority in the Forty-
First Congress (1869–71),[146] Trumbull introduced his proposal yet again early in
the new session. After some haggling over alternative plans and extensive discus-

[140] *Cong. Globe*, 40th Cong., 3rd Sess. 1366 (1869) (Lyman Trumbull): "By relieving members of
the Supreme bench from circuit duties . . . they will have more time to discharge their duties on the
Supreme bench, and it is thought this will relieve that difficulty."

[141] Trumbull admitted that he was "bringing the subject before the Senate and the country, but without being . . . committed to the particular bill." *Cong. Globe*, 38th Cong., 2nd Sess. 292 (1865) (Lyman
Trumbull).

[142] Similar ideas had been proposed, but not debated, in 1848 and 1854. Frankfurter and Landis, *The
Business of the Supreme Court*, 70nn53–54.

[143] Charles Fairman, *Reconstruction and Reunion, 1864–88, Part One* (New York: Macmillan, 1971),
163, blames the bill's failure on the meddling of Chief Justice Chase.

[144] *Cong. Globe*, 39th Cong., 1st Sess. 1711–19, 1738–42, 1762–64 (1866).

[145] The reasons for Johnson's (in)action are wholly unclear, though Kutler, *Judicial Power and Reconstruction Politics*, 58, suggests that the president may have opposed the idea of circuit judges on
principle, and Frankfurter and Landis, *The Business of the Supreme Court*, 74, refer to a belief that the
bill was pocket vetoed "by accident."

[146] In the Fortieth Congress, Republicans enjoyed a 48-seat majority in the Senate (57–9) and a 126-
seat majority in the House (173–47, not including two Conservatives, one Conservative Republican,
and one Independent Republican). In the Forty-First Congress, the Republican majority grew to 50

sion over the provision authorizing retirement (at full pay) of federal judges who had served ten years and reached the age of seventy,[147] legislators seemed to realize both that reform was gravely necessary and that imperfect reform was better than no reform at all.[148] Accordingly, the bill passed with "bipartisan and cross-sectional support,"[149] and Grant signed it into law just over one month after taking office.

Even though the statute was ultimately passed under Grant, the fact that Trumbull proposed substantial judicial reform during the final weeks of the Johnson administration instead of waiting for the beginning of Grant's presidency implies that partisan political calculations—specifically, providing Grant the immediate opportunity to influence the personnel of both the Supreme Court and the lower courts—had little to do with the Circuit Judges Act. Indeed, both the timing of Trumbull's proposal and the tenor of the Senate debate surrounding it in February 1869 suggest that the core issues were not, as is often emphasized, the addition of a ninth justice or the patronage possibilities of appointing nine circuit court judges at once but instead the proper method of easing the steadily growing dockets of the federal courts.[150] The House and Senate debates of February and March 1869, in fact, featured disagreement over a great many things—whether the reduction in circuit-riding duties would place too much distance between the judiciary and the people, whether the system required moderate change or radical transformation, whether a Court of fifteen members was too large, whether a rotation of justices between the capital and the circuits would result in either partisan manipulation of judicial structure or unwanted volatility in the law, whether the idea of circuit judges was tainted by the failed Judiciary Act of 1801, whether a retirement provision would contribute to a noticeable improvement in the functioning of the Court—but not a single criticism that Trumbull's reform plan was a partisan scheme. Like the Judiciary Act of 1866 before it, the Circuit Judges Act was, irrespective of potential political ramifications, motivated by decidedly performance-oriented considerations.

The Consolidation of the Republican Judiciary and the Slow Death of Circuit Riding

The fact that both the Judiciary Act of 1866 and the Circuit Judges Act of 1869 were Republican attempts to satisfy performance (rather than policy or political) goals does not mean that they did not result in political advantage. Indeed, one of the two major achievements of these acts was the completion of the task set by the early 1860s reforms. Where the Judiciary Acts of 1862 and 1863 sought to shatter

---

seats in the Senate (62–12) but shrunk slightly to 104 seats in the House (171–67, not including five Conservatives).

[147] *Cong. Globe*, 41st Cong., 1st Sess. 207–19, 336–45, 574–76, 649–50 (1869).

[148] Kutler, *Judicial Power and Reconstruction Politics*, 59.

[149] Hall, "The Civil War Era as a Crucible for Nationalizing the Lower Federal Courts," 185.

[150] For the conventional emphasis on partisan politics, see, for example, Warren, *The Supreme Court in United States History*, 2:501–8. For the actual debate , see *Cong. Globe*, 40th Cong., 3rd Sess. 1366–67, 1483–89 (1869).

Southern dominance of the federal judiciary, the Judiciary Act of 1866 and the Circuit Judges Act protected and perpetuated Northern dominance. Beginning in 1866, there was only one purely Southern circuit,[151] and in turn, only one Supreme Court seat dedicated to a Southerner. Moreover, since the Court's lone Southern resident, Georgia's James Wayne, was one of the first three justices to leave the Court after the Judiciary Act of 1866 (he died in 1867), his seat—the sole Southern seat—was eliminated upon the end of his service. With the next three vacancies resulting from the departures of Northern justices and with Grant choosing to fill the newly created ninth seat with a reliable economic nationalist from the North,[152] it would be ten years until a Southerner—Kentucky's John Marshall Harlan, appointed by Rutherford B. Hayes to replace David Davis in 1877—sat on the Court again. For those ten years between the death of Wayne and the confirmation of Harlan, neither the all-Southern Fifth Circuit nor the mostly Southern Fourth Circuit claimed a representative on the Court; instead, the Appalachian Sixth Circuit and (as of 1870) the mid-Atlantic Third Circuit were each represented by two justices.[153] Thus, by reorganizing the circuits yet again and by not allowing Andrew Johnson to undo Lincoln's triumph or dilute the advantage Republicans had gained in the early 1860s, the reforms of the late 1860s effectively consolidated Republican control of the judicial branch in Lincoln's memory.

The second major consequence of the judicial reforms of the late 1860s was the beginning of the end for circuit riding, a feature that had been central to federal judicial structure since the Judiciary Act of 1789. Notwithstanding the requirement that Supreme Court justices visit each district in their respective circuits once every two years, the shift from circuit-riding justices to independent (even if residential) circuit judges signified a momentous step toward the intermediate appellate courts that Trumbull and Harris had proposed a few years earlier.[154] Even if it is true that the Circuit Judges Act's failure to establish a fully functional tier of intermediate appellate courts between the Supreme Court and the district courts "underscored the reluctant commitment of Republicans to nationalize the federal judicial system,"[155] it is still the case that it constituted the single most significant alteration of the 1789 federal judicial structure—the single most significant episode of judicial institution building—in American history to that point. Accordingly, it seems patently false to

[151]The Fifth Circuit comprised Alabama, Florida, Georgia, Louisiana, Mississippi, and Texas. The Fourth (Maryland, North Carolina, South Carolina, Virginia, and West Virginia), Sixth (Kentucky, Michigan, Ohio, and Tennessee), and Eighth (Arkansas, Iowa, Kansas, Minnesota, and Missouri) Circuits were each mixed circuits.

[152]Grant's four appointments were Pennsylvania's William Strong, named to replace Robert Grier in 1870; New Jersey's Joseph Bradley, appointed to the ninth seat created by the Circuit Judges Act of 1869; New York's Ward Hunt, who replaced Samuel Nelson in 1873; and Ohio's Morrison Waite, who succeeded Salmon Chase as chief justice in 1874.

[153]Two Ohioans—Chase and Noah Swayne—served the Sixth Circuit while Strong and Bradley hailed from the Third Circuit.

[154]See Kutler, *Judicial Power and Reconstruction Politics*, 59, calling the Circuit Judges Act of 1869 a "bridge between the Federalists' abortive scheme of 1801 and the climactic Republican Act of March 3, 1891."

[155]Hall, "The Civil War Era as a Crucible for Nationalizing the Lower Federal Courts," 184.

Table 4.2.
Circuit Organization and Supreme Court Representation
Judiciary Act of 1866 and Circuit Judges Act of 1869

Circuit	States	Supreme Court Justice
First	Maine, Massachusetts, New Hampshire, Rhode Island	Nathan Clifford (ME)
Second	Connecticut, New York, Vermont	Samuel Nelson (NY)
Third	Delaware, New Jersey, Pennsylvania	William Strong (PA)* Joseph Bradley (PA)*
Fourth	Maryland, North Carolina, South Carolina, Virginia, West Virginia	———
Fifth	Alabama, Florida, Georgia, Louisiana, Mississippi, Texas	———
Sixth	Kentucky, Michigan, Ohio, Tennessee	Salmon Chase (OH)* Noah Swayne (OH)*
Seventh	Illinois, Indiana, Wisconsin	David Davis (IL)*
Eighth	Arkansas, Iowa, Kansas, Minnesota, Missouri	Samuel Miller (IA)*
Ninth	California, Oregon, Nevada	Stephen Field (CA)*

Note: *Indicates a Lincoln or Grant appointee.

claim that the changes of the 1860s were "more cosmetic than substantial" or that the structure of the federal judiciary was "resistant to the impact of the Civil War and the first years of Reconstruction."[156] Republicans would push more aggressively in the direction of judicial nationalization in the 1870s, but, considering that the nine-member Supreme Court has lasted nearly 150 years and that many others had tried and failed to resurrect the Federalists' idea of circuit judges over the preceding sixty years, they had accomplished quite a bit in the meantime.

The Judicial Leviathan, 1870–1877

Out of the federal government's postwar role as the "political receiver of the southern states"[157] came the birth of central state authority;[158] concomitant with the birth of central state authority came the rise of centralized *judicial* authority. Indeed,

[156] Ibid., 186.
[157] Frankfurter and Landis, *The Business of the Supreme Court*, 58.
[158] See, generally, Richard Franklin Bensel, *Yankee Leviathan: The Origins of Central State Authority in America, 1859–1877* (Cambridge: Cambridge University Press, 1990). Cf. Frankfurter and Landis, *The Business of the Supreme Court*, 64: "Nationalism was triumphant; in national administration was sought its vindication."

with issues such as transportation and education—formerly the province of state governments—increasingly becoming the subjects of federal legislation, federal judicial power was increasingly the instrument for the protection of national interests from hostile state action. Unlike in the 1860s, however, that hostile action was neither directed solely toward freedmen and Unionists nor occurring exclusively in Southern states. Rather, the rise of the National Grange and the general agrarianism of the Great Plains states meant considerable Midwestern legislative and judicial opposition toward corporate power and industrial development,[159] both of which had become central to the postwar Republican Party. At the same time, though the Circuit Judges Act of 1869 had allowed Supreme Court justices to devote more time to Supreme Court (rather than circuit court) cases, it had not yet enabled them to keep up with the steady stream of cases flowing through the federal court system. In fact, with the ratification of the Fourteenth Amendment in July 1868 and the passage of the Force Act of 1871 and the Ku Klux Klan Act of 1871 opening up new avenues of litigation and expanding old ones,[160] federal judicial caseloads continued to rise. Having doubled in size from 1860 to 1870, the Court's docket would nearly double yet again by the end of Reconstruction.[161]

This juxtaposition between agrarian state hostility toward the development of a national capitalist market, on the one hand, and a judicial system faced with more work than it could reasonably handle, on the other, presented Republicans with a clear choice: either they could empower the judiciary to serve economic nationalism or they could reform the judicial apparatus in a more neutral and functional manner. If they chose the former, they could advance the cause of industrial growth, but only at the risk of potentially overwhelming judges; if they chose the latter, they would provide the judiciary with much needed relief, but in a way that did nothing to push the nation closer to the economic system they wished for it. Perhaps since they had already attempted to improve the administration of justice by providing circuit judges in 1869, Republicans in the 1870s elevated their chief policy goal over judicial performance by passing the Jurisdiction and Removal Act of 1875,[162] landmark legislation that granted the circuit courts either original or removal jurisdiction over virtually all cases arising under the Constitution or federal law. Although passed on the final day of unified Republican control of government, there is little evidence to suggest that lame-duck political concerns were responsible for this episode of institution building.[163] Indeed, hoping to do for

---

[159] Wiecek, "The Reconstruction of Federal Judicial Power," 341, refers to the "middlewestern courts and legislatures infected with Granger resentment toward eastern capitalists."

[160] 17 Stat. 13 (April 20, 1871); 16 Stat. 433 (February 28, 1871); Frankfurter and Landis, *The Business of the Supreme Court*, 64.

[161] Justice Miller was particularly concerned with the swollen Supreme Court docket and devised a reform plan to address it in 1872. Frankfurter and Landis, *The Business of the Supreme Court*, 76–77; Charles Fairman, *Reconstruction and Reunion, 1864–88, Part Two* (New York: Macmillan, 1971), 420–24.

[162] 18 Stat. 470 (March 3, 1875).

[163] Cf. Gillman, "How Political Parties Can Use the Courts to Advance Their Agendas."

business and industry what the early Reconstruction removal statutes had done (albeit on a smaller scale) for freedmen and Unionists, Republicans began deliberating about judicial reform well in advance of the 1874 midterm election. When that reform finally arrived after the election, it was—despite the appearance lent by its timing—less a surreptitious ploy to entrench Republican policy preferences in the judiciary before the Democrats took control of Congress than an attempt to complete the reconstitution of federal judicial structure and authority that had begun during the Lincoln administration. By radically increasing federal jurisdiction and thoroughly broadening the types of cases that could be removed from state to federal court, it not only expanded the reach of judicial power but also unequivocally affirmed the federal judiciary as a crucial partner in the emerging Republican economic regime.[164]

A National Judiciary for a National Economy

Republicans pursued judicial reform in the mid-1870s with the objective of making federal courts into agents of economic nationalism.[165] More specifically, they sought to shift civil litigation involving business and industry from state to federal courts. The rapid economic growth that followed the Civil War had created a multitude of such lawsuits, but most were destined for state courts, which Republicans deemed less favorable venues than federal courts for economic issues. Unlike state judges, federal judges, many of whom owed their lifetime appointments to corporate pressure, tended to treat cases involving railroads and capital-labor disputes as "matters of national, rather than regional, concern."[166] Since it was in large part reliance on and concern for "[l]ocal practices and customs" that inhibited the creation of a fully national market, Republicans—not to mention businessmen—were eager to move cases to federal court, where judges were more willing and more able to "temper the effects of antibusiness state laws or ignore them altogether."[167] Accordingly, Republicans desired not only to expand federal jurisdiction but also to widen the class of cases that were eligible for removal to federal court. By allowing a host of new cases to begin in federal court and a host more that had begun in state court to finish in federal court, expanded jurisdiction and broadened removal offered Republicans a simple way to effect a mass transfer of relevant cases out of hostile state judicial systems and into the more friendly confines of federal court.

---

[164] On how this partnership worked in the last quarter of the nineteenth century, see Richard Franklin Bensel, *The Political Economy of American Industrialization, 1877–1900* (Cambridge: Cambridge University Press, 2000), esp. 289-354.

[165] See Gillman, "How Political Parties Can Use the Courts to Advance Their Agendas"; and Philip L. Merkel, "The Origins of an Expanded Federal Court Jurisdiction: Railroad Development and the Ascendance of the Federal Judiciary," *Business History Review* 58 (1984): 336–58.

[166] Merkel, "The Origins of an Expanded Federal Court Jurisdiction," 337.

[167] Ibid.

Although this Republican desire to utilize the judiciary as a partner in the development of a national industrial economy only fully displaced the party's prior emphasis on protecting African Americans in the South in the mid-1870s,[168] the idea had been percolating for several years. Beginning in 1867, three statutes—the Bankruptcy Act of 1867,[169] the Removal Act of 1868,[170] and an 1869 amendment to the Habeas Corpus Act of 1863[171]—all embodied the Republican sentiment that expanded federal judicial power could be used in the service of economic nationalism. The Bankruptcy Act, for example, gave federal district courts jurisdiction over bankruptcy cases, thus making receivership and railroad organization cases "staples in the business of the lower federal courts,"[172] which proved receptive venues for the hearing of corporate insolvency claims.[173] Similarly, the Removal Act allowed the removal to federal court of cases involving federally chartered corporations, and the 1869 habeas corpus amendment authorized the removal of cases involving transportation companies. Yet despite the potential authority inherent within these three predecessors of the Jurisdiction and Removal Act, they did little more than evince a synergy between the Republicans' probusiness interests and the exercise of federal judicial power. Not even the combination of the economically motivated removal statutes (the Bankruptcy Act of 1867, the Removal Act of 1868, the 1869 amendment to the Habeas Corpus Act of 1863) and the contemporaneous politically and socially motivated removal statutes discussed earlier (the Separable Controversies Act of 1866, the Internal Revenue Act of 1866, the Civil Rights Act of 1866, the Local Prejudice Act of 1867, the Habeas Corpus Act of 1867) constituted the comprehensive removal scheme Republicans thought necessary to make their economic policy vision a reality. In order to make the federal judiciary into the national institution they wanted it to be, Republicans needed to jettison such a patchwork arrangement in favor of a more aggressive and widespread system of removal.

With sizable majorities in both the House and Senate of the Forty-Third Congress (1873–75),[174] the Republican plan to combine expanded jurisdiction with broadened removal faced only one serious obstacle to passage: a motion by House

---

[168] Cf. Wiecek, "The Reconstruction of Federal Judicial Power," 341.

[169] 14 Stat. 517 (March 2, 1867). For the political and legislative history behind this act, see Merkel, "The Origins of an Expanded Federal Court Jurisdiction."

[170] 15 Stat. 226 (July 27, 1868).

[171] 15 Stat. 267 (January 22, 1869).

[172] Wiecek, "The Reconstruction of Federal Judicial Power," 357.

[173] Peter Graham Fish, *The Politics of Federal Judicial Administration* (Princeton, NJ: Princeton University Press, 1973).

[174] After losing nearly 40 House seats in the 1870 midterm election, Republicans enjoyed only a 32-seat advantage over Democrats (136–104, not including 2 Liberal Republicans and 1 Independent Republican) in the Forty-Second Congress (1871–73) before riding Grant's presidential coattails in the 1872 election to a 111-seat advantage (199–88, not including 4 Liberal Republicans and 1 Independent Democrat) in the Forty-Third Congress. In the Senate, Republicans actually lost seats in the 1872 election, with their 39 seat majority (56–17, not including 1 Liberal Republican) in the Forty-Second Congress shrinking to 28 seats (47–19, not including 7 Liberal Republicans) in the Forty-Third Congress.

Democrat Charles Eldredge of Wisconsin to strike the first section of the bill, which sidestepped the Supreme Court's recent decision in *The Sewing Machine Cases*.[175] By holding that the Separable Controversies Act and the Local Prejudice Act could not remove an entire suit to federal court if any adverse parties shared citizenship,[176] *The Sewing Machine Cases* effectively allowed strategic Southerners to preclude removal by adding to one side of a case a litigant that resided in the same state as a litigant on the other side of the case. In order to prevent such manipulation, and thus limit the number of cases that could not be transferred to federal court, the Jurisdiction and Removal Act authorized removal as long as any one of the defendants was "a citizen of a State other than that in which the suit is brought."[177]

In the brief debate surrounding Eldredge's motion to strike Section 1,[178] New York Democrat Clarkson Potter cautioned his fellow legislators that it was likely to "crowd and clog the Federal courts as in effect to amount to a denial of all justice,"[179] while Massachusetts Republican Ebenezer Hoar, who had successfully argued *The Sewing Machine Cases*, declared his opinion that the provision was unconstitutional.[180] House Judiciary Committee spokesman Luke Poland of Vermont tried to neutralize Hoar's criticism by claiming that his colleague was confusing the Constitution with the Judiciary Act of 1789 and that, regardless of what the latter said, the bill was consistent with the language of the former,[181] but to no avail. Together with Potter and Hoard, Eldredge, who was particularly worried about the "fraudulent procurement" of removal through the inclusion of nominal litigants who lived in a different state,[182] convinced the House to strike Section 1 from the bill.[183] Within a month, however, Republican senator Matthew Carpenter of Wisconsin had offered a substitute bill, reinstating Section 1 of the House bill and adding "substantially more jurisdictional authority."[184] Despite the fact that the new bill both granted "federal question" jurisdiction and allowed removal from state court whenever an issue of federal law was at stake,[185] the Senate debated minor

---

[175] 85 U.S. 553 (1874).

[176] This argument essentially applied the logic of John Marshall's opinion in *Strawbridge v. Curtiss* (see note 84).

[177] 2 *Cong. Rec.* 4301 (1874).

[178] 2 *Cong. Rec.* 4301–4 (1874).

[179] 2 *Cong. Rec.* 4302 (1874) (Clarkson N. Potter).

[180] 2 *Cong. Rec.* 4303 (1874) (Ebenezer R. Hoar).

[181] 2 *Cong. Rec.* 4303 (1874) (Luke P. Poland): "My friend has referred to the old judiciary act. I know that lawyers who have lived long enough to have their heads get white are very apt to refer to the old judiciary act of 1789 as part of the Constitution, as about as sacred as the Constitution."

[182] 2 *Cong. Rec.* 4302 (1874) (Charles A. Eldredge). Effectively, he was concerned about Northerners doing the reverse of what Southerners had been doing to prompt the bill in the first place.

[183] The vote on the question to strike Section 1 is reported only as "ayes 96, noes [sic] not counted," 2 *Cong. Rec.* 4304 (1874).

[184] Kutler, *Judicial Power and Reconstruction Politics*, 155.

[185] Federal question jurisdiction refers to the full scope of jurisdiction stipulated by the first line of Article III, Section 2 of the Constitution: "The judicial power shall extend to all cases, in law and equity arising under this Constitution, the laws of the United States, and treaties made, or which shall

procedural aspects of the legislation for a day before passing it 33–22.[186] Even with Eldredge serving as one of the House members on the subsequent conference, the House agreed to "recede from their disagreements to the amendments of the Senate,"[187] allowing Grant to sign the bill into law on the final day of the Forty-Third Congress.

With only the Eldredge amendment to the House bill impeding the movement toward a more comprehensive removal statute, Republicans had little need for a catalyst to help them accomplish reform. While it is true that the midterm election of 1874—occurring after the Carpenter bill had passed the Senate but before the two houses met in conference—was a landslide victory for the Democrats,[188] the fact that probusiness removal had its origins in the late 1860s and that a version of the ultimate act had been passed months before the election casts doubt on any interpretation that regards the Republicans' lame-duck status as the driving force behind either the content or timing of the Jurisdiction and Removal Act of 1875. In other words, simply because sweeping judicial reform was "finalized just as Republican Party domination of national politics was coming to an end" does not mean it was pursued *because* that domination was coming to an end.[189]

The Federal(ist) Judiciary Reborn

The immediate consequence of the Jurisdiction and Removal Act of 1875 was to shift the "center of judicial power over the nation's major commercial activity . . . from the states to the federal government";[190] the ultimate consequence was to nationalize federal judicial power to an extent that would have scarcely seemed possible in the antebellum period. In the short term, the Republican decision to entrust federal judges with primary authority to interpret (and develop) law related to transportation, corporations, and commerce clarified the intentions of previous removal statutes and transcended the "particularist animosities of state court judges and juries" to facilitate the creation of a federal common law.[191] In the

be made, under their authority. . . ." Controversial in the early republic, this type of jurisdiction was deliberately excluded from the Judiciary Act of 1789 as part of Senator Oliver Ellsworth's compromise with localists before becoming central to the Federalists' ill-fated Judiciary Act of 1801. See chapter 2.

[186] 2 *Cong. Rec.* 4978-4988 (1874). One Democrat (Kentucky's John W. Stevenson) joined thirty-two Republicans in favor of the bill while five Republicans (James L. Alcorn of Mississippi, John H. Mitchell of Oregon, Carl Schurz of Missouri, William Sprague of Rhode Island, and Bainbridge Wadleigh of New Hampshire) joined sixteen Democrats and one Liberal Republican (Morgan C. Hamilton of Texas) in opposition.

[187] 3 *Cong. Rec.* 2168, 2240 (1875).

[188] Capitalizing on the Panic of 1873, Democrats picked up nine seats in the Senate and ninety-four in the House en route to capturing their first majority in either chamber since before the Lincoln administration. The last Democratic majority in the Senate had been in the Thirty-Sixth Congress (1859–61) while the last Democratic majority in the House had been in the Thirty-Fifth Congress (1857–59).

[189] Gillman, "How Political Parties Can Use the Courts to Advance Their Agendas," 517.

[190] Merkel, "The Origins of an Expanded Federal Court Jurisdiction," 348.

[191] Wiecek, "The Reconstruction of Federal Judicial Power," 342.

longer term, the Republican decision to allow virtually any case involving a federal right or claim to begin in federal court and virtually any case involving a federal right or claim that began in state court to finish in federal court granted federal judges the full extent of constitutional power contemplated by Article III.

In this way, the Jurisdiction and Removal Act represented both a bridge between Reconstruction and Gilded Age Republicans and a throwback to the Federalists.[192] On the one hand, it used the tools relied upon by Republicans of the 1860s—notably, expanded jurisdiction and broadened removal—to achieve the economic nationalism sought by Republicans beginning in the 1870s. On the other hand, it reaffirmed and vindicated the Federalist vision of a three-tiered judiciary as a fundamentally nationalizing institution. Thus, the Republican conviction that the judicial system envisioned by the Judiciary Act of 1789 had grown inadequate for the United States of 1875 both enabled the construction of a national market during the waning years of Reconstruction and fundamentally transformed the exercise of judicial power in American politics. For the first time in American history, federal courts "ceased to be restricted tribunals of fair dealing between citizens of different states and became the primary and powerful reliances for vindicating every right given by the Constitution, the laws, and treaties of the United States."[193]

As federal judges would soon see, however, such a capacious conception of the judicial role exacted a substantial toll on the administration of justice. With the Supreme Court simultaneously acknowledging the Republican desire for more frequent removal and interpreting both jurisdictional and removal provisions to include corporations,[194] the subsequent influx of new cases was enough to make the entire judicial system (at least as constituted in 1875) basically unworkable. In essence, the problem was that the judicial workload had changed but the judicial apparatus to deal with that workload had remained the same. Since "new tasks could not be absorbed by old machinery,"[195] the nagging problem of judicial arrears continued to plague the Supreme Court, circuit courts, and district courts alike. Yet despite the need for a reconfiguration of judicial structure to accommodate the reconstitution of judicial power accomplished by the Jurisdiction and Removal Act, comprehensive reorganization failed to generate much support in the final Congress before the end of Reconstruction. Both Democratic attempts to arrest industrialization by limiting removal and an ambitious 1876 performance-oriented plan by Republican representative (and later federal judge) George McCrary of Iowa to establish intermediate appellate courts and make circuit riding voluntary met the same fate: approval in the House, where Democrats had gained

---

[192] See Kutler, *Judicial Power and Reconstruction Politics*, 159, calling the act "truly transitional" and a "bridge between ideas and views advanced by older Republicans and those represented by the party's new breed which prevailed after 1875."

[193] Frankfurter and Landis, *The Business of the Supreme Court*, 65.

[194] Kutler, *Judicial Power and Reconstruction Politics*, 156–59; Tony A. Freyer, "The Federal Courts, Localism, and the National Economy, 1865–1900," *Business History Review* 53 (1978): 354.

[195] Frankfurter and Landis, *The Business of the Supreme Court*, 69.

control, followed by inevitable death in the Senate, where Republicans remained the majority.[196] Thus, even as unified Republican government (temporarily) died out, the Republican judicial leviathan lived on.

• • •

The history of judicial institution building during the Civil War and Reconstruction unfolded in four stages: the remaking of the circuit system with the Judiciary Acts of 1862 and 1863, the aggressive use of removal provisions and the writ of habeas corpus in the postwar South, the performance-oriented but politically significant Judiciary Act of 1866 and Circuit Judges Act of 1869, and the centralization of judicial power in the Jurisdiction and Removal Act of 1875. In examining each of these stages, I have explored both the causes and consequences of judicial institution building. As usual, I have explained why judicial institution building was pursued, how it was accomplished, and what it achieved.

Why was judicial institution building during the Civil War and Reconstruction pursued? Throughout the era, institution building was pursued almost exclusively by Republicans seeking first to mold the federal judiciary into a more Republican institution and subsequently to empower it to help carry out Republican policy objectives. More specifically, the Judiciary Acts of 1862 and 1863 were prompted by Abraham Lincoln's desire to reorganize the circuit system (and, by extension, alter the membership of the Supreme Court) so as to transform the federal judiciary from an institution beholden to Southern slavery to an institution supportive of Northern abolition. The removal and habeas corpus statutes of the early Reconstruction years were intended to fill the Republican need for institutional devices that could protect Unionists and freedmen from biased treatment in the South. The Judiciary Act of 1866 and the Circuit Judges Act of 1869 were attempts to improve the administration of justice by making the Supreme Court more effective, caseloads more manageable, and federal judicial power more visible in the South. The Jurisdiction and Removal Act of 1875 was spurred by Republicans' belief that the federal judiciary could help overcome Midwestern hostility to industrial development and, in turn, be a useful partner in their economic policy regime.

How was judicial institution building during the Civil War and Reconstruction accomplished? Remarkably, nearly all significant institution building during these years was enabled by one momentous event: the change in governing coalition following Abraham Lincoln's election to the presidency in 1860. With Lincoln's election came the secession of the Southern states and the Civil War, and with secession and war came the withdrawal of Southern legislators from Congress. Combined with the dwindling number of Northern Democrats, the absence of Southerners provided Republicans unprecedented majorities in both the House and Senate for well over a decade. As a result, regardless of their intent or presumed effect, Re-

---

[196] Ibid., 77–79, 88–89.

publican judicial reforms went virtually unchallenged from the dawn of the Thirty-Seventh Congress through the close of the Forty-Third Congress. To the extent that Republicans were constrained in building the judiciary, it was less by political opposition than by either their own imagination or disagreement within their own ranks.

What did judicial institution building during the Civil War and Reconstruction achieve? It completely reversed the Southern slaveholding bias built into the structural configuration of the federal judiciary, added a new layer of judicial personnel, vastly expanded federal judicial power vis-à-vis the states, and greatly exacerbated existing problems of judicial performance. Characterized more by success than failure, the period resulted in a judicial system that, although not fully dislodged from its founding era roots, had been given significantly more cases to hear, more judges to hear them, and more powers to exercise. In other words, in empowering the judiciary as an integral partner in their governing coalition, Republicans aggressively and thoroughly transformed it.

Beyond these insights, the course of judicial institution building from 1850 to 1877 both reinforces two lessons learned about the politics of institutional development from earlier periods and offers a new lesson of its own. First, like the early republic and the eras of Jeffersonian and Jacksonian democracy, the Civil War and Reconstruction demonstrates that judicial power is politically constructed. Far from considering the federal judiciary a hostile institution in need of reproach, Republicans viewed courts as potential allies and sought to handle them accordingly. To this end, they both molded judicial structure and personnel to serve their policy objectives and then provided judges with the tools necessary to be an effective regime partner. Predictably eschewing questions of grand design in favor of specific and immediate policy interests (halting the spread of slavery, protecting Unionists and freedmen, constructing a national capitalist market), the actions of wartime and postwar Republicans provide yet further evidence for the idea that political actors—including those in the majority party—can and often do perceive a powerful judiciary to be a virtue rather than a vice.

Second, as they had in antebellum America, prior episodes of institutional development proved capable of not only structuring debates about judicial reform but also encouraging or precluding specific reform options from those debates. The 1789 requirement that Supreme Court justices ride circuit, for example, often featured in debates over how Congress could relieve the Court's congested docket. Though just one provision in an act that had been passed over seventy years earlier, circuit riding had become both an important link between citizens and government and a cherished feature of regional representation in the federal government. As a result, almost any comprehensive reform plan that suggested either serious alterations to it or abolition of it stood little chance of success. With the justices still in need of relief but the possibility of more sweeping reform effectively off the table, Congress eventually created circuit court judges to supplement rather than replace circuit riding. Similarly, when Republicans sought to break the

Southern stranglehold on judicial power, the post-1807 norm of geographically representative Supreme Court appointments reared its head. To the extent that Lincoln did not want to be the first president to flout the norm since it began in Jefferson's second term,[197] Republicans needed to restructure the circuit system in a way that guaranteed the president would be able to shape the Court in favor of the North and to the detriment of the South.

Finally, the constraints of institutional residue from previous reform notwithstanding, the events of the Civil War and Reconstruction suggest that, in the right political climate, landmark reform can occur swiftly and easily. In this case, that climate was the rather remarkable withdrawal from Congress of entire Southern legislative delegations, thereby creating artificially large majorities for Republicans in both houses. Regardless of whether or not they had earned such large majorities in electoral politics, Republicans capitalized on them by restructuring the circuit system, reshaping the Supreme Court, and empowering lower courts to protect favored constituencies—all with seeming effortlessness. Although this situation is almost certainly the exception rather than the rule, it nonetheless suggests that building the judiciary need not always be a contested and difficult process.

The Civil War and Reconstruction era marked both the most radical period of political change in American history and the most aggressive period of judicial institution building in American history. By the end of that period, the federal judiciary, which had been a Democratic stronghold as late as 1861, emerged as the most Republican arm of the national government. Contemporaneous with the reconstruction of the South and the reunification of the nation, then, had occurred a fundamental transformation of the judicial branch. The relatively decentralized and circumscribed judiciary of the antebellum era was gone, replaced by an institution with a larger role and more extensive power than ever before. With the state-building epoch of the Gilded Age about to begin,[198] the judiciary was, perhaps for the first time, undeniably central to America.

---

[197] Of course, with the appointment of Salmon Chase to replace Roger Taney as chief justice in 1864, he did break the norm, but his first three appointments actually reinstituted and then maintained the "one justice per circuit" principle that developed over the course of the Jeffersonian and Jacksonian eras. See notes 69–72 and their accompanying discussion in the text.

[198] See, generally, Stephen Skowronek, *Building a New American State: The Expansion of National Administrative Capacities, 1877–1920* (Cambridge: Cambridge University Press, 1982).

CHAPTER FIVE

The Gilded Age and the Progressive Era

RESTRUCTURING

Although the end of Reconstruction in 1877 brought a close to the bloodiest and most divisive period in American history, the transformation of American politics and society unleashed by the Civil War and its aftermath continued into the last quarter of the nineteenth century and the first decade of the twentieth.[1] With the twin processes of industrialization and governmental centralization accelerating substantially,[2] these years encompassed both the triumph of an industrial economy and the growth of an administrative state. Originating in the 1870s shift of Republican priorities from securing political and social equality for African Americans to facilitating economic prosperity for large corporations, the creation of industrial and administrative America was not only accompanied by the emergence of Jim Crow segregation in the post-Redemption South but also sparked the rise of antibusiness agrarianism in the Midwest,[3] the birth of class conflict between

---

[1] Relevant histories of the period include Alfred D. Chandler Jr., *The Visible Hand: The Managerial Revolution in American Business* (Cambridge, MA: Belknap Press, 1977); Sean Dennis Cashman, *America in the Gilded Age: From the Death of Lincoln to the Rise of Theodore Roosevelt* (New York: New York University Press, 1984); Sean Dennis Cashman, *America in the Age of the Titans: The Progressive Era and World War I* (New York: New York University Press, 1988); Eric F. Goldman, *Rendezvous with Destiny: A History of Modern American Reform* (New York: Knopf, 1952); Samuel P. Hays, *The Response to Industrialism, 1885–1914* (Chicago: University of Chicago Press, 1957); Richard Hofstadter, *The Age of Reform: From Bryan to F.D.R.* (New York: Knopf, 1955); Morton Keller, *Affairs of State: Public Life in Late Nineteenth Century America* (Cambridge, MA: Belknap Press, 1977); Glenn Porter, *The Rise of Big Business, 1860–1910* (New York: Crowell, 1973); Daniel T. Rodgers, *Atlantic Crossings: Social Politics in a Progressive Age* (Cambridge, MA: Belknap Press, 1998); Martin J. Sklar, *The Corporate Reconstruction of American Capitalism, 1890–1916: The Market, the Law, and Politics* (Cambridge: Cambridge University Press, 1988); and Robert H. Wiebe, *The Search for Order, 1877–1920* (New York: Hill and Wang, 1967).

[2] See Richard Franklin Bensel, *The Political Economy of American Industrialization, 1877–1900* (Cambridge: Cambridge University Press 2000); Richard Franklin Bensel, *Yankee Leviathan: The Origins of Central State Authority in America, 1859–1877* (Cambridge: Cambridge University Press, 1990); and Stephen Skowronek, *Building a New American State: The Expansion of National Administrative Capacities, 1877–1920* (Cambridge: Cambridge University Press, 1982).

[3] Rogers M. Smith, *Civic Ideals: Conflicting Visions of Citizenship in U.S. History* (New Haven, CT: Yale University Press, 1997), 347–409; Richard M. Valelly, *The Two Reconstructions: The Struggle for Black Enfranchisement* (Chicago: University of Chicago Press, 2004); Elizabeth Sanders, *Roots of Reform: Farmers, Workers, and the American State, 1877–1917* (Chicago: University of Chicago Press, 1999).

capital and labor,[4] and the beginning of extensive federal government regulation of private industry. Despite prolonged Republican control of national (and especially presidential) politics,[5] then, the Gilded Age and the Progressive Era were dynamic and contested periods of political debate.

Since the Civil War and Reconstruction had effectively made the federal judiciary an arm of the Republican Party, courts and judges were firm supporters of business and staunch opponents of regulation. Indeed, by the conclusion of Ulysses S. Grant's presidency in 1877, eight of the nine justices of the Supreme Court had been appointed by either Grant or Abraham Lincoln—only Nathan Clifford, appointed by James Buchanan in 1858, predated the pivotal 1860 election[6]—and fully 85 percent of lower federal court judges were Republicans.[7] Empowered by the sweeping Jurisdiction and Removal Act of 1875 to hear a wider range of cases involving corporate litigants, these judges had ample opportunities to craft legal and constitutional rules that favored industry over agriculture, capital over labor, and federal over state authority.[8] Utilizing laissez faire doctrines such as substantive due process and liberty of contract to circumscribe the exercise of state police powers and strike down economic regulation,[9] federal courts made it virtually impossible for states to impede the construction of a national market.[10] Such action provoked a firestorm of controversy among populists, progressives, and those representing the labor forces,[11] who respectively criticized the federal judiciary for its probusiness bias, for preventing reformers from addressing social ills, and for consistently and repeatedly siding with management. Regardless of its specific complaint, each group—along with Southern and Midwestern Democrats,

[4]Victoria C. Hattam, *Labor Visions and State Power: The Origins of Business Unionism in the United States* (Princeton, NJ: Princeton University Press, 1993); David Brian Robertson, *Capital, Labor, and State: The Battle for American Labor Markets from the Civil War to the New Deal* (Lanham, MD: Rowman and Littlefield, 2000).

[5]From 1876 until 1912, only one man—Grover Cleveland, in both 1888 and 1896—was elected president as a Democrat.

[6]Following Clifford's death in 1881, the Court was comprised entirely of Republican appointees until Grover Cleveland appointed Lucius Quintus Cincinnatus Lamar in 1888.

[7]Deborah J. Barrow, Gary Zuk, and Gerard S. Gryski, *The Federal Judiciary and Institutional Change* (Ann Arbor: University of Michigan Press, 1996), 28–30.

[8]The causes and consequence of this act are analyzed in chapter 4. See also Tony A. Freyer, "The Federal Courts, Localism, and the National Economy, 1865–1900," *Business History Review* 53 (1978): 343–63; Tony Allan Freyer, *Forums of Order: The Federal Courts and Business in American History* (Greenwich, CT: JAI, 1979); Philip L. Merkel, "The Origins of an Expanded Federal Court Jurisdiction: Railroad Development and the Ascendance of the Federal Judiciary," *Business History Review* 58 (1984): 336–58; and Edward A. Purcell, *Litigation and Inequality: Federal Diversity Jurisdiction in Industrial America, 1870–1958* (New York: Oxford University Press, 1992).

[9]Howard Gillman, *The Constitution Besieged: The Rise and Demise of Lochner Era Police Powers Jurisprudence* (Durham, NC: Duke University Press, 1993).

[10]Bensel, *The Political Economy of American Industrialization*, 321–54.

[11]William G. Ross, *A Muted Fury: Populists, Progressives, and Labor Unions Confront the Courts, 1890–1937* (Princeton, NJ: Princeton University Press, 1994).

whose antipathy to Northeastern finance ran high—at one point viewed the post-Reconstruction federal judiciary as an enemy.

With attention to conflicts over industrialization and centralization, as well as the role of the courts in both processes, this chapter analyzes judicial institution building from the inauguration of Rutherford B. Hayes in 1877 to the inauguration of Woodrow Wilson in 1913. In addition to representing the approximate beginning and end of more than three decades of post-Reconstruction Republican dominance, these two inaugurations also demarcate a distinct period of judicial institution building—a period characterized chiefly by concerns over how to restructure the judicial system to deal with a growing federal judicial docket and over inefficiency and confusion in the judicial process more broadly. As in previous chapters, my task is to explain why judicial institution building was pursued, how it was accomplished, and what it achieved. My argument is that Gilded Age and Progressive Era institution building, though linked by the common challenge of repairing a malfunctioning court system, actually occurred in two separate stages, each with its own political dynamics and its own landmark reform episode. In the first stage (1877–91), institution building was advocated by Republicans seeking to satisfy the performance goal of an efficient and expeditious judicial system by alleviating the Supreme Court's workload, as well as by Democrats seeking to reduce the judicial workload and limit corporate access to the federal courts; made possible by the political entrepreneurship of New York senator William Evarts; and resulted in the creation of an entirely new level of the federal judicial hierarchy. In the second stage (1892–1913), institution building was advocated by progressive Republicans who favored simplifying, streamlining, and standardizing various features of the institutional judiciary;[12] made possible by the widespread (but mistaken) impression that a performance reform was automatically insignificant housekeeping; and resulted in the abolition of circuit courts and the end of circuit riding by Supreme Court justices. After analyzing the politics of institutional development in each stage, I reflect on judicial institution building in the Gilded Age and the Progressive Era and its lessons for the process of building the judiciary more generally.

Industrialists, Agrarians, and the Bloated Supreme Court Docket, 1877–1891

In the years following Reconstruction, the docket of the Supreme Court swelled "beyond all control."[13] The Republican judicial reforms of the 1860s and '70s, particularly the Habeas Corpus Act of 1867 and the Jurisdiction and Removal Act of 1875, had shifted a large and diverse set of cases—from bonds to admiralty,

---

[12] As we shall see in chapter 6, these aims persisted—and amplified—over the twenty years that followed.

[13] Felix Frankfurter and James M. Landis, *The Business of the Supreme Court: A Study in the Federal Judicial System* (New York: Macmillan, 1928), 86.

railroad regulation to receivership—into the federal judiciary, and, with no other exclusively appellate court and an automatic right of appeal to the Court in many instances, the losing parties in such cases inevitably brought their claims to the justices. With the dual ability to file under diversity jurisdiction in federal court and to remove cases from state to federal court, ambitious corporate lawyers were able to engage in "forum shopping" for the judicial venue most likely to support their clients' interests.[14] More often than not, that venue was federal court, where judges applied uniform federal common law rules, local prejudice was absent from the process, and juries were drawn from a wider geographical area and thus more likely to include commercial middle- and upper-class citizens.[15] Unlike state courts, federal courts were concerned with business development and prone to promote nationalism over regionalism. Staffed by judges from corporate (and often railroad) backgrounds, they usually gave corporate litigants the benefit of the doubt on procedural issues, making it easy to remove cases from state courts and difficult for noncorporate parties to evade federal authority.[16] With such a range of advantages to filing in the federal system, corporate law was disproportionately litigated in federal court.

Far from simply an unwitting recipient of the corporate caseload explosion, the Court actively contributed to the workload crisis through its own decisions. Even after *Murdock v. Memphis*,[17] in which the Court narrowly interpreted the Habeas Corpus Act of 1867 so as to deny itself appellate jurisdiction over questions of state law,[18] the federal judicial docket continued to grow, largely because the justices upheld an expansive conception of removal, both generally and as it related to corporations more specifically.[19] In fact, in a series of cases spanning the late 1870s and early '80s,[20] the Court not only affirmed the broad nationalizing intent behind

[14] Freyer, "The Federal Courts, Localism, and the National Economy"; Freyer, *Forums of Order*; Merkel, "The Origins of an Expanded Federal Court Jurisdiction"; Purcell, *Litigation and Inequality*.

[15] Purcell, *Litigation and Inequality*, 23–27.

[16] Merkel, "The Origins of an Expanded Federal Court Jurisdiction," 349–50. Moreover, the "higher costs and burdens" of federal litigation weighed more heavily on "weaker individual parties" than on corporations. Purcell, *Litigation and Inequality*, 27.

[17] 87 U.S. 590 (1875).

[18] Habeas Corpus Act of 1867, 14 Stat. 385 (February 5, 1867). See William M. Wiecek, "*Murdock v. Memphis*: Section 25 of the Judiciary Act of 1789 and Judicial Federalism," in *Origins of the Federal Judiciary: Essays on the Judiciary Act of 1789*, ed. Maeva Marcus (New York: Oxford University Press, 1992), 223–47.

[19] Charles Gardner Geyh, *When Courts and Congress Collide: The Struggle for Control of America's Judicial System* (Ann Arbor: University of Michigan Press, 2006), 96; Howard Gillman, "How Political Parties Can Use the Courts to Advance Their Agendas: Federal Courts in the United States, 1875–1891," *American Political Science Review* 96 (2002): 518–19; Stanley I. Kutler, *Judicial Power and Reconstruction Politics* (Chicago: University of Chicago Press, 1968), 156–57; Purcell, *Litigation and Inequality*, 17–18.

[20] *Gold-Washing and Water Company v. Keyes*, 96 U.S. 199 (1878); *The Removal Cases*, 100 U.S. 457 (1879); *Barney v. Latham*, 103 U.S. 205 (1880); *Railroad Company v. Mississippi*, 102 U.S. 135 (1880); *The Pacific Railroad Removal Cases*, 115 U.S. 1 (1885). Cf. Kutler, *Judicial Power and Reconstruction Politics*, 157: "The Supreme Court thus accepted the responsibilities imposed on the federal judicial system by

the judicial reforms of the Reconstruction Congresses but also began to develop a doctrine of "corporate citizenship" that facilitated removal to federal courts.[21] Together, the effect of the Court's decisions was to keep a steady stream of cases flowing through the federal judicial system and a steady stream of appeals headed directly for the Court itself.

While the scope of federal jurisdiction—and, thus, the potential amount of federal litigation—increased substantially as a consequence of both congressional and judicial action in the 1870s and '80s, the structure of the federal judiciary went unchanged. The result was a judicial system, and especially a Supreme Court, "staggering under a load which made speedy and effective judicial administration impossible."[22] This, of course, had been the problem in the late 1860s, when the multiple reforms of the Thirty-Ninth Congress (1865–67) drowned federal judges with more cases than they could handle. The creation of circuit judges (as part of the Circuit Judges Act of 1869) had briefly alleviated the problem, but by the 1880s (if not earlier), the ills of the late 1860s—overburdened dockets, overworked judges, delayed proceedings—"were revived in aggravated form."[23] Faced with an increasing number of appeals in Washington, D.C., Supreme Court justices rarely sat on circuit courts, instead leaving the work for the new circuit judges, who were in turn sufficiently overwhelmed by appellate work so as to entrust all the trial work of the circuit courts to district judges, who were also responsible for trials at the district court level.[24] The congressional decision to legislate (and the judicial decision to ratify) new sources of federal judicial business without also providing new machinery for the disposal of that business, had once again left the judicial system teetering on the edge of collapse.

With the judiciary virtually unable to function as constituted, Congress debated potential remedies for more than a decade before finally settling on the Circuit Courts of Appeals (or Evarts) Act of 1891.[25] A landmark reform that established an intermediate appellate court (or, more accurately, nine three-judge intermediate appellate court panels), authorized the appointment of one additional circuit judge per circuit, and limited the right of automatic appeal to the Supreme Court, the Circuit Courts of Appeals Act has been interpreted both as an instance of lame-duck partisan entrenchment by Republicans to further their agenda of economic nationalism and as a legislative manifestation of growing hos-

---

Congress and, accordingly, widened the scope of federal authority." See also Gillman, "How Political Parties Can Use the Courts to Advance Their Agendas," 519, concurring that "conservative Supreme Court justices were quite willing to support Congress's efforts to expand the control of federal courts over commercial litigation."

[21] *Railroad Company v. Harris*, 79 U.S. 65 (1870); *Ex parte Schollenberger*, 96 U.S. 369 (1878). Under the doctrine of corporate citizenship, a corporation was considered a citizen of its chartering state and thus satisfied the diversity requirement to remove in every state except that one.

[22] Frankfurter and Landis, *The Business of the Supreme Court*, 86.

[23] Ibid., 129: "The new business which came to the courts exceeded the capacity of the new judges."

[24] Robert W. Breckons, "The Judicial Code of United States with Some Incidental Observations on Its Application to Hawaii," 22 *Yale Law Journal* 453, 455–56 (1912–13).

[25] 26 Stat. 826 (March 3, 1891).

tility against the probusiness federal judiciary.[26] The entrenchment thesis emphasizes the fact that the legislation, which provided for the appointment of nine new
circuit judges, arrived "just in time for Republicans"[27]—that is to say, just before
control of the House swung back to the more agrarian Democratic Party for the
start of the Fifty-Second Congress (1891–93), thus diminishing the likelihood of
the two chambers agreeing on a bill authorizing more judgeships—to suggest that
legislators were motivated chiefly by the desire to entrench their economic policy
preferences in the judiciary. The hostility thesis emphasizes comments by "legislators who saw federal judges as high-handed, lazy, and overly-politicized" and the
fact that the legislation was a compromise bill of sorts to suggest that the Circuit
Courts of Appeals Act was proof of the desire "to rein in the perceived excesses of
federal trial courts" and make the judiciary "more accountable to itself."[28] While
it is true that the Circuit Courts of Appeals Act was ultimately signed into law
during the lame-duck session of the Fifty-First Congress (1889–91),[29] and while
some legislators (mostly Democratic ones) certainly were interested in curtailing
judicial power, neither entrenchment nor hostility accurately explains why the act
was pursued, let alone how it was accomplished.

As we shall see, reform was driven much less by policy goals regarding business
and industry than by performance concerns about the workload of the federal
judiciary—particularly the Supreme Court.[30] Though these concerns were bipartisan—an earlier version of the Circuit Courts of Appeals Act was actually proposed
by a Democrat and the vote on the final bill reflected Republican and Democratic
support—the legislation was nonetheless impeded by Southern traditionalists and
Midwestern populists who supported the existing 1789 system and feared the consolidation of federal judicial power. Thus, despite the act's relatively benign purposes, it ultimately required the political entrepreneurship—the favorable identity,
carefully tailored ideas, and well-executed tactics—of New York senator William
Evarts in order to gain passage. Simply because part of that entrepreneurship occurred in a lame-duck session does not mean the act was colored by lame-duck
concerns; simply because much of that entrepreneurship was aimed at appealing
to legislators who had previously supported more restrictive measures does not
mean the eventual reform actually served the interests of those legislators. Indeed,
since the bill was principally drafted before partisan control of the House switched
hands, ultimately supported by both Democrats and Republicans, and contained
not a single feature that actually limited judicial power, neither the entrenchment
nor hostility interpretations do much to explain the origins of the Circuit Courts
of Appeals Act.

[26] For the entrenchment thesis, see Gillman, "How Political Parties Can Use the Courts to Advance
Their Agendas"; for the hostility thesis, see Geyh, When Courts and Congress Collide.

[27] Gillman, "How Political Parties Can Use the Courts to Advance Their Agendas," 521.

[28] Geyh, When Courts and Congress Collide, 95, 101.

[29] It was, however, drafted, debated, and passed by the Senate more than a month before the 1890
midterm elections.

[30] This is roughly consistent with Frankfurter and Landis, The Business of the Supreme Court, 77–102.

The Varied Responses to the Caseload Crisis

The problem of rising federal judicial caseloads existed before 1891, and the core idea behind the Circuit Courts of Appeals Act—the creation of an intermediate appellate court—had been proposed, in some form or another, as a potential solution to that problem since before the Civil War.[31] Among legislators,[32] Missouri representative James Bowlin (1848), Illinois senators Stephen Douglas (1854) and Lyman Trumbull (1864), New York senator Ira Harris (1865), and Iowa representative (and future circuit judge) George McCrary (1876) all proposed establishing at least one intermediate appellate court before the close of Reconstruction.[33] Despite the failure to establish such a court, Congress was "not indifferent" to the caseload problem.[34] Most legislators did not deny "the need for relief";[35] they did, however, disagree widely about precisely what such relief should look like.[36]

By the early 1880s, these disagreements had calcified into two distinct responses to the caseload crisis.[37] On one side, corporate Republicans attempted to satisfy their performance goal of a well-functioning and efficient judicial branch. Hoping to preserve judicial power but lighten judicial workload, they advocated expanding the judicial force in order to handle the caseload increase brought about by industrialism. A prominent 1882 proposal by independent senator (and former Supreme Court justice) David Davis of Illinois, for example, called for the fusion of district and circuit courts; the abolition of circuit riding; the appointment of two additional circuit judges in each circuit (for a total of eighteen new judges); and, most important, the establishment of nine circuit courts of appeals, each comprising three individuals drawn from Supreme Court justices, circuit judges, and district judges.[38] Like the Trumbull, Harris, and McCrary proposals before it, the Davis bill envisioned one court of appeals in each circuit with final appellate authority over nearly all cases originating in district and circuit courts, thereby greatly winnowing the number of appeals that could possibly reach the Supreme Court.

[31] Ibid., 70–71, 78–79; Erwin C. Surrency, *History of the Federal Courts* (Dobbs Ferry, NY: Oceana, 2002), 86.

[32] A group of eleven district court judges also recommended the creation of an intermediate appellate court after an 1865 meeting. Frankfurter and Landis, *The Business of the Supreme Court*, 86.

[33] Trumbull, Harris, and McCrary all proposed creating nine intermediate appellate courts. After both Trumbull's original bill and Harris's bill sparked intense opposition, Trumbull revised his reform plan to include nine circuit *judges* rather than nine circuit *courts*, eventually leading to the Circuit Judges Act of 1869.

[34] Frankfurter and Landis, *The Business of the Supreme Court*, 88.

[35] Ibid.

[36] Ibid., 80–81, recounting the range of different reform proposals—creating an intermediate appellate court, increasing the size of the Supreme Court, dividing the Court into smaller blocs of justices for the purpose of hearing cases, abolishing circuit riding, limiting jurisdiction—made in the late 1870s and early '80s.

[37] Ibid., referring to "a fierce clash over remedies" and "a story of strife" between rival camps.

[38] Variations on the Davis bill included proposals for a single court of appeals with two divisions of five judges each, a single court of appeals with seven judges, and an enlarged Supreme Court with justices rotating from the Court to an intermediate court of appeals. Ibid., 81–85.

On the other side, agrarian Democrats sought to satisfy both performance and policy goals by simultaneously unclogging judicial dockets and disturbing the symbiosis between the business community and the federal judiciary. Disliking the Reconstruction-era augmentation of judicial power as well as the biased exercise of such power in favor of business and industry, they proposed curtailing federal jurisdiction in cases involving corporations. An annual proposal (from 1877 to 1910) by Democratic representative David Culberson of Texas or one of his allies,[39] for example, sought both to increase the minimum value of a suit for which federal courts could exercise jurisdiction and to eliminate corporate citizenship, which, per the Supreme Court's decisions, satisfied the diversity of citizenship necessary for removal. Since the vast majority of corporate litigation involved only small amounts of money and reached federal court through diversity jurisdiction, the combination of these two changes would have greatly restricted corporate access to the federal judiciary. To the extent that business-related cases represented a sizable portion of the Court's appellate docket, limiting the number of those cases in the federal system at large would inevitably reduce the number that might make their way to the justices.

Throughout much of the 1880s, the attempt to unburden the Supreme Court was essentially impeded by a deadlock between the House and the Senate over the best course for significant judicial reform.[40] Although various versions of both the Davis and Culberson bills were debated extensively in their respective chambers,[41] the fact that Republicans were mostly in control of the Senate from 1877 through 1891 and Democrats were mostly in control of the House during the same period[42]—only the Forty-Sixth Congress (1879–81) saw one party (the Democrats) control both houses[43]—meant that neither bill received bicameral consideration. The Davis bill was approved by the Senate in 1882, only to be ignored by the House; the Culberson bill passed the House in 1880, 1883, and 1884 before dying in the Senate Judiciary Committee.[44] The two chambers were able to agree on a handful of smaller reforms—an 1885 restoration of the jurisdiction at issue in the *McCardle* repealer,[45] an 1887 amendment to the Jurisdiction and Removal Act of 1875,[46]

---

[39] Freyer, *Forums of Order*, 131.

[40] Cf. Frankfurter and Landis, *The Business of the Supreme Court*, 83: "By common consent something had to be done, and yet again it all ended in futility."

[41] For an extensive series of debates, see 13 *Cong. Rec.* 3464–67, 3501–10, 3541–50, 3596–3605, 3696–3703, 3785–94, 3866–71, 3826–34 (1882).

[42] Democrats held a Senate majority in only the Forty-Sixth Congress (1879–81) while Republicans held a House majority in only the Forty-Seventh (1881–83) and Fifty-First (1889–91) Congresses.

[43] Even then, however, Republican Rutherford B. Hayes occupied the White House.

[44] Frankfurter and Landis, *The Business of the Supreme Court*, 84, 90.

[45] William M. Wiecek, "The Great Writ and Reconstruction: The Habeas Corpus Act of 1867," *Journal of Southern History* 36 (1970): 543.

[46] 24 Stat. 552 (March 3, 1887). Compromise legislation passed as a small concession to the South and Midwest, this act raised the jurisdictional minimum from $500 to $2000 and narrowed diversity and removal jurisdiction slightly, but it was ambiguously written and proved difficult for courts to interpret. Frankfurter and Landis, *The Business of the Supreme Court*, 94–96; Freyer, *Forums of Order*, 133–34; Purcell, *Litigation and Inequality*, 14; Surrency, *History of the Federal Courts*, 154.

an 1888 amendment to clarify confusion wrought by the 1887 amendment[47]—but these statutes did little to relieve judicial workload. Even the 1887 act, which had the same general thrust (albeit in a milder form) as the Culberson bill, failed to make much of an impact, alleviating the work of lower courts only marginally and the Supreme Court not at all while actually having a deleterious effect on the conduct of interstate commerce.[48] The result was a continually growing docket at the Court and increasingly more desperate calls—from lawyers,[49] from the American Bar Association,[50] from attorneys general,[51] from presidents,[52] and from the justices themselves[53]—for Congress to unburden the Court.

Even in the Fifty-First Congress (1889–91), when Culberson himself, realizing that some sort—any sort—of reform was "absolutely necessary,"[54] temporarily subordinated his policy goals to his performance ones and joined fellow Democrat John Rogers of Arkansas in support of an updated version of the Davis bill,[55] reform was still constrained by the Democratic opposition of Southern traditionalists and Midwestern populists. While House Republicans—in the majority for the first time since 1883—strongly supported reform and proreform House Democrats

---

[47] 25 Stat. 433 (August 13, 1888).

[48] Since some Eastern businesses did not want to be forced to litigate in biased state courts, they simply cut off business with Southern and Midwestern states. Freyer, *Forums of Order*, 133–34.

[49] See, for instance, Robert M. Hughes, "Reorganization of the Federal Courts," 10 *Virginia Law Journal* 193, 200 (1886): "It would almost be a crime for the present Congress to adjourn without passing some measure of relief to overworked courts and long-waiting suitors." See also Freyer, *Forums of Order*, 139n38.

[50] The American Bar Association convinced Benjamin Harrison to include a section on judicial reform in his first annual message to Congress in 1889. Frankfurter and Landis, *The Business of the Supreme Court*, 97.

[51] Beginning in 1877, Rutherford B. Hayes's attorney general, Charles Devens, strongly urged relief for the Court in four consecutive annual reports to Congress. Eight years later, Grover Cleveland's attorney general, A. H. Garland, who had previously served on the Senate Judiciary Committee, similarly encouraged Congress to act in three reports of his own. Frankfurter and Landis, *The Business of the Supreme Court*, 81, 93; Surrency, *History of the Federal Courts*, 86–87.

[52] The need for judicial reform to unburden the Supreme Court was a fixture of presidential messages to Congress during the Gilded Age. See Rutherford B. Hayes, First Annual Message to Congress (December 3, 1877); Rutherford B. Hayes, Second Annual Message to Congress (December 2, 1878); Rutherford B. Hayes, Third Annual Message to Congress (December 1, 1879); Rutherford B. Hayes, Fourth Annual Message to Congress (December 6, 1880); Chester A. Arthur, First Annual Message to Congress (December 6, 1881); Grover Cleveland, First Annual Message to Congress—First Term (December 8, 1885); Grover Cleveland, Second Annual Message to Congress—First Term (December 6, 1886); Grover Cleveland, Fourth Annual Message to Congress—First Term (December 3, 1888); Benjamin Harrison, First Annual Message to Congress (December 3, 1889); and Benjamin Harrison, Second Annual Message to Congress (December 1, 1890).

[53] Morrison Waite, John Marshall Harlan, and Stephen Field all delivered addresses intended "to enlist public opinion to secure Congressional action." Frankfurter and Landis, *The Business of the Supreme Court*, 97.

[54] 21 *Cong. Rec.* 3403 (1890) (David B. Culberson).

[55] Culberson did not cease to advocate restricting corporate access to federal courts as a way of managing judicial reform; rather, he simply also advocated for the creation of an intermediate appellate court.

such as Culberson (who was then serving his third and final term as chairman of the House Judiciary Committee) and Rogers argued that an intermediate appellate court was necessary both to allow the judiciary to keep pace with demographic change and to ensure that the administration of justice was equitable and efficient,[56] antireform House Democrats from the South and Midwest were unconvinced. In particular, they warned of the increasingly hierarchical and national character of judicial power,[57] expressed concern about making sweeping changes (at great monetary cost) to a system that had served the nation well for a century,[58] and hinted that the creation of new circuit judgeships to be filled by Republican President Benjamin Harrison corrupted the bill with partisanship.[59] Though the Rogers bill ultimately passed the House by a wide margin (131–13, but with 183 members not voting),[60] it encountered renewed and surprisingly stiff resistance in the more conservative Senate, where Southerners still harbored (from Reconstruction) a strong distaste for federal courts and Midwestern populists opposed the centralization of judicial power that would result from more circuit court judges and the elimination of circuit riding.[61] Thus, after the glimmer of opportu-

[56] 21 *Cong. Rec.* 3403 (1890) (David B. Culberson): "While the other departments of the Government have been advanced as the civilization and business of the country have expanded, the Federal judicial system has been left to struggle with the increased business of the country, with a judicial force provided for other and far less exacting conditions." 21 *Cong. Rec.* 3399 (1890) (John H. Rogers): "We are trying to modify or reform the present system, to place it upon a basis which shall be practical, under which justice shall be administrated speedily in all our United States courts."

[57] 21 *Cong. Rec.* 3407 (1890) (William C. Oates): "There is one alarming feature in the tendency of the times, in the tendency of Congress, and in the tendency of our Federal judiciary, and that is towards the centralization of Federal power."

[58] 21 *Cong. Rec.* 3398 (1890) (William C. Oates): "A bill which revolutionizes our judicial system . . . is a measure that requires to be carefully considered, not to be taken up hastily." 21 *Cong. Rec.* 3406 (1890) (William C. Oates): "So, by the provisions of this bill, you are enlarging, yes, doubling the judicial force of the United States, and you will double the expenditure for that purpose. I maintain that there is no necessity for this increase of judges and this increase of expenditure."

[59] 21 *Cong. Rec.* 3407 (1890) (Roger Q. Mills):
Mr. Speaker, if there is anything in our Government that ought to be elevated above and beyond all party prejudices, it is our judiciary; and the way to keep it in order and in the confidence of our people is to have the judges divided between the two great political parties, so that the decisions of the courts of the country will command the respect, confidence, and obedience of the people. In my judgment there can be no greater calamity befall the American people than for the whole body of the people to come to the conclusion that the judgments of the courts were partisan and therefore corrupt. I believe we ought to stand by the precedent we have already established and keep, as far as it is possible to do so, all of our courts from the reach of partisan prejudice.

[60] Of the 131 votes in favor of the bill, all but 12—11 Democrats and Labor Party member Lewis Featherstone of Arkansas—came from Republicans; all 13 nay votes came from Democrats. Unfortunately, there are few clues in the legislative record that might help explain the 136 Democrats and 47 Republicans who cast no vote at all.

[61] 21 *Cong. Rec.* 10230 (John T. Morgan):
At this particular moment of time it is a very embarrassing question to a man from the region of the country to which I belong [the South], because we know that there are pending certain political questions which affect very seriously the people of that country, where

nity presented by the convergence of Republican and some Democratic opinion on the best remedy to solve the caseload crisis in the House, the path to establishing an intermediate appellate court found itself blocked once again in the Senate.

William Evarts and the Moderate Manipulation of Perceptions

Amid this climate of Senate hostility toward the idea of an intermediate appellate court, it was the strategic political action, or entrepreneurship, of Republican senator William Evarts of New York that overcame constraints and enabled landmark reform. Despite the fact that he had—as a member of an 1881 American Bar Association committee charged with reporting on possible remedies for the judicial caseload problem—previously supported an alternative plan,[62] and despite the fact that, by the time he tackled judicial reform in September 1890, he "labored under an infirmity of advanced age in the serious and permanent impairment of his eyesight that made reading and writing an impossibility,"[63] Evarts was the unquestioned Senate leader of the plan that would bear his namesake and become his greatest legacy. Over the course of Evarts's last six months in Congress, he modified the Rogers bill significantly,[64] defended his revised bill on the Senate floor, and served as chair for a conference committee with the House.[65] In drafting a new plan for an intermediate appellate court and then guiding it through the final days of the Fifty-First Congress, three aspects of Evarts's entrepreneurship were crucial: his identity as a knowledgeable lawyer and moderate politician, ideas that held appeal for both traditionalists and reformers, and tactics that gained Evarts valuable allies and preempted the objections of reform critics.

---

it is proposed to link together the political and judicial establishments of the United States in such a way as that it causes our people greatly to suspect the Federal judiciary, to look upon them with apprehension and awe instead of as the agencies of mercy, and justice, and honest, and truth, and decent living.

21 *Cong. Rec.* 10224 (George G. Vest): "But they are under the shadow of the Capitol; they have no constituency to whom they are responsible; they are not elected."

[62] Chester L. Barrows, *William M. Evarts: Lawyer, Diplomat, Statesman* (Chapel Hill: University of North Carolina Press, 1941), 480. Evarts was one of four minority members of the committee who preferred to divide the Supreme Court into smaller quorums rather than establish an intermediate appellate court.

[63] *Arguments and Speeches of William Maxwell Evarts*, vol. 3, ed. Sherman Evarts (New York: Macmillan, 1919), 324. See also Barrows, *William M. Evarts*, 481, noting that when Evarts was unable to read "he spoke from memory, calling on the clerk to read portions of the bill when needed."

[64] Though the Rogers bill was actually referred to a three-member Senate Judiciary subcommittee, the other two members—Democrat James Pugh of Alabama and Republican George Frisbie Hoar of Massachusetts—"relied almost entirely" upon Evarts. *Arguments and Speeches of William Maxwell Evarts*, 323.

[65] For a chronology of legislative debate about and action on the Evarts and Rogers bills, see Williamjames Hull Hoffer, "Leviathan Bound: Changing Congressional Concepts of the U.S. Administrative State, 1858–1891" (PhD diss., Johns Hopkins University, 2002), 304–33.

Evarts's identity comprised both his extensive legal experience and his reputation as a political moderate.[66] As an attorney, Evarts had gained much experience, made many connections, and enjoyed much success. The grandson of Declaration of Independence signer, Philadelphia Convention delegate, and former Connecticut senator Roger Sherman, Evarts had been an impressive law student at Harvard University, a successful New York litigator for railroads and other corporate interests, a leader of the New York bar, an assistant United States district attorney, a member of a New York constitutional convention, a frequent participant in Supreme Court arguments, attorney general under President Andrew Johnson, the lead Republican counsel in the electoral dispute of 1876, secretary of state under President Rutherford B. Hayes, and a prominent member of the American Bar Association. In fact, Evarts's legal background was sterling enough that, after successfully arguing *The Prize Cases* for the government in 1863,[67] he became the preferred choice of many leading politicians to replace the deceased Roger Taney as chief justice.[68] On the Senate Judiciary Committee, where Evarts's "legal knowledge showed to best advantage," he was "active in the minor improvements of the judiciary system" and interested in a range of issues, including the "drawing of judicial districts, determining places for court sessions, creation of new judgeships, questions of jurisdiction, and the increase of judicial salaries."[69] Moreover, his political reputation—distinct from his legal acumen—was that of a loyal but moderate Republican. Though he had helped organize the Republican Party and was a devoted partisan, Evarts rejected the party's more radical tendencies. After the Civil War he allied himself with Andrew Johnson, going so far as to defend the president at his impeachment trial. As attorney general he supported enfranchisement but opposed more aggressive measures for protecting the rights of African Americans. Consonant with Hayes's conciliatory approach and desire to end military occupation of the South, he advocated a narrow interpretation of Reconstruction that focused more on business development than black equality. As a result of these moderate political sensibilities, Evarts did not alienate Democrats or conservative Republicans; rather, at a time when Democrats were slowly reclaiming a place on the national stage, he positioned himself as a legal mind that could be trusted and respected by all.

Evarts's ideas about judicial reform did little to squander the moderate reputation he enjoyed prior to his one term in the Senate. Equally convinced that reform

[66] For a summary of Evarts's life, see Barrows, *William M. Evarts*; and Brainerd Dyer, *The Public Career of William M. Evarts* (Berkeley and Los Angeles: University of California Press, 1933).

[67] 67 U.S. 635 (1863).

[68] Despite the fact that the justices of the Court themselves were "unanimously favorable" toward Evarts's appointment and the claim of one member of Congress that Taney had, just prior to his death, expressed a wish that Evarts succeed him, Lincoln appointed his secretary of the treasury, Ohio's Salmon Chase, instead. See Barrows, *William M. Evarts*, 124–26; and Dyer, *The Public Career of William M. Evarts*, 156–58. When Chase died in 1873, Evarts's name was again put forth, but Grant, after struggling to find a nominee who both wanted the job and could be confirmed by the Senate, somewhat surprisingly chose Ohio lawyer Morrison Waite. Barrows, *William M. Evarts*, 225–26; Dyer, *The Public Career of William M. Evarts*, 158–59.

[69] Barrows, *William M. Evarts*, 479.

was necessary and that neither his preferred plan (dividing the Supreme Court into smaller blocs so that it could hear more cases) nor the Rogers bill would pass the Senate, Evarts devised a new scheme.[70] Seeking to concede to Southern and Midwestern critics no more than strictly necessary in order to assuage their localist fears about the federal judiciary growing increasingly distant from the people, Evarts's revised bill kept Rogers's (and Davis's) idea of nine intermediate appellate courts staffed by three judges each but reduced the number of new circuit judges by half (from two per circuit for a total of eighteen to one per circuit for a total of nine), kept (but abolished the appellate jurisdiction of) the circuit courts, and preserved the right of automatic appeal from district and circuit courts to the Supreme Court in select instances. Aside from the number of new judgeships created, the crucial distinction between the Rogers bill and the Evarts bill was that, while both created circuit courts of appeals to ease the appellate docket of the Court, the latter did so in a way that appeared to retain a semblance of the original judicial structure. In other words, by not abolishing the circuit courts or formally ending circuit riding (which ostensibly brought justices out among the citizens to dispense justice), on the one hand, and by allowing for direct appeal to the Supreme Court in cases involving the constitutionality of a federal statute or treaty, on the other hand, Evarts maintained—even if only symbolically—the linkages between citizens and the Court that Democratic reform opponents regarded as a chief virtue of the Judiciary Act of 1789. Given that Evarts himself was not particularly wedded to this linkage on principle and kept it only because explicitly eliminating it would likely have proved an insuperable barrier to meaningful reform, it is not surprising that he structured it in a way that rendered it virtually obsolete. Though circuit courts lived on, the abolition of their appellate jurisdiction meant that their caseloads—and, in turn, their need for a circuit-riding justice—would be greatly diminished.[71] Far from satisfying "the extremists who still thought of the pioneer days when the Justices were active on circuit and thus, supposedly, kept the common touch,"[72] Evarts drafted a bill that gave a symbolic victory to moderate supporters of circuit riding but a substantive victory to opponents of the long-contested practice.

In addition to careful legislative drafting and a willingness to set aside his preferred remedy in favor of a less personally appealing measure with a better chance

[70] Ibid., 480–81, noting that Evarts "felt something must be done, but was convinced Congress would never accept the quorum plan" and that "[r]ather than have no reform, he shifted to the plan of an intermediate court." See also *Arguments and Speeches of William Maxwell Evarts*, 321: "It was not any change in his opinion as to which of the two methods of relief should be preferred that led Mr. Evarts to give his support to the method that finally prevailed. It was rather because his observation and judgment informed him that it would not be possible to obtain the necessary votes in Congress to adopt the plan he had advocated before the Bar Association, and the imperative need of immediate relief to the court became a paramount consideration." Barrows, *William Maxwell Evarts*, 482, notes that for his apparent reversal on the proper course for judicial reform, Evarts "did not escape criticism."

[71] Technically, justices were still statutorily required to visit each district in their respective circuits once every two years, but with the shift of the circuit courts' appellate jurisdiction to the courts of appeals making their presence unnecessary, most justices simply stopped riding circuit.

[72] Frankfurter and Landis, *The Business of the Supreme Court*, 100.

of securing passage, Evarts employed two tactics that aided his reform effort. First, he rhetorically positioned his bill in different ways in response to different critiques. Against claims that he was motivated by the political goal of creating new judicial appointments for a Republican president to fill, he framed the bill as nothing more than a politically neutral performance attempt to relieve the workload of the Supreme Court and, consequently, improve the administration of justice.[73] Against claims that his reform would increase the power of unelected and unresponsive judges, he framed the bill as a product of responsiveness to the "preponderence [sic] of opinion, judicial and professional, and of the community interested in litigation."[74] Against claims that his proposed changes were disrespectful to the judicial system created by the Judiciary Act of 1789, he framed the bill as a simple updating of that original judicial structure to account for "the great growth of this nation."[75] Second, already embedded in cross-cutting networks of support, Evarts drew on allies for both advice and favors. For example, after initially drafting his bill, he "submitted it to the justices of the Supreme Court and several Circuit Court judges for criticism and suggestion,"[76] a fact that offered no small degree of credibility in debates with fellow legislators. Similarly, when alternative proposals began to appear in the Senate, he convinced an influential friend at the American Bar Association to have the organization, which had long advocated judicial reform, endorse his bill specifically at its annual meeting.[77] With this potent combination of framing and networking, Evarts was able both to manipulate perception of his reform bill and to cultivate a natural constituency in support of it.

As a result of Evarts's entrepreneurial identity, ideas, and tactics, his judicial reform bill passed the Senate (44–6) with only minor revisions in September 1890 before heading to separate conference committees with the House and with representatives of the American Bar Association in late February 1891.[78] Evarts's "judgment dominated" in both instances,[79] making it certain that his bill would win out—over Rogers's strenuous objection.[80] With the close of the Fifty-First Congress only days away, the recognition that the Supreme Court was in dire need of relief,[81] and the realization that it was probably wise to pass some reform measure now even if it needed to be revised later,[82] the House acquiesced to Evarts's bill in

---

[73] 21 *Cong. Rec.* 10220–23 (1890) (William M. Evarts).

[74] 21 *Cong. Rec.* 10306 (1890) (William M. Evarts).

[75] Ibid.

[76] Barrows, *William Maxwell Evarts*, 481.

[77] Ibid.

[78] Ibid., 482.

[79] Ibid.

[80] 22 *Cong. Rec.* 3584–85 (1891) (John H. Rogers).

[81] 22 *Cong. Rec.* 3585–87 (1891).

[82] 22 *Cong. Rec.* 3587 (1891) (Lucien B. Caswell): "If we adopt this report we will have broken in upon the system and have lifted it from the judicial rut where we now find it. It can not be expected that with one bound we will secure a complete plan. Subsequent Congresses will find it easier to amend and improve the law which we now enact than we have found it in securing the passage of this bill, and soon we may find complete relief for the Supreme Court, which we all so much desire to see."

conference and then quickly approved it in chamber (107–62).[83] Though it is true that, by this point, the Democratic triumph in the 1890 election had made House Republicans a lame-duck majority and at least raised the question of whether reform would come this close again with a Democratic House, there is little evidence that such consideration played a role in the bill's passage.[84] More than four decades after the idea was first floated in Congress, the federal judiciary finally included an intermediate appellate court.

Reconfiguring Ellsworth's Architecture, Part I

In terms of unburdening the Supreme Court, the Circuit Courts of Appeals Act was an immediate and unqualified success,[85] largely because it offered a two-pronged solution to the caseload problems that had plagued the judiciary for over a decade. First, the creation of an intermediate appellate court facilitated a useful division of judicial labor, sending the "intrinsically more important issues straight to the Supreme Court" while "diverting the more numerous but less difficult issues to the nine new appellate courts."[86] Second, the shift away from the automatic right of appeal toward certiorari (or discretionary) jurisdiction gave the Court greater leeway in choosing which cases to hear.[87] The first mechanism reduced the number of cases that reached the Court at all; the second reduced the number of cases that, of all those that reached the Court, the justices were required to hear. With these two elements operating in tandem, the result was an appreciable reduction—39 percent after one year and an additional 27 percent after a second year[88]—in the number of cases on the Court's docket.

That the Circuit Courts of Appeals Act "worked to the entire satisfaction of the bar and of the country"[89] distinguished it from the rest of Gilded Age judicial institution building. Indeed, of the handful of judiciary-related acts from 1877 to 1891, only the Circuit Courts of Appeals Act was of any real significance. In 1879, for example, Congress modified the criminal jurisdiction of circuit courts to include writs of error.[90] In 1887, an additional circuit judge was appointed to the Second

---

[83] The votes of individual members were not recorded. 22 *Cong. Rec.* 3585–87 (1891).

[84] After all, two Democrats (Rogers and Culberson) had led the charge for reform while in the minority and presumably could do so again as members of the majority.

[85] See Henry B. Brown, "The New Federal Judicial Code," 73 *Central Law Journal* 275, 278 (1911): "relief to the supreme court was immediate, and its docket was soon reduced." See also Frankfurter and Landis, *The Business of the Supreme Court*, 101: "The remedy was decisive. The Supreme Court at once felt its benefits. A flood of litigation had indeed been shut off."

[86] Frankfurter and Landis, *The Business of the Supreme Court*, 98.

[87] A vast expansion of certiorari jurisdiction in the Judiciary Act of 1925 gave the Court near complete control over its docket. See chapter 6.

[88] From 623 cases in 1890 (the last full year before the Circuit Courts of Appeals Act) to 379 cases in 1891 (with almost ten months under the new system) to 275 cases in 1892 (the first full year operating under the new legislation). Frankfurter and Landis, *The Business of the Supreme Court*, 102.

[89] Brown, "The New Federal Judicial Code," 280.

[90] 20 Stat. 354 (March 3, 1879).

Circuit,[91] which had rapidly become backlogged with financial cases from New York City, and a set of minor amendments was made to the Jurisdiction and Removal Act of 1875.[92] In 1888, Congress mandated that liens on property issued by a federal judge be treated the same as liens on property issued by state judges.[93] In 1889, Congress prescribed the manner of distribution for Supreme Court reports,[94] provided for writs of error to the Supreme Court in both capital cases and cases where the jurisdiction of the circuit court was in question,[95] and abolished the circuit court jurisdiction of three particular district courts.[96] In other words, with the possible exception of the 1891 act equalizing the salaries of all federal district court judges,[97] which made judicial compensation independent of congressional perception of individual judges' workloads,[98] the judicial reforms of the Gilded Age were housekeeping initiatives of little consequence.

Despite its failure to abolish the circuit courts or officially release Supreme Court justices from their circuit-riding duties, then, the Circuit Courts of Appeals Act easily represented the single most important episode of judicial institution building during the Gilded Age. By creating exclusively appellate courts of general jurisdiction (the circuit courts of appeals) for the first time in American history,[99] transferring to those courts the entire appellate jurisdiction of the circuit courts, providing them final jurisdiction over most of their cases,[100] and introducing the writ of certiorari—previously used sparingly and only to summon the record of a case—as a means by which cases could be appealed from the circuit courts of appeals to the Supreme Court, the act went significantly further than either the Judiciary Act of 1801 or the Circuit Judges Act of 1869. Whereas those reforms created new sets of *judges*, the Circuit Courts of Appeals Act created a new layer of *courts*. Similarly, to the extent that the Circuit Judges Act initiated the slow death of circuit riding—a practice that had, despite many attempts to eliminate it, endured for over a century—then the Circuit Courts of

---

[91] 24 Stat. 492 (March 3, 1887).

[92] 24 Stat. 552 (March 3, 1887). These amendments were amended once again the following year. 25 Stat. 433 (August 13, 1888).

[93] 25 Stat. 357 (August 1, 1888).

[94] 25 Stat. 661 (February 12, 1889).

[95] 25 Stat. 655 (February 6, 1890) (regarding capital cases); 25 Stat. 693 (February 25, 1889) (regarding the jurisdiction of the circuit court).

[96] 25 Stat. 655 (February 6, 1890). The existence of district courts with circuit court jurisdiction was an organizational relic from the Jacksonian era, when various new states were excluded from the circuit system for various periods of time. On the politics surrounding territorial expansion and the circuit system, see chapter 3.

[97] 26 Stat. 783 (February 24, 1891).

[98] Surrency, *History of the Federal Courts*, 411–13.

[99] The circuit courts and the Supreme Court were each granted a mix of original and appellate jurisdiction by the Judiciary Act of 1789 and Article III of the Constitution, respectively.

[100] In certain types of cases—those involving capital crimes or the constitutionality of a federal statute or treaty—district and circuit court appeals could still be filed directly with the Supreme Court.

Appeals Act accelerated that death considerably.[101] Rather than either entrench Republican partisans in life-tenured judicial positions,[102] as the entrenchment thesis argues, or rein in the power wielded by lower court judges, as the hostility thesis holds, the Circuit Courts of Appeals Act modified federal judicial structure to handle the scope of jurisdiction granted by the Jurisdiction and Removal Act of 1875, removed "some of the traditional localizing pressures" of circuit riding,[103] and "laid the foundation for the judicial and administrative ascendancy of the appellate courts during the twentieth century."[104] As a result, it is far more accurate to say that the political entrepreneurship of William Evarts substantially restructured the judicial system than claim that it resulted in only "patchwork reform."[105] If the Circuit Courts of Appeals Act did not represent fundamental institutional change, then—short of redrafting Article III or the Judiciary Act of 1789—it is difficult to imagine what would.

Progressive Sensibilities and Judicial Organization, 1892–1913

Due in large part to the success of the Circuit Courts of Appeals Act, the 1890s marked a decade of relative quietude in the politics of judicial institution building. By all accounts, the new circuit courts of appeals were working as planned, the Supreme Court's docket had returned to a manageable level, and the institutional judiciary hummed along with nary a problem.[106] A few lingering issues from the Circuit Courts of Appeals Act compelled Congress to pass a handful of minor judicial reform bills,[107] and the continuous stream of probusiness, antireform decisions from the Supreme Court—particularly the 1895 troika of *United States v. E.C. Knight Company*,[108] *Pollock v. Farmers' Loan & Trust Company*,[109] and *In re*

---

[101]The Judiciary Act of 1801, of course, eliminated circuit riding entirely before the practice was reinstituted when the act was repealed the following year. See chapter 2.

[102]Cf. Gillman, "How Political Parties Can Use the Courts to Advance Their Agendas."

[103]Gillman, "How Political Parties Can Use the Courts to Advance Their Agendas," 521.

[104]Peter Graham Fish, *The Politics of Federal Judicial Administration* (Princeton, NJ: Princeton University Press, 1973), 11.

[105]Ibid., 521.

[106]See, for example, Grover Cleveland, Second Annual Message to Congress—Second Term (December 3, 1894): "The report of the Attorney-General notes the gratifying progress made by the Supreme Court in overcoming the arrears of its business and in reaching a condition in which it will be able to dispose of cases as they arise without any unreasonable delay. This result is of course very largely due to the successful working of the plan inaugurating circuit courts of appeals."

[107]Included among such issues were the scope of Supreme Court review in criminal cases, the extent of the Supreme Court's appellate jurisdiction over litigation arising in the District of Columbia, and the process of appealing denials of interlocutory injunctions. See Frankfurter and Landis, *The Business of the Supreme Court*, 107–27.

[108]156 U.S. 1 (1895) (upholding the Sherman Anti-Trust Act but declaring that it did not apply to manufacturing).

[109]157 U.S. 429 (1895) (striking down a national income tax).

Debs[110]—angered Populists enough to place the Court (and, specifically, the idea of punishing it) at the center of their 1896 campaign,[111] but the former were just small modifications and the latter was simply ineffectual and transient bluster.[112] In other words, though decidedly unpopular with certain groups, the federal judiciary approached the turn of the century as functionally sound and stable as it had even been.

With the Progressive Era proliferation of social and economic regulation and the subsequent rise of administrative government after 1900, however, the judiciary soon found its reach "extended inordinately."[113] Dockets grew, delays once again became commonplace, and complaints about defects and contradictions in the organization of federal courts began to circulate.[114] These problems were not as immediately obvious (and perhaps not as important) as the caseload crisis of the 1880s had been, but progressives, drawing on their growing romance with managerial precision, maintained that they were impeding the efficient exercise of judicial power nonetheless. Thus began the gradual campaign to rectify the flaws in judicial organization, a campaign that culminated—after more than a decade of legislative effort—in the Judicial Code of 1911.[115] Advocated mostly by progressives who thought the judicial system was incredibly complicated, outmoded, and inefficient, the Judicial Code reflected a belief that the competent administration of justice required not only procedures that were impartial and expeditious but also a system that was intelligible and internally consistent. In other words, it represented an attempt to satisfy performance concerns by streamlining and simplifying judicial organization for the benefit of litigants, attorneys, and judges alike. Despite the fact that it abolished circuit courts entirely, eliminated circuit riding completely, and collected all statutes related to the judiciary in one place for the first time in American history, the code sparked only token resistance from lawyers and legislators clinging to the Jeffersonian-Jacksonian ideal of a federal judiciary that was closely connected to local communities. Since most legislators considered the code little more than a necessary act of constituent service and institutional housekeeping, it encountered little opposition en route to passage. Simply because it was performance-oriented, however, does not mean it was unimportant. Indeed, in addition to eliminating an entire layer of courts from the 1789 judicial system and finally (after numerous failed attempts since the First Congress) liberating

---

[110] 158 U.S. 564 (1895) (upholding a federal injunction commanding rail workers to end a strike).

[111] Alan Furman Westin, "The Supreme Court, the Populist Movement, and the Campaign of 1896," *Journal of Politics* 15 (1953): 3–41; Ross, *A Muted Fury*, 27–38.

[112] After the 1896 election, the court-curbing rhetoric dissipated before returning a decade later. Ross, *A Muted Fury*, 57–58, 94–95.

[113] Frankfurter and Landis, *The Business of the Supreme Court*, 105.

[114] See Roscoe Pound, "The Causes of Popular Dissatisfaction with the Administration of Justice," 14 *American Lawyer* 445 (1906); Theodore Roosevelt, Eighth Annual Message to Congress (December 8, 1908); William Howard Taft, First Annual Message to Congress (December 7, 1909); William Howard Taft, Second Annual Message to Congress (December 6, 1910); and William Howard Taft, Third Annual Message to Congress (December 5, 1911)

[115] 36 Stat. 1087 (March 3, 1911).

the justices from the responsibility of riding circuit, the Judicial Code made the federal judiciary a more progressive institution. Per the Progressive Era obsession with scientific administration, the code made the federal judicial system more uniform in its organization, more consistent in its procedures, and more efficient in fulfilling its constitutional duties.

Trimming Judicial Waste

If there was one defect in the Circuit Courts of Appeals Act, it was that, unlike most reforms proposing the creation of an intermediate appellate court, it did not abolish the circuit courts.[116] Even though William Evarts had preserved them only as a means of securing approval from Senate skeptics of reform, and even though he had transferred the entirety of their appellate jurisdiction to the circuit courts of appeals, the continued existence of the original circuit courts meant that the federal judiciary included "two courts substantially of concurrent jurisdiction, with no little uncertainty and confusion in determining the few instances in which their jurisdiction was not concurrent."[117] Moreover, with district court judges performing "substantially all of the work of the circuit court in every circuit in the land,"[118] the work of those two overlapping trial courts—each with its own clerks and own records—was increasingly performed by one set of judges.[119] Serving as a symbol of the "cumbersome, impracticable, confusing, and expensive judicial system,"[120] the abolition of a court that was "wholly unnecessary and . . . long since fallen into disuse" became one of the prime motivations behind judicial reform.[121]

Simply put, progressive legislators pursued reform for performance reasons. They considered the judicial system—including, and perhaps especially, the district-circuit court redundancy—antiquated, confusing, and inefficient, and they reasoned that a standardization of all laws relating to the judiciary would help solve the problems afflicting the administration of justice. Epitomized by future Harvard Law School Dean Roscoe Pound's address to the American Bar Association in 1906, the progressive attack on the judicial system was blunt; "our system of courts," Pound noted, "is archaic and our procedure behind the times. Uncertainty, delay and expense, and above all, the injustice of deciding cases upon points of practice, which are the mere etiquette of justice, direct results of the organiza-

---

[116] See 46 *Cong. Rec.* 87 (1910) (Reuben O. Moon) (noting that the defect "in continuing the original jurisdiction of the circuit court has grown more obvious year by year").

[117] Frankfurter and Landis, *The Business of the Supreme Court*, 129.

[118] 46 *Cong. Rec.* 88 (1910) (Reuben O. Moon).

[119] There was apparently some argument that this development was actually beneficial to the judicial system because "better results were obtained" when the district judge—a resident of the state who knew the local conditions and was better acquainted with local law—held the circuit. Breckons, "The Judicial Code of the United States with Some Incidental Observation on Its Application to Hawaii," 458.

[120] 46 *Cong. Rec.* 88 (1910) (Reuben O. Moon). See also Frankfurter and Landis, *The Business of the Supreme Court*, 128, referring to the "perversion of an outworn system" and the "cluttering and costly forms" of judicial organization.

[121] 46 *Cong. Rec.* 88 (1910) (Reuben O. Moon).

tion of our courts and the backwardness of our procedure, have created a deep-seated desire to keep out of court, right or wrong, on the part of every sensible business man in the community."[122] Directing his criticism specifically at the "multiplicity of courts," the preservation of concurrent jurisdictions, and the "waste of judicial power,"[123] Pound—like then secretary of war (and future president and chief justice) William Howard Taft and many other progressives[124]—believed that courts were crucial societal institutions, but he was equally convinced that a more precise and systematic approach to administration was necessary in order for the judiciary to serve the nation best.

Pound's desire to trim the "weeds of procedural anachronism" had appealed to some legislators since Reconstruction,[125] when Congress twice attempted to impose some uniformity upon federal courts. The first attempt, the Conformity Act of 1872,[126] sought to eradicate differences between federal and state court proceedings in the same state by requiring federal courts to adhere to the procedures of the state in which they were located but actually spawned an even greater diversity of federal court procedures—and more confusion among lawyers and litigants about those procedures—than had previously been utilized.[127] The second attempt, the Revised Statutes of 1874,[128] aimed to compile more than eight decades of ad hoc legislation regulating, among other things, the terms (time and place) of federal court sessions in one code (as many states had already done) but was later "found to be so inaccurate in its details" that it was virtually useless.[129] Twenty-five years later, Congress enlarged the power of a commission that had been created to revise and codify all criminal laws to codify all laws concerning the jurisdiction and practice of the federal courts instead.[130] Over the next several years, Congress repeatedly modified the commission's project—authorizing it to draft a revision of all permanent federal laws and instructing it to incorporate changes that had occurred between reports,[131] for instance—before finally introducing a bill constituting the Judicial Code in 1910.[132]

Mostly because it was seen as a neutral but necessary housekeeping measure, the Judicial Code was virtually uncontested in the Republican-dominated Sixty-

[122]Pound, "The Causes of Popular Dissatisfaction with the Administration of Justice," 448.
[123]Ibid.
[124]As we shall see in chapter 6, Taft was an aggressive and successful judicial reformer in his own right.
[125]Ross, *A Muted Fury*, 76.
[126]17 Stat. 196 (June 1, 1872).
[127]Fish, *The Politics of Federal Judicial Administration*, 21–22.
[128]18 Stat. 1 (1878). For the statute authorizing the endeavor, see 14 Stat. 74 (June 27, 1866).
[129]Brown, "The New Federal Judicial Code," 277.
[130]For the original creation of the commission, see 30 Stat. 58 (June 4, 1897); for the augmentation of its purpose, see 30 Stat. 1116 (March 3, 1899).
[131]31 Stat. 1181 (March 3, 1901); 33 Stat. 1285 (March 3, 1905).
[132]For a summary of congressional action relating to the duties of the codification commission, see Frankfurter and Landis, *The Business of the Supreme Court*, 132–33; and Surrency, *History of the Federal Courts*, 104–5.

First Congress (1909–11).[133] As Pennsylvania Republican Reuben Moon, chairman of the committee charged with reviewing the code, explained upon introducing the measure in the House, the code was simply a collection "from hundreds and thousands of pages scattered through the Statutes at Large, the laws relating to the judiciary."[134] It did abolish the circuit courts, but it did not "displace a single judge or change the present general practice of the courts";[135] nor did it require the creation of any new judgeships. "We do not," Moon remarked of the code drafters, "alter the arrangement of business. We do not alter the compensation of the judges, we do not enlarge or diminish the judiciary, or in any sense make any change" in jurisdiction or personnel.[136] While Moon's depiction of the code as an uncomplicated and uncontroversial endeavor represented a basic factual account more than strategic framing, it nonetheless may have helped convince legislators that the reform was valuable.

Though the code received extensive floor attention, especially in the House,[137] the vast majority of debate was focused not on objections to the idea of the code but on specific minutiae that had been hashed out in committee or conference.[138] Of the little opposition the code did engender, much of it came in the form of memorials from distinguished lawyers and bar associations that maintained "professional affections" for the circuit courts or from circuit court clerks who were faced with losing their jobs.[139] Refusing to allow legislators to attach to the Judicial Code "measures that for years had been vainly sponsored" in other bills,[140] Moon and his Senate partner, Republican Weldon Heyburn of Idaho, successfully fought off amendments related to the salaries of circuit judges, the geographic boundaries of districts, and corporate removal to federal court before gaining passage—without recorded votes—in each chamber. More than a decade after Congress first authorized its creation, the Judicial Code had materialized without either difficulty or controversy.

Reconfiguring Ellsworth's Architecture, Part II

Having "aimed to bring ... conflicting, varying provisions into a consistent whole, if possible, and where not possible to substitute some provision best suited to

---

[133] Republicans held a forty-seven-seat majority (219–172, excluding one Independent Republican) in the House and a twenty-eight-seat majority (60–32) in the Senate.

[134] 46 *Cong. Rec.* 84 (1910) (Reuben O. Moon). Cf. Robert E. Bunker, 'The Judicial Code of March 3, 1911," 9 *Michigan Law Review* 697, 698 (1911), remarking that the code had "little to do save to eliminate the obsolete and to reject what was unnecessary to present requirements."

[135] 46 *Cong. Rec.* 88 (1910) (Reuben O. Moon).

[136] 46 *Cong. Rec.* 84 (1910) (Reuben O. Moon).

[137] 46 *Cong. Rec.* 83–97, 298–321, 564–67, 568–76 (1910); 46 *Cong. Rec.* 805–11, 1060–79, 1536–45, 2131–40, 3216–3222, 3760–65, 3998–4012 (1911).

[138] For a summary of many of these changes, see Frankfurter and Landis, *The Business of the Supreme Court*, 144n174.

[139] Ibid., 133.

[140] Ibid., 143.

conditions,"[141] the Judicial Code of 1911 "did little more than address the problem of organization of the courts, consolidate some sections [of old judiciary acts] and eliminate references to the circuit courts."[142] It lacked sections on pleading, evidence, or habeas corpus and failed to eliminate some provisions that had long since "outlasted their usefulness."[143] Even with reintroduction of the old Culberson bill and the proposal of similar bills,[144] the code left federal jurisdiction—both the sweeping expansion of it in the Jurisdiction and Removal Act of 1875 and the small contraction of it in 1887 and 1888—untouched, except for increasing the jurisdictional minimum for diversity cases from $2,000 to $3,000.

Yet, despite the recognition that it created "little, if anything,"[145] the Judicial Code was a significant piece of judicial institution building. First, by abolishing circuit courts once and for all, it not only eliminated circuit riding and allowed circuit judges to focus exclusively on their work in the circuit courts of appeals but also made the district courts the sole trial courts of the federal system. Except for the rare cases qualifying under the Supreme Court's constitutionally specified original jurisdiction, all federal judicial action began in district court. Second, the code standardized the laws relating to the organization and jurisdiction of the federal courts—that is to say, it standardized the institutional judiciary with a "systematic statement of the structural principles defining the role of the federal courts in the American constitutional scheme."[146] Effectively substituting a single act for the mass of assorted, piecemeal, ad hoc, often overlapping, and sometimes contradictory judiciary-related statutes, the code marked the first time since 1789 that Congress had made a single piece of legislation applicable to all federal courts.[147] More important, it meant that lawyers and judges were "relieved from spending hours and sometimes days hunting through the biennial Acts of Congress, the Statutes at Large, to ascertain definitely what the statute on any particular question is,"[148] thereby making the practice of law less time-consuming for attorneys and subsequently less expensive for litigants.

Although less significant in the long term, other Progressive Era judicial reforms also targeted—with limited success—inefficiencies in the judicial system. On at least nine occasions between 1892 and 1912, for instance, Congress sought to limit delay in the lower courts by authorizing the appointment of an additional judge to a specific judicial circuit,[149] but these new judgeships represented tempo-

---

[141] Breckons, "The Judicial Code of the United States with Some Incidental Observations on Its Application to Hawaii," 458.

[142] Surrency, *History of the Federal Courts*, 107.

[143] Ibid., 106.

[144] Frankfurter and Landis, *The Business of the Supreme Court*, 136–40.

[145] Bunker, "The Judicial Code of March 3, 1911," 698.

[146] Frankfurter and Landis, *The Business of the Supreme Court*, 145.

[147] Surrency, *History of the Federal Courts*, 107.

[148] Jacob Trieber, "The New Federal Judicial Code," 46 *American Law Review* 702, 710 (1912).

[149] 28 Stat. 115 (July 23, 1894) (Eighth Circuit); 28 Stat. 643 (February 8, 1895) (Seventh Circuit); 28 Stat. 665 (February 18, 1895) (Ninth Circuit); 30 Stat. 803 (January 25, 1899) (Fifth and Sixth Circuits);

rary and functional rather than lasting and systemic reform. Similarly, recognizing that "[p]roblems of law became problems of administration,"[150] Congress twice established courts of specialized jurisdiction[151]—the Court of Customs Appeals (later changed to the Court of Customs and Patent Appeals) in 1910 and the Commerce Court in 1910[152]—in the hope of developing, harnessing, and then better utilizing judicial expertise in particular areas of law, but the Court of Customs Appeals was slow getting off the ground and the Commerce Court was abolished after only three years.[153] Even two legislative attempts to reduce the (once again) growing caseload of the Supreme Court by shifting many noncapital criminal cases to the courts of appeals and restricting the right of appeal to the Court in habeas corpus cases did little to prevent the regeneration of the Court's docket.[154]

Compared to these other reforms, the Judicial Code of 1911—even if it was neither a "complete reorganization" of nor a "radical departure" from the existing system,[155] and even if its "aims were limited and its details ephemeral"[156]—stands as a "creative achievement."[157] Serving as the last phase in a three-part diminution and eventual elimination of the circuit courts,[158] which represented fully one-third of the judicial structure inherited from the early republic, the code left the 1789 judicial system more than "slightly mutilated and much changed in phraseology."[159] Indeed, with a court that Oliver Ellsworth and others had thought necessary—a court around which their system pivoted—having become obsolete, redundant, and useless, its elimination in the Judicial Code meant that the judiciary did not emerge out of the Progressive Era "practically unaltered."[160] By contrast, it emerged a more progressive institution—"a simple, concrete, elastic, and logical" system that was more concerned with and more oriented around the prevailing ideals of efficiency and precision.[161]

---

30 Stat. 846 (February 23, 1899) (Third Circuit); 32 Stat. 106 (April 17, 1902) (Second Circuit); 32 Stat. 791 (January 31, 1903) (Eighth Circuit); 33 Stat. 611 (January 21, 1905) (First Circuit).

[150] Frankfurter and Landis, *The Business of the Supreme Court*, 146.

[151] Although occurring occasionally throughout American history, the move toward courts of specialized jurisdiction was most prevalent during—and, indeed, the fundamental feature of judicial institution building in—the late twentieth century. See chapter 7.

[152] Court of Customs Appeals, 36 Stat. 11 (August 5, 1909); Commerce Court, 36 Stat. 529 (June 18, 1910).

[153] 38 Stat. 208 (December 31, 1913). See Frankfurter and Landis, *The Business of the Supreme Court*, 153–74; and Skowronek, *Building a New American State*, 261–67.

[154] 29 Stat. 492 (January 20, 1897) (shifting noncapital criminal cases); 35 Stat. 40 (March 10, 1908) (restricting the right of appeal).

[155] Brown, "The New Federal Judicial Code," 278.

[156] Frankfurter and Landis, *The Business of the Supreme Court*, 145.

[157] Ibid.

[158] The first two parts were the Circuit Judges Act of 1869 and the Circuit Courts of Appeals Act of 1891.

[159] Brown, "The New Federal Judicial Code," 278.

[160] Ibid.

[161] 46 *Cong. Rec.* 88 (1910) (Reuben O. Moon).

• • •

The history of judicial institution building in the Gilded Age and the Progressive Era unfolded in two stages: the Gilded Age attempt to unburden the Supreme Court with the Circuit Courts of Appeals Act of 1891 and the Progressive Era unification and synchronization of all laws concerning the judiciary in the Judicial Code of 1911. In examining these two stages, I have explored both the causes and consequences of judicial institution building. As in the previous chapters, I have explained why judicial institution building was pursued, how it was accomplished, and what it achieved.

Why was judicial institution building in the Gilded Age and the Progressive Era pursued? In both stages, institution building was motivated predominantly by the performance-oriented desire to have a well-functioning judicial branch. In the Gilded Age, the flood of corporate litigation throughout the federal court system generally and at the Supreme Court specifically surpassed the capacity of the judges and justices to dispose of it. In order to alleviate the Court's workload, corporate Republicans sought to abolish circuit riding and establish an intermediate appellate court while agrarian Democrats proposed restricting corporate access to the federal judiciary, thereby evincing a policy goal as well. In the Progressive Era, the judicial system was sufficiently complicated and inefficient so as to create confusion among lawyers and litigants and produce delays in the dispatch of justice. Demonstrating their commitment to organizational rationality and administrative precision, progressive legislators attempted to improve the judicial process by simplifying and streamlining the structure of the entire system.

How was judicial institution building in the Gilded Age and the Progressive Era accomplished? The Circuit Courts of Appeals Act of 1891 was enabled by the political entrepreneurship of New York senator William Evarts; the Judicial Code of 1911 was made possible by the general legislative feeling that the reform was practically necessary but politically unimportant. In the first instance, Evarts, facing opposition from Southern traditionalists and Midwestern populists who feared both the continued centralization of judicial power and the political ramifications of allowing a Republican president to fill eighteen new circuit judgeships, realized that a more aggressive House reform bill was unlikely to pass the Senate and offered his own, slightly milder, proposal in its place. Exploiting his identity as a respected and reasonable statesman, offering proposals that embodied moderate ideas for solving the caseload problem while still holding some appeal for his opponents, and employing tactics like framing and networking to sidestep potential pitfalls, Evarts nearly single-handedly ushered landmark reform through Congress. Two decades later, the Judicial Code faced little opposition as most legislators (erroneously) assumed that performance reform was simply inconsequential housekeeping.

What did judicial institution building in the Gilded Age and the Progressive Era achieve? Together, the Circuit Courts of Appeals Act and the Judicial Code alleviated the burden of the Supreme Court, eliminated circuit riding, simplified the judicial system, and completed a fundamental restructuring of Oliver Ellsworth's 1789 judicial architecture by eliminating one tier of unstaffed courts and replacing it with a new tier of fully staffed courts. Independently, the two reforms each altered the character of the judiciary to align it more precisely with the concerns of its era. Consistent with the Gilded Age movement toward expanding and centralizing authority in the national government, the creation of the circuit courts of appeals simultaneously thickened the institutional judiciary and distanced it from its localized roots. Similarly harmonious with the Progressive Era attraction to scientific administration, the abolition of the circuit courts and collection of all judiciary-related statutes in one document made the judiciary a more consistent, more efficient, and more uniform institution. Neither act significantly influenced the scope of judicial power per se, but each solved concrete problems that had been impairing judicial performance and, in turn, enabled the judiciary to exercise the powers it did possess more effectively. Thus, to the extent that making the exercise of power more efficient can actually make that power itself more potent, the Circuit Courts of Appeals Act and the Judicial Code did, in fact, strengthen and empower the institutional judiciary.

More generally, judicial institution building during the Gilded Age and the Progressive Era confirmed two enduring lessons about the politics of institutional development. First, even though institution building during these time periods was dominated mostly by performance goals, judicial reform remained—as it had been in all prior time periods—a politically constructed process. Whether legislators pursued reform to satisfy a substantive policy aim, secure partisan and electoral advantages, or maintain a functionally efficient judicial branch, it was still the case that political actors, rather than judges, were the ones who built the judiciary. Second, as in the eras of Jeffersonian and Jacksonian democracy, the judiciary was simply not capable of adjusting its structure or powers of its own volition. From 1810 to 1840, continued territorial expansion presented difficulty for the institutional judiciary; from the 1880s through the first decade of the twentieth century, the litigation explosion resulting from industrialization and increased government regulation overwhelmed Supreme Court justices and lower federal court judges alike. In both instances, however, the judiciary proved unable to rectify the problem on its own. In fact, in the Gilded Age and the Progressive Era, the Court's decisions affirming broad congressional intent in the Reconstruction era reforms actually exacerbated rather than ameliorated the caseload problem, thereby encouraging—perhaps forcing—Congress to provide relief.

While similar to prior epochs of institution building in some ways, the thirty-five years following Reconstruction were distinct in at least three other ways. First, whereas other epochs illustrated the strength of major reform episodes and demonstrated the difficulty of overcoming such episodes, the Gilded Age and the Progressive Era suggest that the institutional residue from landmark moments and enactments need not be insurmountable. For instance, the elimination of circuit riding—a practice unsuccessfully targeted by reformers almost since its establishment—may have taken a multitude of failed attempts and more than one successful attempt, but Supreme Court justices were ultimately relieved of the burden in 1911. Second, although narratives of policy making through—and partisan entrenchment in—the judiciary may seem more intriguing explanations for landmark judicial reform, they are not always correct explanations. As the Circuit Courts of Appeals Act of 1891 and the Judicial Code of 1911 reveal, performance concerns can both drive the pursuit of judicial reform and (not infrequently) result in significant institutional change. Unlike the Civil War and Reconstruction, where most institution building was based in Republican policy preferences for the end of slavery, the protection of freedmen, or the development of business, the Gilded Age and the Progressive Era were dominated by performance goals. The fact that such goals were realized through a substantial renovation of the status quo provides strong evidence that performance reforms can be more than trivialities or routine banalities. Third, and finally, the Gilded Age and the Progressive Era witnessed, for the first time, the exertion of substantial influence by outside interest groups. Indeed, with populists and labor serving as core elements of Democratic opposition to the Court and progressives urging more efficient courts, the Gilded Age and Progressive Era made clear that, by the end of the nineteenth century, judicial reform was no longer simply a task for elected officials but instead an opportunity for interest groups and citizens to shape the direction of federal institutions themselves.

Although the federal judiciary was not explicitly empowered during the Gilded Age and the Progressive Era, as it had been during the Civil War and Reconstruction, its structure was significantly modified and its performance substantially improved. That is to say, after the aggressive judicial institution building of the 1860s and '70s placed extreme strain on the federal judicial machinery, the Circuit Courts of Appeals Act of 1891 and the Judicial Code of 1911 were conceived as forms of relief; restructuring the institutional judiciary was conceived as a practical solution to concrete problems of institutional functioning. For a short time during Woodrow Wilson's first term as president, those problems appeared to be solved, and there was little dispute about the benefits of an efficient judicial branch. With World War I and Prohibition on the horizon, however, the third branch would soon be in need of assistance once again. Not only would Congress provide the judiciary such assistance in the 1920s but, for the first time in American history and despite burgeoning skepticism about the implications of judicial efficiency for judicial power, it would do so in a way that made the judicial branch more independent and more autonomous to solve future problems on its own.

CHAPTER SIX

The Interwar and New Deal Years

BUREAUCRATIZATION

World War I began as America reached a crossroads.[1] By that point, the "promise of American life" had been challenged,[2] and it was not yet clear which course the nation would take in restoring it. The continued growth of business and industry meant more economic development but also more conflicts between labor and management over unionization, yellow dog contracts, and injunctions. The continued expansion of regulatory government meant the protection of consumers and citizens from the harsh realities of the market but also a rapidly expanding executive bureaucracy. The American rise to international prominence meant financial and diplomatic interests around the globe but also the need to defend those interests through armed conflict. As World War I faded into history, unpredictability took hold, with the nation experiencing a decade of unstable prosperity (the so-called Roaring Twenties) before rapidly descending into an economic crisis. Out of the Great Depression, of course, came the political revolution of the New Deal: massive growth of the federal government, broad expansion of presidential authority, and extensive governmental regulation of the national economy. By the time the nation prepared for entrance into yet another global war, political, economic, and military supremacy seemed almost imminent.

Just as the interwar and New Deal years were pivotal in shaping what would become "modern" America, so too were they pivotal in shaping what would become the "modern" judiciary. Far from simply and naturally evolving out of the institution as it stood before World War I, that judiciary was unquestionably forged in response to the particular climate of politics before World War II. Indeed, to the extent that the major reforms of the Gilded Age and the Progressive Era—the establishment of the circuit courts of appeals in 1891 and the creation of a unified judicial code in 1911—brought the workload of the federal judiciary under control, the events of interwar and New Deal America exploded it yet again. With the af-

---

[1] See, among others, William E. Leuchtenburg, *The Perils of Prosperity, 1914–1932*, 2nd ed. (Chicago: University of Chicago Press, 1993); Nathan Miller, *New World Coming: The 1920s and the Making of Modern America* (New York: Scribner's, 2003); and Michael E. Parrish, *Anxious Decades: America in Prosperity and Depression, 1920–1941* (New York: Norton, 1992).

[2] Herbert Croly, *The Promise of American Life* (New York: Macmillan, 1912).

termath of World War I came cases involving both economic production from the prewar mobilization and espionage during the war itself. With Prohibition came aggressive prosecution against organized crime. With the emerging administrative state came legislation (and the inevitable challenges to such legislation) concerning monopolies, child labor, taxation, production, and manufacturing. Within the context of this workload resurgence, the interwar and New Deal judiciary faced an unprecedented level of hostility from citizens, interest groups, and other branches of government.[3] Approaching the 1930s, federal judges were the targets of heated court-curbing rhetoric from populists, progressives, and members of the labor movement. During the 1930s, Democrats grew frustrated with the Supreme Court striking down New Deal legislation, and President Franklin Delano Roosevelt proposed his infamous Court-packing plan to bring the recalcitrant judiciary under closer political control.[4] In other words, from World War I to World War II, through normalcy and the New Deal, the federal judiciary not only faced a caseload vastly greater than its capacity but also a diverse set of political actors that seemed decidedly hostile to its work.

Animated by rising federal judicial caseloads, on the one hand, and potent hostility toward judicial power, on the other, this chapter examines judicial institution building during the quarter century between the dawn of World War I in July 1914 and the dawn of World War II in September 1939. As we shall see, this period of institution building was defined by a series of reforms expanding judicial discretion over both caseload and procedure and providing an administrative apparatus—separate from either the legislative or executive branches—for judges to formulate, implement, and assess policy related to their own institution. My goal in this chapter is to illuminate the causes and consequences of those reforms. As in the previous four chapters, I do so by asking why judicial institution building was pursued, how it was accomplished, and what it achieved. Judicial institution building during the interwar and New Deal years was, I argue, prompted by a variety of performance concerns about the workload and administration of the judicial branch; enabled in three separate instances by the political entrepreneurship of Chief Justice William Howard Taft, the political entrepreneurship of Attorney General Homer Cummings, and limited opposition to moderate reform following Roosevelt's more hostile Court-packing plan; and resulted in the metamorphosis of the federal judiciary into a self-governing policy-making institution with not only its own interests but also the capability to pursue and satisfy those interests. This bureaucratization of the judiciary—this transmogrification of an institution that did little more than adjudicate disputes into an institution that recommended policy, lobbied political officials, and governed its own affairs in addition to adju-

---

[3] William G. Ross, *A Muted Fury: Populists, Progressives, and Labor Unions Confront the Courts, 1890–1937* (Princeton, NJ: Princeton University Press, 1994).

[4] William E. Leuchtenburg, *The Supreme Court Reborn: The Constitutional Revolution in the Age of Roosevelt* (New York: Oxford University Press, 1995); Barry Cushman, *Rethinking the New Deal Court: The Structure of a Constitutional Revolution* (New York: Oxford University Press, 1998).

dicating disputes—occurred in three stages: first, Taft's success in forging judicial autonomy over the Supreme Court's docket and creating a policy-making body within the judicial branch (1913–29); second, Cummings's realization of a twenty-year American Bar Association goal to vest the authority to promulgate uniform rules of civil procedure in the hands of the justices (1930–35); and, third, the complete separation of the judiciary's budget and administration from the executive branch control of the Department of Justice (1936–39). After treating each stage in turn, I conclude with a glance back at this critical period of institution building and an assessment of the state of the institutional judiciary at the brink of modern America.

William Howard Taft and the Forging of Judicial Autonomy, 1913–1929

By the time Warren G. Harding was elected president in 1920, the federal judiciary was, in the words of former president and soon-to-be chief justice William Howard Taft, "likely to be swamped, and delay of justice" was "inevitable."[5] The combination of several factors—increased government regulation of the national economy; the first cases of income tax violations; the prosecution of espionage cases lingering from World War I; the rise in civil litigation from canceled wartime contracts; the growing federalization of crime (narcotics, smuggling, auto theft, and white slave trafficking); and, of course, with the ratification of the Eighteenth Amendment (Prohibition) and the passage of the Volstead Act,[6] prosecutions against organized crime and alcohol distributors—left the courts, still highly decentralized and laboring under cumbersome procedures like automatic appeals to the Supreme Court, with a bloated and substantially backlogged docket. In less than a decade, the criminal caseload of the federal judiciary had swelled by nearly 800 percent,[7] and the number of petitions to the Supreme Court for certiorari had nearly doubled (from 270 to 539).[8] At the Court alone, the average time from filing to hearing was more than fourteen months.[9] There had been a few functionalist attempts to deal with the growing judicial caseload in the early twentieth century,[10] but they had been largely piecemeal, modifying the problem only for a short time

---

[5] William Howard Taft, "Three Needed Steps of Progress," *American Bar Association Journal* 8 (1922): 34.

[6] 41 Stat. 205 (October 28, 1919).

[7] See Deborah J. Barrow, Gary Zuk, and Gerard S. Gryski, *The Federal Judiciary and Institutional Change* (Ann Arbor: University of Michigan Press, 1996), 32. On the issue of workload, see Gerhard Casper and Richard A. Posner, *The Workload of the Supreme Court* (Chicago: American Bar Association, 1976).

[8] Felix Frankfurter and James M. Landis, *The Business of the Supreme Court: A Study in the Federal Judicial System* (New York: Macmillan, 1928), 295.

[9] Alpheus Thomas Mason, *William Howard Taft: Chief Justice* (Lanham, MD: University Press of America, 1984), 108.

[10] 38 Stat. 203 (October 3, 1913); 38 Stat. 790 (December 23, 1914); 39 Stat. 726 (September 6, 1916).

and, even then, only at the margins.[11] In order to survive the swell of cases crashing down upon it, the post–World War I judiciary required less tinkering and more transformation.

Over the next several years, two landmark reforms wrought precisely that transformation. The first, the Judicial Conference Act of 1922,[12] provided twenty-four additional district court judges; granted the chief justice authority to transfer judges from overstaffed districts in one circuit to understaffed districts in other circuits[13]; and established the Conference of Senior Circuit Judges (later known as the Judicial Conference), an annual meeting of the nation's top judges that, under the direction of the chief justice, would survey the state of judicial affairs and make proposals to Congress. The second, the Judiciary Act of 1925,[14] drastically redefined the role of the Supreme Court by converting much of its obligatory jurisdiction into certiorari jurisdiction.[15] The former established the chief justice as the "head" of the entire judicial branch, imposed greater structural hierarchy within the court system, and infused "executive principle" into the tasks of judicial governance; the latter unburdened the Court from hearing a multitude of insignificant appeals and allowed it to return to its "higher function" of constitutional interpretation.[16] Although enacted three years apart, these two reforms shared a common purpose and a common benefactor: both were motivated by performance concerns about efficient judicial administration, and both were made possible—overcoming the "muted fury" surrounding federal courts at the time[17]—by Taft's political entrepreneurship. Together, they resulted in both the forging of "judicial autonomy" and the introduction of judicial bureaucracy.[18]

[11] See William Howard Taft, "The Attacks on the Courts and Legal Procedure," 5 *Kentucky Law Journal* 3, 14 (1916–17): "From time to time, some remedial measure is adopted, but only by piecemeal. Some steps have been taken but nothing radical although the subject calls for broad measures."

[12] 42 Stat. 837 (September 14, 1922).

[13] Such authority, which was contingent upon the approval of the senior circuit judges from both circuits involved in the transfer, complemented another power conferred by the 1922 act: the ability of senior circuit judges to transfer judges between districts within a given circuit.

[14] 43 Stat. 936 (February 13, 1925). The statute is also known as the "Judges' Bill" because, as we shall see, judges—Supreme Court justices, in fact—authored and testified in favor of it.

[15] Though similar to the Circuit Courts of Appeals Act of 1891 (see chapter 5) in this shift, the Judiciary Act of 1925 was far more sweeping in its overall effect on the Court's docket.

[16] In practice, of course, constitutional interpretation represents a relatively small percentage of the Court's work.

[17] Ross, *A Muted Fury*.

[18] I borrow this idea of institutional autonomy from Daniel P. Carpenter, *The Forging of Bureaucratic Autonomy* (Princeton, NJ: Princeton University Press, 2001). For a full application of Carpenter's theory to Taft's judicial reform campaign, see Justin Crowe, "The Forging of Judicial Autonomy: Political Entrepreneurship and the Reforms of William Howard Taft," *Journal of Politics* 69 (2007): 73–87. For other, more descriptive, accounts of Taft's reform campaign, see Jeremy Buchman, "Judicial Lobbying and the Politics of Judicial Structure: An Examination of the Judiciary Act of 1925," *Justice System Journal* 24 (2003): 1–22; Peter G. Fish, "William Howard Taft and Charles Evans Hughes: Conservative Politicians as Chief Judicial Reformers," *Supreme Court Review* 1975 (1975): 123–45; Edward A. Hartnett, "Questioning Certiorari: Some Reflections Seventy-Five Years after the Judges' Bill," 100 *Columbia Law Review* 1643 (2000); Mason, *William Howard Taft*; Walter F. Murphy, "In His Own Image: Mr. Chief

"Reasonable Betterment by Practical Means":
Taft's Judicial Reform Campaign

As World War I and Prohibition quickly rendered the previous decade's solutions to the rising judicial caseload moot, comprehensive judicial reform was urged by legal academics, by bar associations, and by judges across the nation. Most prominently, it was urged by William Howard Taft. Taft's suggestions for reform, which he had offered as president (1909–13), as president of the American Bar Association (1913–14), as a law professor at Yale University (1913–21), and, beginning in 1921, as chief justice of the United States, were not only the most prominent but also the most extensive. Among other things, he proposed granting the chief justice broad administrative powers to direct the federal judiciary, establishing an annual meeting of judges to survey judicial business, allowing the Supreme Court greater control over its docket, and consolidating the various forms of judicial procedure into a uniform code.[19] Intended to streamline the judicial process and make the administration of justice cheaper, quicker, and more predictable, these proposals represented a holistic and performance-oriented platform for "reasonable betterment by practical means."[20]

Although Taft and his allies in the bar and on the bench viewed this platform in terms of improving judicial functioning, the potential policy implications of a more efficient—and, consequently, more powerful—judicial system proved a source of disagreement in the deeply fractured Republican Party. On one side, the dominant, probusiness old guard supported reform, albeit for reasons different than Taft. For these legislators, reform was not an end in and of itself but a means to serve policy ends. Recognizing that the judiciary had become a loyal friend to business and industry, reform offered conservatives an opportunity to break the back of labor. On the other side, a smaller but vocal group of progressives were staunch opponents of judicial reform. Looking back at court decisions of the previous two decades,[21] progressives feared that an improved and empowered judiciary might be even more aggressive in thwarting the labor movement and eviscerating protective legislation.[22] Across the aisle, Democrats expressed a

Justice Taft and Supreme Court Appointments," *Supreme Court Review* 1961 (1961): 159–93; Walter F. Murphy, "Chief Justice Taft and the Lower Court Bureaucracy: A Study in Judicial Administration," *Journal of Politics* 24 (1962): 453–76; and Robert Post, "Judicial Management and Judicial Disinterest: The Achievements and Perils of Chief Justice William Howard Taft," *Journal of Supreme Court History* 1998 (1998): 50–70.

[19] See Taft, "Three Needed Steps of Progress"; William Howard Taft, "Adequate Machinery for Judicial Business," *American Bar Association Journal* 7 (1921): 453–54; and William Howard Taft, "Possible and Needed Reforms in Administration of Justice in Federal Courts," *American Bar Association Journal* 8 (1922): 601–7.

[20] Taft, "The Attacks on the Courts and Legal Procedure," 10.

[21] See, for instance, *Hammer v. Dagenhart*, 247 U.S. 251 (1918) (striking down a law prohibiting child labor); *Bailey v. Drexel Furniture Company*, 259 U.S. 20 (1922) (striking down a tax on products of child labor); and *Lochner v. New York*, 198 U.S. 45 (1905) (striking down maximum working hours legislation).

[22] Ross, *A Muted Fury*.

variety of concerns with judicial reform, ranging from the effects of centralized judicial administration on the tradition of judicial localism to the potential triumph of big business over agrarian society to the wisdom, ethics, and constitutionality of placing extensive administrative authority in the hands of federal judges.[23] Even when conservative Republicans—who controlled both houses of Congress and the presidency after the 1920 election—were seemingly poised to enact their legislative agenda, then, the combined opposition of progressives (who formed a sizable bloc on the pivotal Senate Judiciary Committee[24]) and some Democrats stood in the way of meaningful reform.[25]

Politics outside Congress posed similar challenges. On the one hand, with the judiciary struggling to deal with the massive spike in litigation,[26] Taft pointed to real problems in need of a solution[27] and proposed to entrench in the judiciary the very aims of professional expertise, scientific administration, and managerial efficiency valued by the late Progressive Era state-building climate. On the other hand, the post–World War I national mood of ambivalence toward centralization meant that Americans were simultaneously enthusiastic about the opportunities offered by an expanded national government and worried about the disintegration of local government that might accompany such expansion.[28] Compounding this ambivalence was the fact that the Court itself—though still firmly supported by conservative Republicans—continued to make numerous enemies in Congress from its invalidation of state and federal economic regulation. In fact, from 1922 to 1924 alone, the justices faced eleven separate Court-curbing proposals from angry progressives,[29] including aggressive attempts to rein in the Court by Senators Robert La Follette (R-WI) and William Borah (R-ID) in 1922 and 1923, respectively.[30] The result was that, by the time Taft adopted the cause of judicial reform as chief

[23] Frankfurter and Landis, *The Business of the Supreme Court*, 218; Charles Gardner Geyh, *When Courts and Congress Collide: The Struggle for Control of America's Judicial System* (Ann Arbor: University of Michigan Press, 2006), 103–5.

[24] Of fifteen members, four—William Borah (R-ID), George Norris (R-NE), Thomas Walsh (D-MT), and John Shields (D-TN)—were progressives. Recognizing the problem, Taft led an uphill, behind-the-scenes battle to reorganize the committee along more favorable ideological lines. His attempt was rebuffed, however, when Frank Kellogg (R-MN), one of the two senators he favored for appointment to the committee, was defeated for reelection in 1922. See Mason, *William Howard Taft*, 95.

[25] Geyh, *When Courts and Congress Collide*, 103; David H. Burton, *Taft, Holmes, and the 1920s Court: An Appraisal* (Madison, NJ: Fairleigh Dickinson University Press, 1998), 118–21.

[26] "Daugherty Wants 18 More Judges," *New York Times*, August 20, 1921.

[27] Taft, "The Attacks on the Courts and Legal Procedure," 11, lamented that the caseload increase had "swamped a system that was adopted in more primitive times and was adapted to conditions of a people living in rural rather than urban communities."

[28] Robert Post, "Federalism in the Taft Court Era: Can it be 'Revived,'" 51 *Duke Law Journal* 1513 (2002).

[29] Stuart S. Nagel, "Court-Curbing Periods in American History," 18 *Vanderbilt Law Review* 925 (1965); Gerald N. Rosenberg, "Judicial Independence and the Reality of Political Power," *Review of Politics* 54 (1992): 369–98.

[30] La Follette, who later advocated Court curbing during his third-party bid for the presidency in 1924, suggested a constitutional amendment authorizing Congress to reenact federal statutes nullified

justice, the political climate for his measures seemed to hold promise as well as present pitfalls.

An Author, a Lobbyist, and an Expert

These constraints upon judicial reform were not overcome, as might be assumed, by a significant event causing fundamental changes in the political environment. Although Republicans did have unified government for the first time in almost a decade in 1921,[31] and although judicial workload did increase sharply that year because of Prohibition, those events alone do not explain the passage of landmark judicial reform. The problem with explaining the Judicial Conference Act and the Judiciary Act of 1925 as products of the 1920 election is the elapsed time between them and the election. While almost two and more than four years, respectively, may not seem like a particularly long period of time, the history of judicial institution building in other eras has shown that when events do successfully catalyze reform, that reform usually follows almost immediately. Following their defeat in 1800, for example, Federalists needed only three months to pass the Judiciary Act of 1801; likewise, following their victory in 1836, Democrats passed the Judiciary Act of 1837 within four months. In this way, the lag between the election of 1920 and the reforms of 1922 and 1925—a period where there was little attention to judicial reform—suggests that, as important as that election may have been in establishing Republican control of the federal government, it was not the catalyst for judicial reform.

Rather than the product of an election resulting in unified government, the Judicial Conference Act and the Judiciary Act of 1925—two of the most substantively important legislative actions relating to the federal courts in American history—were made possible through Taft's political entrepreneurship. Over the course of several years, Taft shepherded reform through every step of the legislative process, serving as the principal author of, the chief lobbyist for, and the leading expert on the proposed reforms along the way.[32] By the end of his fourth year as chief justice, Taft had sparked a "double revolution"[33]: he not only accomplished what a decade earlier would have seemed an impossibility—he had lain the groundwork for the federal judiciary in general, and the Supreme Court in particular, to become a powerful institution of American governance—but also accomplished it with active judicial intervention in the legislative process. As with

---

by the Court; Borah promoted legislation requiring a seven-member Court majority to declare an act of Congress unconstitutional. Ross, *A Muted Fury*, 191–232.

    [31] Prior to the Sixty-Seventh Congress (1921–23), Republicans had not controlled the House, Senate, and White House since the Sixty-First Congress (1911–13).

    [32] "Taft Favors More Judges," *New York Times*, November 8, 1921; "Taft Urges Need for More Judges," *New York Times*, October 6, 1921; "To Reorganize Judiciary," *New York Times*, August 19, 1921; "Taft Urges Steps to Speed Justice," *New York Times*, August 11, 1922.

    [33] Kenneth W. Starr, "William Howard Taft: The Chief Justice as Judicial Architect," 60 *University of Cincinnati Law Review* 965 (1991–92).

both Oliver Ellsworth (relative to the Judiciary Act of 1789) and William Evarts (relative to the Circuit Courts of Appeals Act of 1891), Taft's success in convincing Congress to approve—nearly without revision—all but one feature of his platform for judicial improvement was a testament to his entrepreneurial identity, ideas, and tactics, each of which was well-suited to the challenge before him.[34]

The key aspects of Taft's identity were his reputation and his networks, both of which furnished him with much-needed political capital. As a prominent national political figure for nearly two decades, Taft brought a set of reputations with him to the Court. Far from universal, these conceptions were varied, diverse, and a source of great controversy.[35] His time as president alone offered contrasting portraits of a would-be reformer, on the one hand, and a weak and bumbling amateur, on the other.[36] As chief justice, Taft layered new images atop the old, less supplanting his prior reputations than complicating their caricatures and correcting their distortions. Perhaps striving to redeem his failed presidency in the eyes of political elites and the public, perhaps because he had long yearned to be chief justice and simply wanted to fulfill his duties with honor, Taft developed a personal reputation as an efficient and effective administrator who cut printing costs, demanded payment of required fees from delinquent lawyers, and reorganized his staff to trim waste and better serve his needs.[37] Tackling traditionally boring administrative details "with great relish," Taft not only organized the associate justices into committees for internal business but also assigned opinions according to a variety of practical criteria, including age, health, backlog of cases, and rate of production.[38] Furthermore,

[34] As we shall see later in this chapter, even that one feature—authorization for the Supreme Court to promulgate a set of uniform instructions governing judicial proceedings in courts across the nation—did ultimately gain congressional approval in 1934, four years after Taft had left the Court and passed away.

[35] While an editorial in the *New York Times* ("Justice Lamar," January 4, 1916) explicitly called for Woodrow Wilson to place Taft on the Court after the death of Justice Joseph Lamar, later editorials in progressive publications such as the *Nation* ("The Chief Justice—A Mistaken Appointment," July 13, 1921) and the *New Republic* ("Taft and the Supreme Court," October 27, 1920; "Mr. Chief Justice Taft," July 27, 1921) sharply criticized Taft's appointment (or prospective appointment) as chief justice.

[36] In tariff reform, Taft was a clumsy executive lacking political awareness and prone to misuse of strategic resources. Attempting to reform civil administration, the army, and business regulation, he was simultaneously burdened by the commitments of Theodore Roosevelt and paralyzed by the fear that any action he might take would alienate some faction of his party. Peri Arnold, "Effecting a Progressive Presidency: Roosevelt, Taft, and the Pursuit of Strategic Resources," *Studies in American Political Development* 17 (2003): 61–81; James David Barber, *The Presidential Character: Predicting Performance in the White House*, 3rd ed. (Englewood Cliffs, NJ: Prentice Hall, 1985), 150–59; Stephen Skowronek, *Building a New American State: The Expansion of National Administrative Capacities, 1877–1920* (Cambridge: Cambridge University Press, 1982); Stephen Skowronek, *The Politics Presidents Make: Leadership from John Adams to Bill Clinton* (Cambridge, MA: Belknap Press, 1997), 252–59.

[37] Mason, *William Howard Taft*, 193, 269.

[38] Ibid., 193–97, 206–9. As to internal committees, Taft designated Justice Louis Brandeis, who had experience with financial matters, for service on the Accounts Committee and Justice Willis Van Devanter, the Court's expert on legal procedure, for the Rules Committee. As to the distribution of opinions, Taft, viewing a united front as important to judicial efficiency, often used his assignment power to promote unanimous (or near unanimous) opinions. For his part, Taft also tried to stem

he increased the Court's control over the responsibilities of the clerk, demanded quicker writing of opinions and scheduling of cases, attempted (albeit unsuccessfully) to shorten the summer recess, rejected his brethren's desire to reduce the pace and rigor of work, and revised the Court's internal rules about the logistics of hearing appeals.[39] Attempting to make promptness at the Supreme Court "a model for the courts of the country,"[40] Taft exhibited "no patience with judges who did not do their work properly."[41] Consequently, he not only reduced the period between the filing and hearing of a suit from fifteen months to eleven but also broke records for the number of cases decided by the Court in his initial year as chief justice.[42]

In demonstrating the depth of his conviction that the federal judiciary operate consistently and expeditiously, Taft's innovations gained him a measure of respect among legislators and fellow judges. The latter group, knowing that Taft was "plugged-in" to the politics of the capital, often wrote to suggest possible changes they hoped he would champion.[43] One judge, desiring a change in one of Taft's reforms, wrote glowingly to the chief justice of his confidence that Taft's "counsel and advice will have great weight" in Congress.[44] And with some members it did. Voting in favor of the 1922 reforms, one congressman remarked of Taft and his fellow justices that "it seems to me that those gentlemen are of such high character that we could without much alarm follow their advice and suggestion."[45] Another replied to Taft's gratitude for his support by citing both his "personal regard" for the chief justice and the "value I place upon any suggestion that you may make."[46] To be sure, not all congressmen felt such adulation toward Taft, but for those who did, their trust in the chief justice was seemingly an integral factor in their decision to support his reform efforts.

With his lengthy résumé in politics,[47] Taft also possessed "an intricate web of vast personal relations" before he ever donned his Supreme Court robe.[48] Upon

---

the tide of mutiny by dissenting extremely infrequently, even when he disagreed with the outcome. David J. Danelski, "The Influence of the Chief Justice in the Decisional Process of the Supreme Court," in *Courts, Judges, and Politics: An Introduction to the Judicial Process*, 4th ed., ed. Walter F. Murphy and C. Hermann Pritchett (New York: Random House, 1986), 568–77; Robert Post, "The Supreme Court Decision as Institutional Practice: Dissent, Legal Scholarship, and Decisionmaking in the Taft Court," 85 *Minnesota Law Review* 1267, 1283–84 (2001).

[39] Mason, *William Howard Taft*, 195.

[40] Starr, "William Howard Taft," 964.

[41] Henry F. Pringle, *The Life and Times of William Howard Taft* (New York: Farrar and Rinehart, 1939), 992.

[42] Mason, *William Howard Taft*, 195.

[43] Ibid., 122.

[44] James F. Smith to William Howard Taft, October 19, 1921, quoted in Mason, *William Howard Taft*, 122.

[45] 62 *Cong. Rec.* 166.

[46] George S. Graham to William Howard Taft, February 20, 1925, quoted in Mason, *William Howard Taft*, 123.

[47] Even before his presidency, Taft had served as secretary of war (1904–8), governor of the Philippines (1901–4), a circuit judge (1892–1900), and solicitor general (1890–92).

[48] Mason, *William Howard Taft*, 121.

joining the Court, Taft exploited these networks to persuade not only members of Congress and fellow judges but also presidents, newspaper editors, and lawyers to support his reforms.[49] When Republicans took back the White House in 1920, Taft offered Warren Harding extensive advice on the matter of judicial appointments.[50] Despite his appointment as chief justice, Taft remained in his advisory role—albeit with mixed success—during the subsequent Republican presidential administrations of Calvin Coolidge and Herbert Hoover.[51] Although Coolidge in particular seemed to tire of Taft's meddling, he nonetheless allowed the chief justice to draft a section of his 1923 State of the Union Address expressing support for increased certiorari jurisdiction[52] and even directly suggested that Congress pass Taft's initiatives.[53] Beyond Pennsylvania Avenue, Taft also curried favor with the media and key interest groups. Contacting newspaper editors directly, he encouraged (and received) press support of his proposals,[54] provided written critiques of his opponents, urged editorials against a proposal to withdraw the Court's diversity jurisdiction, and generally utilized the press to inform lawmakers and the public about his reforms and to repel future attacks against them.[55] Similarly, Taft spared no effort to enlist the support of organizations of lawyers,[56] especially the American Bar Association (ABA), of which he had served as president for the year following his departure from the White House and from which he had aggressively campaigned for the same reforms he proposed as chief justice. The rise of legal professionalism in the early twentieth century had helped establish the ABA as a powerful interest group,[57] and

[49] Facing the tremendous challenge of unifying lower court judges behind reform, Taft sent personal letters to every district judge asking for suggested reforms in judicial procedure, to every circuit judge requesting information and advice on any problems with overcrowded dockets, and to every state supreme court chief justice proposing to bring all courts of last resort closer together. Murphy, "Chief Justice Taft and the Lower Court Bureaucracy," 454. Among Taft's other efforts to establish or exploit networks were his participation in numerous voluntary organizations, his back-channel involvement in partisan politics (assessing the credentials of Republican candidates), and his intervention in diplomatic relations (encouraging American membership in the International Court of Justice). Mason, *William Howard Taft*, 273–86.

[50] Murphy, "In His Own Image"; Murphy, "Chief Justice Taft and the Lower Court Bureaucracy."

[51] From soliciting names of candidates from lawyers, politicians, and newspapermen to ushering his favored nominee (Pierce Butler) through the confirmation process to discouraging the nomination of candidates unsympathetic with his own views (Benjamin Cardozo and Learned Hand), Taft had a greater hand in selecting both his Supreme Court colleagues and lower court judges than perhaps any other chief justice before or since.

[52] Hartnett, "Questioning Certiorari," 1674.

[53] Mason, *William Howard Taft*, 113.

[54] "Helping the Courts," *New York Times*, December 24, 1924; "Speedier Justice," *New York Times*, November 29, 1924; "To Relieve the Supreme Court," *New York Times*, February 6, 1925.

[55] Mason, *William Howard Taft*, 127–29.

[56] "Taft Backs Bill to Speed Trials," *New York Times*, February 19, 1922; "Taft Urges Steps to Speed Justice," *New York Times*, August 29, 1923.

[57] James Willard Hurst, *The Growth of American Law: The Law Makers* (Boston: Little, Brown, 1950), 287–91, 359–67; Edson Sunderland, *History of the American Bar Association and Its Work* (Chicago: American Bar Foundation, 1953).

the organization proved a crucial ally in Taft's reform campaign,[58] telling Congress that the bill was too technical even for lawyers and that legislators should simply defer to the judiciary, pass the bill, and observe its effects in action.

In addition to an identity that provided valuable political capital, Taft advocated ideas that were consonant with the progressive romance with the science of organization and management. In fact, his entire reform platform pivoted around the idea of infusing "executive principle"[59]—practices or procedures explicitly designed to increase administrative precision and efficiency—into the tasks and governance of the judicial branch. By proposing strategic management of lower court judges by the chief justice, Taft sought to address the problem of underutilized or lazy judges.[60] By suggesting the Judicial Conference, he sought to create an institutional structure whereby the judiciary could address its own flaws. By recommending a reduction in the Court's obligatory jurisdiction and subsequent increase in its certiorari jurisdiction, he sought to facilitate a more expedient appeals process. Besides furthering widely held progressive aims, each of these ideas also had the advantage of seeming relatively banal. With the courts continuously under political attack, Taft eschewed reforms that had the impression of strong judicial empowerment, opting instead for innovations that appeared—at least on the surface—largely clerical. In other words, rather than explicitly attempt to make the judiciary stronger (by expanding jurisdiction or broadening causes for removal, for example), Taft's reforms sought to make it more effective; rather than encourage expanding the powers of the judiciary, his reforms simply advocated a more competent exercise of existing powers.

Taft's tactics for pursuing these acutely tailored reform ideas were carefully planned and executed. Three tactics—framing, compromise and measured action, and the strategic deployment of colleagues—proved especially useful. First, as already noted, sensitive to the dangers of negative perception and progressive worries about a fortified Court, Taft drew on the progressive commitment to scientific administration to preempt opposition by framing his reforms as a response to real problems rather than judicial aggrandizement and stressed the "broadly felt benefits of a more efficient federal bench."[61] Although his opponents—chiefly progressives and the American Federation of Labor—excoriated the lower courts for their unresponsiveness,[62] Taft maintained that the judiciary's problems stemmed less from objectionable decisions than inefficient administration.[63] As a result,

---

[58] Taft also succeeded in persuading the bar to resist congressional measures he opposed, such as the withdrawal of diversity jurisdiction and the restriction of judicial discretion in jury trials.

[59] Taft, "Adequate Machinery for Judicial Business," 454.

[60] Geyh, *When Courts and Congress Collide*, 103.

[61] Buchman, "Judicial Lobbying and the Politics of Judicial Structure," 13.

[62] Walter F. Murphy, *Congress and the Court: A Case Study in the American Political Process* (Chicago: University of Chicago Press, 1962), 48–53; Ross, *A Muted Fury.*

[63] "Federal Judges doubtless have their faults, but they are not chiefly responsible for the present defects in the administration of justice in the Federal Courts." Taft, "Possible and Needed Reforms in Administration of Justice in Federal Courts," 607.

he claimed, the necessary remedy was not the curtailment of judicial power but managerial innovation.[64] Thus, by framing his innovations as efficiency measures designed to increase judicial efficacy as well as preserve the "dignity and influence of the Court,"[65] Taft successfully invoked the language of progressivism in order to sidestep trenchant and vocal critiques of federal judicial power offered by progressives themselves.[66]

Second, Taft demonstrated his willingness to compromise and pursued change through measured action. When he realized that his proposal for a "flying squadron" of two new "roving" judges per circuit (for a total of eighteen "judges at large") would fail to gain approval,[67] he endorsed a milder version that provided additional judges to twenty-one specific districts without upsetting local patronage arrangements.[68] Astutely aware that Congress could take away the newfound power to transfer judges between districts, Taft urged senior circuit judges to use the power cautiously.[69] In general, Taft recognized that reform could be fleeting and aimed to set his innovations on the firmest possible ground. His ultimate goal was not just more judges or a lighter workload but an improved and empowered judiciary; his focus was not on gaining power in the short term but on consolidating it for the long term.

Third, Taft carefully dispatched his fellow justices to take advantage of their reputations and their networks. In 1924, instead of testifying before the Senate Judiciary Committee himself, he sent Justices George Sutherland (a former ABA president and Senate Judiciary Committee member), James McReynolds (a Democrat), and Willis Van Devanter (the Court's expert on jurisdiction) in his place. Sensitive to the dangers of negative perception caused by his advocacy of a bill advancing his own power (in front of a congressional committee, no less!),[70] Taft had Justice Van Devanter assure Congress that no justice—not even the chief justice—wanted to enter the legislative field. When an opportunity to purchase a Boston

---

[64] Taft also guarded against moves that he perceived might dilute the Court's prestige, including issues relating to judicial salaries, diplomatic rank, and social protocol at official state functions. Similarly, as a way of acknowledging the Court's "public responsibility," Taft set standards for the attire, behavior, and opinion-writing style of his fellow justices. Mason, *William Howard Taft*, 267–71.

[65] Keith E. Whittington, "Preserving the 'Dignity and Influence of the Court': Political Supports for Judicial Review in the United States," in *Rethinking Political Institutions: The Art of the State*, ed. Ian Shapiro, Stephen Skowronek, and Daniel Galvin (New York: New York University Press, 2006), 283–302.

[66] Needless to say, the judicial reforms of the 1920s had a complicated and uneasy relationship to progressivism. Although they were framed in progressive terms, they were offered by a progressive apostate (Taft) and resisted by many progressives in Congress who disliked the Court's antiprogressive jurisprudence.

[67] Taft, "Possible and Needed Reforms in Administration of Justice in Federal Courts," 601.

[68] Murphy, "Chief Justice Taft and the Lower Court Bureaucracy," 455–58.

[69] Mason, *William Howard Taft*, 106.

[70] Indeed, to some, Taft's active lobbying and influence with legislators—calling the chairmen of the House and Senate Judiciary Committees after the annual Judicial Conference and requesting authority to devise a plan to address new problems, for instance—seemed presumptuous at best, an outright violation of separation of powers at worst. Ibid., 122–26.

law library presented itself, Taft brought Justices Oliver Wendell Holmes and Louis Brandeis—both Massachusetts residents, and Holmes the circuit justice for the First Circuit—along with him to a House Appropriations subcommittee hearing for symbolic support.[71] In each situation, Taft was astute enough to realize that his identity was not the only one with the potential to yield political capital and not the only one capable of facilitating the passage of reform.

With a carefully constructed identity, favorable ideas, and deft tactics, Taft's dynamic and sustained political entrepreneurship neutralized progressive and Democratic opposition and enabled landmark institution building. Indeed, neither the Judicial Conference Act nor the Judiciary Act of 1925 endured a particularly challenging legislative fight, with perfunctory committee hearings and limited floor debate.[72] Neither the House nor the Senate demonstrated "awareness that it was passing a bill involving great changes,"[73] with the former behaving "like an uninformed and indifferent ratifying body" and the latter debating the issues but deferring "to the prestige of the Supreme Court and its Chief Justice."[74] In the end, both acts passed Congress by comfortable margins,[75] and Taft's judicial reforms—and, to the extent that the chief justice himself had conceived definite programs and launched them, they were indeed *Taft's* reforms—were signed into law by Warren G. Harding and Calvin Coolidge, respectively. Substantially empowering the chief justice in the discretionary administration of the judicial branch and engaging in aggressive jurisdictional housecleaning, they constituted exactly the sort of institutionally transformative reform that had been needed before Taft but hardly been considered in his absence.

The Trappings of Judicial Bureaucracy

The genius of Taft's reforms was that they recognized a central problem—the fact that Congress had created a hierarchy of courts but not a hierarchy of judges[76]—and set out to rectify it. Adding executive principle into the administration of an institution that had been little more than a collection of functionally disparate and geographically dispersed judicial fiefdoms, Taft accomplished his dual desire of centralization and managerial efficiency. Although the judiciary was not completely transformed into a hierarchical and centrally managed institution capable of understanding and

---

[71] Ibid., 126–27.

[72] See Frankfurter and Landis, *The Business of the Supreme Court*, 279–80, lamenting that the debates appeared "meager and uninformed in comparison with the great arguments evoked by judiciary bills in 1825, 1869, 1890" and contending that prior statesmen with an interest in judicial reform—Ellsworth, Van Buren, Webster, and Evarts, for example—"had no counterparts" in the 1920s.

[73] Ibid., 275.

[74] Ibid.

[75] The final vote on the Conference of Senior Circuit Judges Act was much closer in the Senate (36–29) than in the House (139–78), while the final vote on the Judiciary Act of 1925 was a landslide in the Senate (76–1) and an unrecorded voice vote in the House.

[76] Frankfurter and Landis, *The Business of the Supreme Court*, 218.

actively addressing its own needs, faults, and weaknesses, the metamorphosis had certainly begun. In other words, the trappings of judicial bureaucracy had arrived.

By granting Taft the authority to transfer judges from overstaffed districts in one circuit to understaffed districts in another circuit, the Judicial Conference Act allowed the chief justice to place "the judges of the country where they can do the most good."[77] Such a turn to "executive management" of judges not only meant that the "whole Federal judicial force of the country would be strategically employed" but also marked the beginning of Taft's seemingly uphill battle to shift the allegiance of federal judges from their states to the nation.[78] As the new judicial allegiance—aided in large part by the collegiality of the Judicial Conference—took hold, lower court judges increasingly looked to the chief justice for relief from crowded dockets and for general guidance in conducting judicial business. In response, Taft's congressional opponents voiced fears about consolidating the power of the entire judicial system in the chief justice. To do so, they claimed, risked converting a government of laws into a government of men—or, in this case, a government of one man.[79] While Taft was correct in denying that he was as powerful as his model judge, the lord chancellor of England, it is certainly true that he was more powerful—as a politician, as an administrator, and certainly as a policy maker—than most of his predecessors had been.

By authorizing an annual meeting of senior circuit judges, the Judicial Conference Act not only offered the chief justice a position from which to promote and comment on legislation related to the federal judiciary but also made him the unequivocal "head of the Federal judicial system."[80] Viewing the conference as a means to achieve solidarity, Taft was convinced that, if individual judges from across the nation could meet (a nearly unprecedented event), exchange information, and garner advice from those facing similar problems, then the disparate judges of America would be well on their way to comprising a unitary judicial "team."[81] Emphasizing "the ordinary business principles in successful executive work,"[82] Taft used the conference to require judges to file reports indicating the business completed and that remaining on the docket,[83] collect statistics on judi-

---

[77] Taft, "Three Needed Steps of Progress," 35.

[78] Taft, "The Attacks on the Courts and Legal Procedure," 17.

[79] Mason, *William Howard Taft*, 101–6.

[80] Taft, "The Attacks on the Courts and Legal Procedure," 14.

[81] Calls for "teamwork" (one of Taft's favorite slogans as chief justice) and the metaphorical conception of the judiciary as a "team" were crucial to the development of a shared judicial allegiance. In turn, it was precisely this allegiance that convinced lower court judges to surrender a substantial measure of their *individual* autonomy in exchange for enhanced *institutional* autonomy vis-à-vis the other branches of government. Cf. Carpenter, *The Forging of Bureaucratic Autonomy*, 23–25, on the role of bureaucratic entrepreneurs in the construction, articulation, and rhetorical selling of "bureaucratic culture"—"the metaphorical complex of language and symbols which defines the self-understanding of an agency."

[82] Taft, "The Attacks on the Courts and Legal Procedure," 16.

[83] Taft, "Adequate Machinery for Judicial Business," 454; Taft, "Possible and Needed Reforms in Administration of Justice in Federal Courts," 601; Taft, "Three Needed Steps of Progress," 34.

cial workload and productivity,[84] and generally supervise judicial administration throughout the nation.[85] With the guiding hand of Taft and under the direction of the initial conferences, therefore, the judiciary became a piece of "quasi-executive" machinery—"reforged with a capacity for self-study, criticism, and reform."[86] The conference was not yet "a central office with managerial power,"[87] but the federal judiciary at last had a legislative arm and judges were, as Taft had long wished they would be, "independent in their judgments, but . . . subject to some executive direction as to the use of their services."[88]

By limiting the automatic right of appeal to the Supreme Court and expanding the types of cases that could be heard only with the justices' assent, the Judiciary Act of 1925 gave the Court near-complete control over its docket for the first time in history.[89] Offering an alternative much preferred to the possibility of restricting jurisdiction, the shift toward certiorari review was considered "the best and safest method" for simultaneously easing the Court's workload and protecting its authority.[90] In fact, since it solved the problem of increasing caseload pressure by decreasing the number of cases the Court was *required* to hear rather than the number it was *permitted* to hear,[91] the shift actually enhanced the authority of the Court by dramatically increasing its discretion to pick and choose cases of interest.[92] With such a complete and thorough revision of its jurisdiction,[93] the Court was finally able to "exercise absolute and arbitrary discretion with respect to all business but constitutional business."[94] The fact that this revision was prompted and undertaken by the justices themselves only further established the Court's ability to participate in policy making that substantially affected it.

[84] Taft, "The Attacks on the Courts and Legal Procedure," 16.

[85] "Calls Council of Judges," *New York Times*, September 21, 1923; "Say Federal Courts Need 5 More Judges," *New York Times*, September 29, 1923.

[86] Starr, "William Howard Taft," 966.

[87] Peter Graham Fish, *The Politics of Federal Judicial Administration* (Princeton, NJ: Princeton University Press, 1973), 39.

[88] Taft, "Three Needed Steps of Progress," 35.

[89] The docket control was only "near-complete" because the act did preserve mandatory jurisdiction in a few select types of cases—notably, those relating to rulings by the Interstate Commerce Commission and injunctions against administrative agencies. In 1988, the right of appeal to the Court was virtually eliminated; 102 Stat. 662 (June 27, 1988).

[90] Taft, "Possible and Needed Reforms in Administration of Justice in Federal Courts," 603.

[91] Taft, "Three Needed Steps of Progress," 35.

[92] Analyses of agenda setting and the Court's certiorari process have further illuminated the importance of this development. See Richard L. Pacelle Jr., *The Transformation of the Supreme Court's Agenda: From the New Deal to the Reagan Administration* (Boulder, CO: Westview, 1991); and H. W. Perry Jr., *Deciding to Decide: Agenda Setting in the United States Supreme Court* (Cambridge, MA: Harvard University Press, 1991).

[93] Taft "Possible and Needed Reforms in Administration of Justice in Federal Courts," 603; Taft, "Three Needed Steps of Progress," 35; William Howard Taft, "The Jurisdiction of the Supreme Court under the Act of February 13, 1925," 35 *Yale Law Journal* 1, 12 (1925–26).

[94] Taft, "The Attacks on the Courts and Legal Procedure," 18. Despite Taft's assurances to the contrary, the Court immediately exercised such discretion with regard to "constitutional business" as well, routinely declining to hear cases raising constitutional issues.

The sum total of Taft's reforms was an institutional judiciary—a lower-court hierarchy, a Supreme Court, a chief justiceship—transformed. Indeed, the judiciary Taft left in 1930 was thoroughly unlike the one he had joined nine years earlier.[95] Though not all of Taft's innovations became consistent features of judicial governance, the three main changes— the reorganization of the federal court system under the chief justice, the establishment of the Judicial Conference, the radical expansion of certiorari jurisdiction[96]—persist more than eighty years since their passage.[97] By creating "explicit institutional structures designed to facilitate reform" and embedding the spirit of executive principle within those structures,[98] Taft was thus able to entrench both structural hierarchy and managerial efficiency within the judicial branch. Moreover, since the structures created were judicial structures—staffed, operated, and evaluated by Taft and his judicial teammates— they catalyzed the emergence of a self-governing judiciary. After more than a century of exclusion from the politics of policy making for their own institution, judges had finally earned the authority to build the judiciary.

Judicial Rule Making and New Deal Politics, 1930–1935

By the early twentieth century, both lawyers and judges were exasperated with the Conformity Act of 1872. Pinpointed as a problem by Supreme Court Justice Samuel Miller as early as 1886 and targeted for revision by the American Bar Association a decade later,[99] the Conformity Act governed civil procedure—the rules by which judges conduct civil trials—in federal court. In the eyes of the legal academy and profession, the statute contained one fatal flaw: rather than compel all federal courts to utilize a common set of federal rules, it instead required that federal

[95] Had Taft lived a few more years he would have witnessed a judiciary transformed even further by two other initiatives he had devised and championed: the creation of the Federal Rules of Civil Procedure and the construction of an independent building for the Supreme Court.

[96] The expansion was certainly radical. In 1924, cases within the Court's obligatory jurisdiction represented 40 percent of all filings; by 1930, such cases represented only 15 percent of all filings. See Casper and Posner, *The Workload of the Supreme Court*, 20.

[97] Though not Taft's innovation per se, it is worth noting that a 1929 statute marked the first reorganization of the circuit system since 1866. From Reconstruction through 1929, all twelve states admitted to the Union were added to the Eighth or Ninth Circuits. By the 1920s, the Eighth Circuit had grown sufficiently large—encompassing thirteen states from Minnesota to New Mexico, Missouri to Utah— that it could scarcely operate effectively. Accordingly, after the ABA's suggestion of a broad reorganization sparked widespread opposition, Congress—at Taft's suggestion—simply divided the Eighth Circuit in half, shifting the circuit's six Southwestern mining states (Colorado, Kansas, New Mexico, Oklahoma, Utah, and Wyoming) into a newly created Tenth Circuit. The seven more agriculturally oriented Midwestern states (Arkansas, Iowa, Minnesota, Missouri, Nebraska, North Dakota, and South Dakota) were left in the Eighth Circuit, and all other circuits remained unchanged; 45 Stat. 1346 (February 28, 1929).

[98] Fish, "William Howard Taft and Charles Evans Hughes," 123–24.

[99] Stephen B. Burbank, "The Rules Enabling Act of 1934," 130 *University of Pennsylvania Law Review* 1015, 1040–41 (1982).

judges "conform" to the civil procedure of the state in which they sat. Although the defects and inconsistencies of the Conformity Act had (in part) prompted the Judicial Code of 1911, the heart of the act remained untouched. For its part, the Judicial Code had succeeded in collecting all judiciary-related statutes into one document, but it did not change any of those statutes and, as such, did not change the fact that actual courtroom procedures remained different in federal courts across the nation. The upshot was that federal trials were being administered according to more than forty sets of rules, leaving the increasing number of lawyers who practiced in more than one state bewildered about the applicable procedure and any judges who sat in more than one state frustrated by the entire enterprise.[100]

Seeking to assuage the aggravation felt by the bar and bench alike, conservative legal reformers—led by the American Bar Association—sought to replace the Conformity Act with a uniform code of federal procedure devised by the Supreme Court justices themselves. Such a code, they reasoned, would allow substantive judgments to displace procedural technicalities at the core of the legal process. It would make the administration of justice more efficient for judges, more expedient for lawyers, and, consequently, more affordable to litigants. Though these potential benefits held obvious appeal for many, the idea of a code was vigorously opposed—and nearly single-handedly impeded—by Democratic senator Thomas Walsh of Montana. After twenty years of stalemate between conservative reformers and the progressive senator, however, the strategic and unremitting efforts of a savvy and respected attorney general created political space where there had previously only been political will. The end result, the passage of the Rules Enabling Act of 1934,[101] was a New Deal measure that did exactly what conservative reformers had hoped it would: delegate procedural rule-making authority to the Supreme Court. By the time the Federal Rules of Civil Procedure became operative two years later, it was clear that the broad delegation of congressional authority in the Rules Enabling Act had not only effected a revolution in civil procedure but also signaled the emergence of federal judges as willing and able policy makers.

The Extended Search for Procedural Uniformity

For its supporters in the ABA, the Rules Enabling Act was a long time coming. Dating back to failed late-nineteenth-century attempts to win membership approval for a plan to replace the Conformity Act with a set of uniform procedural rules, reformers had argued the mechanics of law and justice failed to work properly. Law, they lamented, had become oriented around procedure rather than substance. Judges found their discretion to make judgments about the law—their ability to ensure justice—confined by rigid, but rarely sensible, rules and regulations. Attorneys spent their time researching technical minutiae and loopholes rather

---

[100] Stephen N. Subrin, "How Equity Conquered Common Law: The Federal Rules of Civil Procedure in Historical Perspective," 135 *University of Pennsylvania Law Review* 909, 957–58 (1987).

[101] 48 Stat. 1064 (June 19, 1934).

than jurisprudential arguments, doctrines, or theories. Litigants encountered exorbitant fees from lawyers and extensive delay in their court proceedings. In response to these developments, spawned in large part by the procedural diversity mandated by the Conformity Act and the strict legal codification of procedure at the state level,[102] late-nineteenth- and early-twentieth-century reformers (Taft among them) sought to reestablish the simplicity and straightforwardness of law, reduce the congestion hampering the business of federal courts, liberate judges to decide matters of substantive law, and minimize the influence of crafty lawyers who could manipulate the complexities of existing procedure to their (and their clients') disproportionate advantage.

Stirred from a decade of dormancy by Roscoe Pound's famous 1906 address to the ABA,[103] the idea of applying, for the first time in American history, a consistent set of rules to all federal courts became especially enticing as the national government grew stronger, national programs grew more numerous, and national litigation—disputes involving transportation, manufacturing, communication, and banking that crossed state lines, for instance—grew more common in the first decade of the twentieth century.[104] Immediately following Pound's speech, in fact, the ABA officially set up the Committee to Suggest Remedies and Formulate Proposed Laws to Prevent Delay and Unnecessary Cost in Litigation,[105] which included Pound himself and which enthusiastically endorsed the idea of a uniform code in 1910. The following year, "the renascence of interest in reform of judicial procedure" intensified as ABA member Thomas Shelton proposed the resolution that would become the heart of the association's twenty-year campaign for procedural reform.[106] By the time Shelton was named the first chair of the ABA's Committee on Uniform Judicial Procedure in 1912, forty-two (of forty-eight) state bar associations and the vast majority of legal academics supported the ABA's endeavor.[107] Desiring both to improve the administration of justice and to reassert the role of law in constructing a just society, Shelton (on behalf of the ABA and in close consultation with then president Taft) advocated authorizing the justices of the Supreme Court to prepare a uniform code of flexible and efficient procedural rules.

In addition to their performance objectives, reformers were also heavily influenced by a "highly charged political climate" in which progressives continued

---

[102] Edward A. Purcell Jr., *Brandeis and the Progressive Constitution: Erie, Judicial Power, and the Politics of the Federal Courts in Twentieth Century America* (New Haven, CT: Yale University Press, 2000), 28.

[103] Roscoe Pound, "The Causes of Popular Dissatisfaction with the Administration of Justice," 14 *The American Lawyer* 445 (1906).

[104] Erwin C. Surrency, *History of the Federal Courts* (Dobbs Ferry, NY: Oceana, 2002), 195.

[105] With such a lengthy name, the committee was commonly referred to as the Committee of Fifteen, a reference to the number of members that composed it.

[106] Burbank, "The Rules Enabling Act of 1934," 1045.

[107] Surrency, *History of the Federal Courts*, 197; Purcell, *Brandeis and the Progressive Constitution*, 31.

to press for judicial recall and other court-curbing initiatives.[108] Just as Taft had sought to shift the focus of anticourt sentiment by blaming poor administration, so too did supporters of judicial rule making advocate a uniform code as a "means of deflecting attention from the conservative positions courts had taken on socio-economic issues."[109] With increased judicial efficiency, they reasoned, the movements for more popular control of judges and stricter judicial accountability to the elected branches of government might dissipate—or, at the very least, lose some of their appeal.[110] In other words, while the main objective of reform was to improve the administration of justice by simplifying legal procedure, reformers also hoped that successful improvement would stem the tide of progressive attacks on the judicial system and buttress the legitimacy of the courts against any future attacks.

Of course, the simple existence of a procedural reform bill did not prompt the Court's opponents to wilt. Indeed, even though the idea of judicial rule making was not novel—the Supreme Court had been given the authority to devise rules of equity as early as 1792,[111] and the widely acclaimed revision of those rules in 1912 suggested both that "procedure could be made simple and less technical" and "that the Supreme Court was an appropriate body to do the drafting"[112]—the idea of having the justices of such a controversial Court determine the procedural rules that would be used in all federal courts sparked substantial hostility. Progressives, in particular, were highly skeptical about the motives of the conservative ABA reformers, but Southern and Western Democrats also resisted a Court-devised code.[113] As both a progressive and a Western Democrat, Montana senator Thomas Walsh quickly emerged as the leader of the opposition to procedural reform.

At the heart of Walsh's twenty-year-battle against the Rules Enabling Act were three objections. First, and most important for Walsh, uniform federal procedure privileged a small group of national lawyers over a larger group of state and local lawyers.[114] To the extent that alleviating the work of the former meant an entirely new set of rules, it imposed a hardship on those local lawyers who had grown accustomed to, and intimately familiar with, their own state's procedures. Second, the promulgation of new procedural rules was likely to cause confusion, mistakes, and further delay in the administration of justice—the exact problems that advocates of reform sought to address. Third, if rule making were to occur, it needed to

---

[108] Subrin, "How Equity Conquered Common Law," 955.

[109] Ibid., 956.

[110] Ibid., 955–56; Purcell, *Brandeis and the Progressive Constitution*, 30; Paul Frymer, "Acting When Elected Officials Won't: Federal Courts and Civil Rights Enforcement in U.S. Labor Unions, 1935–85," *American Political Science Review* 97 (2003): 487.

[111] *Equity* refers to types of procedure or relief (injunctions, restraining orders, or decrees to commit some action, for instance) that can be used when more strictly "legal" remedies (such as monetary damages) are considered insufficient.

[112] Subrin, "How Equity Conquered Common Law," 954.

[113] Fish, "William Howard Taft and Charles Evans Hughes," 138; Purcell, *Brandeis and the Progressive Constitution*, 29–30.

[114] Walsh proudly pronounced himself "for the one hundred who stay at home as against the one who goes abroad"; quoted in Burbank, "The Rules Enabling Act of 1934," 1063–64.

come from Congress rather than from the Supreme Court. To invest judges with the effective authority to make law was an unconstitutional delegation of powers, and to burden them with the duties of drafting new rules would undoubtedly sap their already limited time and energy.

With these three objections and a series of dilatory techniques, Walsh stymied progress on the Rules Enabling Act through five presidential administrations—those of William Howard Taft, Woodrow Wilson, Warren G. Harding, Calvin Coolidge, and Herbert Hoover. At several points between that first Senate hearing in 1913 and Roosevelt's inauguration in 1933, it appeared procedural uniformity might be realized, only to fall prey to Walsh's obstruction each time. In 1916, for instance, it was "mistakenly reported" at the ABA annual meeting that the uniform procedure bill had passed when, in fact, Walsh had bottled it up in committee while allowing a smaller reform bill to reach the Senate floor.[115] The prospects for success seemed almost certain following the 1924 elections, which resulted in Republicans holding onto the White House as well as gaining one seat in the Senate and twenty-two in the House.[116] Procedural reform had not only secured the endorsements of Chief Justice Taft, President Coolidge, every state bar association, many local bar associations, civic and business organizations, and law review editors and law school deans but also commanded a large majority in the House.[117] Yet even after the Senate Judiciary Committee approved the bill without amendment, Walsh somehow "succeeded in having it recommitted."[118] Despite Shelton's claim to some ABA members that Walsh had agreed to report the bill eventually, the proposal died in committee once again.[119] Procedural reform came one step closer to fruition in 1926, emerging—over Walsh's minority views—out of the Senate Judiciary Committee after an extensive study and with a positive majority report that rebutted each of Walsh's objections individually.[120] But, even then, Walsh maneuvered on the floor to prevent consideration of the bill by the whole Senate, and the ABA was left frustrated once again. In each of these instances, the specific details and sponsorship of the procedural reform bill changed, but the core of the proposed legislation and its ultimate fate remained the same.

The "Startlingly Stunning Success" of Homer Cummings

That fate changed rapidly with Roosevelt's landslide victory over Hoover in 1932 and his appointment of Connecticut lawyer and Democratic Party stalwart Homer Cummings as attorney general in 1933. In advance of that point, the possibility of

---

[115]Burbank, "The Rules Enabling Act of 1934," 1065.

[116]This increased the Republican majority over Democrats in the Sixty-Ninth Congress (1925–27) to thirteen seats in the Senate (54–41, not including one Farmer-Laborer) and sixty-four seats in the House (247–183, not including three Farmer-Laborers, one American-Laborer, and one Socialist).

[117]Purcell, *Brandeis and the Progressive Constitution*, 31.

[118]Burbank, "The Rules Enabling Act of 1934," 1082.

[119]Ibid.

[120]Ibid., 1083–85.

reform had looked increasingly grim for the ABA. With both a string of defeats and disappointments—a key Senate ally (Albert Cummins of Iowa) died in 1926, a majority of the Senate Judiciary Committee opposed the procedural reform bill in 1928, Shelton stepped down as chairman of the Committee on Uniform Judicial Procedure in 1930, Democrats nearly took control of both houses of Congress in the 1930 midterm elections[121]—and President-elect Roosevelt initially naming none other than ABA nemesis Walsh as his original attorney general–designate, the association stood ready to abandon its extended quest for procedural uniformity. Yet almost immediately upon the ABA allowing the Committee on Uniform Judicial Procedure to lapse, Walsh died—en route to the capital to accept his appointment from Roosevelt, in fact—and was replaced (initially on an interim basis but soon thereafter on a permanent one) by Cummings, a nationalist and an enthusiastic supporter of procedural reform. With the plan for judicial rule making freed from the hands of the conservative ABA, Cummings moved with great celerity, gaining Roosevelt's trust, convincing him to support the idea, and, believing that procedural reform would help federal courts implement New Deal legislation, throwing the administration's support behind a renewed attempt at a uniform federal code. In quick succession, the House and Senate Judiciary Committees reported the bill favorably, both houses passed it "with only modest resistance" and after only "perfunctory" debate,[122] and Roosevelt signed it into law. With Cummings's entrepreneurship—his reputation as a loyal but nonideological Democrat, his opportunistic idea to rebrand procedural reform as a Democratic initiative, his perseverance in keeping the issue on the agenda and persuading Congress to pass it—leading the way, twenty years of failure by the ABA had been wiped away in the first few months of the New Deal, twenty years of obstacles and obstruction overcome with "startlingly stunning success."[123]

Cummings was, in many ways, "perfectly typecast" for the role of procedural reform.[124] Of an "aristocratic and well-educated background,"[125] he brought to the Justice Department a delicate blend of seemingly disparate, yet somehow consonant, identities: an experienced lawyer who was also a deft politician, a loyal Democrat concerned with party coherence and unity who maintained a reputation as a moderate statesman.[126] With background in both criminal law—as a prosecutor

[121] In the Senate, Democrats gained eight seats to trim the Republican majority to one seat (48–47); in the House, Democrats gained fifty-two seats to cut the Republican majority to two seats (218–216).
[122] Subrin, "How Equity Conquered Common Law," 970; Burbank, "The Rules Enabling Act of 1934," 1097.
[123] "Congress Strengthens the Machinery of Justice," *American Bar Association Journal* 20 (1934): 422.
[124] Subrin, "How Equity Conquered Common Law," 969.
[125] Leonard Baker, *Back to Back: The Duel Between FDR and the Supreme Court* (New York: Macmillan, 1967), 12.
[126] Cordell Hull, Roosevelt's first and longtime secretary of state, strongly recommended Cummings for attorney general: "I have heard twelve or fifteen senators during the last week casually remark that Mr. Cummings is exceptionally well equipped to make an outstanding attorney general. His great legal ability, which all recognize, his poise, his fine intellect, his fundamental, sane, and practical realism, preeminently fit him for the Attorney General." Frank Freidel, *Franklin D. Roosevelt: Launching the New Deal* (Boston: Little, Brown, 1973), 158. Nebraska attorney general and prominent Western Demo-

in Fairfield County, Connecticut, Cummings gained wide acclaim for his motion to dismiss a case against a young murder defendant he became convinced was innocent[127]—and vast areas of civil law,[128] Cummings was, on one level, a lawyer's lawyer. He knew the dynamics of both the courtroom and the office, could relate to both the judge and the client, and understood both public service and private practice. Of course, at the same time that he was thoroughly immersed in the conventions of law, he was intimately familiar with the customs of politics. A former mayor of Stamford, president of the Mayors Association of Connecticut, and candidate for a variety of state and federal offices (including both the House and the Senate), Cummings had carefully cultivated "wide personal acquaintance in every state"[129] as well as meaningful affiliations with a host of social clubs, civic organizations, and interest groups along the Eastern seaboard.

His most enduring and most powerful network was, of course, the Democratic Party.[130] Having served twenty-four years as a member of the Democratic National Committee, including terms as both chairman and vice chairman, Cummings was thoroughly enmeshed in Democratic political circles,[131] where he was widely respected on account of his powerful keynote speech in the 1920 Democratic National Convention and his dramatic public "plea for party harmony" during the "bitterly divided" convention four years later.[132] (On both occasions, Cummings's addresses were sufficiently popular as to yield him "substantial votes for the presidential nomination."[133]) By 1932, even though most of his active party

crat Arthur Mullen later noted that Cummings was "destined to be, permanently, the best man for a job which to require every ounce of ability which any lawyer would have." Arthur F. Mullen, *Western Democrat* (New York: Wilfred Funk, 1940), 307.

[127] See S. J. Woolf, "Cummings Sees the Law as a Living Thing," *New York Times*, September 3, 1933: "Despite the circumstantial evidence and the confession, the prosecuting attorney was skeptical of the prisoner's guilt. He conducted an investigation of his own and became convinced that Israel [the defendant] was innocent. Then, in the face of popular feeling, and resisting all the pressure which the police force could bring to bear, he appeared in court and asked to have the indictment dismissed." Speaking before the court, Cummings emphasized that "it is just as important for a State's Attorney to use the great powers of his office to protect the innocent as to convict the guilty."

[128] Cummings spent the 1920s and '30s in full-time legal practice. Carl Brent Swisher, "Biographical Note," in *Selected Papers of Homer Cummings: Attorney General of the United States, 1933-1939*, ed. Carl Brent Swisher (New York: Scribner's, 1939), xiii.

[129] William A. Kelly, "Honorable Homer Cummings, Attorney General of the United States—A Biographical Sketch," *Bulletin of the New Haven County Bar Association* 14 (January 1934): 13–16, 15.

[130] On Cummings's service to the Democratic Party before the New Deal, see David L. Mazza, "Homer S. Cummings and Progressive Politics from Bryan through Wilson, 1896–1925" (PhD diss., St. John's University, 1978).

[131] Indeed, Mullen referred to Cummings as "one of the stalwarts of the Democratic Party," a man who led the party at "one of its most trying times" and "carried the torch through long, dark hours" when few still liked Wilsonian idealism. Mullen, *Western Democrat*, 307.

[132] Woolf, "Cummings Sees the Law as a Living Thing"; *Dictionary of American Biography: Supplement Six, 1956–1960*, s.v. "Cummings, Homer Stille." For a detailed account of Cumming's role in the two conventions, see Mazza, "Homer S. Cummings and Progressive Politics from Bryan through Wilson, 1896–1925."

[133] Swisher, "Biographical Note," xiii.

service was over and he was more of an "elder statesman" of the party than a lead-ing operative in it, Cummings was nonetheless instrumental in Roosevelt securing the Democratic nomination. Leading up to the Democratic National Convention that year, he "helped persuade twenty-four senators and numerous congressmen to announce their support" for his "close friend";[134] at the convention itself, he "planned strategy, operated as floor manager, and delivered a resounding second-ing speech."[135] As a result of his service to Roosevelt's campaign, Cummings was "mentioned for various cabinet positions," with initial attorney general–designate Walsh recommending that Cummings be appointed assistant attorney general in charge of judicial and executive appointments.[136] Yet even as Cummings was a Roosevelt loyalist whose ultimate appointment as attorney general "boded well for the continuance of . . . Democratic ideals,"[137] he was also someone who, earlier in his career, had been elected Mayor of Stamford only with "the support of a large number of Republican voters" and, even as a member of the Roosevelt adminis-tration, seemed capable of mustering bipartisan appeal on occasion.[138] Whether because he allowed Republican holdovers in the Justice Department during his tenure or because even his critics admitted at the time that he was "doing a good job administratively,"[139] Republicans, while no doubt disagreeing with him on a great many issues, found him difficult to detest.[140]

Cummings's identity was far more important to the success of judicial reform than any ideas he may have harbored about it. Indeed, aside from one word, the bill Cummings introduced (the one that would ultimately become the Rules En-abling Act) was an exact replica of the final incarnation of the ABA bill;[141] even Cummings, long identified with the progressives and their desire to improve ju-dicial administration,[142] "saw himself as reviving the ABA's campaign and, with the advantages of his position and political approach, leading it to a successful

---

[134] *Dictionary of American Biography: Supplement Six, 1956–1960*, s.v. "Cummings, Homer Stille"; Associated Press, "Cummings Regarded as Walsh Successor," *Los Angeles Times*, March 3, 1933. Cum-mings's close connection to Roosevelt dates at least back to 1920, when he delivered, at Roosevelt's home in Hyde Park, New York, the address at the notification ceremony for Roosevelt's selection as James Cox's vice presidential running mate. Swisher, "Biographical Note," xiii.

[135] *Dictionary of American Biography: Supplement Six, 1956–1960*, s.v. "Cummings, Homer Stille." Cummings also delivered a seconding speech on behalf of Roosevelt's nomination in 1936.

[136] Swisher, "Biographical Note," xiv.

[137] Mullen, *Western Democrat*, 307.

[138] *Encyclopedia of Biography*, vol. 15, s.v. "Cummings, Homer Stille."

[139] George Creel, "The Tall Man," *Colliers*, January 1936, 23, 32.

[140] Though it is difficult to know quite how much stock to place in these sorts of assessments, there are also reports—perhaps hagiographic ones—that Cummings also possessed a series of positive per-sonality traits, including a genial disposition and affable manner, intellectual confidence, and emo-tional calm. See Kelly, "Honorable Homer Cummings, Attorney General of the United States," 15–16; and *Encyclopedia of Biography*, vol. 15, s.v. "Cummings, Homer Stille."

[141] Burbank, "The Rules Enabling Act of 1934," 1097.

[142] Kelly, "Honorable Homer Cummings, Attorney General of the United States," 15. On Cummings's embrace of progressivism generally, see Mazza, "Homer S. Cummings and Progressive Politics from Bryan through Wilson, 1896–1925."

conclusion."[143] Yet though he contributed not a single new idea to the substance of
the reform itself, Cummings's procedural idea—his decision to pick a forsaken proposal up off the Senate floor and recast it as a Roosevelt administration initiative—
proved not only amenable to the New Deal's moment of triumph but also crucial
to the bill's success. After all, as the Great Depression began to erode Republican
support in the late 1920s and early 1930s, procedural reform was effectively dead in
the hands of a conservative legal group such as the ABA. Once the ABA effectively
abandoned the cause, however, Cummings recognized the opportunity to co-opt
the opposition's project—the merits of which he did not dispute—for the benefit
of his president and his party, writing letters to Roosevelt recommending the bill
as an "important and vital step toward the simplification of legal procedure" and to
the chairmen of the House and Senate Judiciary Committees formally requesting
its reintroduction.[144] By lending his prominent Democratic imprimatur to what
had traditionally been a conservative proposal, then, Cummings assuaged the partisan fears of not only Roosevelt—who, having not yet found his domestic agenda
impeded by the Supreme Court,[145] was still eager to demonstrate his support for
business and his willingness to assist the courts[146]— but also Democratic legislators seeking to remain faithful to the political program of the New Deal.

With the refashioning of reform into a New Deal idea helping to overcome
the potentially reflexive opposition of Democrats, Cummings utilized both private
and public tactics to attain passage. First, behind the scenes, he "labored with"
congressional committees and haggled with "recalcitrant" members of Congress,[147]
spending virtually all his time at the Capitol,[148] where he was frequently seen "slip-

[143] Burbank, "The Rules Enabling Act of 1934," 1096. In an article on the subject at the time, Cummings noted, following an acknowledgment that the ABA had spearheaded the campaign for procedural reform for more than twenty years, "I sought to revive the issue." Homer S. Cummings, "The New
Law Relating to Federal Procedure," *United States Law Week* 1, no. 42 (1934): 16.

[144] Homer S. Cummings, "Letter to the President, Recommending Approval of Legislation Authorizing the Formulation of Uniform and Simplified Rules of Civil Procedure under the Supervision of
the Supreme Court," June 12, 1934, reprinted in *Selected Papers of Homer Cummings*, 188; Homer S.
Cummings, "Letters to Chairmen of Senate and House Judiciary Committees," March 1, 1934, reprinted
in *Selected Papers of Homer Cummings*, 186.

[145] Recall that the Court did not begin actively striking down New Deal measures until 1935. See
Schechter Poultry Corporation v. United States, 295 U.S. 495 (1935) (invalidating the National Indus-
trial Recovery Act as a violation of the nondelegation doctrine and beyond the reach of congressional
Commerce Clause authority); *United States v. Butler*, 297 U.S. 1 (1936) (invalidating the Agricultural
Adjustment Act as a violation of the Tenth Amendment); and *Carter v. Carter Coal Company*, 298 U.S.
238 (1936) (invalidating the Bituminous Coal Conservation Act as beyond the reach of congressional
Commerce Clause authority).

[146] Purcell, *Brandeis and the Progressive Constitution*, 32.

[147] Several years later, Cummings noted that it took "personal appeals, pathetic persuasion, and
something approaching imprecations" to overcome the opposition. Homer S. Cummings, "From an
Address before the Chicago Bar Association at a Dinner in Honor of Lord Macmillan," August 2, 1938,
reprinted in *Selected Papers of Homer Cummings*, 187.

[148] See Herbert Corey, "Stream-Lined Justice," *Nation's Business*, July 1938, 30: "It is also true that
the committeemen from the A.B.A. had other fish to fry. They could put down their frying pans for a
few days at a time, but they could not come to Washington for an indefinite stay. The best they could

ping in and out of committee-rooms."[149] Relentless yet polite with hesitant legislators, many of whom he knew personally, Cummings managed to "speak their language," offering them "the respect and deference for their position they believed
they deserved" and generally eschewing "the blare of trumpets" for "friendly per-
sistence" that ultimately wore down his doubters.[150]

Second, even if these claims of active legislative politicking—many of which
are either somewhat vague or originate from Cummings himself—are exagger-
ated, Cummings still employed a series of more public entrepreneurial tactics that
demonstrated not only his thorough understanding of the issues surrounding procedural reform but also the importance and the desirability of such reform.[151] Most
notably, convinced that the technicality of the issues and the accompanying inertia
were the primary obstacles to passage,[152] he launched an aggressive publicity campaign designed both to raise awareness about and spark enthusiasm for reform.
Whether by addressing legal organizations or writing for legal publications,[153]
Cummings advocated for the bill "without reserve,"[154] simultaneously emphasizing that reform was supported by nearly everyone and that reform would benefit
nearly everyone. To illustrate his broad base of political support, Cummings repeatedly reminded his audiences that reform had been endorsed, at one point or
another, by a distinguished list of prominent individuals, including four presidents
(Taft, Wilson, Coolidge, and Roosevelt); five attorneys general (James McReynolds, Thomas Gregory, A. Mitchell Palmer, Harlan Fiske Stone, and John Sargent);
"outstanding jurists" (and previous judicial reformers) Taft and Pound; the deans

---

do was to appear before a committee of the House or Senate, say what they had to say, file a bundle of
papers with the clerk and catch the eight o'clock plane for home. Attorney General Cummings is here
all the time"; emphasis added.

[149] Creel, "The Tall Man," 32.

[150] Baker, *Back to Back*, 13; Creel, "The Tall Man," 32 (also describing Cummings behaving "softly,
inconspicuously and almost piteously," like a "widowed mother of eighteen children who is about to be
thrown out on the street by a cruel landlord"); Corey, "Stream-Lined Justice," 30 (also noting that Cummings "kept on pegging away without the use of woodwinds or brasses"). Cummings tells the story
of one particular House member, someone who had "made speeches against the idea" of procedural
reform and "would be obliged to protest when it came to a vote, whom, after hours of compromise, he
convinced "to absent himself . . . when the matter came up," thereby not reversing his prior position
but not inhibiting the unanimous consent needed for the passage of reform at that particular juncture
either; Cummings, "From an Address before the Chicago Bar Association," 187.

[151] Cummings, "The New Law Related to Federal Procedure," 2, called it "one of the most sweeping
legal reforms in the history of the United States."

[152] Carl Brent Swisher, "Introduction," in *Selected Papers of Homer Cummings*, xxv, notes that the
issue offered "none of the glamour of a war on crime or a series of battles over constitutional questions invoking the immediate well-being of the people." Cummings framed the situation succinctly:
"Our one great enemy is inertia. But surely the hour has struck. Let us not confess that we are so disorganized, so indifferent, so lazy, so ineffectual, and so impotent that we cannot marshal our forces in
[*sic*] behalf of a measure of reform which the leaders of the bar have so long and so overwhelmingly
approved." Homer S. Cummings, "From an address at the Silver Anniversary Banquet of the New York
County Lawyers' Association," March 14, 1934, reprinted in *Selected Papers of Homer Cummings*, 184.

[153] At least one such address was broadcast nationally over the radio.

[154] "Congress Strengthens the Machinery of Justice," 422.

of "many important law schools including Harvard, Yale, Cornell, and Virginia"; and, in a 1921 poll, more than 80 percent of circuit judges and 75 percent of district judges.[155] Among leading professional organizations, the reform carried the approval of forty-six state bar associations, the executive committee of the Association of American Law Schools, the U.S. Chamber of Commerce, the Commercial Law League, the National Civic Federation, and—of course—the ABA.[156]

To suggest the wisdom and appeal of his proposal, Cummings stressed the ways in which reform, far from catering exclusively to the professional legal elite, would make the judicial system "less complicated, less expensive, and far more speedy" for all Americans.[157] He promised, in classic progressive fashion, that reform would remedy the flaws of "an outworn system" that served "to delay justice or entrap the unwary."[158] He argued, counter to the traditional localist critique long articulated by Thomas Walsh, that procedural uniformity would actually simplify (rather than complicate) the lawyer's job by reducing the number of procedural schemes he would need to master to one.[159] He asserted that judicial rule making would "center authority and responsibility in qualified hands," thereby resulting in "fewer decisions based upon technical questions of procedure" and allowing attention "to be directed to the substance of right rather than to its form."[160] He downplayed the notion of judicial aggrandizement by maintaining that the proposed reform was "in harmony with basic constitutional principles" about the "true balance between the legislative and judicial branches" and portraying it as a natural extension of prior and "highly satisfactory" efforts to vest administrative authority in the judges themselves.[161] Together with his demonstration that procedural uniformity was popular among political and legal leaders, Cummings's ardent promotion of the virtues of reform helped to transform the image of the bill from a mundane piece of conservative special-interest legislation not worthy of political capital to a rare opportunity for meaningful improvement of a critical governmental institution.

Utilizing a favorable reputation and extensive networks both to lend credibility to a counterintuitive idea and to garner support for that idea both inside and outside the Capitol, Cummings and his "earnest and persuasive efforts" built substantial momentum for his reform agenda.[162] With neither progressive Republicans nor Southern and Western Democrats "willing to fight the New Deal,"[163] they joined liberals (who accepted Cummings's suggestion that judicial reform might actually further the aims of New Deal legislation) and conservative Republicans (who—

---

[155] Cummings, "The New Law Relating to Federal Procedure," 2.
[156] Ibid.
[157] "Legislation of the Seventy-Third Congress," *American Bar Association Journal* 20 (1934): 460.
[158] Ibid; Cummings, "From an Address at the Silver Anniversary Banquet," 182.
[159] "Powerful Support for Rule-Making Measure," *American Bar Association Journal* 20 (1934): 224.
[160] Cummings, "From an Address at the Silver Anniversary Banquet," 183.
[161] Ibid.
[162] Charles Evans Hughes, "Address of Chief Justice Hughes," *American Bar Association Journal* 21 (1935): 340.
[163] Purcell, *Brandeis and the Progressive Constitution*, 33.

whether or not they received credit for it—had finally obtained the reform they had long desired) in support of procedural reform. Only ninety days after he began his campaign in favor of it, Cummings's bill passed Congress and made its way to a receptive president's desk "almost as a matter of course."[164]

To what extent is Cummings's success in this endeavor almost accidental, simply a case of having the good fortune to be in the right place (the Roosevelt administration) at the right time (the moment Walsh died)? Undoubtedly, Cummings's triumph was in some sense dependent on a favorable historical moment, but the fact that the conditions for transformative change were propitious—that Roosevelt's victory in 1932 prompted the ABA to abandon its campaign, thus creating political space for a Democratic attorney general to lead the charge in favor of procedural reform without accusations of partisan or ideological apostasy; that Walsh's sudden death removed the most formidable opponent to procedural reform from a position where he would have been in a position to kill it with ease—does not mean that transformative change was inevitable or probable. For one thing, another attorney general was certainly possible or even likely. Indeed, Cummings, who was initially tasked with leading the Justice Department on a temporary basis only,[165] was far from the only or most obvious choice, and according to a newspaper report at the time, the short list for the permanent position contained eight prominent names[166]—none of them Cummings's. While some of those men may well have supported procedural reform as attorney general—it is not clear whether any had ever expressed definitive views on the subject—it is unlikely that they would have tackled the initiative with the energy and enthusiasm of a longtime supporter such as Cummings. Even if we assume (incorrectly) that Cummings's appointment was a foregone conclusion, the tasks of overcoming apathy and negotiating a formerly Republican initiative through a Congress with a new—and overwhelming—Democratic majority remained formidable. Far from preordained with the election of Roosevelt, the death of Walsh, or even the appointment of Cummings, then, the passage of Rules Enabling Act was a steep challenge requiring both substantial personal effort and strategic political action. Whether or not Cummings's effort and action—his taking advantage of the opportunities that presented themselves—were the sole determining factors in reform, they were certainly the decisive factors. In that way, even if the "seed . . . had been sown" and the "soil had been cultivated,"[167] Homer Cummings's seemingly serendipitous success was still a paradigmatic example of political entrepreneurship.

[164]"Powerful Support for Rule-Making Measure," 422.

[165]The Los Angeles Times reported at the time that Cummings "will hold the office temporarily and eventually go on to the important insular post" of Governor of the Philippines. Associated Press, "Cummings Regarded as Walsh Successor."

[166]The list included, among others, Harvard Law School professor (and future Supreme Court justice) Felix Frankfurter, former assistant attorney general and former Federal Trade Commission chairman Huston Thompson, former Nebraska attorney general Arthur Mullen, former representative J. Swagar Sherley of Kentucky, and Senator Robert Wagner of New York.

[167]"Powerful Support for Rule-Making Measure," 422.

The Judicial Wielding of Legislative Power

In a literal sense, the Rules Enabling Act was not landmark judicial reform in and of itself but congressional authorization for the Court to engage in landmark judicial reform. After all, the *real* change—the real transformation of American civil procedure—came not with the Rules Enabling Act in 1934 but with the adoption of the Federal Rules of Civil Procedure two years later.[168] The rules, which were actually drafted by a politically diverse committee of lawyers and law professors who answered to the Court and functioned under guidelines it had established,[169] sent a clear substantive message: "procedure should step aside and not interfere with substance."[170] They merged the theretofore separate jurisprudential realms of law and equity, introduced new procedures such as summary judgments, and generally used procedure as an aid to understanding particular cases rather than restricting parties.[171] Straightforward yet innovative, the rules made civil litigation "a more appealing political strategy" for many interest groups by opening up new jurisdictional avenues, making it easy for plaintiffs to discover damaging evidence, and broadening judicial discretion to award damages.[172] In all these ways, it was the Federal Rules of Civil Procedure rather than the Rules Enabling Act that made a lasting impact on the conduct of business in federal courts.

In a more symbolic sense, however, the Rules Enabling Act was actually *more* important than the Federal Rules of Civil Procedure—and would have remained so regardless of what the Court did (or did not do) with the power delegated to it. The sheer fact that Congress was compelled to delegate power to the Court in the first place suggests that the federal judiciary had arrived as a power player on the national political scene. For an institution that had long had even its most mundane institutional arrangements dictated to it by Congress, the legislative cession of the power to make rules—the power to make procedural law, in essence—governing judicial practice across the entire nation can only be regarded as a momentous step toward the realization of full institutional independence and autonomy. Indeed, following the creation of a judicial policy-making institution (in the Judicial Conference Act of 1922) and the growth of the Court's control over its own docket (in the Judiciary Act of 1925), the Rules Enabling Act marked the fortification of a new and growing conception of the judiciary as an institution that could and should govern its own internal affairs.

---

[168] As required by statute, the Court presented a final draft of the rules to Congress, after which the rules became effective without the need for a congressional vote in favor.

[169] Subrin, "How Equity Conquered Common Law," 971, remarks that the committee's composition "reflected both the conservatives, and the professional, professorial liberals who had joined in supporting uniform federal rules."

[170] Ibid., 973.

[171] Surrency, *History of the Federal Courts*, 200.

[172] Frymer, "Acting When Elected Officials Won't," 484.

This same conception of the institutional judiciary was equally reflected in three other institution-building episodes during the early New Deal period.[173] First, the creation of an independent building for the Supreme Court, which had been a hobbyhorse of Taft's when he was chief justice, eliminated the Court's reliance on Congress for physical space and provided some tangible distance between the lawmaking and law-interpreting branches of the federal government.[174] Second, Congress authorizing the Court to devise a code of criminal rules allowed the justices to shape and unify criminal procedure in precisely the way the Rules Enabling Act had enabled them to shape and unify civil procedure.[175] Third, the Uniform Declaratory Judgment Act,[176] which was proposed as early as 1921 and considered in Congress throughout the 1920s, granted federal judges the authority to issue binding rulings about the claims involved in a particular case without ordering action or awarding damages.[177] The first reform symbolized not only the newfound independence of the Court but also the growing conception that it was an institutional equal to, rather than dependent of, Congress. The second signified both legislative trust of judicial expertise and deference to judicial autonomy on matters relating to the conduct of courts. The third enhanced federal judicial power not—as had often been the case—by expanding jurisdiction but by offering judges an additional remedy to utilize in cases already under their jurisdiction. Thus, although all three reforms were less politically contested and less institutionally transformative than the Rules Enabling Act, all three nonetheless contributed to the independence, autonomy, and power of the federal judiciary as the Supreme Court headed toward confrontation with Franklin Roosevelt.

The Bureaucratic Arm of Judicial Administration, 1936–1939

The titanic clash that occurred between Franklin Roosevelt and the Supreme Court at the close of Roosevelt's first term may have demonstrated—at least initially—the Court's jurisprudential independence in opposing the political program of a popular president, but it occurred against the largely ignored backdrop of the Court's severe organizational dependence on the executive branch. Even by that point,

---

[173] Notable exceptions to this conception included contemporaneous attempts to deprive the federal judiciary of diversity jurisdiction and withdraw the power to issue a labor injunction. Though the former failed, the latter was accomplished in the Norris-LaGuardia Act of 1932. 40 Stat. 70 (March 23, 1932). On both measures, see Purcell, *Brandeis and the Progressive Constitution*, 81–89.

[174] The creation of the building was authorized in 1928 and appropriated in 1929; 45 Stat. 1066 (December 21, 1928); 46 Stat. 51 (December 20, 1929). Construction formally began in 1932 and was completed three years later.

[175] Congress originally (in 1933) authorized the Court to draft a set of rules applying only to criminal appeals procedure, 47 Stat. 904 (February 24, 1933). Seven years later, after the appeals rules had gone into effect, Congress expanded the Court's mandate to include rules for criminal trial procedure as well; 54 Stat. 688 (June 29, 1940). Those rules finally became effective in 1946.

[176] 48 Stat. 955 (June 14, 1934).

[177] See Purcell, *Brandeis and the Progressive Constitution*, 125–32.

with the Court having recently earned some measure of spatial separation from Congress by moving out of the Capitol and across First Street to its own building, the federal judiciary did not have full control over its own administration or any control, for that matter, over its own finances. From 1789 to 1849, such control was vested in the Department of the Treasury; from 1849 to 1870, the Department of the Interior; and from 1870 to 1939, the Department of Justice.[178] The creation of the Judicial Conference in 1922 had established some measure of administrative self-sufficiency for federal courts, but it did not make them wholly (or even mostly) independent of executive branch administration, and it certainly did not grant them budgetary autonomy. Consistent with the tradition of other institutions (usually Congress) attending to the housekeeping of the judicial branch, the federal judiciary still appealed for administrative and clerical personnel to Justice Department officials, still submitted a summary for the attorney general to include in his annual report to Congress, and—perhaps most important—still shared the money appropriated under the headline "Judiciary" with the Justice Department.[179] Since the attorney general had authority not only to dispense funds appropriated to the judiciary but also to cut budget requests made by the Judicial Conference, the pre–World War II judiciary annually faced the challenge of "persuading the executive branch of its financial requirements."[180] Exacerbated by the fact that the chief administrative and financial officers of the judicial branch—the marshals—were subordinates of the attorney general, the "relatively insignificant place of the courts in the department's total administrative realm,"[181] and the lack of any real consultation between the attorney general and the Judicial Conference, such financial dependence led to persistent tension and consistent conflicts between federal judges, who criticized "indifferent bureaucracy,"[182] and the Department of Justice, which grew frustrated with the haphazard organization and administration of courts.[183]

With these tensions and conflicts fresh in their minds, federal judges—including Chief Justice Charles Evans Hughes—sought to place some distance between the executive and judicial branches of government. Like the campaign for the Rules Enabling Act, this reform drive was predominantly performance oriented but tinged with slight political concerns. At base, judges believed that removing the judiciary from the administration of the attorney general and providing it with an extensive administrative apparatus all its own would make the institution more efficient as well as reduce the possibility of executive branch encroachment upon the judiciary. Unlike the campaign for uniform procedural rules, however, this reform drive provoked little active resistance. Yet even as it had few opponents,

---

[178] For a summary of this last period, see Fish, *The Politics of Federal Judicial Administration*, 91–124.

[179] Surrency, *History of the Federal Courts*, 119.

[180] Thomas G. Walker and Deborah J. Barrow, "Funding the Federal Judiciary: The Congressional Connection," *Judicature* 69 (1985–86): 44.

[181] Fish, *The Politics of Federal Judicial Administration*, 101.

[182] Ibid., 102.

[183] Ibid.

the idea of a thicker and more detached judicial bureaucracy also had few active nonjudicial supporters—at least until Roosevelt's ill-fated Court-packing plan in 1937. In the aftermath of that controversy, legislators joined judges in an attempt to protect judicial independence and the separation of powers from executive imperialism. The resulting reform, the Administrative Office of the Courts Act of 1939,[184] established the Administrative Office of the Courts, created circuit judicial councils, and regularized circuit judicial conferences. These innovations—which, in the wake of the failed attempt at more aggressive reform, were actually supported (at least publicly) by the Roosevelt administration—not only enhanced judicial communication and increased judicial capacity for branch governance but also made the judiciary, which had been financially tied to the Justice Department for seven decades, wholly and completely independent of the executive in terms of its budget and its administration.

Administration in the Face of Attack

The campaign to move judicial appropriations and personnel control out of the Justice Department—to move toward a judicial administration of judicial matters—first began in the mid-1920s, after the Justice Department sought to establish "uniformity in administration of the courts and professionalization of court personnel."[185] Manifested in the attorney general's successful move to take control over the salaries of lower court clerks and deputies, the idea of shifting administrative tasks that previously fell to individual judges to a more centralized location in the executive branch irked many in the judicial branch. Judges already resented the Justice Department's "influence in the selection and promotion of judges, its investigations of courts and court officers, and . . . its prominent and sometimes questionable role in the inter-circuit assignment of judges,"[186] but the turf wars only escalated as finances grew lean during the Great Depression. Simple cost-cutting measures—not summoning juries at the end of the fiscal year and minimizing travel (and thus travel expenses) for judicial branch officials—met little judicial resistance, but the Justice Department's attempt to eliminate bailiffs, criers, and messengers "came as a bitter blow to many judges."[187] By the time the attorney general reduced federal judges' per diem allowances by 50 percent (from ten to five dollars) as part of applying the Economy Act of 1932 and unsuccessfully attempted to reduce judicial salaries by 15 percent in the Independent Office Appropriations Act of 1933,[188] federal judges were fed up and resolved to do something about it.

---

[184] 53 Stat. 1223 (August 7, 1939).

[185] Peter Graham Fish, "Crises, Politics, and Federal Judicial Reform: The Administrative Office Act of 1939," *Journal of Politics* 32 (1970): 605.

[186] Ibid., 607.

[187] Ibid., 608.

[188] 47 Stat. 405 (June 30, 1932); 48 Stat. 307 (June 16, 1933). The latter statute was struck down as unconstitutional by the Supreme Court in *Booth v United States*, 291 U.S. 339 (1934).

Fearful of an "accelerating worldwide trend toward national executive-centered government,"[189] judges decided that the administration of the judiciary needed to be specific to—and perhaps come from within—the judiciary itself. This desire for a bureaucratic division for the judiciary reflected two distinct performance concerns about the institutional workings of the judicial branch. First, echoing Roscoe Pound's 1906 observation that much dissatisfaction with the judiciary stemmed from poor organization, reform-minded judges believed the "administrative side of the judicial system" in need of substantial improvement.[190] In part, they hoped to fill the administrative void left by the Judicial Conference,[191] which, though a successful annual meeting and useful forum for generating ideas about judicial policy, was plainly not a centralized administrative organ. To the extent that much administrative power remained in the Justice Department, the conference neither actively supervised the "business management of the courts" nor provided the judiciary with the systematic informational support it needed in order to identify and address problems.[192] Second, judges became convinced that the interconnection of judicial branch and Justice Department administration not only impeded the prompt dispatch of judicial business but also threatened the integrity of the separation of powers. If the courts were to be truly "independent agencies of impartial justice,"[193] then the executive branch—the single most frequent litigant in the federal court system[194]—could not be permitted to exercise any control over the process relating to, officials implicated in, or financing of the distribution of that justice. More simply, if the judiciary were to be seen as independent in its judgments, then it needed actually to be independent in its administration.

As sensible as the idea of a separate administrative body for the judicial system may have seemed to judges, it went virtually unnoticed by legislators until Roosevelt's proposal of his Court-packing plan in February 1937.[195] Despite framing his complaints in conservative language about the delays, expense, and complexities associated with the administration of justice, the details of the Judicial Reorganization Bill revealed the real motive behind Roosevelt's sudden enthusiasm for judicial reform: to overcome the bloc of conservative justices—the "Four Horsemen"[196]—that consistently voted to nullify New Deal legislation. After all, in just one year, the Court had nullified (part of) the National Industrial Recovery

[189] Fish, "William Howard Taft and Charles Evans Hughes," 132.

[190] William L. Ransom, "Improving the Administration of Justice," *Journal of the American Judicature Society* 20 (1936–37): 223.

[191] Fish, "Crises, Politics, and Federal Judicial Reform," 601.

[192] Henry P. Chandler, "The Administration of the Federal Courts," *Law and Contemporary Problems* 13 (1948): 186.

[193] Ransom, "Improving the Administration of Justice," 222.

[194] Chandler, "The Administration of the Federal Courts," 186.

[195] For a thorough account detailing the creation of the bill, see Leuchtenburg, *The Supreme Court Reborn*, 82–131.

[196] The moniker referred to Justices Willis Van Devanter (appointed by William Howard Taft in 1911), James McReynolds (appointed by Woodrow Wilson in 1914), George Sutherland (appointed by Warren G. Harding in 1922), and Pierce Butler (appointed by Warren G. Harding in 1923).

Act (*Schechter Poultry Corporation v. United States*), the Agricultural Adjustment Act (*United States v. Butler*), and the Bituminous Coal Conservation Act (*Carter v. Carter Coal Company*), provoking Roosevelt's ire to the point of counterattack. Criticizing the Court for having "cast doubts on the ability of the elected Congress to protect us against catastrophe" and lamenting that the "three-horse team" of American government featured one branch not "pulling in unison" with the others, Roosevelt sought to "infuse new blood" into the judiciary through a scheme to supplement older (anti–New Deal) judges with younger (pro–New Deal) judges.[197] More specifically, the plan authorized the president to nominate (for Senate confirmation) an additional judge for every federal judge (including Supreme Court justices) who had not retired within six months of his seventieth birthday. Although Roosevelt himself explicitly denied that he was trying to control the federal government through the appointment of "spineless puppets" to the bench,[198] his opponents—including Democrats who both favored and opposed the New Deal—quickly objected to the way in which the proposal "applie[d] force to the judiciary,"[199] attacking not only judicial independence specifically but the American constitutional tradition more broadly. Roosevelt attempted to push forward into the summer, but a series of events—the Court's decision in *West Coast Hotel v. Parrish* in March,[200] the retirement of William Van Devanter in May, an adverse report from the Senate Judiciary Committee in June, the death of Senate majority leader (and Court-packing proponent) Joseph Robinson of Arkansas in July—combined to blunt much of his criticism (about the Court's obstructionism toward economic regulation, as well as the fact that, despite more than four years in office, he had yet to have an opportunity to place a justice on the Court), deprive him of

[197] Franklin Roosevelt, Fireside Chat on Reorganization of the Judiciary, March 9, 1937.
[198] Ibid.
[199] Senate Committee on the Judiciary, Report on Reorganization of the Federal Judiciary, June 14, 1937.
[200] 300 U.S. 379 (1937) (upholding a Washington minimum wage law as a legitimate exercise of state police power against complaints that it violated "liberty of contract" as protected by the Due Process Clause of the Fourteenth Amendment). Although not a challenge to New Deal legislation itself, *West Coast Hotel*—and Justice Owen Roberts's notorious "switch-in-time-that-saved-nine"—signaled a decisive shift in the Court's treatment of economic regulation during the 1920s and '30s at large. With Roberts decamping from the Four Horsemen to join fellow moderate Chief Justice Charles Evans Hughes and the liberal Three Musketeers (Justices Louis Brandeis, Benjamin Cardozo, and Harlan Fiske Stone), the Court upheld the National Labor Relations Act and the Social Security Act in the succeeding two months alone. For rival interpretations of the Court's shift from *Morehead v. Tipaldo*, 298 U.S. 587 (1936) (striking down a New York minimum wage law as a violation of the Due Process Clause of the Fourteenth Amendment), to *West Coast Hotel*, compare Leuchtenburg, *The Supreme Court Reborn*, 132–62 (emphasizing the "externalist" factors of Roosevelt's opposition and the looming Court-packing plan), with Cushman, *Rethinking the New Deal Court*, 11–43, 84–105 (emphasizing the "internalist" factors of changing fact patterns and doctrinal evolution). For the cases immediately following *West Coast Hotel*, see *National Labor Relations Board v. Jones & Laughlin Steel Corporation*, 301 U.S. 1 (1937) (upholding the National Labor Relations Act as a legitimate exercise of congressional Commerce Clause authority); and *Steward Machine Company v. Davis*, 30 U.S. 548 (1937) (upholding the Social Security Act against claims that it violated the Tenth Amendment).

his most crucial legislative ally, and, in turn, render his reorganization proposal a virtual impossibility.

While the Court-packing plan ultimately failed,[201] the mere proposal of such an aggressive reform, especially following so soon after Roosevelt's rout of Alf Landon, the Republican governor of Kansas, in the 1936 presidential election,[202] proved important in the judicial quest for budgetary independence from the executive in two ways. First, the Court-packing plan placed the idea of administrative, performance-oriented reform into the public mind and onto the legislative agenda. Although Roosevelt's neo-progressive rhetoric of administrative efficiency was designed to make Court-packing more palatable (and seemingly more legitimate) to hesitant legislators and a skeptical public, one of its effects was actually to lend a Democratic voice to the Republican idea—utilized by Taft two decades earlier and by the ABA after that—that the central problems of the federal court system were administrative (and not doctrinal) at their core. In the wake of the Court-packing defeat, judges and legislators reconsidered these problems and discovered—upon taking stock of the "adequacy of the judiciary's administrative institutions"[203]—that the Judicial Conference was desperately in need of an independent (of the executive branch) bureaucratic entity to gather information, compile statistics, and serve as a strategic liaison between the judicial and legislative branches of government. Second, the perceived antijudicial hostility behind Roosevelt's plan forged an alliance between judges who desired reform and legislators who feared an omnipotent presidency. After all, for many judges and legislators, the Court-packing plan was a wake-up call about the need to free the judiciary's budget from the Department of Justice. Taking the plan as proof that a "hostile and power-grasping executive branch" threatened judicial independence,[204] reformers grew all the more hesitant about leaving Roosevelt's attorney general in control of the judicial budget. In neither way did the Court-packing plan function as an immediate catalyst to overcome a set of entrenched constraints, but it did place the issue more prominently in the national political spotlight, where it had few enemies, and earn for it some measure of support that it may have not possessed previously.

Viewing Roosevelt's Court-packing plan in light of his landslide reelection the previous year—or, more precisely, viewing his Court-packing plan as evidence of his increasing desire for unchecked executive power following an emphatic governing mandate from the people—judges and legislators used his failed case for judicial reform against him, turning what would have been an antagonistic measure into a constructive one. Despite slight opposition from one handful of judges who felt the Justice Department was "better situated to secure appropriations from

[201] Of course, there is debate about whether—with the Court reliably affirming New Deal legislation beginning in March 1937—Roosevelt may have won the long-term jurisprudential war even as he lost the immediate political battle.

[202] In one of the most lopsided contests in American history, Roosevelt carried 46 of 48 states, won 523 of 531 electoral votes, and received more than 60 percent of the popular vote nationwide.

[203] Fish, "Crises, Politics, and Federal Judicial Reform," 614.

[204] Ibid., 615.

Congress" and another handful who objected to the idea of a centralized administrative agency as anathema to the spirit of judicial localism,[205] the Administrative Office of the Courts Act passed easily, in part because it combined a centralizing feature that would provide national uniformity (the Administrative Office of the Courts) with more decentralizing features (the circuit judicial councils and circuit judicial conferences) that would assure sensitivity to local circumstances.[206] In the end, the bill was widely supported by judges (including a nearly unanimous Supreme Court), by the ABA, and even by the Roosevelt administration, which sought, somewhat disingenuously, to recast the act's passage as a victory for the cause of judicial reform generally rather than as a bitter defeat of its Court-packing plan specifically.[207] A reform that had been percolating since the mid-1920s had been realized, and improved administration of the courts had triumphed in the face of an attack upon them.

The Disentanglement of Executive Administration and Judicial Power

As described by its inaugural director, the Administrative Office of the Courts served four functions.[208] The first three of these functions—"providing personnel and facilities for the courts," "promoting promptness in the dispatch of judicial business," and "promoting efficient procedures"—were essentially housekeeping duties. Of course, since the judiciary had previously been forced to perform such functions itself (if they were to be performed at all), having a true administrative apparatus—rather than judges moonlighting as administrators during the Judicial Conference—was a most welcome development. Functioning as the official bureaucratic arm of the conference, which was itself the legislative and quasi-administrative arm of the federal judiciary, the Administrative Office served a multitude of roles.[209] Among other things, it allotted the salaries of administrative officials; fixed the number of clerks, probation officers, and deputies; obtained suitable quarters for judicial proceedings and made arrangements with the agencies in charge of those quarters; supervised the construction and operation of buildings; maintained extensive statistics from clerk reports and site visits; and offered friendly, empirically based suggestions about how to improve judicial administration. In other words, the Administrative Office became the "secretariat

---

[205] Fish, "William Howard Taft and Charles Evans Hughes," 111; Fish, "Crises, Politics, and Federal Judicial Reform," 603.

[206] Such a balance was struck at the suggestion of Chief Justice Charles Evans Hughes. See Fish, "William Howard Taft and Charles Evans Hughes," 141–43.

[207] In his role as attorney general, Homer Cummings both drafted two reports in favor of the bill and offered a supportive statement about it to the Senate Judiciary Committee. Of course, since these actions followed the demise of the Court-packing plan, of which Cummings was a central drafter and main proponent, and given the willingness and ability to take an opposition initiative and repackage it as his own that he demonstrated only a few years earlier in securing the Rules Enabling Act, one might reasonably doubt his sincerity.

[208] Chandler, "The Administration of the Federal Courts," 188.

[209] Ibid., 188–95.

for the Judicial Conference" and the "fact gatherer and business assistant of the courts" more broadly.[210]

The last of the four stated functions of the Administrative Office—"promoting legislation for the courts"—effectively established a legislative liaison for the federal judiciary.[211] Acting as the link between the Judicial Conference and Congress, the Administrative Office offered a more efficient "medium for expression of the collective opinion of the federal judiciary" concerning federal courts legislation.[212] Under the supervision of the conference, the Administrative Office presented recommendations to Congress on appropriations as well as the number and location of needed judgeships, provided congressional committees (chiefly the Judiciary and Appropriations Committees) with information and statistics, and acted as a "clearing house for legislation pending in Congress."[213] In so doing, it made the judicial lobby "more routine, systematic, and widespread" and "labored to smooth the way for Conference policies."[214] By lending "institutional memory" and "stable and professionalized leadership" to the project of judicial administration,[215] the Administrative Office thus liberated the Judicial Conference from its original tasks of bureaucratic management and legislative lobbying and allowed it to focus instead on its role as a "centralized policy-making institution."[216]

Just as the Administrative Office helped empower the Judicial Conference to formulate and implement national policies relating to the federal judiciary, so too did the two other features of the Administrative Office of the Courts Act—the circuit judicial councils and the circuit judicial conferences—assist lower federal judges in more targeted judicial administration. With the ability to issue orders that were binding upon district court judges, the councils,[217] composed of all the courts of appeals judges for a given circuit, were given "broad power to supervise and direct the administration of the federal courts in the respective circuits, to the end that the business may be effectively and expeditiously transacted."[218] The conferences—small-scale geographic versions of the national Judicial Conference that were recommended by the Judicial Conference Act and occurred occasionally during the 1920s and '30s[219]—were less potent, but not necessarily less important,

[210] Fish, "Crises, Politics, and Federal Judicial Reform," 602; Fred M. Vinson, "The Business of Judicial Administration," *Journal of the American Judicature Society* 33 (1949–50): 76.

[211] See, generally, John W. Winkle III, "Interbranch Politics: The Administrative Office of U.S. Courts as Liaison," *Justice System Journal* 24 (2003): 45.

[212] Chandler, "The Administration of the Federal Courts," 196.

[213] Fish, *The Politics of Federal Judicial Administration*, 206.

[214] Winkle, "Interbranch Politics," 50; Fish, *The Politics of Federal Judicial Administration*, 208.

[215] Lori A. Johnson, "Institutionalization of the Judicial Branch," paper presented at the Western Political Science Association Meeting, March 12, 2004, 29.

[216] Fish, *The Politics of Federal Judicial Administration*, 228.

[217] On these "grassroots" institutions of judicial administration, see Peter Graham Fish, "The Circuit Councils: Rusty Hinges of Federal Judicial Administration," 37 *University of Chicago Law Review* 203 (1970).

[218] Chandler, "The Administration of the Federal Courts," 185.

[219] Fish, "Crises, Politics, and Federal Judicial Reform"; Surrency, *History of the Federal Courts*, 120.

tools of judicial administration.[220] Indeed, since they provided an opportunity for trial and appellate judges to discuss common problems and formulate mutually agreeable solutions, they facilitated judicial teamwork and further contributed to the understanding of the judicial system as a national system devoted to national purposes. Considered in combination, the circuit judicial councils and conferences assured that, despite the centralizing influence of the Administrative Office of the Courts, much judicial governance would, just as Chief Justice Hughes hoped,[221] continue to be performed on the local level.

In addition to these pragmatic and concrete functions, the Administrative Office of the Courts Act also served, in the words of future chief justice Fred Vinson, as "something of a Declaration of Independence for the federal courts."[222] The fact that virtually all responsibilities for judicial administration (including budgetary requests and appropriation dispersal) were transferred from the Justice Department, where they were ultimately under the direction of the attorney general, to the Administrative Office, where they were ultimately under the direction of the Judicial Conference, meant that courts had become "separate and independent of the Executive."[223] Whereas previously judges had answered to bureaucrats (in the Justice Department), under the new system bureaucrats (in the Administrative Office) answered to judges. Unlike Roosevelt's Court-packing plan (which proposed a "proctor" to supervise judicial administration) and other proposals for a strong judicial bureaucracy, the Administrative Office of the Courts Act resisted a "ubiquitous central administrator" in favor of a configuration whereby judges yielded administration but not power.[224] The director of the Administrative Office supervised housekeeping, fact-finding, and lobbying, but the Judicial Conference—the judges of the federal judiciary—supervised the director. In this way, the "locus of ultimate control" remained in the hands of the judges themselves.[225]

The Administrative Office of the Courts Act represented the culmination of a gradual, long-term shift in views on and practices of judicial branch governance. By 1939, the tradition of legislative and executive branch attention to internal judicial plumbing had virtually disappeared, with the Administrative Office of the Courts assuming most functions previously performed by Congress or the Department of Justice. From the conclusion of World War I to the brink of World War II, the federal judiciary developed a policy-making arm, gained substantial control over its docket (at least at the Supreme Court level), developed a uniform

---

[220] See Vinson, "The Business of Judicial Administration," 76: "For, every minute spent by the judges in these conferences and every dollar expended has been repaid many hundredfold in enhanced efficiency in court administration."

[221] Part of Hughes's attachment to judicial federalism was his belief that "diffusing administrative responsibilities among the several circuits" would serve as "a defense against politically inspired attacks on the judicial establishment in Washington." Fish, "Crises, Politics, and Federal Judicial Reform," 624.

[222] Vinson, "The Business of Judicial Administration," 76.

[223] Ibid.

[224] Fish, "Crises, Politics, and Federal Judicial Reform," 623.

[225] Ibid., 621.

federal code of civil procedure, and fully separated its finances and administration from the reach of an overzealous executive branch.[226] The judicial branch
had grown more powerful in previous periods of judicial institution building, but
never had its independence and autonomy been greater than at the brink of modern America.

• • •

The history of judicial institution building during the interwar and New Deal years
unfolded in three stages: the creation of the Judicial Conference and expansion of
certiorari jurisdiction in the Judicial Conference Act of 1922 and the Judiciary Act
of 1925, respectively; the congressional delegation of rule-making authority to the
Court in the Rules Enabling Act of 1934; and the creation of a bureaucratic judicial
apparatus in the Administrative Office of the Courts Act of 1939. In examining
these stages, I have uncovered both the causes and consequences of judicial institution building; I have explained why judicial institution building was pursued,
how it was accomplished, and what it achieved.

*Why was judicial institution building during the interwar and New Deal years
pursued?* In all three stages, institution building was pursued primarily by lawyers,
judges, and legal academics for performance reasons. During the 1920s, judicial
reform was pursued by Chief Justice William Howard Taft in order to improve the
administration of justice and, consequently, insulate the judiciary against political attacks. More specifically, the Judicial Conference Act of 1922 was guided by
Taft's vision of encompassing an institutional arena whereby judges might com-
municate about problems and ideas, a federal judicial branch under the leadership of the chief justice, and a system of courts governed by "executive principle."
Similarly, the Judiciary Act of 1925 was prompted by caseloads sufficiently heavy
and a docket sufficiently backlogged so as to create widespread delay throughout the justice system. In the procedural reform campaign that formally stretched
from the beginning of the Wilson administration through the early 1930s before
culminating in the Rules Enabling Act of 1934, institution building was motivated
by a desire to make the law more substantive and less procedural, thereby reducing delay, confusion, and unpredictability. Finally, the Administrative Office of the
Courts Act of 1939 was an attempt not only to provide the judiciary with a house-

---

[226] With the creation of the Federal Judicial Center in 1967, 81 Stat. 664 (December 20, 1967), the judiciary would also gain an internal education, research, and outeach division to assist both the policy-
making judges of the Judicial Conference and the managerial professionals of the Administrative Office
of the Courts. To the extent that the Federal Judicial Center effectively split off from the other two bodies, providing similar functions in a more sustained and more thorough fashion, it serves as something
of a (delayed) coda to the more transformative enactments of the interwar and New Deal years. On
the center's establishment and functioning, see William Schwarzer, "The Federal Judicial Center and
the Administration of Justice in the Federal Courts," 28 *U.C. Davis Law Review* 1129 (1995); and Russell
Wheeler, "Empirical Research and the Politics of Judicial Administration: Creating the Federal Judicial
Center," *Law and Contemporary Problems* 51 (1988): 31–53.

keeping and fact-finding division but also to lessen improper (and potentially cor-
rosive) executive branch influence on the judiciary through control of the federal
judicial budget.

*How was judicial institution building during the interwar and New Deal years
accomplished?* The judicial reforms of the 1920s, which faced resistance from
both Democrats and influential progressives, were made possible only through
the political entrepreneurship of Taft. Utilizing an identity based on a rapidly improving reputation and myriad political networks, a set of ideas that was harmonious with the late Progressive Era emphasis on scientific administration, and a
series of tactics—from framing to compromise and measured action to strategic
deployment of colleagues—that built valuable political capital, Taft managed to
orchestrate not one but two major reform efforts. In much the same way, the Rules
Enabling Act was facilitated by the political entrepreneurship of Attorney General
Homer Cummings. Building upon a reputation that was respected by both Democrats and Republicans and exploiting extensive political and legal networks, Cummings buttressed his idea to pursue the abandoned ABA idea of procedural reform
with both diligent lobbying and an aggressive publicity campaign to guide what
had long been considered a conservative idea to successful passage in a Democratic Congress and during a Democratic administration. In contrast to both the
Taft reforms and the campaign for procedural uniformity, which required political
entrepreneurship to overcome substantial constraints militating against passage,
the creation of the Administrative Office of the Courts was accomplished relatively
easily following an enabling event. Here, legislators supported reform less because
they possessed a strong desire to thicken the institutional judiciary per se than
because, in the wake of Roosevelt's overwhelming reelection and failed Court-
packing plan, judicial reform offered a compelling means of resisting the executive
aggrandizement of governmental power more generally.

*What did judicial institution building during the interwar and New Deal years
achieve?* By the end of the 1930s, as the nation mobilized for war once again, the
federal judiciary had been bureaucratized and remade anew. The Judiciary Act
of 1925 had provided the Supreme Court greater discretion over what cases to
hear. The Rules Enabling Act of 1934 had provided judges greater influence in how
those cases would be handled in lower courts. The Judicial Conference Act of 1922
and the Administrative Office of the Courts Act of 1939 had each provided the
judicial branch greater command over how it would be administered. Although
these changes were "seemingly prosaic reforms of court organization, jurisdiction, administration, and procedure,"[227] they actually offered judges considerable
control over each aspect of the institutional judiciary. The expansion of certiorari
and promulgation of uniform procedural rules offered control over functions, the
Judicial Conference over individuals, and the Administrative Office of the Courts

---

[227] Fish, "William Howard Taft and Charles Evans Hughes," 124.

over resources. Moreover, with both the legislative branch (in the Rules Enabling Act) and the executive branch (in the Administrative Office of the Courts Act) effectively ceding power to the judiciary, the reforms of the interwar and New Deal period made clear that the federal judiciary was no longer a skeletal institution largely dependent on other branches in order to operate properly. Indeed, for the first time in 150 years, the judiciary—though built mostly by legislators—was governed almost entirely by judges.

Reflecting on the period more broadly, it is clear that the process of building the judiciary during the interwar and New Deal years reflected that of other periods in meaningful ways. First, as has been the case throughout American history, the judiciary was built through political decisions rather than judicial ones, through committee work and roll calls rather than oral argument and opinion assignment. Though judges—along with legislators, interest groups, and legal academics— played a significant role in institution building, that role consisted more of proposing, pursuing, and lobbying on behalf of reform than issuing legal decisions that effected institutional change. In other words, the idea that judicial institution building is a politically constructed process—a process whereby diverse actors attempt to satisfy diverse goals—remained as true in interwar and New Deal America as it had been in any other period of American political development. Second, as a comparison of prior eras suggests, institution building is often unpredictable. Like the Civil War reorganization of the federal judiciary along more Yankee lines following Abraham Lincoln's successful presidential campaign, some initiatives (like the Administrative Office of the Courts Act of 1939) coast to passage with little opposition at all. Like the attempts to adapt the federal circuit system to population growth and statehood admission during the Era of Mixed Feelings, other initiatives (such as the Rules Enabling Act of 1934) are impeded at every step. Third, as institution building during the Gilded Age and Progressive Era demonstrated, many reforms are pursued not because they further policy aims or facilitate partisan entrenchment but because they promise tangible improvements in the administration of justice. Simply because such concerns are less salient does not mean they are any less influential in the process of institution building. Fourth, and finally, judicial institution building in interwar and New Deal America continued the Gilded Age and Progressive Era shift toward moving judicial reform debates outside the halls of Congress. While Congress still played an important role, not least since it enacted each reform in statute, nonlegislative—and, in fact, nongovernmental—actors played more important roles than ever before. In each stage of institution building during this period, either lawyers, lawyers' groups (such as the American Bar Association), legal academics, or judges had a significant hand in shaping the ultimate reforms.

Yet even as it followed the patterns of previous eras, so too did the interwar and New Deal years illuminate theretofore unrecognized aspects of judicial institution building. First, although the interwar and New Deal period was not the first time judicial branch actors either formulated, expressed, or acted upon their own judicial reform ideas—that had occurred as early as 1790, when the first Supreme Court justices bitterly complained about circuit riding—there was something distinct about the way in which those actors implicated themselves in the institution-building task during these years. In large part, this uniqueness can be attributed to the fact that judges involved in judicial reform were not simply trying to secure a lighter workload or a more comfortable institutional environment but instead trying to fight off political attacks. Their aims were more performance oriented than anything else, but one of those performance goals was institutional survival. Second, and related, interwar and New Deal institution building suggested not only that antagonism toward the judicial branch can prompt landmark institution building but also that such antagonism might prompt judicial allies (as well as enemies) to pursue such reform. Indeed, the fact that this extensive and transformative period of institution building coincided with the longest period of sustained judicial antipathy in American history may not be a coincidence. As we have seen, it was partly the prevalence of court-curbing attacks that motivated Taft's desire for "executive principle" and partly the Roosevelt administration's Court-packing attempt that forged a judicial-legislative alliance in the quest to remove judicial administration from executive oversight. Third, and finally, in contrast to the eras of Jeffersonian and Jacksonian democracy and the Gilded Age and the Progressive Era, the interwar and New Deal years proved that judges were, in fact, capable of adapting their practices to changing circumstances when necessary. Judges had failed to attend to their own institutional needs in the past not (for the most part) because they were unwilling or unable but because Congress had not provided the means or the authority, opting to fix the problems for the judiciary rather than provide the judiciary the tools to fix them itself. But, as became clear in the case of all four major interwar and New Deal reforms, judges were more than willing to adjust or modify existing structures and procedures in order to make them more efficient so long as they were empowered and equipped to do so.

With the high-water mark of New Deal–Great Society liberalism still to come, the ultimate shape of the federal government that would define late-twentieth-century America—and the ultimate shape of the federal judiciary that would feature so prominently in American politics during that period—was not yet fully determined. But, at the close of the 1930s, one thing was abundantly clear: with the prerogative and responsibilities of the institutional judiciary centralized in the hands of judges and coordinated by their judicial bureaucrats, the largely dependent (even if increasingly powerful) judiciary of pre–New Deal America was but a distant memory. Much like the enhanced role of the federal government in regulating the nation's economic activity, the unification and consolidation of the tools necessary to judicial governance simultaneously provoked principled opposition among outsiders and suggested the need for practical alterations to insiders. As the remainder of the twentieth century would show, those alterations would come in the form of more specialized tasks and competencies that, far from diluting political influence as critics wished, would only focus, solidify, and extend the judiciary's role in the daily functioning of the American polity.

CHAPTER SEVEN

Modern America

SPECIALIZATION

As America emerged triumphant from its wartime engagements, it found itself both a consolidated administrative state and a critical world power.[1] Indeed, if the nation faced any lingering questions about either the character of its regime or its role in the world when Pearl Harbor was attacked in 1941, it almost certainly had clear answers by the time Hiroshima and Nagasaki were bombed nearly four years later. Domestically, the wartime mobilization had fully eradicated the last remaining vestiges of the 1930s economic doldrums, in the process necessitating closer governmental supervision of growth and distribution through measures such as production boards and price controls.[2] Internationally, the economic devastation across much of Europe and concomitant decline of both the United Kingdom and Germany as global powers left the United States and the Soviet Union, nominally allies in World War II, opposite one another in geopolitical bipolarity.[3] Far from fleeting and idiosyncratic effects of the immediate postwar period, these developments only ossified in the decades that followed. For its part, the spirit (if not the actual substance) of Franklin Roosevelt's New Deal not only averted extinction at the hands of Dwight D. Eisenhower in the 1950s but also evolved and expanded into Lyndon Johnson's Great Society in the 1960s. Similarly, the Cold War—and its manifestations in the Berlin

---

[1]Perhaps because the era is somewhat sprawling, perhaps because of changes in the academic interests of historians, there are few period political histories of modern America. One exception is William H. Chafe, *The Unfinished Journey: American History since World War II*, 5th ed. (New York: Oxford University Press, 2003). There are, of course, numerous histories of both particular postwar decades and specific themes stretching across those decades. See, for example, Lizabeth Cohen, *A Consumers' Republic: The Politics of Mass Consumption in Postwar America* (New York: Knopf, 2003); Elaine Tyler May, *Homeward Bound: American Families in the Cold War Era*, rev. ed. (New York: Basic, 1999); Lisa McGirr, *Suburban Warriors: The Origins of the New American Right* (Princeton, NJ: Princeton University Press, 2001); James T. Patterson, *Grand Expectations: The United States, 1945–1974* (New York: Oxford University Press, 1996); Bruce J. Schulman, *The Seventies: The Great Shift in American Culture, Society, and Politics* (New York: Free Press, 2001); and Sean Wilentz, *The Age of Reagan: A History, 1974–2008* (New York: Harper, 2008).

[2]Bartholomew H. Sparrow, *From the Outside In: World War II and the American State* (Princeton, NJ: Princeton University Press, 1996).

[3]G. John Ikenberry, *After Victory: Institutions, Strategic Retreat, and the Rebuilding of Order after Major Wars* (Princeton, NJ: Princeton University Press, 2000), 163–214.

Blockade, the Korean War, and the Cuban Missile Crisis, among other conflicts—
kept America deeply engaged in foreign affairs as the prospect of a third world war
simmered barely under the surface of American-Soviet relations. Whether looking
inward or outward, then, modern America was growing—enhancing its authority
within its borders, extending its influence well beyond them.

These parallel processes provoked much consternation among policy makers
and citizens alike. By the time Johnson—who decisively defeated Arizona senator Barry Goldwater in the 1964 presidential election only to find his substantial
domestic policy achievements (the Civil Rights Act of 1964 and the Voting Rights
Act of 1965 chief among them[4]) dwarfed by his ill-fated escalation of involvement
in Vietnam—declined to run for reelection in 1968, the consternation had ignited,
albeit for different reasons, both liberal restlessness and conservative counterrevo-
lution. At the heart of the former, which would manifest in protests and demonstrations from Berkeley, California, to Washington, D.C., lay a deep concern with
the exercise of military might amid a robust embrace of "countercultural" ideas
about sex, drugs, and identity politics. At the heart of the latter, which would propel
Richard Nixon and later Ronald Reagan to the White House, lay a pointed critique
of the federal government's role in regulating economic activity accompanied by
wistful longing for a return to both more decentralized governance and more traditional social mores. Though by no means the incipient cause of these currents of
controversy, the Supreme Court, at once symbolizing the vanguard of the liberal establishment and serving as a primary target of the conservative ascendancy, proved
a chief interlocutor in them. With former California governor Earl Warren having
joined the Court as chief justice in 1953, the justices quickly adopted a more aggressive judicial role and advanced a more progressive constitutional vision. From racial segregation to school prayer to criminal process,[5] the Court tackled sufficiently
contentious issues and issued sufficiently divisive rulings so as to place it very much
in the national spotlight. And with that spotlight often substantially more hostile
than flattering,[6] the power of the judiciary—from the Court's willingness to strike
down state legislation to district judges implementing the Court's orders,[7] all en-
veloped by the commanding language of "judicial supremacy"[8]—was very much a
fertile source of national debate.

[4] 78 Stat. 241 (July 2, 1964); 79 Stat. 437 (August 6, 1965).
[5] *Brown v. Board of Education*, 347 U.S. 483 (1954) (striking down racially segregated educational facilities as a violation of the Equal Protection Clause of the Fourteenth Amendment); *Engel v. Vitale*, 370
U.S. 421 (1962) (prohibiting denominationally neutral and voluntary state-sponsored prayer in public
schools as a violation of the Establishment Clause of the First Amendment); *Miranda v. Arizona*, 384
U.S. 436 (1968) (holding that the Fifth Amendment requires law enforcement to inform criminal suspects of their procedural rights before interrogating them).
[6] See, generally, Lucas A. Powe Jr., *The Warren Court in American Politics* (Cambridge, MA: Belknap
Press, 2000).
[7] J. W. Peltason, *58 Lonely Men: Southern Federal Judges and School Desegregation* (Urbana: University of Illinois Press, 1971).
[8] *Cooper v. Aaron*, 358 U.S. 1 (1958) (declaring that the Supremacy Clause of Article VI requires state
officers to enforce the decisions of the Supreme Court).

Against the backdrop of—and building discontent with either or both—increasing authority at home and increasing influence abroad, this chapter considers judicial institution building from the start of World War II in 1939 to the election of Bill Clinton's presidential successor in 2000. Despite the extreme tumultuousness of national and international politics during much of this period, the process of institution building was, for the most part, mundane (though by no means unimportant), operating less in the crosshairs of the volatility than in the shadow of it, existing less as a mirror of acute events than a relatively uncontroversial response to more enduring trends. As has been my strategy throughout this book, I uncover the contours of this process with an eye toward why judicial institution building was pursued, how it was accomplished, and what it achieved. Judicial institution building in modern America was, I argue, pursued by legislators, judges, and academics seeking to modify the judiciary so as to enable it to serve (and, in one case, check) a bigger and (by any measure) more interventionist government more expertly. It was then made possible by the lack of any substantial opposition to seemingly consensus structural innovation, by the recognition of a workload crisis sufficiently threatening to judicial capacity so as to make moderate reform (offered following the failure of more aggressive reform) uncontroversial, and by a facilitating event creating a bipartisan, cross-institutional reform coalition; it resulted in the simultaneous refinement of judicial capacity and adaptation of the federal judiciary to a growing set of institutional responsibilities. This move past mere Progressive Era concerns with efficiency and extension of the bureaucratizing impulses of the interwar and New Deal years to deliberate specialization of the (theretofore largely generalist) institutional judiciary occurred in three stages: the enhancement and expansion of judicial adjuncts both to execute administrative duties for and to relieve the growing caseload burden on federal district court judges (1939–79), the reorganization of existing courts and judges in order to develop and utilize expertise to handle the particularly complicated matter of patent law (1969–98), and the creation of a new tribunal to provide some measure of judicial scrutiny over the increasingly important domains of domestic surveillance and intelligence gathering (1972–2000). Following my analysis of each of these stages, I recap this last era in the process of building the judiciary and situate it within the longer historical trajectory of judicial institution building at large.

Augmenting the Quasi-Judiciary, 1939–1979

With the 1940s and much of the 1950s "handicapped by the abnormalities of war and postwar government,"[9] judicial institution building took a decided back seat to more pressing matters for more than two decades. Congress did pass the landmark

---

[9] William F. Swindler, "The Chief Justice and Law Reform, 1921–1971," *The Supreme Court Review* 1971 (1971): 255.

Administrative Procedure Act of 1946,[10] but that legislation, which (among other things) established processes and standards for judicial review over the decisions of administrative agencies, was less transformative of the judiciary per se than of the bureaucracy, regulating as it did the ways in which agencies functioned in American government. Yet the act, the culmination of a decade-long struggle over the exact shape of congressional and judicial oversight over bureaucratic action, neatly tied up the politics of one era as it presaged the central institution-building tension of a new one. Indeed, even as late as June 1946, more than a year after the death of Franklin Roosevelt landed Harry Truman in the White House, the episode served both as one of the final battles over New Deal politics and fore-shadowed the need to attend more closely to the burgeoning administrative state it left behind.[11] Although that institutional configuration had been building for some time—in earnest since Roosevelt's initial election in 1932, in somewhat modified form tracing back to the Gilded Age—the close of the New Deal shifted attention from whether America wanted or needed an administrative state to how it would either maximize (in supportive corners) or manage (in oppositional ones) the one it had already constructed.

Far from forgotten in those debates and considerations, the judiciary (as the Administrative Procedure Act demonstrated) was central to the modern state-building project. With the federal government seeking to do more than ever be-fore, federal courts were being called on to supervise more than ever before. Pro-jecting power from the center to the periphery by implementing and enforcing governmental programs, by forcing states to do what the national bureaucracy wanted but could not yet do, the judiciary had, quite simply, become indispensable in post–New Deal America. Indispensability, of course, placed substantial stress on the institutional judiciary, with federal judges—especially at the district court level—swamped with overburdened dockets and the substantial clerical tasks that accompanied them. In response to these workload struggles, which were hardly unique to the judiciary of this era but which seemed to bring a unity of reform energy absent from earlier periods of American history, Congress heeded the performance-oriented calls of federal judges to relieve the burden—and, by ex-tension, increase the effectiveness—of the judicial system. Although piecemeal ideas were broached and occasionally enacted, the central thrust of the reform agenda during the 1960s especially was the thorough replacement of the outdated commissioner system with a more robust army of quasi-judicial magistrates. Seen both as necessary updating to what had become a weak link in the federal judi-cial apparatus and as a clever means for the federal government to squeeze more production out of a strained judicial branch in a relatively cost-efficient manner,

[10] 60 Stat. 238 (June 11, 1946).
[11] McNollgast [Mathew D. McCubbins, Roger G. Noll, and Barry R. Weingast], "The Political Ori-gins of the Administrative Procedure Act," *Journal of Law, Economics, and Organization* 15 (1999): 180–217; Martin Shapiro, "APA: Past, Present, and Future," 72 *Virginia Law Review* 447 (1986); George B. Shephard, "Fierce Compromise: The Administrative Procedure Act Emerges from New Deal Politics," 90 *Northwestern University Law Review* 1557 (1996).

the legislation providing for these new officers—the Federal Magistrates Act of 1968[12]—was enacted in a spirit of cooperation between legislators and federal judges and with hardly any voices of opposition within either group. Together with a series of amendments and modifications over the succeeding decade, it provided federal district court judges with a valuable and multifaceted resource to assist in the disposition of their workload and to facilitate the smooth performance of their role in the governmental system.

An Antiquated Office in a Modern Nation

As early as 1793, Congress had realized the need to provide federal judges with some sort of quasi-judicial assistance, authorizing circuits courts in 1793 to appoint "one or more discreet persons learned in the law" to help dispatch the business of their court.[13] Originally authorized simply to take bail in criminal cases, these learned persons, known initially as "circuit court commissioners" and later as United States Commissioners, found the contours of their office continually expanded as both the nation and its judicial business grew. In 1842, commissioners were granted the authority to perform for federal offenders the same functions that justices of the peace performed for state offenders.[14] In 1896, following the extension of increased duties to enforce legislation ranging from the Fugitive Slave Act of 1850 to the Civil Rights Act of 1866,[15] they were granted four-year terms in office, albeit subject to removal by a district court at any time.[16] Within several decades, the institutional portfolios of commissioners had broadened to include four central functions: conducting preliminary exams for those charged before a grand jury, issuing search and arrest warrants, setting bail, and appointing legal counsel for indigent defendants.[17] (Following authorization from Congress in 1940, and at the urging of their district judge supervisors, some commissioners also tried cases for and sentenced those convicted of petty offenses.[18]) Although officially defined as part-time "subordinate magistrate[s]" with "certain independent judicial functions,"[19] commissioners had become the "front-line of the judicial process" and a citizen's likely "first contact with the administration of federal justice."[20]

Judicial workload increased so substantially during the 1940s, however, that the commissioner system, which had seemingly served the nation well throughout the

[12] 82 Stat. 1107 (October 17, 1968).
[13] 1 Stat. 333 (March 2, 1793).
[14] 5 Stat. 516 (August 23, 1842).
[15] 9 Stat. 462 (September 18, 1850); 14 Stat. 27 (April 9, 1866).
[16] 29 Stat. 140 (May 28, 1896). This statute also established, for the first time, a uniform fee schedule for commissioners.
[17] Charles A. Lindquist, "The Origin and Development of the United States Commissioner System," *American Journal of Legal History* 14 (1970): 1–2.
[18] 54 Stat. 1058 (October 9, 1940).
[19] Lindquist, "The Origin and Development of the United States Commissioner System," 1.
[20] Ibid.

nineteenth and even into the early twentieth century, was considered ill-designed "to meet the present-day requirements" of a modern judiciary.[21] Following a 1942 report authorized by the Judicial Conference and issued by the director of the Administrative Office of the Courts that recommended substantial changes to the commissioner system,[22] Congress passed minor administrative reforms (simplifying the fee schedule and providing for essential office expenses),[23] but the relatively limited jurisdiction possessed by and inadequate duties performed by commissioners continued to be a source of agitation. District court judges, in particular, made their concerns clear to legislators on multiple occasions and in various ways.[24] After more than a decade of doing nothing save request from the Judicial Conference a further (never completed) study focused on jurisdictional issues,[25] Congress, recognizing that it had been actively creating new areas for federal litigation over the preceding years, suddenly took seriously the calls to reform the "obsolete and ineffective system" of commissioners in 1965.[26] Armed with a list of suggestions from the Judicial Conference, the Senate Judiciary Subcommittee on Improvements in Judicial Machinery opened exploratory hearings "to record the nature of the present system and to point out its inherent defects."[27] And, with expert testimony from judges and academics revealing "widespread dissatisfaction" with the status quo,[28] those defects were numerous. In addition to concerns about most commissioners not being members of the bar, about the fee system being confusing and the fees inadequate, and about the "insufficiency of support services" for commissioners,[29] the hearings revealed that commissioners did not "have a clear idea of . . . their functions" and that there existed "great disparity from district to district on how even fundamental problems were handled."[30] The commissioner system, Congress discovered, was in dire need of thorough renovation and perhaps even replacement.

In the course of the Senate hearings, two divergent reform paths emerged from members of the subcommittee: either demote (or even eliminate) the commissioner and transfer his responsibilities to the supervising district court judge, or

[21] Frank Sanders, "The Organization and Functions of the Commissioner System," *Western Political Quarterly* 21 (1968): 435.

[22] Joseph F. Spaniol, "The Federal Magistrates Act: History and Development," *Arizona Law Review* 1974: 566.

[23] 68 Stat. 703 (August 13, 1954).

[24] Lucinda M. Finley, "Article III Limits on Article I Courts: The Constitutionality of the Bankruptcy Court and the 1979 Magistrate Act," 80 *Columbia Law Review* 560, 565 (1980).

[25] Spaniol, "The Federal Magistrates Act," 566–67.

[26] Brendan Linehan Shannon, "The Federal Magistrates Act: A New Article III Analysis for a New Breed of Judicial Officer," 33 *William and Mary Law Review* 257 (1991).

[27] Hearings on the U.S. Commissioner System before the Subcommittee on Improvements in Judicial Machinery of the Senate Committee on the Judiciary, 89th Cong., 1st and 2nd sess. (1965–66), 90th Cong., 1st sess. (1967).

[28] Spaniol, "The Federal Magistrates Act," 567.

[29] Peter G. McCabe, "The Federal Magistrate Act of 1979," 16 *Harvard Journal on Legislation* 343, 347 (1979).

[30] Hearings on the U.S. Commissioner System.

elevate the commissioner in a manner that could help address workload inequities and inefficiencies at the district court level. With the witness judges overwhelmingly favoring the latter and legislators pointing out ways in which the former was "inefficient and impractical" in its use of judicial manpower,[31] the subcommittee drafted a bill that manifested decidedly performance-oriented sensibilities. Seeking to "reform the first echelon of the Federal judiciary into an effective component of justice,"[32] the legislation aimed to "relieve district judges of certain ministerial or subordinate duties" and thereby free them "for more productive case management and trial work."[33] More specifically, it proposed abolishing the office of United States Commissioner and replacing it with the newly created office of United States Magistrate.[34] Unlike commissioners, who were part-time officials, magistrates could be either part-time (and serve four-year terms) or full-time (and serve eight-year terms). Unlike commissioners, who were rarely lawyers, magistrates would be required to become members of the bar of the highest court in their respective states. Unlike commissioners, who, despite consistent empowerment during the nineteenth century, were still relatively limited in the duties they could perform, magistrates would possess all authority already wielded by their predecessors as well as select additional powers—conducting pretrial and discovery proceedings, reviewing habeas corpus petitions, acting as special masters—and the possibility for executing further duties as sanctioned by district court judges.[35] If the commissioner system had become an institutional relic, then the magistrate system represented the drive to modernize an archaic mechanism of judicial governance.

Much like the Judicial Code of 1911,[36] the creation of magistrates garnered consensus support in the overwhelmingly Democratic Ninetieth Congress (1967–69). In large part, the bill's smooth legislative path is attributable to the fact that the idea to create a new system of magistrates was not regarded as a radical reform proposal but an "attempt at designing a flexible, beneficial innovation for assisting in the administration and efficiency of the federal courts."[37] Armed with evidence and testimony that there was widespread belief among judges that workload relief—whether through reform of the commissioner system or some other alternative—was not simply attractive but actually crucial, faced with the reality that "a multitude of new federal statutes and regulations had created an avalanche of additional work for the district courts which could be performed" only with

[31] McCabe, "The Federal Magistrate Act of 1979," 348.
[32] Senate Report No. 371, 90th Cong., 1st sess. (1967).
[33] Shannon, "The Federal Magistrates Act," 257.
[34] In 1990, the title of the office was changed to United States Magistrate Judge.
[35] The new system of magistrates was modeled, at least in part, on the system of bankruptcy referees, which would itself be the subject of reform the following decade.
[36] See chapter 5.
[37] Christopher E. Smith, "Assessing the Consequences of Judicial Innovation: U.S. Magistrates' Trials and Related Tribulations," 23 *Wake Forest Law Review* 455 (1988).

either more judges or more support for existing judges,[38] and comforted by the fact that there was no obvious way in which magistrates appeared to benefit either Democratic or Republican policy or political goals, legislators were content to act in a spirit of institutional cooperation, aiding the judiciary in the performance of its functions and, by extension, providing for litigants a "fair, inexpensive, and expeditious resolution of their disputes."[39] With nary a voice of opposition[40]—in the House, Republican William Cahill of New Jersey lodged vigorous objection,[41] but his motion to recommit was overwhelmingly defeated (258–64)—and not a single serious constraint inhibiting it, the Federal Magistrates Act coasted to easy passage (without roll call votes) in both chambers, and a superior version of an inferior judicial officer was born.

The Arrival of "Para-Judges"

Following a one-year pilot program, individuals were officially appointed in late 1970, and the new—more extensive and more efficacious—system of magistrates was fully in place by July 1971. More cost effective than establishing new judgeships,[42] but more useful in alleviating workload than providing more clerical staff, the magistrate's role was initially somewhat undefined. Under the original terms of the Federal Magistrates Act, the position had "few enumerated powers, and final decision-making authority remained at all times with a federal judge."[43] Congress, however, "did not intend the terms of the Act to establish an exhaustive list," assuming instead that the statutory grants of authority would "serve as a guide . . . for district judges to experiment freely in delegating tasks to magistrates."[44] Designed to "encourage judges to be creative in their utilization of magistrates and not to constrain them to the tasks and duties mentioned explicitly,"[45] the statute established a framework that has "allowed for the considered growth of the magistrate judges system to augment the United States district courts."[46]

[38] Jack B. Streepy, "The Developing Role of the Magistrate in the Federal Courts," 29 *Cleveland State Law Review* 81 (1980).

[39] Philip M. Pro and Thomas C. Hnatowski, "Measured Progress: The Evolution and Administration of the Federal Magistrate Judges System," 44 *American University Law Review* 1503, 1505 (1995).

[40] Outside of Congress, there was apparently some objection from part-time commissioners who preferred to be grandfathered into the system and not forced to join the bar in order to maintain their positions. See Leslie G. Foschio, "A History of the Development of the Office of United States Commissioner and Magistrate Judge System," 1999 *Federal Courts Law Review* 4 (1999).

[41] Christopher E. Smith, *United States Magistrates in the Federal Courts: Subordinate Judges* (New York: Praeger, 1990), 18.

[42] Caroll Seron, "The Professional Project of Parajudges: The Case of U.S. Magistrates," 22 *Law & Society Review* 559 (1988).

[43] Shannon, "The Federal Magistrates Act," 253.

[44] Ibid., 257.

[45] Ibid., 259.

[46] Pro and Hnatowski, "Measured Progress," 1504.

Over the decade that followed the original enactment, however, such growth emanated as much (if not more) from legislative modification by Congress as it did from judicial delegation via the Judicial Conference, the Administrative Office of the Courts, circuit judicial councils, or district court judges themselves. Two years after a 1974 Supreme Court decision holding that the Federal Magistrates Act did not allow magistrates to conduct evidentiary hearings in habeas cases,[47] Congress explicitly authorized district judges to refer various case-dispositive pretrial matters, including motions to dismiss, suppress evidence, and grant summary judgment or injunctive relief,[48] generally allowing magistrates to conduct pretrial hearings as needed before reporting back and recommending a ruling. Three years later, in 1979, Congress tinkered with the original act again, this time permitting magistrates to conduct civil trials with or without juries so long as the parties consented and expanding the classes of criminal cases magistrates could hear to include all federal misdemeanors rather than just petty offenses.[49] Together, these two amendments "resulted in a new breed" and a "unique corps" of judicial officers capable of exercising many of the same powers[50]—from hearing motions to instructing juries to rendering final decisions—as the district court judges who controlled their appointment, tenure, salary, and dockets.

Much more than bureaucrats but decidedly less than full Article III judges, magistrates continue to occupy something of a liminal space in the institutional judiciary. Indeed, with a combination of judicial and quasi-judicial tasks,[51] they are effectively "para-judges." Acting in a judicial capacity, they "decide discovery disputes in both civil and criminal cases, conduct civil jury and bench trials, and report and recommend on dispositive motions over a broad range of civil and criminal matters, ranging from social security benefits to habeas corpus petitions to requests for injunctive relief."[52] Acting in a quasi-judicial capacity, they "assign counsel, conduct detention hearings, set release conditions, take pleas and impose sentences in petty offense and misdemeanor cases; handle removal, prison transfer, extradition and competency hearings; and handle supervised release and probation revocation hearings."[53] With this flexibility to fill a variety of nuanced and overlapping roles in the judicial process, magistrates quickly became—and have long since remained—both key fixtures of the federal judicial apparatus and

---

[47] *Wingo v. Wedding*, 418 U.S. 461 (1974).

[48] 90 Stat. 2729 (October 21, 1976).

[49] 93 Stat. 643 (October 10, 1979). This statute also provided for merit selection for magistrates. See, generally, McCabe, "The Federal Magistrate Act of 1979"; and Smith, "Assessing the Consequences of Judicial Innovation," 462–66.

[50] Shannon, "The Federal Magistrates Act," 253; Pro and Hnatowski, "Measured Progress," 1504.

[51] See also Seron, "The Professional Project of Parajudges," 560–62, describing three distinct identities held by magistrates: additional judges to perform pretrial tasks, intrajudicial specialists empowered to act on certain aspects of the docket, and assistant or junior judges charged with preparing cases for hearing and disposition by district judges.

[52] Foschio, "A History of the Development of the Office of United States Commissioner and Magistrate Judge System," 6.

[53] Ibid.

crucial components in the quest to control judicial workload and improve judicial performance.[54]

In the same general spirit and at the same general time, but with some critical differences, Congress also established a series of courts to handle bankruptcy issues as part of the Bankruptcy Reform Act of 1978.[55] Part of a larger, decade-long bankruptcy reform struggle engendered by "dissatisfaction with the bankruptcy laws in the 1960s,"[56] the creation of these courts—and the appointment of judges to populate them—harbored the same impulse toward efficiency through specialization that characterized the magistrate system. Like magistrates, bankruptcy judges were designed as "auxiliaries to the district courts"; like magistrates, they were "empowered to enter binding judgments in a broad range of cases."[57] Yet while these courts—staffed by judges serving fourteen-year terms, with unprotected salaries, and removable for nonimpeachable offenses—presently operate in the shadow of Article III judges just like magistrates, they initially seemed, at least until the Supreme Court struck them down in 1982,[58] considerably closer to emerging from that shadow. Indeed, unlike both bankruptcy referees,[59] their institutional predecessors who possessed narrow jurisdiction and lacked any firm measure of independence from the district courts, the Administrative Office of the Courts, or the Judicial Conference,[60] and magistrates, who (even if more powerful than the commissioners that had been before them) are clearly subordinate to and dependent on grants of authority from district judges, bankruptcy judges as established in 1978 were substantially in control of their own decisions and their own dockets.[61] Moreover, even though power was conferred on both magistrates and bankruptcy judges through an "internal delegation of judicial power" from the district

---

[54] On the various benefits of and practical challenges faced by magistrates, see Steven Puro and Roger Goldman, "U.S. Magistrates: Changing Dimensions of First-Echelon Federal Judicial Officers," in *The Politics of Judicial Reform*, ed. Philip L. Dubois (Lexington, MA: Lexington, 1982), 137–48; and Smith, *United States Magistrates in the Federal Courts*.

[55] 92 Stat. 2549 (November 6, 1978). A decade earlier, and only one year after the Federal Magistrates Act, Congress reclassified the United States Tax Court, formerly an independent executive agency tasked with adjudicating income tax disputes brought by citizens who had not yet paid the taxes in question, as an Article I legislative court. 83 Stat. 487 (December 30, 1969).

[56] Eric A. Posner, "The Political Economy of the Bankruptcy Reform Act of 1978," 96 *Michigan Law Review* 47, 67 (1997). On the reform struggle more generally, see Carroll Seron, "Court Reorganization and the Politics of Reform: The Case of the Bankruptcy Court," in *The Politics of Judicial Reform*, ed. Philip L. Dubois (Lexington, MA: Lexington, 1982), 87–98.

[57] Finley, "Article III Limits on Article I Courts," 562.

[58] *Northern Pipeline Construction Company v. Marathon Pipe Line Company*, 458 U.S. 50 (1982) (invalidating the jurisdiction granted to bankruptcy courts under the Bankruptcy Act of 1978 as an unconstitutional exercise of congressional authority to establish inferior tribunals under Article III).

[59] For an account of the role and work of bankruptcy referees and the various attempts to reform them, see Carroll Seron, *Judicial Reorganization: The Politics of Reform in the Federal Bankruptcy Court* (Lexington, MA: Lexington, 1978).

[60] Finley, "Article III Limits on Article I Courts," 562; Posner, "The Political Economy of the Bankruptcy Reform Act of 1978," 61.

[61] Finley, "Article III Limits on Article I Courts," 564.

courts, the transfer of jurisdiction to magistrates is wholly discretionary whereas the transfer of jurisdiction to bankruptcy judges might be read as "mandatory."[62] That is to say, while district judges can choose when and how to utilize magistrates, they were briefly statutorily required to transmit the entirety of their expanded jurisdiction over bankruptcy issues to the bankruptcy judges.[63] The sum of these institutional differences placed magistrates and bankruptcy judges—both specialized judicial officers, neither Article III judges—in decidedly distinct institutional spheres, with the former assisting Article III judges as subordinate assistants and the latter substituting for them as parallel judges under Article I. After the Supreme Court—recognizing the import of these differences—struck down the 1978 conception of bankruptcy judges, Congress reauthorized them in modified form two years later, this time as a much closer analog to magistrates than they had previously been.[64]

In addition to augmenting the quasi-judiciary with judicial adjuncts like magistrates and bankruptcy judges, Congress also attended to both the "supply side" (judges) and the "demand side" (litigation) of judicial workload in a series of sometimes counteracting statutes during the 1970s. First, supplementing magistrates and bankruptcy judges with Article III judges, it authorized the largest expansion of the federal judiciary in history in the Omnibus Judgeship Act of 1978.[65] Second, extending the supervisory reach of the judiciary to match the regulatory reach of the federal government, it granted the federal courts jurisdiction over a variety of specific issues of federal regulation, including toxic waste, public utilities, and energy conservation.[66] Third, exhibiting concern with increased court filings contributing to a delay in the administration of justice (including a delay in the dispatch of government business), it removed federal court jurisdiction over other issues, including those involving, among other things, social benefits and law enforcement.[67] None of these reforms were about specialization per se, but all three had ramifications for the same phenomenon specialization aimed to tackle: the growing workload of the federal judiciary, and the need for Congress to find multifaceted ways to address it that did not include neutering an administrative state that, though relatively new in the scheme of the American political experience, politicians had grown accustomed to and citizens now relied upon.

---

[62] Ibid., 569.

[63] Ibid.

[64] 98 Stat. 333 (July 10, 1984).

[65] 92 Stat. 1629 (October 20, 1978).

[66] See, among others, the Toxic Substances Control Act of 1976, 90 Stat. 2003 (October 11, 1976); the Public Utility Regulatory Policies Act of 1978, 92 Stat. 3117 (November 9, 1978); and the Emergency Energy Conservation Act of 1979, 93 Stat. 749 (November 5, 1979).

[67] See Dawn M. Chutkow, "Jurisdiction Stripping: Litigation, Ideology, and Congressional Control of the Courts," *Journal of Politics* 70 (2008): 1053–64. Congress also passed legislation significantly curtailing the use of three-judge district courts and the right of direct appeals to the Supreme Court from such courts; 90 Stat. 1119 (August 12, 1976).

The Cultivation of Judicial Expertise and the Extension of Judicial Supervision, 1969–1998

When Warren Burger replaced Earl Warren as chief justice of the United States in 1969, he brought with him a concern for the institutional judiciary unseen since the tenure of William Howard Taft. The judiciary Burger inherited, much like the one Taft encountered almost fifty years prior, was swamped by filings and paralyzed by delays. With overburdened judges, frustrated citizens, and no natural resolution in sight, the state of the judiciary was—again, inadvertently mimicking the dynamics of Taft's time—in desperate need of ameliorative measures. Seemingly more interested in these performance-oriented issues surrounding the smooth administration of justice than halting the heyday of constitutional liberalism or leaving a potent conservative counterrevolutionary mark in jurisprudence, Burger forcefully and frequently pushed the idea of judicial reform both in speeches to bar associations and in testimony to Congress. And while he did not assume quite the active entrepreneurial role in the process that Taft did, Burger did place the weight of the chief justiceship behind the need for institutional maintenance, modification, and innovation. In doing so, he firmly placed the judicial imprimatur behind the cause of judicial reform even as he largely left the details to be worked out and daily battles to be waged by like-minded souls of substantially less importance.

From members of Congress to Article III judges to leading law professors, those like-minded souls all seemed to identify the problem as one of workload and suggest that the best resolution was one that could either reduce it or allow judges to dispatch it more expeditiously. The exact proposals they designed to effect these desired changes, of course, varied widely in substance as well as popularity. But even with a series of distinct—and, at times, controversial—reform possibilities offered up during the early 1970s, the path to success ultimately proved relatively smooth. More specifically, even as a pair of dramatic reform proposals threatened to overwhelm the seeming consensus agreement on the need to reduce the docket burden on both the Supreme Court and the circuit courts of appeals, they created political space for a more limited performance-oriented alternative to succeed. That alternative—the creation of a national appellate court to deal with patent disputes almost exclusively—was hardly of the scale that Burger had contemplated and encouraged, but its embodiment in the Federal Courts Improvement Act of 1982 was far from trivial either.[68] To the extent that the increasing complexity surrounding patent law was emblematic of the increasing complexity surrounding the work of the federal government during the 1970s and '80s, tackling the issue directly suggested a frank recognition that the judiciary, central to the regulatory apparatus that had developed since the New Deal, was simultaneously behind in its workload and simply behind the times.

[68] 96 Stat. 25 (April 2, 1982).

Of Consistency, Coherence, and Commissions on the Caseload Crisis

The judicial reforms of the 1960s and '70s had addressed some problems of judicial performance but inadvertently—though, in retrospect, not necessarily unexpectedly—either created or exacerbated others. From the replacement of commissioners with magistrates to the conversion of referees into bankruptcy judges to the establishment of a large slate of new federal district court judgeships, Congress had focused its judicial institution-building attention primarily on district courts and the rising caseloads that faced the judges who staffed them. That focus was hardly unwarranted—and the reforms it generated hardly ineffectual—but, rather than simply alleviate the burdens of district courts without affecting the circuit courts of appeals that supervised them (or the Supreme Court that supervised them), it sufficiently increased the number of lower court decisions in need of appellate review so as to leave the federal judiciary at large with a caseload dilemma that was actually "worsening rather than being solved."[69] Authorizing new district court judgeships, as Congress had done in 1978, only created the possibility for more intracircuit conflicts in need of resolution by the circuit courts of appeals; creating new circuits, as Congress had done in 1980 (transferring three of the states in the Fifth Circuit into a newly established Eleventh Circuit),[70] only created the possibility for more intercircuit conflicts in need of resolution by the Supreme Court.[71] And with the caseload of the circuit courts of appeals having increased dramatically over the past several decades but the capacity of the Supreme Court to dispose of that caseload having "remained essentially static" since the turn to a predominantly discretionary docket in the Judiciary Act of 1925,[72] the Court, swamped by the increasing number of certiorari petitions in need of review, found itself "less able to resolve conflicts between the circuits."[73] From rapid caseload growth came more conflicts, and from more conflicts came both repetitious litigation (resulting from litigant forum shopping) and greater uncertainty in several areas of federal law.[74] The result, the Department of Justice noted, was a crisis "not . . . for the courts alone" but one "for litigants who seek justice, for claims of human rights, for the rule of law, and . . . therefore . . . for the Nation."[75]

In response to these developments, both the judiciary and Congress established commissions to study backlogs in judicial business, inadequacies in judicial performance, and potential reforms in judicial organization or administration.

[69] House of Representatives Report No. 312, 97th Cong., 1st Sess. (1981).
[70] 94 Stat. 1994 (October 14, 1980). See, generally, Deborah J. Barrow and Thomas G. Walker, *A Court Divided: The Fifth Circuit Court of Appeals and the Politics of Judicial Reform* (New Haven, CT: Yale University Press, 1988).
[71] Charles W. Adams, "The Court of Appeals for the Federal Circuit: More Than a National Patent Court," 49 *Missouri Law Review* 43, 45 (1984).
[72] Ibid., 44–45.
[73] Adams, "The Court of Appeals for the Federal Circuit," 45. By that point, the Court already reviewed less than 1 percent of cases decided by the circuit courts of appeals.
[74] Ibid.
[75] Quoted in House of Representatives Report No. 312, 97th Cong., 1st Sess. (1981).

First, in 1971, Warren Burger appointed Paul Freund of Harvard Law School to lead a commission of prominent lawyers and legal academics known as the Study Group on the Caseload of the Supreme Court.[76] In its report the following year, the Freund Study Group emphasized how caseload was impeding the Court's ability to carry out its most integral duties by forcing it to avoid deciding cases in need of resolution and to devote less time to those cases it did decide. In order to address these lamentable developments, the group proposed a National Court of Appeals to screen petitions and appeals to the Supreme Court.[77] This central idea, however, provoked a range of "overwhelmingly hostile" complaints and objections—the new court would be ineffectual and useless, it would increase rather than decrease delay, it would diminish the prestige of either or both the circuit courts of appeals or the Supreme Court, it would lack respect in the legal community[78]—and the Freund Study Group's recommendations gained little traction among policy makers. Second, in 1972, Congress named Republican senator Roman Hruska of Nebraska to chair a commission of legislators, lawyers, judges, and academics known as the Commission on Revision of the Appellate System. Releasing one report in 1973 and a second in 1975, the Hruska Commission focused its attention less on the Supreme Court and more on the geographic organization of the circuit courts of appeals (in the first report) and the internal structure of them (in the second),[79] citing in particular the lengthy delays in case disposition caused by, inordinately extensive time spent resolving, and undesirable uncertainty produced by litigation from intercircuit conflicts. Like the Freund Study Group, the Hruska Commission suggested a National Court of Appeals, but, seeking to avoid the controversy that befell its predecessor, the commission envisioned a tribunal that would handle referrals from the Supreme Court (among other courts) rather than screen petitions for the Supreme Court. Though this difference was far from insignificant, the Hruska Commission's report provoked similar, though slightly less pointed, criticism as had the Freund Study Group's report; as a result, it "received little political support" and failed to progress "past the hearing stage."[80]

Though their particular targets were distinct—the Freund Study Group concerned with the Supreme Court, the Hruska Commission concerned with the circuit courts of appeals—both panels were focused on the caseload crisis afflicting the federal judiciary, and both viewed the issue in terms of the performance-oriented problems of consistency and coherence. Despite their inability to mo-

---

[76] Among others, the group included Alexander Bickel of Yale Law School and Charles Alan Wright of the University of Texas Law School.

[77] Federal Judicial Center, "Report of the Study Group on the Caseload of the Supreme Court," *Federal Rules Decisions* 57 (1972): 573–628.

[78] Adams, "The Court of Appeals for the Federal Circuit," 48.

[79] Commission on Revision of the Federal Appellate System, "The Geographical Boundaries of the Several Judicial Circuits: Recommendations for Change," *Federal Rules Decisions* 62 (1973): 223–50; Commission on Revision of the Federal Appellate System, "Structure and Internal Procedures: Recommendations for Change," *Federal Rules Decisions* 67 (1975): 195–409.

[80] Adams, "The Court of Appeals for the Federal Circuit," 49.

tivate immediate action, their combined work, together with frequent speeches from Warren Burger himself, dramatically raised awareness about the substantial challenges facing the two appellate tiers of the federal judicial hierarchy. As a result, by the mid- to late 1970s, the issue of reform was not only firmly entrenched on the political agenda but also beginning to find consensus support. There remained, of course, a range of different ideas about how best to remedy the ills of the caseload crisis, but there was seeming agreement both that change was needed to "increase the capacity of the federal judicial system to adjudicate issues of national law" and that the respective proposals of the Freund Study Group and Hruska Commission "would have made more extensive revisions" than were deemed desirable.[81] With Freund and Hruska having staked out positions that were deemed overly aggressive, it was clear that there were obstacles to radical reform, but, despite the lack of a natural motivated constituency within Congress and the existence of other demands for congressional time and attention, it was far from clear that they had not effectively softened the ground to enable more moderate reform aimed at the caseload crisis to succeed where they had failed.

That moderate initiative ultimately emerged from a 1977 study by and 1978 proposal from the Office for Improvements in the Administration of Justice at the Department of Justice.[82] Similar to a 1975 idea from Judge Harold Leventhal of the Court of Appeals for the District of Columbia Circuit,[83] the Justice Department proposal focused exclusively on those areas of law "where the need for reform was thought to be the greatest,"[84] specifically suggesting patent, tax, and environmental law.[85] Whereas the Freund Study Group had called for a national appellate court of general jurisdiction that would serve as a gatekeeper for the Supreme Court, and the Hruska Commission had called for a national appellate court of general jurisdiction that would be referred cases from the Supreme Court, the Justice Department called for a national appellate court of specialized jurisdiction that would neither screen cases for nor be referred cases from the Supreme Court. Instead, it called for a new circuit court of appeals defined by its (relatively limited) subject matter rather than its geography, a unique blend of characteristics that offered a possible solution to the very performance-oriented problems the Freund Study Group and Hruska Commission had identified. As a national court, it could help to forge uniform understandings and achieve much needed legal consistency; as a specialized court, it could "acquire expertise" in its substantive areas and work toward greater legal coherence.[86] Possessing most of the benefits but seemingly

---

[81] Harold C. Petrowitz, "Federal Court Reform: The Federal Courts Improvement Act of 1982—and Beyond," 32 *American University Law Review* 543, 549 (1983).

[82] Adams, "The Court of Appeals for the Federal Circuit," 60.

[83] Harold Leventhal, "A Modest Proposal for a Multi-Circuit Court of Appeals," 24 *American University Law Review* 881 (1975). See also Petrowitz, "Federal Court Reform," 547–48.

[84] Adams, "The Court of Appeals for the Federal Circuit," 60.

[85] Leventhal's proposal had, in addition to those three realms of law, also suggested labor law and securities law.

[86] Adams, "The Court of Appeals for the Federal Circuit," 46.

none of the liabilities of prior iterations, this idea of a specialized subject matter appellate court held far greater chance of passage than either of its predecessors.

Facing opposition from some of the "highly organized" bar associations—those focused on tax law and government contracts were particularly fearful of dramatic changes in their appellate practices[87]—the Senate Judiciary Committee of the Ninety-Sixth Congress (1979–81), to whom the Justice Department had forwarded its bill, modified the proposal in two key ways. First, it reduced the number of judges from fifteen to twelve. Second, and more important, it narrowed the court's jurisdiction from patent, tax, and environmental law to predominantly patent law. Despite lingering mild objections from foes of specialization generally, who feared that taking patents "out of the mainstream of legal thought" would lead to a "one-sided view of the issues" destined to produce "substantively inferior law,"[88] these two modifications effectively cleared the proposal's path to enactment. After all, there was widespread recognition in legal circles that the effects of the caseload crisis—specifically the lack of consistency and coherence that came from intercircuit conflicts—had been particularly troublesome for patent law, a fact that was specifically noted (as a secondary finding) by the Hruska Commission itself.[89] And unlike a specialized appellate court for other realms of law, the idea of a specialized patent court was hardly novel, with more than forty bills on the subject having been introduced in—though ultimately rejected by—Congress since the late nineteenth century.[90] In addition to easing the burden of the workload crisis on the circuit courts of appeals, "where the technical nature of patent disputes required a disproportionate amount of time from . . . generalist judges," the idea of a single forum for most patent disputes offered the stability, uniformity, and predictability needed to "foster technological growth and industrial innovation" as well as "facilitate business planning."[91] In light of the legal confusion that made "enforceability of patents uncertain and reduced public confidence" in the patent system,[92] the promise of such substantial performance-oriented benefits gained the support of most of the patent bar, the judges on the Court of Customs and Patent Appeals and the Court of Claims, and the Judicial Conference.[93] Having sidestepped the criticisms of earlier proposals and having focused chiefly on the ills plaguing patent law, the proposal for a specialized appellate tribunal, though withdrawn from consideration in the Ninety-Sixth Congress, passed easily in the Ninety-Seventh

[87] Petrowitz, "Federal Court Reform," 551.

[88] Rochelle Cooper Dreyfuss, "The Federal Circuit: A Case Study in Specialized Courts," 64 *New York University Law Review* 1, 25 (1989).

[89] David T. DeZern, "Federal Circuit Antitrust Law and the Legislative History of the Federal Courts Improvement Act of 1982," *Review of Litigation* 26 (2007): 469; Dreyfuss, "The Federal Circuit," 6–7.

[90] Adams, "The Court of Appeals for the Federal Circuit," 59n121.

[91] Dreyfuss, "The Federal Circuit," 7.

[92] Ibid.

[93] Adams, "The Court of Appeals for the Federal Circuit," 63.

Congress (1981–83).[94] The widespread recognition (at least among legal academics and policy makers) of the caseload crisis that was prompted by the work of the Freund Study Group and the Hruska Commission had made the Federal Courts Improvement Act a possibility, but only the retreat from the bold proposals of both groups to a milder and more focused alternative made it a reality.

The Flexibility of Specialized Justice

The centerpiece of the Federal Courts Improvement Act—the Court of Appeals for the Federal Circuit—was actually a merger of (and addition to) both the jurisdiction and personnel of two existing federal courts: the Court of Customs and Patent Appeals (originally established in 1910) and the appellate division of the Court of Claims (originally established in 1855).[95] Somewhat "less specialized than either of its predecessors" but "much more specialized than any of the regular federal courts of appeals,"[96] the Court of Appeals for the Federal Circuit possessed exclusive jurisdiction over appeals in four types of cases: orders and decisions of the Merit System Protection Board (which adjudicates conflicts between federal agencies and their employees), nontax and nontort federal court decisions on civil actions against the federal government for $10,000 or less, various interlocutory orders, and federal district court patent decisions. Yet although its jurisdiction obviously extended beyond patents to include elements of tariff and customs law, technological transfer regulations, and government labor disputes, and although it technically had jurisdiction only over the vast majority of (rather than all) patent issues, the Court of Appeals for the Federal Circuit is effectively the nation's patent court, making patents the "most important area of specialized federal appellate jurisdiction" in the nation.[97]

Despite the existence (both then and now) of a range of general concerns about judicial specialization,[98] the creation of a specialized patent court proved generally salutary. By providing "a forum to which Congress can assign other catego-

---

[94] Both the House and Senate passed reform bills—and agreed on a compromise bill in conference—during the Ninety-Sixth Congress, only to see final action in the Senate delayed by "an attempt to add a controversial amendment." Petrowitz, "Federal Court Reform," 552.

[95] The act also transferred the entirety of trial jurisdiction (over monetary claims against the federal government) possessed by the Court of Claims, which had gained Article III status in 1953, to a new Article I United States Court of Claims (later to be renamed the Court of Federal Claims). This change, which reverted the court back to its pre-1953 status and promoted the "commissioners" who had served on the old court to (Article I) judges with fifteen-year terms on the new court, allowed the court to handle cases referred by Congress.

[96] Richard A. Posner, "Will the Federal Courts of Appeals Survive until 1984? An Essay on Delegation and Specialization of the Judicial Function," 56 *Southern California Law Review* 761, 776 (1983).

[97] Ibid., 777.

[98] Posner, "Will the Federal Courts of Appeals Survive until 1984? An Essay on Delegation and Specialization of the Judicial Function," 783–88, summarizes a series of them, including a "reduction in the caliber of judges," an increase in "the concentration of government power," and greater difficulty coping with "unforeseen changes in the caseload mix."

ries of cases" without disrespecting the geographically oriented circuit courts of appeals,[99] reducing access to the Supreme Court, or fundamentally reworking the judicial hierarchy,[100] the Court of Appeals for the Federal Circuit, like the creation and expansion of magistrates before it, promised increased efficiency through additional flexibility. Unlike its closest predecessor—the ill-fated Commerce Court of the early twentieth century,[101] which was also "established to adjudicate technical complex disputes where national uniformity and administrative efficiency were prime concerns"[102]—the Court of Appeals for the Federal Circuit was actually "situated to retain public confidence."[103] Whereas the Commerce Court was staffed with highly controversial appointments, tasked with reviewing a popular regulatory body, lacked an existing body of law to employ, and operated with a bias toward powerful groups during a time at which the federal judiciary was already seen as a reactionary impediment to social progress, the Court of Appeals for the Federal Circuit was composed of already confirmed federal judges, who were not seen as hostile to reform, who inherited a body of commonly accepted common law, and who were not beholden to any of the parties likely to appear before the court.[104] And with a single, respected, and national appellate court supervising patent decisions, intercircuit conflicts and the negative externalities that emanated from them—not least, widespread forum shopping by litigants and, consequently, a flood of unnecessary litigation—decreased, and the improvements in judicial performance long desired by legal reformers had at last become a reality. At least in the realm of patents, judicial institution building had yielded law that was "both more rational and easier to apply."[105]

Though successful in promoting both legal consistency and legal coherence in its own right, the Court of Appeals for the Federal Circuit hardly established a trend for judicial institution building going forward. Indeed, far from a "portent" of a growing reliance on specialized justice,[106] the reform is better conceptualized as part of the continual congressional effort "to squeeze more efficiency out of

[99] Adams, "The Court of Appeals for the Federal Circuit," 61.

[100] Petrowitz, "Federal Court Reform," 553.

[101] See chapter 5; Felix Frankfurter and James M. Landis, *The Business of the Supreme Court: A Study in the Federal Judicial System* (New York: Macmillan, 1928), 153–74; and Stephen Skowronek, *Building a New American State: The Expansion of National Administrative Capacities, 1877-1920* (New York: Cambridge University Press, 1982), 261–67.

[102] Dreyfuss, "The Federal Circuit," 64.

[103] Ibid., 65.

[104] Ibid., 64–65. At the same time, it can hardly be denied that "specialization may create conditions that cause a court to take a distinctive path" and that neutral performance-oriented reforms may well have ramifications that are partial to particular ideas, arguments, or constituencies. Lawrence Baum, "Judicial Specialization, Litigant Influence, and Substantive Policy: The Court of Customs and Patent Appeals," *Law & Society Review* 11 (1977): 846.

[105] Dreyfuss, "The Federal Circuit," 52.

[106] Posner, "Will the Federal Courts of Appeals Survive Until 1984? An Essay on Delegation and Specialization of the Judicial Function," 776.

the existing system."[107] The Federal Courts Improvement Act accomplished that goal with reorganization and jurisdictional reallocation, but it offered only modest caseload relief to either the other circuit courts of appeals or the Supreme Court, especially compared with the broader relief promised by the proposals from the Freund Study Group and Hruska Commission.[108] In other words, as substantial as the creation of the new court was for the refinement of justice in the late twentieth century, it was still, like many instances of judicial institution building throughout American history, something of a stopgap measure that left significant work still to be done.[109]

Part of that work certainly involved specialized courts, with Congress establishing a series of them—including the Temporary Emergency Court of Appeals,[110] the Regional Rail Reorganization Court,[111] the division of the Court of Appeals for the District of Columbia Circuit that appoints independent counsel,[112] and the Court of International Trade (a reorganized and renamed version of the Customs Court, which was itself formerly known as the Board of General Appraisers)[113]— from 1973 to 1980.[114] But that momentum slowed substantially in the 1980s—only the Court of Appeals for Veterans Claims followed the Court of Appeals for the Federal Circuit in terms of new specialized appellate tribunals[115]—as Congress largely ignored calls for specialized courts for domains such as science and the environment and redirected its institution-building attention toward a series of other performance-oriented modifications. In 1980, following the advice of the first Hruska Commission report,[116] Congress reorganized the circuit alignment for the first time since it carved the Tenth Circuit out of part of the Eighth Circuit in

[107] Petrowitz, "Federal Court Reform," 562.

[108] At the time, patent cases constituted only 1 percent of the docket of the circuit courts of appeals, though those cases did tend to involve some of the most complex and time-consuming intricacies of law. Adams, "The Court of Appeals for the Federal Circuit," 62.

[109] Petrowitz, "Federal Court Reform," 562.

[110] Economic Stabilization Act Amendments of 1971, 85 Stat. 743 (December 22, 1971). See James R. Elkins, "The Temporary Emergency Court of Appeals Act: A Study in the Abdication of Judicial Responsibility," 1978 Duke Law Journal 113 (1978).

[111] Regional Rail Reorganization Act of 1973, 87 Stat. 985 (January 2, 1974).

[112] Ethics in Government Act of 1978, 92 Stat. 1824 (October 26, 1978).

[113] 94 Stat. 1727 (October 10, 1980). See, generally, Isaac Unah, The Courts of International Trade: Judicial Specialization, Expertise, and Bureaucratic Policymaking (Ann Arbor: University of Michigan Press, 1998). Rulings of the Court of International Trade, which hears cases related to imported goods and tariff assessment, can be appealed to the Court of Appeals for the Federal Circuit.

[114] On the movement toward specialized courts generally, see Ellen R. Jordan, "Specialized Courts: A Choice?" 76 Northwestern University Law Review 745 (1981); and Richard L. Revesz, "Specialized Courts and the Administrative Lawmaking System," 138 University of Pennsylvania Law Review 1111(1990).

[115] The Court of Appeals for Veterans Claims was established by the Veterans' Judicial Review Act, 102 Stat. 4105 (November 18, 1988).

[116] Commission on Revision of the Federal Appellate System, "The Geographical Boundaries of the Several Judicial Circuits."

1929,[117] shifting some states from the Fifth Circuit into a newly created Eleventh Circuit.[118] Although reminiscent of the antebellum, Civil War, and Reconstruction era battles over the size and organization of the federal circuit system,[119] these shifts were decidedly performance oriented, devoid of much of the policy and political motivations (though not necessarily the policy and political ramifications) that characterized the debates over judicial organization in earlier periods of American history. Several times from 1988 to 1990, Congress tinkered with issues of jurisdiction, civil procedure, and citizen access to the courts,[120] with one statute completing the task begun by the Judiciary Act of 1925 and making nearly the entirety of the Supreme Court's docket discretionary.[121] Throughout the 1980s and '90s, it also passed a series of acts adding or modifying staff positions—the Supreme Court police or an administrative assistant for the chief justice, for example—to attend to the daily administrative and governance needs of the growing institutional judiciary.[122] And with recognition of the fact that the extent of judicial supervision of American government outpaced the extent of political or public supervision of individual judges' behavior, Congress sought to impose enhanced measures of accountability to protect citizens against judicial misconduct.[123] The institutional judiciary had grown not only in depth of power and range of authority but also (and, following World War II, perhaps especially) in administrative size and organizational complexity, and in search of the highest level of institutional performance possible, Congress continued to address problems as they arose and, largely, in the manner judges desired.

Judging the National Security State, 1972–2000

Since the process of state building had begun in the aftermath of the Civil War, "the state" had always been focused largely on domestic policy—on the development of bureaucratic capacity both to regulate industry and to provide for citizen

---

[117] 45 Stat. 1346 (February 28, 1929). The statute, which emerged largely out of the context of an American Bar Association suggestion to redistribute appellate workload more equitably without the appointment of more judges, grouped Colorado, Kansas, New Mexico, Oklahoma, Utah, and Wyoming in the newly created Tenth Circuit, leaving Arkansas, Iowa, Minnesota, Missouri, Nebraska, North Dakota, and South Dakota behind in the Eighth Circuit.

[118] 94 Stat. 1994 (October 14, 1980). Following substantial negotiation, the statute ultimately constituted Louisiana, Mississippi, and Texas as the Fifth Circuit and Alabama, Florida, and Georgia as the Eleventh Circuit. For the long saga preceding this compromise, see Barrow and Walker, *A Court Divided*.

[119] See chapters 3 and 4.

[120] Judicial Improvements and Access to Justice Act of 1988, 102 Stat. 4642 (November 19, 1988); Judicial Improvements Act of 1990, 104 Stat. 5089 (December 1, 1990).

[121] On the Judiciary Act of 1925, see chapter 6; on the subsequent reform, see the Supreme Court Case Selections Act of 1988, 102 Stat. 662 (June 27, 1988).

[122] 96 Stat. 1957 (December 29, 1982); 104 Stat. 1097 (October 30, 1990); 110 Stat. 3359 (October 9, 1996); 112 Stat. 1535 (August 13, 1998).

[123] Judicial Conduct and Disability Act of 1990, 94 Stat. 2035 (October 15, 1980).

welfare.[124] Beginning at the close of World War II, and especially progressing into the 1950s and '60s, however, America's administrative state evolved on decidedly parallel tracks. With the ambitious social programs of the Great Society requiring modifications to and, in some cases, expansion of the New Deal institutional architecture, the makings of an (albeit distinctive) welfare state emerged in the realms of health care and poverty assistance. At the same time, the tensions of the Cold War and the protest fervor of the 1960s gave rise to a national security state— perhaps unique in the world—that simultaneously faced clear hostility from other nations and sought to prevent percolating grassroots challenges to its authority from its own citizens.[125] Nascent early in the 1960s but an increasingly large and consequential part of the administrative state in the decades to come (before escalating even further following the terrorist attacks of September 11, 2001, and the ensuing War on Terror), the national security state was premised on the idea that America faced enemies—both external and internal—and that government, in the words of Alexander Hamilton, "ought to be clothed with all the powers requisite" to enable protection against them.[126]

To the extent that governmental officials might, in the vigorous execution of their duties, exercise those powers too forcefully, and to the extent that those powers held the potential for substantial intrusion into the lives of ordinary (and perhaps innocent) Americans in the first place, Congress eventually—after decades of inaction—sought to subject them to judicial limitation. That limitation, which gained legislative traction only after the executive branch had acted so egregiously as to spark national controversy, came in the form of the Foreign Intelligence Surveillance Act of 1978,[127] which established two federal courts charged solely with authorizing government requests for electronic surveillance of American citizens suspected to be agents of "foreign power." Motivated chiefly by legislators' performance-oriented desires to clarify existing gaps in the law surrounding intelligence gathering and their policy goal of reasserting limitations on the executive branch in the aftermath of an overzealous president, the legislation seemingly materialized with little warning, little buildup, and (relatively) little controversy. In fact, facilitated largely by the investigations into executive wrongdoing that became so prevalent in the early to mid-1970s, the act's only notable opposition came

[124]On regulating industry, see Martin J. Sklar, *The Corporate Reconstruction of American Capitalism, 1890–1916: The Market, the Law, and Politics* (New York: Cambridge University Press, 1988); and Skowronek, *Building a New American State*. On providing for citizen welfare, see Theda Skocpol, *Protecting Soldiers and Mothers: The Political Origins of Social Policy in the United States* (Cambridge, MA: Belknap Press, 1992); Christopher Howard, *The Hidden Welfare State: Tax Expenditures and Social Policy in the United States* (Princeton, NJ: Princeton University Press, 1997); and Ira Katznelson, *When Affirmative Action Was White: An Untold Story of Racial Inequality in Twentieth Century America* (New York: Norton, 2005).

[125]On the earlier origins of this development in the National Security Act of 1947, see Douglas T. Stuart, *Creating the National Security State: A History of the Law That Transformed America* (Princeton, NJ: Princeton University Press, 2008).

[126]Alexander Hamilton, *The Federalist 23*, December 18, 1787.

[127]92 Stat. 1783 (October 25, 1978).

not out of any view that it was unwise or unnecessary to regulate the intelligence community but instead from the position that reform needed to embody more aggressive and more stringent regulations of it. When that mild resistance ultimately relented, the federal judiciary ostensibly found itself squarely in the realm of judging the national security state. Yet though the Foreign Intelligence Surveillance Act (and the courts it created) has stood, albeit with amendment, as a quintessential example of the modern institution building thrust toward specialization for more than thirty years since its enactment, its ultimate legacy seems to be somewhere between vigilantly supervising surveillance activities (as some original advocates may have hoped) and automatically sanctioning them behind a shroud of secrecy (as many current critics fear).

Countering Intelligence in the Wake of Watergate

From roughly the presidency of Herbert Hoover through the presidency of Lyndon Johnson, or the forty years prior to the buildup to the Foreign Intelligence Surveillance Act, American citizens possessed no constitutional protection against electronic surveillance by the federal government. Indeed, since the Supreme Court's holding in *Olmstead v. United States* in 1928 that the Fourth Amendment applied only to physical trespass,[128] any limitations on wiretapping for domestic surveillance had been left to the determination of Congress, an institution that proved heavily influenced by the state of international affairs at the time. During peacetime, Congress acted with some sensitivity to the concerns of civil libertarians, passing (most significantly) the Communications Act of 1934,[129] which prohibited "both unauthorized intercept of any private radio or wire communication and unauthorized use or publicity of any information contained in such communication."[130] During wartime, however, Congress deferred to presidential claims of inherent authority under Article II to conduct electronic surveillance for national security purposes. As a result, with armed conflict of one form or another a relative fixture in American affairs during the three decades following the start of World War II, the widespread anticommunist hysteria and witch hunts of McCarthyism, and the Federal Bureau of Investigation's controversial Counter Intelligence Program (COINTELPRO) to disrupt "subversive" groups (a category spanning organizations from the National Association for the Advancement of Colored People to the Ku Klux Klan), electronic surveillance became a crucial and oft-used law enforcement tool during the 1940s, '50s, and '60s.

Given the marked advances in intelligence practices and the increased usage of electronic surveillance in the time since its initial foray into this domain, the Court

[128] 277 U.S. 438 (1928) (upholding a conviction based on evidence obtained through wiretapped telephone conversations on the grounds that wiretapping constitutes neither "search and seizure" nor "self-incrimination" as protected by the Fourth and Fifth Amendments).

[129] 48 Stat. 1064 (June 19, 1934).

[130] "The Foreign Intelligence Surveillance Act: Legislating a Judicial Role in National Security Surveillance," 78 *Michigan Law Review* 1116, 1119 (1980).

sought to establish some jurisprudential contours for congressional action in 1967, overruling *Olmstead* in *Katz v. United States* by extending the Fourth Amendment to cover electronic surveillance as well as physical trespass.[131] But, even as it did so, the Court carved out a possible exception for matters of national security, a path Congress itself would reify legislatively the following year.[132] By establishing "a detailed procedure" requiring a warrant, based on a judicial determination of probable cause, that "a serious crime had been or was about to be committed" for electronic surveillance but exempting surveillance for national security purposes from that procedure,[133] Congress, whether purposefully or inadvertently, seemed to expand the Court's exception into a category the executive could exploit. And between the consolidation of the Central Intelligence Agency's Operation CHAOS and the FBI's increasingly aggressive use of COINTELPRO during the late 1960s, Richard Nixon seemed eager to use the guise of national security as justification for thorough and systematic intimidation of various manifestations of the New Left, including feminists, black nationalists, student activists, and antiwar protesters. The law concerning national security–related electronic surveillance was, if not outright permissive, at the very least ambiguously flexible, and in the power vacuum resulting from an absence of clear congressional guidelines or judicial principles, the executive had "unilaterally adopted warrantless electronic surveillance standards and procedures" as it saw fit.[134]

To the extent that concerns about electronic surveillance, though heightened under Nixon, actually preceded his administration, attempts to limit surveillance had appeared on the political agenda occasionally since World War II. In 1941, for example, the House Judiciary Committee contemplated a number of bills that would have required a judicial warrant for wiretapping, but none made it out of committee.[135] In 1953, the same committee held hearings on the subject of wiretapping for national security purposes, and the House at large even passed a bill requiring a court order, only to watch its companion bill fail to reach the Senate floor.[136] Even after the details of the 1972 Watergate break-in began to emerge, shifting the congressional mood toward Nixon to "one of antagonism,"[137] the project of limiting surveillance proved "adversarial and futile."[138] As the Senate Watergate Committee conducted hearings throughout 1973 and into 1974, senators began to

[131] 389 U.S. 347 (1967) (overturning a conviction based on evidence obtained through wiretapped telephone conversations on the grounds that the Fourth Amendment protects a citizen's privacy irrespective of whether physical intrusion occurs).

[132] 82 Stat. 197 (June 19, 1968).

[133] Americo R. Cinquegrana, "The Walls (and Wires) Have Ears: The Background and First Ten Years of the Foreign Intelligence Surveillance Act of 1978," 137 *University of Pennsylvania Law Review* 793, 801 (1989).

[134] Ibid., 806.

[135] Ira S. Shapiro, "The Foreign Intelligence Surveillance Act: Legislative Balancing of National Security and the Fourth Amendment," 15 *Harvard Journal on Legislation* 119, 130 (1977–78).

[136] Ibid., 130–31.

[137] Cinquegrana, "The Walls (and Wires) Have Ears," 806.

[138] Shapiro, "The Foreign Intelligence Surveillance Act," 121.

argue that the president lacked authority to disregard the Fourth Amendment even with national security at stake and introduced legislation to prohibit warrantless electronic surveillance completely.[139] Pressing the familiar presidential argument of inherent authority, Nixon vigorously opposed such legislation as an unconstitutional restriction on the duty of the executive to protect the nation against foreign threat, and, following the president's lead, both the chairman and ranking members of the Senate Judiciary subcommittee in charge of the legislation stymied the bill's progress at that stage.[140]

Over the next two years, however, the national political climate changed substantially. Nixon, facing certain impeachment in Congress, resigned in August 1974. Just over four months later, investigative reporter Seymour Hersh published a front page story in the *New York Times* detailing how the CIA had "conducted a massive, illegal domestic intelligence operation during the Nixon administration."[141] In direct response, and amid rising "anxiety over the executive's exclusive exercise of the surveillance power,"[142] Gerald R. Ford established the Rockefeller Commission, and Congress established the Church Committee, to investigate the practices of and potential abuses by the American intelligence agencies. By late 1975, the combination of hearings and reports had cataloged a host of "illegal and improper intelligence community activities" that drastically exceeded legitimate governmental authority and unambiguously infringed upon individual rights,[143] and the costs of several decades of congressional deference to presidential authority on intelligence matters instantly became clear to all.

The report of the Church Committee, in particular, served to consolidate fears about executive overreaching and galvanize support for reform to curb it. Detailing how intelligence agencies had, since the early 1930s and without seeking a warrant, wiretapped Americans—including members of Congress, journalists, and leaders of political organizations and associations—"who engaged in no criminal activity and who posed no genuine threat to the national security,"[144] the thorough and meticulous report made clear that the problem of warrantless electronic surveillance was unequivocally not simply "an aberration of the Nixon years."[145] Indeed, even as it excoriated the Nixon administration for using the guise of "national security" to discredit and attack social movements and political causes with which it disagreed, the report pinpointed as the problem Congress's "failure to apply the wisdom of the constitutional system of checks and balances to intelligence activities,"[146] either

[139] Ibid.

[140] Ibid.

[141] Seymour Hersh, "Huge C.I.A. Operation Reported in U.S. Against Antiwar Forces, Other Dissidents in Nixon Years," *New York Times*, December 22, 1974.

[142] "The Foreign Intelligence Surveillance Act," 1116–17.

[143] Duncan L. Clarke and Edward L. Neveleff, "Secrecy, Foreign Intelligence, and Civil Liberties: Has the Pendulum Swung Too Far?" *Political Science Quarterly* 99 (1984): 493.

[144] Senate Report No. 755, 94th Cong., 2nd sess. (1976).

[145] Shapiro, "The Foreign Intelligence Surveillance Act," 121.

[146] Senate Report No. 755, 94th Cong., 2nd sess. (1976).

by statutorily specifying what intelligence agencies could and could not do or by exercising its bureaucratic oversight function.[147] Even the respected legal scholar Edward Levi, who, upon becoming attorney general in 1975, sought to forestall the passage of legislation that would weaken presidential authority by pledging "to personally review applications for warrantless electronic surveillance and require scrupulous evidence indicating probable collaboration,"[148] ultimately conceded that the restoration of "public confidence in intelligence operations" probably required closer oversight by nonexecutive actors.[149]

Having already established legislative oversight through the House and Senate Select Committees on Intelligence (the latter a formalized replacement for the Church Committee), members of Congress, and the Senate in particular, turned in 1976 to "cooperative efforts" with the White House to draft legislation providing some form of judicial oversight as well.[150] Though the two sides still disagreed over whether the president possessed inherent powers to authorize electronic surveillance, they agreed that, even if he did, such surveillance should, whether as a matter of constitutional requirement (in Congress's view) or simply one of prudence (in the Ford administration's view), "be authorized by a neutral and detached magistrate."[151] And though there were some early questions about "whether it was permissible to involve federal judges in approving requests for electronic surveillance conducted for national security purposes," legislators were reassured by the fact that similar functions, including bankruptcy proceedings, had been delegated to the judiciary already.[152] With Congress serving the interests of civil libertarians and the attorney general protecting the president's interests in gathering intelligence information, the two sides worked behind the scenes to forge an "effective compromise on the respective roles of the executive and the judiciary."[153] At the heart of this compromise was the creation of an independent judicial body that would review, but largely act deferentially toward, executive branch requests for a warrant to wiretap for the purpose of obtaining foreign intelligence. Under this scheme, the executive could not act unilaterally, thereby addressing the concerns of civil libertarians, but the judiciary would not seek to impede good-faith presidential action, thereby assuaging the fears of the intelligence community.

Although the initial bill embodying this compromise did not reach the Senate floor before the Ninety-Fourth Congress (1975–77) adjourned, the wide support it garnered along the way—as evidenced by bipartisan cosponsorship from conservatives and liberals as well as quick progression through the Senate Judiciary

[147] Shapiro, "The Foreign Intelligence Surveillance Act," 189–90n239.
[148] Ibid., 143–44.
[149] Ibid., 121.
[150] Ibid., 122.
[151] Allan N. Kornblum and Lubomyr M. Jachnycky, "America's Secret Court: Listening In on Espionage and Terrorism," *Judges Journal* 24 (1985): 16.
[152] Cinquegrana, "The Walls (and Wires) Have Ears," 808.
[153] Shapiro, "The Foreign Intelligence Surveillance Act," 188.

and Intelligence Committees[154]—left it with relatively favorable prospects heading into the Ninety-Fifth Congress (1977–79). Moreover, with Jimmy Carter having defeated Gerald Ford in the 1976 presidential election, key Senate sponsors like Democrat Edward Kennedy of Massachusetts suspected (correctly, it turns out) increased support for intelligence reform from the White House.[155] In fact, with the Carter administration favoring reform, the only obstacle came from certain liberal senators (Walter Mondale of Minnesota, for example) who worried that the reform proposal would not actually protect citizens against governmental intrusion into their private lives. Even that, however, proved virtually inconsequential, as Kennedy and others convinced their colleagues that the present reform was the most stringent they were likely to pass.[156] Ultimately, with the wake of Watergate—and, more specifically, the Church Committee—having brought the issue of intelligence oversight to the agenda and supplied it with a ready constituency among politicians as well as the public, it passed with substantially greater ease than its importance might have suggested.[157]

America's Covert Court and America's Role in the World

The Foreign Intelligence Surveillance Act actually created two courts: first, the Foreign Intelligence Surveillance Court, which was initially composed of seven existing district court judges designated by the chief justice of the United States and tasked with individually hearing requests from the federal government for warrants to engage in electronic surveillance within the United States for the purposes of national security;[158] and, second, the Foreign Intelligence Surveillance Court of Review, which is staffed by a panel of three existing circuit courts of appeals judges and authorized to hear appeals from the government in the instance that a judge on the lower surveillance court denies or modifies a warrant request.[159] In embedding its courts within a three-tiered system where district judges take direct action on disputes, subject to review by circuit courts of appeals judges, who are themselves subject to review by the Supreme Court, the act created a hierarchical mini judicial system that bears striking resemblance to the American federal judiciary at large.[160] In terms of actual operations, however, it created a pair of courts that function unlike any other federal court in America. Sessions can be convened on

---

[154] Ibid., 122–23.

[155] Following the spirit of a Ford administration directive banning the CIA from engaging in electronic surveillance in the United States, Carter issued an executive order prohibiting agencies other than the FBI from engaging in physical surveillance of American citizens. See Executive Order 11905 (1976); and Executive Order 12036 (1978).

[156] Shapiro, "The Foreign Intelligence Surveillance Act," 124–25.

[157] The Senate passed the bill on a voice vote; the House passed it 226–176.

[158] In 2001, Congress expanded the FISC to include eleven judges; 115 Stat. 272 (October 26, 2001).

[159] In both cases, any foreign intelligence surveillance judging is performed in addition to rather than in place of the judges' regular dockets.

[160] Judges on both courts serve seven-year, nonrenewable terms.

any day and at any time. Parties are never notified. Business is conducted in secret. Proceedings are nonadversarial.[161] Records are confidential.[162]

These very features of the Foreign Intelligence Surveillance Court (FISC) make it exceedingly difficult to assess either the immediate effects or long-term legacy of this particular episode of judicial institution building. On the one hand, the Foreign Intelligence Surveillance Act did, for the first time, establish judicial principles governing the circumstances under which warrants for electronic surveillance of American citizens would be granted. Formerly granted solely at the discretion of the executive and the intelligence community and subject to virtually no accountability whatsoever, the vesting of some sort of oversight authority in an independent judicial forum was undoubtedly an improvement. On the other hand, the jurisdiction of the FISC is limited to "the function that judges perform every day in their courtrooms—evaluating facts and deciding questions of law" and the substantive scope of its review limited to instances in which the government's certification that the purpose of the requested surveillance is to collect foreign intelligence seems "clearly erroneous."[163] Given this standard, it should be little surprise that, in its first thirty years of operation (through 2007), the FISC denied only nine out of more than 25,000 governmental requests (and not a single one before 2003, when the number of requests began to increase substantially).[164]

While it is impossible to determine conclusively whether the government's remarkable success in obtaining its desired warrants is a reflection of a judicial "rubber stamp," thereby suggesting that reform failed, or "carefully prepared and rigorously reviewed" petitions, thereby suggesting that reform succeeded,[165] the fact that the FISC seems inclined to limit only egregious intelligence behavior (otherwise allowing the government leeway in pursuing national security objectives) does not seem out of line with either the motivating desires behind the act or the legislative-executive compromise at the heart of it. After all, with even the Church Committee acknowledging that electronic surveillance had become "a valuable technique for the collection of intelligence and counter-intelligence,"[166] and with even staunch congressional reform advocates having eschewed aggressive prohibition of electronic surveillance in favor of a more modest requirement for a warrant in order to engage in it, more active judicial supervision of intelligence activities, while no doubt pleasing to civil libertarian advocates, would prove anathema to

---

[161] In the lower court, the determination about whether or not to issue a warrant is based solely upon the presentation of the Department of Justice—specifically, the Office of Intelligence Policy and Review. In the review court, outside groups may be invited or permitted to submit *amicus curiae* briefs.

[162] The authorizing act does, however, require an annual report to Congress indicating the number of requests it heard and the number it granted and denied.

[163] Kornblum and Jachnycky, "America's Secret Court," 16.

[164] See Foreign Intelligence Surveillance Act Court Orders 1979-2010, accessed September 3, 2010, at http://epic.org/privacy/wiretap/stats/fisa_stats.html. During this same time period, however, the FISC did modify a number of government requests for a warrant.

[165] Kornblum and Jachnycky, "America's Secret Court," 16.

[166] Senate Report No. 755, 94th Cong., 2nd sess. (1976).

the delicate balance between security and rights at stake. In this way, even though the Foreign Intelligence Surveillance Act may initially seem less about increasing governmental efficiency and more about limiting governmental intrusion, it actually serves a similar purpose as most other postwar institution-building initiatives: ensuring that the growing American state works as fluidly, as competently, and as productively as possible.

In an age where the role of that state in the world at large is perpetually a source of deliberation, the story of the Foreign Intelligence Surveillance Act and its judicial progeny is perpetually evolving.[167] In 1994, Congress extended the act to give the FISC the power to grant warrants to enter premises rather than simply to install wiretaps.[168] In 1998, it further amended the act to give the federal government authority "to reengage in 'roving' wiretaps, install 'pen registers,' and place 'trap and trace' devices on communication lines" in order to further national security interests.[169] In 2002, the Foreign Intelligence Surveillance Court of Review met and issued an opinion for the first time since its creation twenty-five years earlier;[170] in 2008, it publicly released a second opinion, though not until five months after the fact.[171] Several times since the inauguration of the War on Terror, Congress passed amendments that seem either to broaden the scope of allowable governmental action under the Foreign Intelligence Surveillance Act or to limit the work of the FISC in overseeing such action.[172] And, of course, the relevance and import of the FISC in the first place was called into question with the revelation that the counterterrorism policies pursued by George W. Bush included a National Security Agency surveillance program that operated without either congressional approval

[167] In the same vein as the FISC, Congress established the Alien Terrorist Removal Court in 1996. Part of a statute that originated in Speaker of the House Newt Gingrich's 1994 "Contract with America" and found bipartisan support in the aftermath of the April 1995 Oklahoma City bombing, the Alien Terrorist Removal Court consists of five existing district court judges (who might also serve or have previously served on the FISC) chosen by the chief justice for renewable five-year terms. See the Anti-Terrorism and Effective Death Penalty Act of 1996, 110 Stat. 1214 (April 24, 1996). Charged with hearing grant applications by the attorney general for the deportation of suspected alien terrorists, this court has not, even with the inauguration of the War on Terror, met a single time in its first fifteen years of existence.

[168] 108 Stat. 3423 (October 14, 1994).

[169] Gerald H. Robinson, "We're Listening! Electronic Eavesdropping, FISA, and the Secret Court," 36 *Willamette Law Review* 51, 55–56 (2000): 55–56. 112 Stat. 2396 (October 20, 1998).

[170] *In re Sealed Case*, 310 F.3d. 717 (2002) (overturning the Foreign Intelligence Surveillance Court's decision to issue but impose restrictions on a wiretapping warrant sought by the federal government and condoning the use of evidence acquired under such a warrant for use in criminal cases).

[171] *In re Directives* [redacted] *Pursuant to Section 105B of the Foreign Intelligence Surveillance Act*, docket no. 08-01 (upholding the constitutionality of the Protect America Act of 2007 against claims that the warrantless wiretapping provisions therein constituted unreasonable search and seizure in violation of the Fourth Amendment).

[172] See, most notably, the Uniting and Strengthening America by Providing Appropriate Tools Required to Intercept and Obstruct Terrorism Act of 2001 (the USA PATRIOT Act), 115 Stat. 272 (October 26, 2001); the Protect America Act of 2007, 121 Stat. 552 (August 5, 2007); and the Foreign Intelligence Surveillance Act Amendments Act of 2008, 122 Stat. 2436 (July 10, 2008).

or judicial sanction.[173] Regardless of what the future may hold for the Foreign Intelligence Surveillance Act, the fact that the national security state it was designed to regulate appears (for the near future, at least) a fixture in American politics suggests that, far from a ephemeral moment in the history of institution building, the place of the judiciary in the realm of foreign policy will surely be a persistent focus of judicial reform as the next era of American history unfolds.[174]

• • •

The history of judicial institution building in modern America unfolded in three stages: the renovation and replacement of the commissioner system with a magistrate system in the Federal Magistrate Act of 1968; the formation of the specialized, patent-focused Court of Appeals for the Federal Circuit as part of the Federal Courts Improvement Act of 1982; and the establishment of two national security–oriented courts in the Foreign Intelligence Surveillance Act of 1978. In examining these stages, I have illuminated both the causes and consequences of judicial institution building. As throughout the book, I have provided an account of why judicial institution building was pursued, how it was accomplished, and what it achieved.

Why was judicial institution building in modern America pursued? In all three stages, institution building was sought by legislators, judges, and academics hoping to improve judicial performance less through increased resources than through increased flexibility in the utilization of existing resources. The move to expand the role and power of judicial adjuncts, as seen most clearly in the use of magistrates, arose largely within the context of crowded dockets—and long delays in the dispatch of justice—at the district court level. The merger of two existing courts into a national appellate court (equivalent in stature to the other circuit courts of appeals) of specialized jurisdiction for domestic (largely economic) affairs was the culmination

---

[173] The program was uncovered in 2005; two federal judges—one in 2006, the other in 2010—subsequently declared it a violation of the Foreign Intelligence Surveillance Act.

[174] Indeed, though it has yet to give rise to a landmark piece of institution building, the War on Terror has certainly increased dialogue (and, occasionally, confrontation) among Congress, the president, and the judiciary over issues such as the legitimate scope of governmental power to protect the citizenry from foreign and domestic threat, the applicability and relevance of constitutional guarantees such as habeas corpus to noncitizens, and the legitimacy of non–Article III military commissions in processing terrorist detainees and enemy combatants. See, for example, *Rasul v. Bush*, 542 U.S. 466 (2004) (affirming federal court jurisdiction over habeas corpus claims filed by suspects held at the American military base at Guantanamo Bay, Cuba); *Hamdi v. Rumsfeld*, 542 U.S. 507 (2004) (holding that the Fifth Amendment guaranteed basic procedural protections, including the right to a trial before a neutral decision-maker, to American citizens held as enemy combatants); and *Hamdan v. Rumsfeld*, 548 U.S. 557 (2006) (declaring military commissions for noncitizens a violation of both the Geneva Convention and the Uniform Code of Military Justice). In response to *Hamdan*, Congress passed the Military Commissions Act of 2006, 120 Stat. 2600 (October 17, 2006), only to see it nullified in *Boumediene v. Bush*, 553 U.S. 723 (2008) (striking down a congressional attempt to establish military commissions by statute as a violation of the Suspension Clause). At the heart of these conflicts sits a dispute between whether the conduct of the War on Terror should be subject to supervision by or deference from the federal judiciary.

of a broader campaign to provide relief to the nation's appellate courts as well as to guarantee greater consistency and coherence in legal realms where such properties were particularly critical. The creation of a mini-judicial hierarchy focused exclusively on matters of national security was an attempt to impose some—but not too much—judicial scrutiny over one segment of the government's intelligence activities.

How was judicial institution building in modern America accomplished? In all three cases of institution building during this period, opposition to substantial judicial reform was fairly minimal, but in each case the absence of such opposition traced to a different source. The Federal Magistrates Act of 1968 was enabled by the virtual absence of any notable objections to what seemed like a moderate and sensible solution to the serious and frustrating dilemma of increasing federal trial court workload. The Federal Courts Improvement Act of 1982 earned passage as a streamlined reform initiative when it became clear that the bolder proposals to address the appellate courts' own caseload crisis were simply too contentious to make any fruitful progress. The Foreign Intelligence Surveillance Act of 1978 was the result of the increased public salience of and political will for reform following a series of revelations about the inappropriate use of intelligence resources in past presidential administrations.

What did judicial institution building in modern America achieve? Collectively, the reforms of the era simultaneously sharpened and extended judicial authority to keep pace with the increasing size—and increasing number of functions—of the federal government in both domestic and foreign policy. The embrace of magistrates and other judicial adjuncts unburdened federal district court judges from either judicial or quasi-judicial duties surrounding various types of cases. The addition of the Court of Appeals for the Federal Circuit allowed for more effective regulation of the complicated but crucial legal realm of patents by funneling all cases in that doctrinal area into one tribunal, thereby substituting the ills produced by intercircuit conflicts for the wisdom of judges who would gradually gain more substantive knowledge of the technical issues involved. The creation of the FISC and the Foreign Intelligence Surveillance Court of Review allowed the government the space it needed to protect the nation and its citizenry while at the same time satisfying civil libertarians with enough judicial oversight to ensure that truly egregious and inappropriate efforts at intelligence gathering stood little chance of gaining approval. In each case, institution building altered the judiciary by specializing either the tasks it performed or the personnel who executed them. In doing so, it brought increased efficiency, increased flexibility, and increased order to an institutional structure that had grown substantially (and perhaps excessively) centralized during the interwar and New Deal years.

Considered within the broader historical context of the process at large, judicial institution building in modern America embodied a series of typical characteristics and dynamics. First, as we initially witnessed in the early republic, the precedential weight of prior institution-building efforts can pivotally shape future ones. Whether the particular contours of bankruptcy judges shadowing those of magistrates or the FISC serving as a model for the Alien Terrorist Removal Court (created in 1996), judicial reform initiatives during this era often set examples for subsequent reform. Second, having been virtually excluded from judicial governance and administration until the 1920s, judges once again proved active and instrumental in encouraging institution building in the second half of the twentieth century. Speaking in large part through the Judicial Conference and aided to no small extent by research from the Administrative Office of the Courts and (later) the Federal Judicial Center, judges made legislators aware of the caseload crisis, the problems emanating from it, and their preferred solutions to it. Third, with—and perhaps even because of—this increased involvement of judicial actors, judicial institution building in modern America continued the interwar and New Deal years trend away from reforms that were fixated on policy and politics toward those chiefly concerned with performance. Throughout the period, legislators seemed less interested in manipulating the institutional judiciary to their advantage than in providing judges the tools to perform their functions competently and dependably. Indeed, more than just a rhetorical frame for more policy or political reform (or a piece of factual background to these more strategic explanations), performance goals were the driving force behind episodes of institution building that made concrete changes to and effected tangible results for the institutional judiciary. The fact that the reforms that provided such tools were performance-oriented did not make them any less consequential; rather, it simply made them somewhat less contestable. Finally, and most plainly, as was true in the early republic, the eras of Jeffersonian and Jacksonian democracy, the Civil War and Reconstruction, the Gilded Age and the Progressive Era, and the interwar and New Deal years, the process of building the judiciary was politically constructed. Even amid a simultaneous broadening of relevant actors (to include judges and academics) and focusing of guiding interests (on performance), judicial institution building retained its most essential and most defining attributes: central involvement on the part of politicians as opposed to merely judges, critical action in the political as opposed to exclusively legal sphere.

At the same time, two key features distinguish institution building in modern America from that of earlier eras. First, although performance had long been a stated goal (sometimes genuinely, sometimes not) of institution builders, the performance in question had always been that of the judiciary in particular. Concomitant with the rise of the administrative state, however, the rationale for performance-oriented reform included improved performance for the national government at large. A reflection of the fact that the federal government had, since the New Deal, continually assumed new functions and provided new services, reforms such as the creation of magistrates or the establishment of the FISC were explicitly conceptualized and framed in terms of the performance benefits they would bring not only for judges but also for the array of governmental agencies and programs that depend upon judges. With post–New Deal (and post–Great

Society) expansion of governmental authority and personnel had come both inefficiencies and excesses, and, for the first time, proponents of institution building advocated building the judiciary to help eradicate those problems and improve the quality of federal governance. Second, serving a role similar to that best executed by the American Bar Association from the late Progressive Era through the New Deal, external study groups, independent commissions, and special congressional committees were prominent players in the reform campaigns of the era. From the Freund Study Group and Hruska Commission on the workload crisis to the Watergate Committee and the Church Committee on executive branch overreaching, these investigative panels—populated by combinations of legislators, judges, lawyers, and legal academics—raised awareness about, dramatized dilemmas involving, and offered policy proposals addressing the status of the institutional judiciary and its role in various aspects of the American political system. In this way, specialized entities had a critical hand in creating the specialized judiciary.

For all the changes wrought by the period following World War II—by the Great Society and the subsequent conservative ascendancy—the institutional judiciary was not transformed fundamentally; it was, however, refined considerably. Having begun the era satisfied with its newfound ability to govern itself, the judiciary ended it structurally thicker, functionally more concentrated, and generally better equipped to serve and better aligned with the modern American nation. There was a wider and more clearly defined set of functions than ever before. There were more judges, more extensive judicial support staff, and more elaborate administrative entities than ever before. There were greater resources (in terms of both finances and physical space) than ever before. Hardly a product of accident or happenstance, these changes were the result of more than two hundred years of institutional development and experimentation. Indeed, by the time the modern Supreme Court tackled perhaps its most stunning task ever by effectively deciding the 2000 presidential election, the federal judiciary had been constructed and reconstructed—made, remade, and modified—countless times. The results—independence, autonomy, and power—were as historically unfathomable as they were empirically unmistakable. Far from the uncertainty and frailty that defined its origins, the judiciary stood at the dawn of the twenty-first century as an institution the nation's founders would have scarcely recognized and one they could have hardly imagined.

CHAPTER EIGHT

Judicial Power in a Political World

"With all due deference to separation of powers," Barack Obama said in his second State of the Union Address in January 2010, "last week the Supreme Court reversed a century of law that, I believe, will open the floodgates for special interests, including foreign corporations, to spend without limit in our elections."[1] A response to the Court's controversial decision in *Citizens United v. Federal Election Commission*,[2] Obama's remarks—including his subsequent plea to Congress to "pass a bill that helps correct some of these problems"[3]—were met with cheers by much of the audience, though not, of course, by the justices of the Court, six of whom were in attendance that evening. Five of the six—John Roberts, Anthony Kennedy, Ruth Bader Ginsburg, Stephen Breyer, and Sonia Sotomayor—remained, as is customary for the members of the Court, still and silent, but, in a much-debated moment that would be replayed repeatedly on television and the Internet, Samuel Alito shook his head in disapproval and appeared to mouth the words "not true, not true." Within minutes of Obama concluding his speech that night, the controversy had erupted, and the questions came fast and furious. Had Obama's aggressive "attack" on a decision of the Court crossed the line? Had Alito's defiant reaction constituted an improper breach of judicial impartiality? Shouldn't the president, as his own reference to the separation of powers suggests, respect the judgments of the Court as authoritative expositions of constitutional principles rather than merely alternative political views? Shouldn't the members of the Court preserve their separation from the ruthlessness of politics through nonpartisan stoicism and disinterest? Wasn't the whole event simply a stain on contemporary American politics, one we would all like to leave in the past and one we would all prefer to avoid in the future?

The intense reactions from both left and right, from supporters of both the president and the Court, implied that something remarkable had occurred. And, indeed, on a superficial level, something remarkable—something between gripping political theater and salacious political melodrama—*had* occurred: the president had chastised the Court with the entirety of Washington society in the room

---

[1] Barack Obama, Second State of the Union Address, January 27, 2010.

[2] 558 U.S. ___ (2010) (striking down a federal regulation of corporate campaign speech as a violation of the First Amendment).

[3] Obama, Second State of the Union Address.

and the entirety of the nation's citizenry able to watch on television, and a justice had reacted with disagreement to a statement in what Chief Justice Roberts would later call a "political pep rally."[4] But, on a deeper level, the State of the Union incident revealed more about our conceptions of the Court than it did about the Court itself—more about our unstated assumptions regarding the place of judiciary in American politics than about its actual place. One set of reactions, largely expressed by those in the media and by elected officeholders, focused on blaming either or both Obama and Alito for their roles in needlessly, inappropriately, and harmfully "politicizing" the judiciary. The Court, we were reminded, was removed from the political sphere, so Obama, a partisan politician, was wrong to draw it into political debate, and Alito, an objective judge, was wrong to take the bait. Another, somewhat smaller, set of reactions, particularly from scholars of the Court and its history, took the incident as simply another instance in a long line of collisions between politicians and the Court. The Court, we were taught, had been targeted by, among other presidents, Thomas Jefferson, Andrew Jackson, Abraham Lincoln, and Franklin Roosevelt; its default position in the political system was one of a foil, a lightning rod, and an oft-criticized "outsider" that could be cowed by harsh words and forced to adapt by intimidating threats. According to one camp, the dispute deviated from a norm of insulation; according to the other, it proved a pattern of discord.[5]

I want to suggest, somewhat counterintuitively, that these two seemingly divergent reactions to the Obama-Alito kerfuffle actually reflect a similar presumption, one shared by both current political rhetoric surrounding the Supreme Court and contemporary academic exegesis about the Supreme Court—namely, that judicial power is separate from and outside the realm of democratic politics. In political rhetoric, this presumption paradoxically gives rise either to an unrepentant defense of the Court's position as above the fray and its integrity as beyond reproach (from "judiciaphiles") or a paranoid skepticism that judicial power was "stolen" from the people and their representatives, that the Court somehow rose to prominence through manipulative action taken when citizens and politicians were not looking or carried out in ways they could not prevent (from "judiciaphobes"). In academic exegesis, it serves as the basis for the conclusion that the relationship between courts and other political institutions (or between judges and other political actors) is characterized by hostility and friction, is defined by antagonism and opposition. Based on the story I have told about judicial institution building from

---

[4] Associated Press, "Chief Justice John Roberts Found State of the Union Scene 'Troubling,'" *Washington Post*, March 10, 2010.

[5] For early scholarly reactions that express, in various forms, both of these reactions, see Douglas E. Edlin, "'It's Not What You Said, It's How You Said It': Criticizing the Supreme Court in the State of the Union," *Yale Law and Policy Review Inter Alia* 28 (2010): 27–36; Mark A. Graber, "A Tale Told by a President," *Yale Law and Policy Review Inter Alia* 28 (2010): 13–25; Bruce Peabody, "What Deference is Due? Constitutional Chiding and the State of the Union," *Yale Law and Policy Review Inter Alia* 28 (2010): 1–11; and Keith E. Whittington, "The State of the Union Is a Presidential Pep Rally," *Yale Law and Policy Review Inter Alia* 28 (2010): 37–50.

the time of the nation's founding to the present, I want to suggest that these various propositions—and, consequently, their shared presumption about judicial power being, in some sense, beyond the sphere of politics—are fundamentally incorrect. In their place, I want to offer a different conception of the relationship between judicial power and democratic politics, one that not only locates the judicial branch squarely within the political arena but also places substantially greater emphasis on its cooperation rather than conflict with those in that arena, most notably federal elected officials. As I attempt to demonstrate in this concluding chapter, such a conception is, on an empirical level, vastly more faithful to the judiciary's place in America's past and, on a normative one, considerably less fatalistic about its place in America's future.

Judicial Institution Building as a Political Project

As this book has made clear, the institutional development of the federal judiciary—including, but not limited to, the Supreme Court—has been an undeniably political project. It has, that is to say, been simultaneously guided by political incentives and subject to political constraints. Far from occurring in a world apart from politics, far from happening in courthouses and judges' chambers, the construction and reconstruction—the making, remaking, and modification—of the institutional judiciary that has unfolded over the course of American political development has been the work of elected politicians acting in political forums and upon political interests. The process of judicial institution building, in other words, has not been removed from or contrary to politics but deeply embedded within it. Indeed, as I describe in chapter 1, to the extent that courts and judges have become central to American politics, it is because elected politicians have *actively, repeatedly*, and *strategically* assisted them in becoming so. In this section, I want to debunk the assumption of judicial separation from politics that structures much contemporary thinking about judicial power by unpacking each of these three claims before suggesting how the idea that judicial power at large—rather than merely judicial review[6]—is politically constructed should prompt us to reevaluate our conceptions of the relationship between the Court and the political branches.

First, judicial power has not been stolen from political society but affirmatively granted by it. Rather than depicting a story of law trumping politics, of institutional development occurring in peculiarly apolitical legal venues, the history of judicial institution building I have sketched in this book illustrates how courts have emerged as powerful less because of judicial decisions than because of political ones. Indeed, despite our reverence for the Court's decisions in *Marbury v.*

---

[6] As noted previously, existing work on the "political construction" of judicial power tends to focus on how the practice of judicial review is maintained and supported by political actors—a subject that, while admittedly important, embodies a relatively limited conception of judicial power and captures a relatively small proportion of interactions between the judiciary and the political branches. See chapter 1.

Madison and *McCulloch v. Maryland*,[7] it is simply not the case that the judiciary became powerful on the basis of John Marshall's pronouncements about judicial review or federal supremacy over the states. While those pronouncements were by no means unimportant, they did little to provide the judiciary with any concrete tools of judicial power. They did not, that is to say, bestow upon the judiciary more functions, new individuals, or increased resources; they did not create, consolidate, or expand the structural and institutional capacities needed to respond to and intervene in the political environment. Instead of arriving concomitant with landmark judicial decisions, nearly all significant steps in the accretion of judicial capacity were effected by acts of Congress. The Judiciary Act of 1789 (see chapter 2), which (among a great many other things) created a tier of lower courts and filled the constitutional gaps in the Court's jurisdiction, did not flow from pen of Chief Justice John Jay; rather, it emerged from the mind and through the efforts of Senator Oliver Ellsworth. The Local Prejudice Act of 1867 (see chapter 4), which empowered federal courts to take control of state court cases where a litigant believed the judge was biased against him, was the product of a Republican legislature rather than a Republican judiciary. The Judiciary Act of 1925, which granted the Court near-complete control over its docket (see chapter 6), was, it is true, the legacy of Chief Justice William Howard Taft, but it was brought to fruition by Taft's proposing, drafting, and lobbying for passage of a legislative bill rather than his marshaling of Court brethren behind a judicial opinion. In each of these instances, judicial power expanded because of, rather than in spite of, political action; in each of these instances, judicial power expanded through, rather than over, political will.

Second, judicial power has not emerged suddenly and spontaneously so much as it has developed consistently and continuously. Indeed, the growth of judicial power was made possible not by a singular event but through a collection of occurrences, the timeline for which has stretched over two hundred years and has encompassed a multitude of different actors and parties. The individual reforms may not have arrived at a regular pace or followed predictable patterns, but neither were they limited to one era, one administration, or one episode; instead, they were multiple, manifold, and recurring, often building upon and modifying one another so as to refine judicial capacity or improve judicial efficiency. The geographic organization initially designed for thirteen states along the Eastern seaboard was the subject of steady attention and the cause of two pivotal reforms, the Judiciary Act of 1807 and the Judiciary Act of 1837 (see chapter 3), in the early to mid-nineteenth century. The early institutional architecture of three tiers of courts but only two sets of judges was made less burdensome on Supreme Court justices through repeated structural innovation, including the appointment of circuit

[7] *Marbury v. Madison*, 5 U.S. 137 (1803) (invalidating Section 13 of the Judiciary Act of 1789 as in conflict with Article III); *McCulloch v. Maryland*, 17 U.S. 316 (1819) (upholding the creation of the Second Bank of the United States as a constitutional exercise of congressional authority under the Necessary and Proper Clause and rejecting the idea that a state could tax an organ of the federal government).

judges in 1869 (see chapter 4) and the creation of circuit courts of appeals in 1891 (see chapter 5), in the mid- to late nineteenth century. The original problems of a decentralized and administratively dependent branch were virtually eradicated by a series of reforms, including the authorization of the Judicial Conference in 1922 and the establishment of the Administrative Office of the Courts in 1939 (see chapter 6) in the early to mid-twentieth century. The steadily mounting caseloads of federal district court judges were alleviated by frequent modifications to the set of tasks that might be delegated to judicial adjuncts like magistrates and bankruptcy judges (see chapter 7) in the mid- to late twentieth century. With these changes part of a gradual process ongoing over the course of two centuries, it is clear that the character of judicial institution building was far more evolutionary than revolutionary.

Third, judicial power has not increased because of clueless or feckless behavior but because of strategic and deliberate action. In other words, politicians have engaged in institution building consciously and tactically, empowering the judiciary because they saw it in their—and often their constituents'—interests to do so. The particular interests being served have varied from the promotion of a specific economic agenda (policy) to the creation of new Supreme Court seats for partisan allies (politics) to the unburdening of a rapidly increasing judicial docket (performance). Regardless of the specific interest at hand, it is clear that politicians have traditionally viewed the judiciary as a potential partner in, rather than an obstacle to, their governing coalitions. In the early republic (see chapter 2), Federalists proposed a strong judiciary under the assumption that such an institution would simultaneously promote the national unity they believed necessary and further the commercial growth they believed desirable. In the late Jeffersonian period (see chapter 3), National Republicans attempted to update the circuit system in order to appease Westerners, whose political support they sought in their partisan fight with Old Republicans. In the Gilded Age (see chapter 5), Republicans substantially expanded the jurisdiction of federal courts in the hope that a strong federal judiciary would help facilitate the triumph of industrial capitalism over the forces of local agrarian opposition. In the modern era (see chapter 7), Democrats and Republicans alike supported specialized courts for matters as disparate as patents and foreign intelligence surveillance in the expectation that the establishment of such courts would lead to greater consistency and enhanced coherence in either technically complicated or politically sensitive legal domains. Across the span of American political development, then, the growth of judicial capacity has furthered rather than impeded the disparate goals politicians sought to achieve.

To the extent that our presumption about the judiciary operating outside the normal scope of political action leads us to ignore these three findings, and, by extension, the centrality of democratic politics to the construction of judicial power more generally, it also casts doubt on the simplistic and essentially conflictual models of interbranch relations proffered in much extant scholarly literature about judicial politics. Indeed, the idea that judicial power has been politically rather than legally constructed, an idea drawn from the history of judicial institution building that I have sketched in this book, suggests that the common conceptions of legislative-judicial dynamics in particular—politicians threatening and punishing judges for wayward decisions, on the one hand, and courts brazenly subverting the democratic will through judicial review of representative lawmaking, on the other—are profoundly misguided. As we have seen, the relationship between Congress and the courts is, on the whole, characterized by a continual give-and-take that reflects neither strict judicial dependence upon nor inevitable judicial intransigence toward the legislature. In other words, legislative-judicial interactions around institution building do not conform to frameworks that envision the Court begging Congress for power or Congress punishing the Court for its indiscretions. Instead of Congress manipulating the Court to its advantage and the Court's detriment or the Court unilaterally thrusting itself into the political arena without invitation or acceptance, the two institutions interact in a more dynamic and complicated fashion. Often those interactions are friendly, occasionally they are neutral, and even less occasionally they are antagonistic, but they are rarely restricted to either a congressional response to a judicial decision or a judicial decision in response to congressional signals.

By emphasizing concepts such as Court-curbing and strategic retreats, then, scholars of judicial politics (and related fields) have perpetuated a fundamental misconception about the nature of the relationship between Congress and the Court. That relationship, as the history of judicial institution building demonstrates, is markedly more supportive than combative. Courts have undoubtedly provoked popular and political dissatisfaction and sparked politicians to try to curb the exercise of judicial power on numerous occasions, but the most common congressional posture toward the federal judiciary has long been—and remains to this day—cooperation rather than conflict. In the more than two hundred years between the start of George Washington's presidency in 1789 and the election of George W. Bush in 2000, Congress, through the variety of enactments already mentioned as well as several others, established (chapter 2), reorganized (chapter 3), empowered (chapter 4), restructured (chapter 5), bureaucratized (chapter 6), and specialized (chapter 7) the federal judiciary. Hardly any of the episodes constituting these dominant modes of institution building represented congressional enmity toward the judiciary; in fact, nearly all of them reflected support of it and, in turn, yielded a meaningful enhancement of either judicial independence, autonomy, or power.

Although most (if not all) of the reforms I have mentioned in this chapter and described elsewhere in this book offered politicians something they wanted, the fact that episodes of judicial institution building have served the policy, political, or performance goals of elite actors makes them neither less important to the growth of judicial capacity nor more hostile to it. After all, if judicial power has been increasing or expanding, if the judiciary has been given *more* work to do or *more* tools to use in doing that work (as has been true in almost all instances through American history), then judicial institution building, regardless of what motivated politicians to pursue it, has been cooperative, helping all branches in their struggle for governmental power. Even in those instances where judicial institution building reorganized or restructured rather than measurably expanded judicial power, it did so in ways that were at best mildly mutualistic, at worst plainly commensalistic, and—above all—not even remotely parasitic. That is to say, even when institution building did not explicitly trigger judicial empowerment—as in the case of the geographic expansion and reorganization of the federal circuit system in Judiciary Act of 1837 (chapter 3), the compilation of all judiciary-related laws into one statute in the Judicial Code of 1911 (chapter 5), or the establishment of the Court of Appeals for the Federal Circuit in 1982 (chapter 7), for example—it hardly signaled judicial endangerment. Throughout American history, elected officials may have pursued institution building because they believed it in their interest to do so, but judges—far from being harmed or limited—have been the actors who benefited most.

Why, then, have scholars of judicial politics continued to view the history of legislative-judicial relations through a primarily conflictual lens, emphasizing political tension and hostility where it simply did and does not exist? Because they have—somewhat peculiarly, given their broader interests in the separation of powers—adopted a view of the judiciary as not simply functionally independent but intrinsically extrapolitical. Because they have assumed, in other words, the same perspective that runs through so much partisan rhetoric about the Supreme Court in American politics. As a result, when scholars of judicial politics see political forces acting on the judiciary, they view the occurrence as an anomaly to be studied. But once we discard the idea that courts are in any way isolated from politics and (more accurately and reasonably) treat the judiciary as behaving like one of American government's "separated institutions *sharing* powers,"[8] then we see that political forces shaping the nature, contour, and extent of judicial power is not the exception but the unequivocal historical rule. And once we recognize this reality, it is not clear why legislators or executives trying to shape the judiciary to serve their interests should be considered hostile court curbers in the least. Especially if we shift our focus from what politicians say about the judiciary to what they do (or do not do) for or to it, then most evidence of an oppositional relationship virtually disappears; especially if we shift our concern from demagoguery surrounding judicial power to the policy making that enables or encumbers the exercise of it, competition reveals itself to be far more isolated and far less central than collaboration.

Judicial Power and Democratic Politics

By moving us away (contra political rhetoric) from the idea of a hermetic separation between judicial power and democratic politics, and by recasting (contra academic exegesis) the historical relationship between politicians and the Court as one of cooperation rather than conflict, the case I have outlined in this book and highlighted

[8] Richard E. Neustadt, *Presidential Power and the Modern Presidents: The Politics of Leadership from Roosevelt to Reagan* (New York: Free Press, 1991), 29. See also Charles O. Jones, *The Presidency in a Separated System* (Washington, DC: Brookings Institution Press, 1994).

in this chapter suggests that the empirical foundations upon which much normative theorizing—both scholarly and popular—about judicial power is based are at best incomplete and at worst outright incorrect. Indeed, the fact that the dramatic expansion of the institutional judiciary has resulted less from countermajoritarian judicial decisions than majoritarian political ones should force us to consider whether the substantial hand-wringing about the supposed democratic deviance of judicial power is truly warranted or whether a model that points toward some degree of democratic pedigree for judicial power might justify somewhat different normative conclusions.

The fact that there is little sense in talking about the institutional development of the judiciary as being either meaningfully estranged from or meaningfully in tension with politics should, as a starting point, be of great comfort to all constituencies, save perhaps those partisan operatives and interest groups on both sides of the aisle who seem to thrive on the escalation of conflicts surrounding the culture war and the Supreme Court's place within it. In concluding this book, I want to outline why this finding—the fact that judicial power is not currently and has not historically been devoid of politics—should be seen as normatively desirable by anyone with one or more of three political commitments: first, protecting judicial independence from democratic politics; second, promoting judicial accountability to democratic politics; and, third, solidifying and revitalizing the participation of "the people" in democratic politics.

First, for those who desire robust independence and limited accountability, the centering of judicial power in a political world should serve to counter overheated discourse about courts and judges and provide a powerfully weighty counterpoint to the arguments of those seeking to curb them. After all, to the extent that antijudicial hostility is often expressed in terms of courts acting in an extrapolitical manner—judges are unelected, their power is constitutionally unspecified, their behavior virtually unchecked by and unaccountable to political branches[9]—the dismantling of that paradigm could serve to deny the critics of judicial power a meaningful rhetorical frame. In a more affirmative fashion, demonstrating the extent to which judicial institution building has been a political project and the extent to which the current shape of the federal judiciary is a political product should indicate that judicial power has a firmer base in the political system than previously thought. In fact, given that such power has been actively, repeatedly, and strategically granted by democratically elected—and, thus, democratically accountable—legislators, one might even suggest that it is cloaked in something of a democratic pedigree.[10] If so, then even though judicial power—as all governmental power—should still be wielded cautiously and

[9] See, most recently and perhaps most aggressively, James McGregor Burns, *Packing the Court: The Rise of Judicial Power and the Coming Crisis of the Supreme Court* (New York: Penguin, 2009). See also Mark Tushnet, *Taking the Constitution away from the Courts* (Princeton, NJ: Princeton University Press, 2000); and Jeremy Waldron, *Law and Disagreement* (Oxford: Oxford University Press, 2001).

[10] Christopher L. Eisgruber, *Constitutional Self-Government* (Cambridge, MA: Harvard University Press, 2001). This is distinct from the idea that the Court has a useful role as a "referee" for the democratic process and a useful function in "reinforcing democracy" even as it technically stands outside

carefully,[11] it can also be wielded without guilt about its origins because those origins lie in the votes and actions of democratic politicians.

Second, for those who desire robust accountability and limited independence, the centering of judicial power in a political world should be comforting because it means that, far from a perversion of American democracy, judicial power was actually constructed by elected actors. In other words, the fact that judicial institution building is suffused with democratic politics—that it is democratic politics that serves as the engine for the acceleration of judicial capacity—should serve to assuage fears about self-aggrandizing and so-called activist judges run amok in the constitutional temple. Having neutralized the rhetoric of accountability by softening some of the bite of the countermajoritarian difficulty, the idea of political construction also aids the reality of accountability by providing evidence that political actors have bestowed judicial power and, thus, can take it away if they desired to do so.[12] With life-tenured judges anything but insulated from political controversy and contestation, attempts by political actors to rein them in seem far less unprecedented and inappropriate than we might previously have thought.

Third, and finally, for those who might desire to triangulate between independence and accountability in any number of ways, the centering of judicial power in a political world should be seen as normatively balanced in a manner that is democratically empowering. Crucially, it offers some—but not too much—of both independence and accountability. In the fusion between decisional sovereignty and institutional responsibility, power is wielded outside the political world but constructed inside it. Striking a particularly delicate equilibrium between two rival aims, this dynamic allows for the formation of moderate virtues and the avoidance of excessive vices. Perhaps even more important, should we collectively decide that we desire more independence and less accountability (or vice versa), the idea of a politically constructed judiciary leaves the political space (and the possibility for democratic agency) needed to make such changes happen.[13] In that way, emphasizing the ways in which courts and judges have historically grown more powerful shifts onto us the responsibility to hold our elected officials—and, by extension, the judges they empower—answerable for the size, scope, and character of judicial power.

---

it. See John Hart Ely, *Democracy and Distrust: A Theory of Judicial Review* (Cambridge, MA: Harvard University Press, 1980).

[11] Alexander M. Bickel, *The Least Dangerous Branch: The Supreme Court at the Bar of Politics* (New Haven, CT: Yale University Press, 1986); Cass R. Sunstein, *One Case at a Time: Judicial Minimalism on the Supreme Court* (Cambridge, MA: Harvard University Press, 1997).

[12] I acknowledge here that politicians may lack either or both the will and incentive to restrict judicial power, but that reality has little bearing on the fact that they have, should they choose to exercise it, the authority to do so.

[13] While it is undeniably true that the forces of path dependence may make such changes difficult and thereby lessen the ability of the citizenry to control (or, at the very least, influence) the extent of judicial power in any meaningful sense, the existence of obstacles to a particular result does not (as the history of judicial institution building clearly illustrates) make attainment of that result impossible. Neither, I would suggest, does it remove the normative force and justification that even the possibility of democratic agency provides.

Let me be clear: my argument is not that judicial power is unproblematic because judges are accountable to citizen preferences or responsive to changes in the political climate in any meaningful sense. (That argument may or may not be true; regardless, I leave it for others to make or dispute.[14]) Nor do I wish to portray the decisions of courts and judges as beyond reproach. We may legitimately and appropriately disagree with the holding or rationale of a particular case—we may think decisions permitting late-term abortion or unlimited corporate campaign contributions wrong on any number of moral, political, legal, or policy dimensions—but when the power to decide those cases is a function of the political process, we lose *some* of our ability to attack it. Under this view, the accusation that the judiciary is at fault for any number of national problems holds little water. We may question the decisions the judiciary makes, but we—through our elected officials—have conferred upon it the power to make them. Once again, the implication here is not that we, as citizens, cannot or should not critique courts and judges for making decisions we do not like or do not think the Constitution supports. Rather, it is that if Americans—on the left, on the right, in the center—do view increased judicial power as problematic (and I am not saying they should), then we have no one to blame but our elected officials. And, if we consider those officials in some sense accountable through linkage mechanisms such as elections or the mass media, then—unless we (seek to) use our democratic power to encourage those officials to strip or limit judicial power according to our interests—we have nobody to blame but ourselves.

[14] The classic account on this point is Robert G. McCloskey, *The American Supreme Court*, 5th ed., rev. Sanford Levinson (Chicago: University of Chicago Press, 2010). For current variations on the theme, see Barry Friedman, *The Will of the People: How Public Opinion Has Influenced the Supreme Court and Shaped the Meaning of the Constitution* (New York: Farrar, Straus and Giroux, 2009); Lucas A. Powe Jr., *The Supreme Court and the American Elite, 1789–2008* (Cambridge, MA: Harvard University Press, 2009); and Jeffrey Rosen, *The Most Democratic Branch: How the Courts Serve America* (Oxford: Oxford University Press, 2006).

Page numbers followed by "t" refer to tables.

97, 187; citizen access to federal courts in, 64; Democratic-Republican responses to, 65–68; legacy of, 79, 82, 130; new judgeships under, 64, 65–66, 67; removal provisions in, 148; repeal of, 67–72, 79
Judiciary Act of 1802, 61, 72–83, 87n6
Judiciary Act of 1807, 87–92, 98–99, 128–31, 273–74; limitation on judicial appointments in, 91–92; link between the circuits and Supreme Court in, 89–92, 118, 128–29; performance-oriented consensus on, 88–89; residency requirements in, 90–92, 103–7
Judiciary Act of 1837, 129–31, 273–74, 276; circuit court reforms under, 118–24; impact of Westerners on, 125–26; slavery policies impacted by, 124–28, 138–39
Judiciary Act of 1862, 137, 142–46
Judiciary Act of 1863, 137, 143–46, 154, 157n138
Judiciary Act of 1866, 147n76, 153–56, 159–61
Judiciary Act of 1925, 13n46, 200, 203–12, 224, 273; certiorari jurisdiction in, 185n87, 200, 211, 234, 250, 257; mandatory jurisdiction in, 211n89
Jurisdiction and Removal Act of 1875, 40n80, 152, 162–66, 173–74; amendment of 1887 to, 178–79, 186
jury system, 29n21, 42

Kansas, 142–43, 145t, 161t, 212n97, 257n117
Kansas-Nebraska Act of 1854, 134
Katz v. United States, 260
Kellogg, Frank, 202n24
Kennedy, Anthony, 270
Kennedy, Edward, 263
Kent, James, 101n66
Kentucky: admission to statehood of, 62n189, 84; federal circuit court of, 77, 91t, 92, 119n158, 125, 143n57, 145t, 161t
Kentucky Resolution of 1798, 60, 85
King, John P., 117
King, Rufus, 35n54, 41n85
Ku Klux Klan Act of 1871, 162

labor movement, 171–72, 197–98, 201, 225n173
La Follette, Robert, 202
Lamar, Joseph, 204n35
Landis, James M., 22n59
Landon, Alf, 230

Langdon, John, 41
Lawrence, William, 150
Lee, Richard Henry, 35n57, 36, 37n65, 40–41
Leventhal, Harold, 252–53
Levi, Edward, 262
Lincoln, Abraham, 271; anti-slavery policies of, 119, 139–40; election of 1860 of, 19, 131, 140–41; judicial appointments by, 125n174, 142, 170, 173, 182n68; judicial reform policies of, 138, 141–43; Republican Party of, 133–34; secession of Southern states under, 137, 140–41; suspension of habeas corpus by, 148
Livermore, Samuel, 41
Livingston, Henry Brockholst, 91t, 101n66
Local Prejudice Act of 1867, 149–50, 164, 165, 273
Louisiana: civil law system of, 116–17; federal circuit court of, 92, 113, 116, 119, 119n158, 127, 142n51, 143n57, 145t, 161t, 257n118; secession of, 139
Louisiana Purchase, 84

Maclay, William, 34, 35n57, 37n67, 41
Madison, James: Constitutional Convention participation of, 26–27, 44n104, 95, 97; judicial appointments of, 101n66, 122; national negative proposal of, 27n11; report on the federal court system by, 69
magistrates, 242–48, 266–67, 274
Maine: admission to statehood of, 84n2; federal circuit court of, 92, 122, 145t, 161t
Marbury, William, 75–76
Marbury v. Madison, 2–3, 5n155, 68n223, 75–77, 272–73
Marshall, John, 55, 56; as Chief Justice, 65, 86n5, 88, 91t, 93, 94n33, 103, 111, 273; conflict with Jefferson of, 75–77; death and replacement of, 119, 120; on judicial reforms, 63; recusal from *Stuart v. Laird* of, 76
Martin v. Hunter's Lessee, 85n3, 94–95, 101
Maryland, 91t, 143n57, 161t
Mason, Jeremiah, 103
Massachusetts, 91t, 145t, 161t
Mayor of New York v. Miln, 120n160
McCarthyism, 259
McCrary, George, 167–68, 177
McCulloch v. Maryland, 94, 101, 273

Princeton Studies in American Politics:
Historical, International, and Comparative Perspectives

Ira Katznelson, Martin Shefter, and Theda Skocpol, Series Editors

Note: the list of series titles is continued from page ii of this book